FREEDOM'S PLOW

FREEDOM'S PLOW

TEACHING IN THE MULTICULTURAL CLASSROOM

EDITED BY
THERESA PERRY
JAMES W. FRASER

ROUTLEDGE

NEW YORK   LONDON

Published in 1993

Reprinted in 1994 by

Routledge
29 West 35th Street
New York, NY 10001

Published in Great Britain by

Routledge
11 New Fetter Lane
London EC4P 4EE

Library of Congress Cataloging-in-Publication Data

Freedom's plow : teaching in the multicultural classroom / [edited by]
  Theresa Perry, James W. Fraser.
      p.   cm.
   Includes bibliographical references and index.
   ISBN 0-415-90699-7.—ISBN 0-415-90700-4 (pbk.)
   1. Intercultural education—United States. I. Perry, Theresa, 1945–   .
II. Fraser, James W., 1944–   . III. Title: Teaching for a
multicultural democracy.
LC1099.3.F74 1993
370.19′6′0973—dc20   92-29648
                                                      CIP

British Library Cataloging-in-Publication Data also available.

A long time ago,
An enslaved people heading toward freedom
Made up a song:
     Keep Your Hand On The Plow! Hold On!
That plow plowed a new furrow
Across the field of history.
Into that furrow the freedom seed was dropped.
From that seed a tree grew, is growing, will ever grow.
That tree is for everybody,
For all America, for all the world.
May its branches spread and its shelter grow
Until all races and all peoples know its shade.

KEEP YOUR HAND ON THE PLOW!
    HOLD ON!

    Langston Hughes
    Freedom's Plow

To Ellen S. Jackson

Contents

CONTENTS

Preface

In February 1991 the editors of this book were invited to participate in an in-service day for the teachers and staff of the Wauwatosa, Wisconsin, public schools. These teachers, like many of their counterparts throughout the nation, were struggling to find the best means of teaching their rapidly changing student population. Wauwatosa is a middle-class suburb of Milwaukee, and until quite recently the students in the schools represented the overwhelmingly white population of the town. Demographic changes in both suburb and city along with a voluntary city-to-suburb busing program have now led this school system to serve a much more diverse student population.

During our visit we found that the vast majority of the teachers, with the strong backing of the Superintendent, were struggling valiantly to find new and better ways to serve their students. At the same time, we found that the resources available to these teachers were severely limited. Quality multicultural curricula, structures, and staffing patterns which could support diversity, and perhaps most important, meaningful intellectual models for re-visioning the purposes of schools, have not been available to today's teachers. This book is designed to help fill that gap. Our hosts in Wauwatosa, a school district that can serve well as a microcosm of schools throughout this nation, have never been far from our minds as this volume has emerged.

While addressed to all people of good will who want to help the United States build on the strengths of its increasingly diverse population, the primary audience of this book is teachers and students in teacher preparation programs. As we argue throughout the book, we believe that teachers are the central players in building a multiracial/multicultural democracy, and the schools where teachers work are one of the primary institutions where the new society is beginning to be born.

The basic starting point of this volume is our belief that if a vision of democracy that includes all the nation's people is to be fostered in this country and modeled in the nation's educational system, then the issue of multicultural education must be at the heart, and not on the margins, of all discussions about education. Multicultural education, we believe, is not the latest new fad on the educational horizon. It is, rather, the fundamental question to be addressed if schools are to be agents of democracy in an increasingly diverse United States.

We have organized this book into four major sections. In Part I we describe the intellectual framework—the theoretical context for reconstructing schools as multiracial/multicultural democracies—in which we believe the discussion of multicultural education must be framed. In Part II we hear the voices of teachers from different racial and ethnic backgrounds as they reflect on the practice of multiculturalism. While a number of works have emerged that focus on the theory and practice of multiculturalism, few include the voices of teachers who struggle daily with the possibilities, constraints, and dilemmas as they attempt to create a multicultural democracy. In chapter 2 we hear from teachers at a Quaker elementary school that has redefined itself as multicultural and anti-racist. Susan Bennett reflects on her initial year at a teaching and learning community which has so clearly defined itself; Bisse Bowman explodes our notion of what is possible for first and second graders, allowing us to envision a lower school as a place for authentic intellectual work; Laraine Morin tells us how important it is for school to be a safe place: she exposes us to possibilities for including African and African American literature in the study of adventure novels and science fiction writing, and she challenges teachers to reflect constantly on what is working and what could be done better.

In the following chapters Judy Richards, a third/fourth grade teacher at a public school in Cambridge, MA, describes how she daily integrates multiculturalism into all aspects of her pedagogy and practice, including mathematics. Sandra Dickerson introduces us to her "majority-minority" urban high school, reflecting on its movement toward becoming an authentic multicultural community and the resistance from those who "stand guard over the Anglo-Saxon Canon." For those who would limit multiculturalism to content, bell hooks, one of the leading African American feminists, reflects on what it means for pedagogy to be transformative. Nitza Hidalgo discusses the process of introspection that white teachers often experience as they prepare themselves for effective work with multicultural populations.

In Part III we have included essays designed to help teachers enter new areas of study and adopt alternative perspectives on newly emerging, contemporary, and traditional disciplines. For those who want to move beyond the traditional white Western story line that has dominated school textbooks and curricular materials, this section explores the contribution of a wide variety of cultures and traditions to the development of a new common culture and a new intellectual canon in the United States. Sau-ling Wong, in her exquisitely crafted chapter, introduces us in perspective and content to Asian-American literature. Edna Acosta-Belén discusses Puerto Rican migration literature and its relationship to the Puerto Rican identity. In her introduction to the music of East and Southeast Asia, Susan Asai, an ethnomusicologist, sees music as a medium for understanding the culture of this region. Violet Harris critically discusses the last 100 years of the literature of resistance in the African American children's literature tradition. Maxine Greene, one of the clearest voices in our time for the democratic possibilities of schooling, speaks as a white woman about questions of "Openness and variety as well as inclusion," as she seeks in a wide-ranging literary review to "draw attention to the absences and silences that are as much a part of our history as the articulate voices, the shimmering faces, the images of emergence and success." Ceasar McDowell and Patricia Sullivan argue for situating movement history in a central place in the story of the United States, beginning with the first act of resistance to slavery, and including the building of alternative institutions by the historically oppressed.

Part IV focuses on the structure—the power arrangements, perspectives, and personnel policies—that are needed if schools are to emerge as truly multiracial, multiethnic democracies. The authors of these chapters describe a wide range of challenging new ventures and perspectives that are helping to shift the basic structures of schooling in this country so that the voices of the traditionally excluded become central to the definition of quality education in the future In this section we are reminded that, while urging schools to "act as if the new community had arrived," we must always work against the effects of oppression and stratification that are daily manifested in our schools.

Kathy Greeley and Linda Mizell speak about how in two different schools, one independent and the other public, they have done anti-racist work. In chapter 14, Peter Murrell critically discusses the current movement to establish Afrocentric Black male immersion schools. Imani Perry analyzes Afrocentricity as reflected in the work of Molefi Asante and popular culture. Robert Lowe enters the contemporary conversation about school choice, and in his analysis exposes this option as a threat to the democracy. Finally, drawing on her interviews with Black intellectuals, and their writings, about the pedagogy and practice of African American teachers in historically Black schools, Lisa Delpit critiques contemporary work on literacy and projects for us a model of teachers who while acknowledging inequalities in society, were able to teach "as if the new community had arrived."

Writing and editing this book has been an extraordinary experience for both of us—an African American female and a white male—to struggle with a set of significant themes, and to struggle with a re-visioning of the fundamental purposes of education in democratic society. It is our hope that this volume will serve as a resource for people of good will who also seek to join in the process of building what has never truly existed before, a fully democratic school for this nation.

Acknowledgments

Our first and most important acknowledgment is to our chapter authors who have worked with us through this process of writing and editing. We are grateful that so many of our fellow educators have been willing to share a part of themselves with us and with our readers as we all try to move forward into a multicultural democracy. Beyond the chapter authors, we have been encouraged by a diverse group of educators who have told us again and again that this book is important, that we need to keep going with this task. We are grateful.

We also want to acknowledge our specific gratitude to the editors of four journals who have allowed us to reprint previously published material in *Freedom's Plow*.

Chapter 8: "Beyond Island Boundaries: Ethnicity, Gender, and Cultural Revitalization in Nuyorican Literature," appeared previously in *Callaloo*, Volume 15, Number 4 (Fall, 1992). Reprinted by permission of the author and the Johns Hopkins University Press.

Chapter 10: "African American Children's Literature: The Last One Hundred Years," appeared previously in *The Journal of Negro Education*, Vol. 59, No. 4 (1990).

Chapter 16: " 'Choice' for the Chosen: The False Promise of Market-Driven Education," appeared in a slightly different form as "The Illusion of 'Choice' " in *Rethinking Schools* 6 (March–April, 1992).

Chapter 17: "The Politics of Teaching Literate Discourse" appeared in different form in *Theory Into Practice* Vol. XXXI, No. 4 (Autumn, 1992).

The poem in the frontpiece is taken from Langston Hughes, "Freedom's Plow," pages 291–297 in *Selected Poems of Langston Hughes* (New York: Random House, 1959).

We are also most grateful to Angela Irving of Lesley College. Without her continuing support for our work we would not have accomplished this task.

Finally, we want to say a special word of thanks to Jayne Fargnoli of Routledge. Without her encouragement, prodding, and support, we would not have completed this project. We are grateful to her as an editor, colleague, and friend in the quest for a multicultural democracy.

Part I

Multicultural Education

An Issue at the Heart of
Democratic Education

1

Reconstructing Schools as Multiracial/Multicultural Democracies

Toward a Theoretical Perspective

Theresa Perry and James W. Fraser

The Present Critical Historical Moment

From the beginning of this nation's history the link between democracy and education has been central to discussions of schooling. While some Americans, for many different reasons, have historically supported public schooling, others have opposed or undermined it, and yet still others—from the slaves who "in danger and darkness" taught each other to read and write and as freed men and women established "native" schools, to nineteenth-century Roman Catholics who founded parochial schools—individuals and groups of individuals have sought alternative means of education. But among proponents of various options, the link of education to the building of differing visions of democracy has been strong.

Today this nation's people is more diverse than ever. If there is to be democracy in the twenty-first century, it must be a multiracial/multicultural democracy. Unless democracy is conceptualized such that all groups are included, democracy loses its meaning. And if a democracy which includes all of America's people is to be fostered and prefigured in this nation's educational system, then multicultural education must be at the heart, and not on the margins, of all discussions about education in this country. In this situation, multicultural education becomes not a matter of simply adding new material to the school curriculum, but of fundamentally re-visioning the relationship of schooling to a democratic society. The purpose of this book is to define multicultural education as the central issue in deliberations about education in the decades ahead.

As the new year of 1991 began, an Australian newspaper, the *Sydney Morning Herald*, in bold letters spanning the entire width of the page, carried the headline, "America in the Grip of a Cultural Centrifuge." In smaller letters, the subheading was carefully placed before the text of the article's first column, as if to make sure that the readers did not miss its point. It read, "Consensus

3

in the cultural and moral life of the United States has collapsed as European models are rejected and ideals of the great, the good, and the true are questioned."

James Woods, the article's author, correctly perceived that something of note, worthy of the attention of Australians, was occurring in the United States, even if his interpretation of those events was questionable. In an attempt to help Australians understand "what is going on in America," he described this "cultural centrifuge" as "the struggle in academia over what Americans need to know, read, and learn." Woods further characterized these struggles as the indulgences of privileged intellectuals on some of the nation's most elite campuses, which have little if anything to do with the real problems faced by America's poor and historically oppressed.

Even as Woods attempts, like many in the United States, to trivialize and narrow the debate to one of what some call a matter of a "politically correct" naming of certain ideas, he presents evidence that the debate is not, in fact, confined to the academy. Alluding to the "struggle over the imminent quincentennial celebrations of Columbus' discovery of America," Woods describes a complaint by organizers of some celebrations that they had been told "to talk of Columbus encountering, not discovering, America." Woods wonders "if this struggle, along with plans to blockade the harbours when replicas of Columbus' boats arrive, would make the celebrations more apologetic than celebratory."

Something significant is occurring in this country, worthy of the attention of Australians thousands of miles away, worthy of the attention of all Americans, especially educators. We are not, as Woods would have it, in the midst of what is essentially an arcane, frivolous debate of privileged intellectuals about what students should know. The debate is not at its core about Europe and its "relevance for a country as diverse, multiracial, and politically corrugated as America." It is not even about universal values and whether America can appeal to them any more. The debate is about the United States of America, and what its definitive values and identity will be in the next century.[1]

In this nation, individuals and groups are in the midst of a national debate, an open conversation, not always carefully orchestrated or well reasoned. This conversation is not confined to a particular place, or restricted in participation. It is occurring on urban street corners, in the feature articles and on the editorial pages of our daily newspapers, in school board meetings and faculty curriculum discussions, and, also, at some of our most prestigious universities.[2] A struggle is occurring over appropriate mythologies and narratives, about what this country can and will become.

The current "political correctness" debate is a small part of this larger conservation, this broad political struggle to redefine American life and culture.[3] The "political correctness" debate has been socially and politically constructed by neoconservatives who understand that the political activity of the 1950s, 1960s, and 1970s and changing demographics have created the conditions for cultural hegemony to be seriously contested, and that a new definition of the democracy, one that is anti-racist, antisexist, antihomophobic, in settings throughout this country, is being created. By constructing a discourse which casts those working against cultural imperialism and for a multiracial, multicultural democracy as undemocratic, conservative forces are attempting to maintain control of conversational terrain. In the midst of this broad-based struggle over the nature and shape of our social and cultural institutions, the role of advocate for multicultural education is to re-vision America, to redefine American life and culture, and to develop metaphors, narratives, practices, and social and power relations consonant with this new definition.

The vision of this country as a melting pot, if ever viable for people of color, is being seriously contested. Even as this contestation is acknowledged and given voice in many different quarters, the question that must take center stage is, "Can we imagine and build a nation, as well as social, cultural, and educational institutions, predicated on a diversity of racial and ethnic identities?" This book assumes that it is not only possible, but also very desirable, to build such a nation, and that the outcome of the struggle will be both a richer curriculum, more equitable and humane schools, and a more worthy society for all of the nation's peoples. It is also predicated on the belief that our educational institutions can and should be places where we both struggle for and prefigure this new vision of society.

The struggle against cultural hegemony is occurring in different and unsuspecting locations throughout this country. It is occurring in urban communities as school board members discuss and pass legislation mandating a multicultural curriculum and reject textbooks whose version of multiculturalism is evaluated as unacceptable. It is occurring on the campuses of elite northeastern prep schools (perhaps because the administrations of these institutions understand that they cannot claim to educate a leadership class that is all White) as these schools one by one decide to participate in the Association of Independent Schools' Multicultural Assessment Plan, unwittingly creating a context in which cultural hegemony can be contested. It is occurring among African American youth as their Rap artists characterize themselves as Afrocentric, make Malcolm X their new cultural hero, display the red, black, and green prominently in their videos, and consciously critique the Eurocentricism of school and the bankruptcy of its practices. It is occurring on college campuses as faculty and students debate the nature and role of Western civilization and consider adding non-Western and multicultural courses to the curriculum. Indeed, the signs of the debate are everywhere.

Who Defines the Culture?

The scene could have been from an old movie idealizing campus life at one of New England's old Ivy League institutions. Music was blaring from the windows, students were bustling onto the green. In the yard, students with a wide assortment of skin colors and hair textures (according to the New Haven

Register, the incoming class was more than 30 percent American minorities)[4] naturally grouped themselves, sitting, standing, and walking together.

A few students were still moving in; most were relaxing after the moving and unpacking ordeal of the last two days. They were preparing for freshperson orientation's one formal occasion, an event clearly reminiscent of the institution's rich heritage. All students were expected to attend, the men to wear jackets and ties. At this occasion, the college's president and dean would welcome students and their parents and deliver formal addresses.

A select group of faculty and academic officers, robed in academic regalia, sat on the stage. The audience was composed of families—mothers, fathers, grandparents, aunts and uncles, siblings—and the young men and women about to begin their first year of college. The institution's elite New England past was quite evident in the self-assurance and the "at homeness" of the families of the sons and daughters who in times past would have constituted the overwhelming majority of the class. The future was scattered throughout the audience, represented in the faces of Asian-American, Latino, African American, and Caribbean families. Some sat nervously, not knowing what to do with their hands or bodies; others sat confidently, waiting to participate in this ritual, comforted that more than a few others like them were in the audience.

In this charged atmosphere, the Dean of the College rose to speak. He threw down the gauntlet, asserting that the study of Western civilization should be at the center of academic thought at the university. Subtly chiding those who are overly critical of the Western heritage, Donald Kagan contended that the mistakes of Western civilization are the mistakes of humanity, the glories unique to Western civilization. Thus began another iteration of the debate at one of the nation's most prestigious universities about what Americans should know, read, and learn. The Yale Political Union would, during the year, take assertions from this speech, making them the subject of its rather formal debates. One member of the faculty asked his students for their final exam to critique the speech, using material they had covered in the class. Clearly, once again, a nerve had been struck which was at the heart of the nature of education in this country.[5]

But, contrary to James Woods' assertion, elite universities are far from being the only locations of debates of this significance. Those who would question the broad, far-reaching, popular nature of this conversation need only view the videos of Rap artists who appeal to African American youth. The video, "You Must Learn," by KRS One, is a case in point. The video opens with KRS One in the position of a teacher standing in front of a class of students. Behind him is a map of Africa. He is lecturing the class about Shim, one of the sons of Noah, who is a Black man. Enter the police, who promptly pull the map of Africa up and drag KRS One out of the school into the streets. In the next frame, we see KRS One outside the school standing on the corner. Instead of lecturing, he is now rapping. The refrain, "I must learn," brackets his exhortations to African American youth to learn about their African heritage.[6]

Countless Rap songs carry a similar message—the obligation of African

American youth to learn about their heritage, and the corresponding failure of America's schools to provide them with this knowledge. A popular, nonmainstream art form, Rap music is a vehicle for Black youth to contest the operative definition of knowledge. As surely as faculty and students on college campuses, textbook publishers, and school committees are engaged in the struggle over what Americans need to know, read, and learn, so too are African American youth in our nation's cities.

It is not simply the demographic shifts, but the contradictions they raise, that have, in part, precipitated America's struggle for redefinition. Demographic shifts are forcing us to reexamine our definition of social and cultural institutions as White mainstream. The story of this country, its mythology as an open, democratic society, is daily experienced as unbelievable in our city schools where students of color sometimes constitute up to 80 percent of the student population of a district and 90 to 100 percent of many individual classrooms, and where their lives, cultures, and traditions are at best marginalized and at worst ignored or denigrated.

Whether these thoughts are consciously articulated or left sitting, or simmering, at the bottoms of their brains, these children have to want to know why all or most of the people in charge of their schools don't look, talk, walk, or move like they do. They have to want to know why the teachers don't come from their communities, and why the curriculum provides them little clue about themselves and their history. They do, and sometimes the contradictions prove too much, even for the young, prompting a Black first-grade girl in a Milwaukee city school to ask her White student teacher, "Why are all the student teachers they send us White?"

Perhaps more telling is a conversation between a student and a teacher in a first-grade classroom where the teacher was exploring an ill-conceived notion of multicultural education which was also developmentally inappropriate. The teacher asked her first-grade students: "Why should children of different races work together?" When silence followed this query, the teacher began prodding the students. She wanted an answer. When the answer was not forthcoming, she announced, "Because all children are the same, because color doesn't matter." A little Black boy in the back of the room raised his hand and said, "What about Rodney King?" He paused and continued, "the police beat him because he was Black." It is important to note that this incident occurred two months before the LA riots. As students get older the questions and the failure of schools to provide meaningful answers, turn to a rage that can barely be contained.

Of course, the questions, and the rage, are not new. Catholic and Jewish immigrants from Europe were met by schools and teachers who held little respect for their religions or their cultures. Chinese immigrants in California a hundred years ago were met with outright hostility in the schools while generations of Latinos in the Southwest were met with contempt. Every generation of African American students who attended white schools has met cultural barriers.

Throughout history there have been examples of resistance to the cultural imperialism of schools. In 1859, hundreds of Catholic students at Boston's Eliot School refused to recite the Protestant versions of the Lord's Prayer and the Ten Commandments after one of them, Thomas Wall, insisted, "I wasn't again going to repeat them damned Yankee prayers."[7] While African Americans in segregated schools struggled for access to a liberal arts curriculum, African American autobiographies record numerous instances where Black teachers attempted to accord African American culture and traditions equal status with the mainstream culture. The Negro National Anthem was often sung along with the National Anthem, Countee Cullen and Langston Hughes were studied along with Shakespeare. As M. Carl Holman notes, "Mr. Watts, Miss Armstrong, Mr. Blanton and Miss Lewis taught us from the 'lillywhite' textbooks prescribed by the St. Louis school system, but they also mounted on their bulletin boards the works and pictures of Langston Hughes, James Weldon Johnson, Claude McKay, Sterling Brown, Countee Cullen and Jean Toomer."[8]

Robert and Helen Lynd reported from Middletown in the depths of the great depression about a teacher who told them, "I am facing a new problem nowadays: My pupils insist on raising questions that I dare not let them discuss though my conscience demands that I not clamp down on their honest questions."[9] Finally Maya Angelou tells the story of her own graduation when, at an unexpected moment, "Not one but two white men came through the door offstage." The content and the tone of the program quickly changed to accommodate the visitors. The Black school leaders immediately lost power, and things got much worse when one of the visiting officials took over the podium. "It was awful to be Negro and have no control over my life," Angelou remembered. "It was brutal to be young and already trained to sit quietly and listen to charges brought against my color with no chance of defense." But that was not the end of the story. The valedictory student, of whom Angelou apparently expected little, changed everything.

> I looked up and saw Henry Reed, the conservative, the proper, the A student, turn his back to the audience and turn to us (the proud graduating class of 1940) and sing, nearly speaking,
>   Lift ev'ry voice and sing
>   Till earth and heaven ring
>   Ring with the harmonies of Liberty . . .
> It was the Negro national anthem. Out of habit we were singing it. . . . We were on top again. As always, again. We survived. The depths had been icy and dark, but now a bright sun spoke to our souls. I was no longer simply a member of the proud graduating class of 1940; I was a proud member of the wonderful, beautiful Negro race.[10]

Clearly, challenging the status quo is not new in the nation's schools.

What is different today is the attitude with which these challenges are raised, these contradictions experienced. While previous generations of the disempowered and historically oppressed wanted their cultures to be respected and in such cases as that of African Americans and Polish Catholics, for their cultures to be incorporated in segregated and Catholic schools, respectively, they did not call for a redefinition of the ruling culture. Today's youth of color are not willing to accept the ruling culture. They have a rage, born of a sense of unrealized possibilities, not seen before.

The perennial question for the children of color (especially caste minorities)[11] in urban schools in this country is whether the rhetoric of democracy makes sense if schools are organized around the principle of White political and cultural hegemony. For all who believe in an open democratic society, the growing diversity of the citizens of this nation gives a new urgency to the question of whether it is possible at the same time to maintain and promote democratic ideals and schools which are organized as hegemonic institutions. It is not hard to imagine the consequences for a nation when the story it tells about itself, its origins and identity, becomes unbelievable or bankrupt for a significant portion of the population.

Who the citizens of the United States are has changed dramatically in the last generation. This is partly a matter of the nation's self-perception, and partly a matter of dramatic demographic shifts in the racial and ethnic composition of the nation. It is important to remember that the United States has never been a White nation, although White institutions and cultural norms have certainly held sway throughout most of the nation's history. Over the last three hundred years, the percentages of Whites, African Americans, Native Americans, and Latinos have shifted radically, A hundred and fifty years ago, several of the southern states had Black majorities, while large areas of the Southwest were overwhelmingly Latino and the majority population of some future states was still Native American. It was only with the massive immigration from Europe in the last century, led by immigrants from southern and eastern Europe, paralleled by the virtual genocide of the native Americans, that the huge White majorities came to be seen in the demography of the United States. But this demography is now changing again.

In Los Angeles there has been a growing realization that the city is quickly approaching the status of a majority Latino city, the same majority which had been dominant there when California was admitted to the Union in 1850. The changes in Los Angeles are symbolic of changes occurring to a greater or lesser degree throughout the nation. Through a combination of new levels of immigration, especially from Central and South America and Southeast Asia, and of differential birthrates among Whites and people of color, the non-White population of the country is mushrooming.[12]

Changing demographics alone cannot account for the new level of multicultural consciousness. Indeed, demographics alone do not automatically translate into a redefinition of a nation's ruling cultural norms. There have been examples, in the United States and in other parts of the world, where a small minority has established the cultural norms for the majority.[13]

Cultural hegemony usually follows political hegemony where those in power, to a greater or lesser extent, institutionalize their definition of culture. According to Pierre Bordieu, "Different classes and class fractions are engaged in a

symbolic struggle to impose their definition of the social world most in conformity with their interests . . . with the field of ideological production reproducing
in transfigured form the field of social positions."[14] Because the issue is not
simply which group has the largest population, but who has power, history has
recorded instances where political power has rested with a minority—sometimes
a very small minority—which has proceeded, in conformity with their interests,
to establish cultural and social norms for the larger society.

The current situation in the United States possibly complicates the notion
that cultural hegemony usually follows political hegemony, raising the question
as to whether, without the prior shifting of political relationships, cultural
hegemony can be seriously contested. Because, in our post-modern society,
inequality is mediated by culture, to contest cultural hegemony is to challenge
the ideological underpinnings that support the structures of inequality. Further,
because the kind of society we are envisioning is a democracy, the culture of
the people necessarily assumes a critical position. For, as John Adams asserted,
political victory was easy because the real American Revolution first happened
in "the minds and hearts of the people," twenty years before the first shots were
fired—thus the primacy of the struggle against cultural hegemony at this stage
in the struggle for democracy in this country.[15]

Additionally, those in power must know that it is increasingly risky to assume
that society can be stabilized, that the rhetoric of democracy will be meaningful
to African American and Latino youth, and that these youth will be engaged
by schools, if schools continue to marginalize their lives, histories, and culture.
Although conservative ideologues might be adamant that social and cultural
institutions retain their definition as White mainstream, changing only at the
edges, those with economic stakes in the society are undoubtedly aware that
the broad consensus in defining our social and cultural institutions as White
mainstream has been fractured and that this definition has ceased to be functional
for the nation.

The Impact of the Civil Rights Movement: Defining a Democratic Culture

Had the current demographic shifts occurred before the Civil Rights movement, they would not have had the same impact. Though poverty, political
disenfranchisement, repression and racism continue to characterize the lives
of the historically oppressed peoples, the Civil Rights movement and the
resultant legislation changed the operative definition of equal opportunity.
The Civil Rights movement dramatically altered patterns of access as well
as the nation's consciousness of what were democratic rights—and whose
rights they were anyway. All of us—notable and ordinary people who
participated in the Civil Rights movement—pushed the boundaries of democ-

racy further outward, prompting its redefinition. Before the sixties, this was essentially a closed society for people of color. There were individual exceptions, but the exceptional nature of a person of color gaining access served to reenforce the reality that only very limited opportunities were available to most non-White citizens of the nation. It is the possibility that our social and cultural institutions could be open, the belief that they should be, the fact that greater numbers of people of color, even if not enough, participate in these institutions—along with changing demographics—that have created the conditions for us to contest the very definition of our social and cultural institutions as White mainstream.

A review of the last thirty years of African Americans' struggle within higher education suggests that the present discussion about the nature and shape of our cultural and social institutions is logically the next step in the democratization of schools and colleges. In the late fifties and early sixties, African Americans entered the academy in small, very small, numbers, unobtrusively in the North, in places where a very few "qualified" Negroes were acceptable, and obtrusively and courageously in the segregated South where custom and law limited access. The goal at this point was access; access nearly always on the terms established by the White institutions.

But that very access led to other demands. From the mid to late 1960s, as part of the Civil Rights movement, not only was access expanded, but those African Americans admitted to the academy demanded that more individuals from their communities be allowed entry and that the terms for entry and the conditions affecting their lives on the campuses be improved. They wanted an opening of the admissions process, scholarships, appropriate supports, and places for themselves—cultural centers, African American Studies courses, centers, and departments.

Thereafter, quickly thereafter, women, Puerto Ricans, Chicanos, Asian-Americans, and Native Americans made similar demands. Within their cultural and sometimes political spaces, and within changed conditions and perceptions of possibilities, mainstream and minority scholars and students, men and women engaged in counterhegemonic activities. They developed courses on the Harlem Renaissance, rediscovered Zora Neale Hurston, Virginia Woolf, and the history of working people. Not only was the content and epistemology being questioned, but also alternative traditions were being developed.

African American Studies, Women's Studies, Asian American, Puerto Rican, Chicano, and Native American Studies, along with programs that focus on the experience of more recent European immigrants and the history of labor, located in departments and centers, though all too often marginalized, are now part of the higher education landscape. And we are not satisfied. Again we are asking that this country's definition of democracy be expanded. We are asking for a redefinition of the normative, we are asking that our social and cultural institutions be redefined. We are asking that our schools and colleges be reconstructed as multiracial, multicultural democracies.

The Historical Struggle for Inclusion

The current generation is not the first to grapple with questions of how to build the good society and the role of schools in that process. As the late Lawrence Cremin never tired of noting, it was Aristotle in the *Politics* who insisted that "it is impossible to talk about education apart from some conception of the good life." Cremin went on to say that "people will inevitably differ in their conceptions of the good life, and hence they will inevitably disagree on matters of education; therefore the discussion of education falls squarely within the domain of politics."[16] If participation in a democratic society is essential to the good life, then it follows that education must foster democracy, but it also follows that just as people disagree about the nature of democracy, they will disagree about education.

It is also a reality that for most of America's history, women and people of color were not included as full participants in the vision of democracy enunciated by many of the nation's most prominent voices. Our democracy has never been defined effectively as a democratic nation state predicated on a diversity of racial and ethnic origins.

Two hundred years ago, Thomas Jefferson gave early voice to the link between education and democracy, even as he failed to include the slaves that he and others held, Native Americans, or white women as participants in that democracy. Notwithstanding, in the midst of the American Revolution, Jefferson proposed a new system of public schools for Virginia, reminding the Virginia legislators

> that experience hath shown, that even under the best forms of government those trusted with power have in time, and by slow operations, perverted it into tyranny; and it is believed that the most effectual means of preventing this would be to illuminate, as far as practicable, the minds of the people at large.[17]

The contradiction of Jefferson, the slave owner, giving voice to the proposition of education for a democratic society has not been lost on subsequent generations. But at the same time the voice itself has remained powerful. As Langston Hughes knew:

> *His name was Jefferson. There were slaves then,*
> *But in their hearts the slaves believed him, too,*
> *And silently took for granted*
> *That what he said was also meant for them.*[18]

In the case of education, the belief in democracy was far from silent.

As the historian James Anderson has noted, the history of education in this country is a story of two competing and contradictory traditions—education for full citizenship and education for second-class citizenship. Extending back to slavery, against the backdrop of laws that made it a crime for slaves to learn to read and write, historians have documented the slaves' tenacious pursuit, sometimes at risk of death, of literacy.[19]

Furthermore, given this experience of literacy, slaves emerged from slavery with not only an insatiable desire to learn to read and write, but also with the belief that literacy was a negation of the status of slave and was, in fact, a means to full citizenship.

Out of an educational tradition that saw the emancipatory possibilities of schooling, from slavery to the present, African Americans have conceptualized school as a context for the social reconstruction of society and engaged in activities aimed at subverting the oppressive intent of much of mainstream schooling. In the late nineteenth and early twentieth centuries, W.E.B. Du Bois, Anna Julia Cooper, and other African American educators, in opposition to the philosophy of northern industrialist/philanthropists, engaged in counter-hegemonic activities and argued that African Americans should have access to the broadest possible education, that they should be educated for first- and not for second-class citizenship.

Acting on this philosophy, Anna Julia Cooper, as principal of the M Street School (later the famous Dunbar High School) in Washington, D.C., "in defiance of her white supervisor—Percy Hughes, who told her colored children should be taught trades—sent several of her students to prestigious schools, including Harvard, Brown, Oberlin, Yale, Amherst, Dartmouth, and Radcliffe."[20] Her insistence on educating African Americans for full citizenship led to the famous "M Street Controversy" and her eventual termination as the school's principal. According to the minutes of the D.C. Board of Education, Cooper was charged with "1) refusing to use a textbook authorized by the Board; 2) being too sympathetic to weak and unqualified students; 3) not being able to maintain discipline [two students had been caught drinking]; and 4) not maintaining a proper spirit of unity and loyalty."[21] The reality, however, was that she had a different vision of African American education, one that would lead to first-class citizenship for her students.

Du Bois, Carter G. Woodson, and others, understanding how curriculum is implicated in the aims and purposes of school, wrote books designed to counter the prevailing stereotypes of African Americans and develop race pride. (Violet Harris, in her chapter in this book, documents the existence and power of this oppositional tradition.) In creating the Organization for the Study of Negro Life and Culture, Woodson institutionalized his efforts to support scholarship and the development of materials that countered stereotypes and documented the history and culture of African Americans.

Even as Woodson believed that African Americans should have access to the broadest possible education, in the *Miseducation of the Negro* he argued that as an oppressed people, African Americans needed a "special education," one which, while prefiguring their status as free men and women, and acknowledging their oppressed status, enkindled in them the desire to cast off the shackles of oppression. In other words, he knew that education that was liberating for the oppressor could indeed be oppressive for the oppressed.[22]

At the turn of the twentieth century, many other thoughtful people also struggled with the meaning of democracy at a time when the nation's population and power arrangements were changing significantly as a result of new patterns of immigration and a changing economy. John Dewey spoke for a larger democratic vision for schools when he insisted that, "A democracy is more than a form of government; it is primarily a mode of associated living, of communal experience."[23] Part of the vision of the progressive educators and their allies was this call to view democracy, the good society, as one which included the diversity of the nation's peoples in building new ways of living together. Thus Jane Addams, the founder of Hull House who worked for reform in turn-of-the-century Chicago, once wrote, "We have learned to say that the good must be extended to all of society before it can be held secure by any one person or any one class; but we have not yet learned to add to that statement, that unless all people and all classes contribute to a good, we cannot even be sure that it is worth having."[24]

The progressive education movement meant many different things to many different people. It certainly had its conservative side, but it also had an inclusionary vision that must be remembered. Thus, in 1899, John Dewey wrote:

> When the school introduces and trains each child of society into membership within such a little community, saturating him [or her] with the spirit of service, and providing them with the instruments of effective self-direction, we shall have the deepest and best guarantee of a larger society which is worthy, lovely, and harmonious.[25]

While it is hard to believe that schools can really provide "the deepest and best guarantee" of the kind of larger society we want, it is the case that the classrooms of the nation are one key element in the ongoing struggle to build an inclusive society in which all children and their families, whatever the cultural heritage and social location, are valued and respected and given voice. This would be a significant step toward the building of a larger society in which power is redistributed, all have voice and all make their contribution to the social good.

The massive immigration of southern and eastern European immigrants in the years around the turn of the twentieth century did not, however, lead to an easy consensus on the nature of the good society. While during the late nineteenth century the United States received about 500,000 immigrants per year, in the decade just before World War I approximately one million people per year immigrated, with the vast majority of them no longer from the nation's old northern European stock.[26] These "new immigrants" were not always greeted with open arms, and—as in every era of the nation's history—the debate arose about the role of the school in "Americanizing" newcomers. The imagery of the melting pot was born in these years with Israel Zangwill's play *The Melting Pot* produced in 1908. Other voices however, were raised in favor of a culture more respectful of diversity. In 1916, Randolph Bourne attacked the melting pot ideology in an essay, "Trans-national America," in which he called for "a cosmopolitan, international definition [of American society and culture] that would be in the making rather than already made."[27]

Although it is important to know that we are heirs to a tradition that has grasped the emancipatory possibilities of schooling, it is equally important to remember that this legacy extends to the present. Indeed, many of us have witnessed and participated in educational struggles predicated on the belief that school is a legitimate place to struggle for freedom and the expansion of the democracy.

It is certainly no accident that the battle for equity and desegregation has been one of the primary battles of late-twentieth-century educational politics. The Supreme Court's 1954 *Brown* v. *Board of Education* decision, which had been decades in the making, set a precedent for many of the educational battles to follow.

At its core, the civil rights movement's focus on education is a matter of building a new vision of the good society, or, in the words of Martin Luther King Jr., the "beloved community."

The history of opposition to cultural dominance dates back at least to the beginning of the nineteenth century, as slaves and recently freed slaves, immigrants from China, and conquered peoples from the Americas, along with immigrants from Ireland and southern and eastern Europe, all participated at certain moments in significant acts of resistance. Throughout most of this history, however, resistance was simply that—a refusal to allow domination to continue in a specific institution at a specific moment. Within the Civil Rights movement, however, something new and quite powerful was emerging with greater clarity than ever before in the United States: a different vision of what society should look like. Building on initial acts of resistance, African Americans and their supporters began to envision a completely different society within the United States, one in which competition and dominance were replaced with cooperation and inclusion. It is this vision of a new society which has given such power to the struggle for inclusive, multicultural education in the last three decades.

Following the *Brown* decision, the struggle for integrated quality education in the North and the South, in public schools and colleges, would take many different forms. For linguistic minorities, as well as for African Americans, the guarantee of access was insufficient: thus the struggles to maintain cultural and linguistic identity and the historic battles which led to and were spawned by the Supreme Court's *Lau* v. *Nichols* decision which mandated bilingual education,[28] and the subsequent campaigns for bilingual/bicultural education.

During the latter part of the 1960s, spurred on by the Civil Rights and Black Power movements, African Americans with their allies, from New York City to Boston to Milwaukee, demanded control of the schools in their communities. The call was for more than accountability. African American parents and community activists wanted to share in the control and governance of the schools their children attended. In settings where African Americans were able to claim a share in the power they implemented changes in the curriculum aimed at giving their children an understanding, both theoretical and practical, of their past and future.

At St. Joseph's Community School in Boston, for example, the seventh- and eighth-grade students learned about the writers of the Harlem Renaissance: Zora Neale Hurston, Countee Cullen, Arna Bontemps, Nella Larson. They also learned about the Registrar of Deeds and studied how to discover who owned the slum property in their neighborhoods, and they followed the process of a court challenge to a landlord's failure to clean up the property.

The community school/community control movement reached its height in New York City between 1967 and 1970 when the creation of experimental community control districts led to a teacher's strike that closed the city's schools for weeks. After the 1968–69 strike, community control was not as central to Civil Rights strategies, but a precedent had been set that would influence political activity in both urban North and rural South for decades.[29]

Reconstruing Schools as Multiracial, Multicultural Democracies

Reconstruing schools as multiracial, multicultural democracies requires that we acknowledge that schools are at the same moment local and national institutions. As such, they should be informed by the social realities of the communities they serve and representative of the vision of the society in which they exist.

As local community institutions schools should respond to the social and cultural realities of the communities they serve. John Dewey, in considering what this meant, maintained that the community should want for all of the children "what the best and wisest parent wants for his or her child."[30] Arguing that Dewey's analogy is not an appropriate way to extend the purposes of education from the individual to the community, Amy Gutmann contends that the principles of nondiscrimination and nonrepressiveness should constrain the policies and practices of the school as a local institution.[31] For us, the school as a local institution is fundamentally constrained by the aims and purposes of school as a national institution: namely, to prepare all students for first-class citizenship in a nation predicated on a diversity of racial and ethnic origins.

Operating out of the Gutmann framework, the local school cannot pursue policies and practices that "render the democracy repressive or discriminatory."[32] Operating out of our framework, the local school similarly cannot pursue policies in opposition to the aims of school as a national institution in a democratic society. Schools must always pursue policies that support the education of all students for full citizenship in a multiracial/multicultural democracy.

To suggest that the purposes of school as a national institution should constrain as well as inform the response of local schools to social realities in the communities they serve is to acknowledge that there will be significant variation in the midst of unity in the nation's schools.

It is essential that schools be shaped by their communities. This is true whether the community be Chicago, Cambridge, or Birmingham, or a small town somewhere in between. For example, let us consider Pharaoh, one of the two boys whose lives are chronicled in the book, *There Are No Children Here*, by Alex Kotlowitz. Pharaoh lives in the Henry Horner Project, in Chicago.[33] In his community there are no parks, banks, stores; the closest laundromat is a mile away. Half the people in the project do not have telephones. Up-close violence is a routine part of his life. How should schools that serve the Pharaohs of this country be construed such that they afford these children the possibility of full citizenship in a democracy predicated on a diversity of racial and ethnic origins? One could speculate about the form, process, and content of these schools. They would probably be linked to or have social services integrated in them. The curriculum would need to offer credible explanations for the violence, for social realities, while also inspiring meaningful hope. The point is that schools that serve the Pharaohs of this country should be different from other schools given the nature of the local communities in which they exist. The local variations, however, would be constrained and informed by the national goal of preparing all children for first- not second-class citizenship, in a multicultural, multiracial democracy.

On the other hand, a school in Cambridge, Massachusetts, which serves a significant Haitian community, if it is to be legitimate, must institutionalize informal and formal aspects of Haitian life, history, and culture. One would not, however, expect this same specific orientation of a school in a southern community which did not have a significant Haitian population.

As national institutions, schools, even if the populations they serve are majority White, cannot exist as White mainstream institutions. Our schools have to prepare our young people for citizenship in an America which fully includes in its self-definition women as well as men, all races and all ethnic groups. Perhaps most important, our schools should represent our visions of the future. Democracy is incompatible with schools as hegemonic institutions, whether these schools are in Chelsea, Massachusetts or Wauwatosa, Wisconsin; Los Angeles, California, or Meridian, Mississippi. If we concede that schools are national as well as local institutions, the question that we too must ask of ourselves is whether the operative definition, the functional reality of our schools, makes sense, given a society that is increasingly multiracial and multicultural. Is the rhetoric of democracy believable to us, to our students, mainstream or minority, if our schools are organized around the principle of cultural and political hegemony? In the face of an increasingly diverse society, schools which continue to function as White mainstream institutions have rendered themselves anachronistic.

We would like to argue that school as a national institution, should prefigure the society we want rather than reinforce existing social and political arrangements. And if the society we want is a democratic nation predicated on a diversity of racial and ethnic origins, we believe we have no choice but to re-vision our schools as multiracial, multiethnic, multigendered democracies. The challenge is to reconstrue schools in such a way that from top to bottom they represent and usher in the future we want. Our challenge is to reconstrue schools so that they are institutions for all of America's children.

Too much of the liberal call for dealing with the "problem" of growing diversity in the schools is far too deeply apologetic, far too unwilling to demand the fundamental restructuring of power relationships and cultural assumptions that must happen if this nation is to live up to its multicultural potential; far too unwilling to celebrate the new multiracial, multiethnic culture that is coming into being. Well-meaning as they are, too many of the current discussions about diversity take the apologetic approach that "problem" of multiculturalism and diversity must be "solved."[34]

But our question is, Why is this a problem? Why isn't it a wonderful opportunity to build a new, more diverse, equitable, and much more interesting society for all of us to live in? To shift the fundamental question in multicultural education from solving a problem to embracing a grand opportunity requires a reordering of our approach to diversity.

One of the central ways power is exercised in democratic societies, schools included, is in structuring discourse. Further, the exercise of power in academia occurs primarily in defining what is legitimate knowledge, who should have access to what kind of knowledge, and who is qualified to transmit knowledge. If diversity is a problem to be solved, then incremental additions to the curriculum, supported by affirmative action programs that lead to incremental changes in the faculty, will be sufficient. If, however, the goal is to grasp the opportunity to fundamentally reorder the ruling definitions of the culture, then something much more profound must happen. It therefore seems clear that if we are to change educational institutions so that they truly embrace a multicultural future, we must begin by defining a new conversational terrain, one that both questions these givens and interrogates the operative definition of school.

To be more specific, there needs to be a means of structuring discourse at the school in such a way that parents, teachers, students, and administrators are asked to seriously engage a vision of school as a multiracial, multicultural democracy, asking what this vision means for the total life of the community. Someone will have to be willing, in an ongoing fashion, and in many different settings, to hold up for the community a vision of what it can become, of what a multiracial, multiethnic democracy would be like. Someone will need to assume responsibility for always raising these questions and pushing the conver-sation to the next level.

In thinking about this task, we are really using the eschatological metaphor of the *parousia*, the coming City of God, both to capture a sense of urgency about re-visioning schools and the possibilities of alternative visions. Whatever one's theological preference—or lack thereof—the question must be posed: Can we, as it were, step over the present, project ourselves and our schools into the future, into our vision of what a school would be like if power were shared among all races, ethnic groups, and social classes, as if the new community (the new multiracial, multiethnic democracy) had actually come into being? Could we as an educational community begin to operate, make hiring and curricular decisions, conduct business, as if the new time were at hand? With this vision of the new school community in mind, what compelling questions would we ask about the work of the institution? How would we talk about its meaning? Who would we want to be included in the school communities? What criteria would be used to determine what knowledge was worth passing on? How would the past be represented? the future envisioned? What metaphors would be used to capture the past? what narratives would be most important to pass on to our children? Who would we want to be our teachers? Who would hold positions of authority and how would authority be exercised? These are the fundamental questions which must be asked if schools, and the nation's society, are to be restructured to meet the promise and possibilities of a truly multicultural future.

The Teacher: A Central Player in the Struggle for a Multicultural Democracy

Reconstruing schools as multiracial, multiethnic democracies of necessity means reconstructing what it means to be a teacher. It is important in this regard to acknowledge that conceptions of teachers are neither given nor universal, but social and cultural constructions, necessarily linked both to how schools are structured and to the social histories of the people for whom schools were created.

The operative conception of teaching is quite powerful in ways that are both liberating and constraining. The operative notion of what it means to be a physician determines not only the activities a physician will or will not engage in while practicing medicine, but also expectations about the nature and conditions of medical work and the jobs a physician will accept or reject. The operative notion of what it means to be a teacher is no less powerful. It is a social construction, critically informed by the role and function of schools in a given sociohistorical community.

If we see the teacher as a central participant in the construction of a new American culture, that means that the teacher must play the key role in allowing the lives, histories, and cultures of the historically oppressed to critically influence the reconceptualization of knowledge that is represented in the curriculum and the classroom. This is much more than a matter of adding the voices of the children and families of urban America to the public school curriculum. This approach is merely additive; it leaves unchanged the primary stories, the dominant metaphors and definitions that frame areas of inquiry from history to literature. What we are talking about is creating a new tradition, telling "new stories" that are fundamentally different by virtue of the role that the lives of the historically oppressed have assumed in their construction. This is a matter of redefining American culture, not once and for all, but in the negotiated meanings that are always emerging out of a curricular process which proceeds on the assumption that new stories, new metaphors, and new interpretations, result from a dynamic interplay of text and context.

It is in the day-to-day interactions of teachers and students, dealing with a transformed curriculum and attempting to create a transformed, democratic classroom, that the new common culture will be created and continually recreated. It is essential that both the curriculum and the classroom context be part of this process and that the teacher be the key negotiator between the two. As central as the reconceptualization of discipline-area knowledge is to the creation of a new common culture, this is not the whole story. It is the negotiated meaning that is important, and negotiated meaning requires real-live people—teachers and students—who participate in an ongoing process of negotiation. The negotiated meaning is informed by the context, the personal and historical identities of those who make up the classroom, the power relations represented in the school and the classroom, and the pedagogical strategies employed. The negotiated meaning is always a result of what is presented by the teacher as legitimate knowledge; who it is—teachers, students, parents—that is negotiating the meaning. Negotiated meanings are always critically informed by the racial, class, and gender identities of the faculty and student participants and by the power relationships represented in the classroom and the larger educational institution.

If we conceive of teachers as central participants in the creation of a new common culture, then nothing short of representing the "community of the future" in the classroom, on the faculty, and in governance is in order. Re-visioning discipline-area study is a necessary step in the creation of the new common culture, but context is a part of, not separate from text, and negotiated meaning is predicated on the presence of African Americans, Latino Americans, Native Americans and Asian-Americans, males and females, as central players.

Reconceptualized Schools: From Utopian Vision to Practical Reality

This is a utopian book. We are taking the risk of being dreamers in raising these issues. We believe that our goal as educators is to follow W.E.B. Du Bois in his plea for education that would produce "young women and men of devotion to lift again the banner of humanity and to walk toward a civilization which will be free and intelligent, which will be healthy and unafraid."[35] Indeed, until we ourselves are unafraid of being branded romantics for using such language, the essential vision which will guide all of our work will remain unattainable.

To say that we need to hold this utopian vision is not, however, to say that its implementation will be easy. It won't. There is a long, hard struggle involved in beginning to build a new world, and there will be opposition.

Diversity can lead to clashes. When we bring people together in school from different races and cultures and from differing positions of power and privilege, it is inevitable that there will be misunderstanding, fear, tense moments. That is part of the process of learning about and from each other. A homogeneous school may be quieter and simpler, but is will not help us in the process of building a better society.

Even more important, if the youth we educate view and experience our democracy as including all of the people, they will inevitably ask all sorts of questions about social and political life outside of the school:

—about the distribution of goods and services in this society;

—about racism, classism, sexism, and homophobia;

—about the concrete manifestation of rights and privileges in the democracy.

And questioning children and youth make people nervous. Thirty years ago, James Baldwin, in a talk to teachers, said:

> The purpose of education, finally, is to create in a person the ability to look at the world for him [or her]self, to make his [or her] own decisions, to say this is black or this is white, to decide whether there is a God in heaven or not. To ask questions of the universe, and then to learn to live with those questions, is the way a person achieves identity. But no society is really anxious to have that kind of person around. What societies really, ideally want is a citizenry which will simply obey the rules of society.[36]

Society's wants have not, unfortunately, changed much in the intervening years.

If educators begin to truly embrace the multicultural future and use that embrace to build a new multicultural, democratic present, there are going to be students asking all sorts of embarrassing, uncomfortable questions of the society. And while people of goodwill will welcome these questions, even when they get uncomfortable, the society we live in today does not welcome such questions. All societies are uncomfortable with dissent, and as American society moved from the 1980s into the 1990s, it grew much more uncomfortable. The conservative reaction in this society is alive and well, and it must be reckoned with.

An education for a new public culture of difference[37] must be one which leads students and educators to reject reaction in any form, to demand—for teachers and for students—the alert, critical, engaged consciousness that can optimally come from thinking minds in dialogue with—and ultimately in community with—each other. It is only when representatives of all races, classes, and cultures, when women and men bring their different stories that a new public culture can emerge.

If we have this kind of education, we will be in trouble, and it will be worth it, for we will be living in a society, at least in our schools, and perhaps in our larger community, which has begun, if only in small ways, to resemble the community we want.

Educational dialogue needs to be practical. But it is also true that the desire to immediately be practical, to immediately be relevant, has impoverished the dialogue about education in this country and kept us from larger goals and larger visions. There has been too much hiding of larger questions, too much reluctance to discuss the meaning and purpose of education in the fear of being impractical. It is time for that larger discussion.

In that discussion, we want to come down on the side of efforts that lead to a larger society quite different from the one we have now: One that is not greedy and mean-spirited; one built on the energies and diversity of all of its peoples, one that does not view diversity as a problem to be solved, but an opportunity to be grasped. We agree with Manning Marable when he says:

> Democracy is not a thing, it is a process of expanding opportunities for all citizens and the ability to control decision making from the bottom up. This requires certain prerequisites for a decent life for all within the political society—full employment, decent housing, education, health care, and so forth. The battle for full democracy leads directly and inevitably toward the promise of economic equality. The challenge of all democracies is not to make the rich richer but for all of us to exercise greater economic and political rights.[38]

It is to building an ever expanding democracy that a multicultural education worthy of the name must be dedicated.

Notes

1. James Woods, "America in the Grip of a Cultural Centrifuge," Sydney, Australia, *Morning Herald*, Jan. 5, 1991; p 15.

2. Institutions as diverse as the University of California at Berkeley or Stanford University and the public schools of Boston, Massachusetts, Baltimore, Maryland, and other large cities have all been involved in this debate.

3. For a fuller discussion of the issue of "political correctness" and the New Right agenda in education, see *Debating P.C.: The Controversy over Political Correctness on College Campuses*, Paul Berman ed. (New York: Dell, 1992).

4. New Haven *Daily Register*, Aug. 29, 1990.

5. Imani Perry (Yale class of 1994), interview with authors, Boston, June 1, 1991.

6. KRS One, *Ghetto Muses, The Blue Point Hiphop*, Jive Records.

7. Stanley K. Schultz, *The Culture Factory: Boston Public Schools, 1789–1860* (New York: Oxford University Press, 1973), 307–308.

8. M. Carl Holman, "Anger and Beyond: The Negro Writer in the U.S. The Afternoon of a Young Poet," in Jay David, ed. *Growing Up Black* (New York: Avon Books, 1992), 44.

9. Robert S. and Helen Merrill Lynd, *Middletown in Transition: A Study in Cultural Conflict* (New York: Harcourt, Brace and World, 1937), 231–241.

10. Maya Angelou, "I Know Why the Caged Bird Sings," in David, ed. *Growing Up Black*, 38–42.

11. See the work of John U. Ogbu. For a discussion of Ogbu's conception of caste-like minorities, see especially: John U. Ogbu, "Minority Status and Schooling in Plural Societies," *Comparative Education Review*, 27:2 (June, 1983), 168–190; "Black Education: A Cultural-Ecological Perspective," in H. P. McAdoo, ed. *Black Families* (Beverly Hills, CA: Sage, 1981), 139–154; and "The Consequences of the American Caste System," in *School Achievement of Minority Children*, U. Niesser, ed. (Hillsdale, N.J.: Lawrence Erlbaum: 1986), 19–56.

12. See Philip Bennett, "The Face of the Future: Welcome to L.A.," *The Boston Globe Magazine*, Oct. 13, 1991: 14–16, 50–54.

13. For a definition of hegemony, see Antonio Gramschi, *Selections from Prison Notebooks* (New York: International Publishers, 1971).

14. Pierre Bordieu, "Systems of Education and Systems of Thought," in *Knowledge and Control: New Direction in the Sociology of Education*, ed, M.F.D. Young, (London: Collier Macmillan, 1971).

15. John Adams to Hezekiah Niles, February 13, 1818, *The Works of John Adams*, Charles Francis Adams, ed. (10 vols.; Boston: Charles C. Little and James Brown, 1851), 10: 282.

16. Lawrence A. Cremin, *Popular Education and Its Discontents* (New York: Harper & Row, 1990), 85.

17. Thomas Jefferson, "A Bill for the More General Diffusion of Knowledge," (1779) in Gordon C. Lee, ed. *Crusade Against Ignorance: Thomas Jefferson on Education* (New York: Teachers College Press, 1961), 83–92.

18. Langston Hughes, "Freedom's Plow," in *Selected Poems of Langston Hughes* (New York: Random House, 1959), 294.

19. James D. Anderson, *The Education of Blacks in the South* (Chapel Hill: University of North Carolina Press, 1988); see also Joel Spring, *The Sorting Machine Revisited: National Educational Policy Since 1945* (New York: Longman, 1989).

20. Mary Helen Washington, "introduction to Anna Julia Cooper," in *a Voice from the South*, Schomburg Edition (New York: Oxford University Press, 1988), xxxiv.

21. ibid.

22. Carter G. Woodson, *The Miseducation of the Negro* (Trenton, NJ: African World Press, 1990).

23. *Democracy & Education*, (New York: Macmillan, 1916; reprint., New York: The Free Press, 1966), 101–2.

24. Cited in Lawrence A. Cremin, *The Transformation of the School* (New York: Alfred A. Knopf, 1961), ix.

25. John Dewey, *The School & Society* rev. ed. 1915 (Chicago: University of Chicago Press, 1900), 29. A significant debate has emerged in the last few years about the best understanding of the role of John Dewey within the history of opposition to cultural imperialism in the United States. For two differing perspectives on this debate, see William Andrew Paringer, *John Dewey and the Paradox of Liberal Reform* (Albany: State University of New York Press, 1990) and Robert B. Westbrook, *John Dewey and American Democracy* (Ithaca, N.Y.: Cornell University Press, 1991). Our intention in this chapter is not to join that debate but to note the long history of the discussion of the relationship of a multicultural perspective to the development of a democratic educational process.

26. Diane Ravitch, *The Great School Wars: New York City, 1805–1973* (New York: Basic Books, 1974), 173.

27. Randolph Bourne, "Trans-national America," in *The History of a Literary Radical & Other Papers*, with an introduction by Van Wyck Brooks (1916. reprint, New York: Russell, 1956), 260–84; cited in Cremin, *Popular Education and Its Discontents*, 109–13.

28. See James Crawford, *Bilingual Education: History, Politics, Theory and Practice* (Trenton, N.J.: Crane, 1989).

29. For a very different interpretation of the community control movement, see Ravitch, *The Great School Wars*, 280–398.

30. John Dewey, *The Child and the Curriculum* and *The School and Society* rev. eds. 1900 and 1915, reprinted in one vol. (Chicago: University of Chicago Press, 1956).

31. Amy Gutmann, *Democratic Education* (Princeton, NJ.: Princeton University Press, 1987).

32. Gutmann, *Democratic Education*, 14.

33. Alex Kotlowitz, *There Are No Children Here* (New York: Doubleday, 1991).

34. As one national report of the 1980s said:

> The broad outlines of the problem can be seen in the numbers. First, Blacks, Hispanics, and Asians account for a rising proportion of the school population. California now has a majority of minorities in the first three grades of its elementary schools, and 23 out of the 25 largest city school systems enroll a majority of minority students. By around the year 2000, one out of three Americans will be a member of a racial minority. (*The Nation Prepared: Teachers for the Twenty-first Century: The Report of the Task Force on Teaching as a Profession* (New York: Carnegie Forum on Education and the Economy, 1986), 79.

35. Cited in *W. E. B. Du Bois: A Reader*, Meyer Weinberg, ed. (New York: Harper, 1970), 153–4.

36. James Baldwin, "A Talk to Teachers," Oct. 16, 1963, reprinted in Rick Simonson and Scott Walker, eds., *The Graywolf Annual Five: Multicultural Literacy* (St. Paul, Minn.: Graywolf Press, 1988), 4.

37. We are indebted to Professor Henry Giroux of Pennsylvania State University for this term.

38. Manning Marable, *The Crisis of Color and Democracy: Essays on Race, Class and Power* (Monroe, Maine: Common Courage Press, 1992), 239.

Part II

The Practice of
Multicultural Education

Doing the Work

Different Ways of Seeing

Teaching in an Anti-Racist School

*Linda Mizell, Susan Benett, Bisse Bowman,
and Laraine Morin*

ambridge Friends School (CFS) is a Quaker elementary day school
located in north Cambridge, Massachusetts, which serves over 200
children in grades kindergarten through eighth. Our evolving reputation
as a multicultural, anti-racist school which "does what it says" has enabled us
to attract—and keep—increasing numbers of students of color, as well as many
other families who value diversity and recognize that a multicultural, anti-racist
community provides the richest experience for all students. Children of color
comprise one quarter of the student body; during the last three years, they have
accounted for as much as 44 percent of incoming students, most of them
kindergartners. Among a faculty and staff of 42, however, there are only 5
people of color: 1 administrator, 1 support staffer, and 3 teachers. Two of the
three teachers arrived in the fall of 1991. I am that one administrator. Both I
(Linda Mizell) and my immediate predecessor are African American women.

I came to CFS in the summer of 1988 as the new Director of Admissions and
Development, following the school's completion of the Multicultural Assessment Plan (MAP). CFS was one of seven independent schools around the
country which had agreed to serve in the pilot phase of MAP, a National
Association of Independent Schools (NAIS) project. At the same time, CFS
was embarking on an ambitious Five Year Plan which placed diversity issues
in the forefront of our institutional priorities.

From its inception 30 years ago, CFS had always considered itself a nonracist,
multicultural community. Peaceful conflict resolution, respect for individual
differences, and concern for social and racial justice are fundamental to Quak-
erism. What was different in 1988 was a new-found commitment to becoming
an *anti-racist* community, a task few schools in this country had undertaken.

As a direct result of MAP, Cambridge Friends School decided that the entire
faculty, staff, and Board of Trustees, along with a number of parents, would
participate in intensive racism-awareness training. With the support of several
nationally and internationally known consultants, CFS began a series of three-
day workshops which were to change the course of the school's existence—

although, arguably, the real impact of the workshops was to clarify the course which had been established in principle in 1961.

Our training was conducted by Dr. Barbara E. Riley and the late Dr. Robert B. Moore, both of them critical forces in the Council on Interracial Books for Children. Our initial goal was to develop a common language, as the first step in (1) developing a long-range strategy for increasing the diversity of the student body and faculty, (2) developing a more multicultural curriculum, and (3) affirming our long-standing commitment to nonracist policies and practices.

Instead, we came out of the workshop experience with a collective commitment to becoming an anti-racist school, galvanized in our collective will to not only confront racism within the CFS community, but also to begin changing the structures which make racism silent, invisible, and inevitable. Since 1988, CFS has gained national recognition for its cutting-edge approach to curriculum and policy reform.

One of the most difficult aspects of this kind of institutional change is the absence of models. No other independent school in the country has embraced such a collective commitment, and so our dual task has been to do the work even as we invent the process—sometimes ineptly—for doing it. Much of our success is owed to the guidance and support which we have received from several recognized experts in the field of anti-racist institutional reform.

Along with Drs. Riley and Moore, Enid Lee has been critical to the development of our "blueprint." Ms. Lee has been described as "one of Canada's most respected authorities on race relations." In addition to her independent consulting, she has served as Race/Ethnic Relations Supervisor for the North York Board of Education.

In March of 1990, Enid came to CFS to lead the annual staff development workshop. We realized that we needed to do a lot more work on our curriculum. All too frequently, our attempts at multicultural curriculum had taken a "tribe-of-the-week" approach, concentrating for brief periods on heroes, celebrations, arts, and artifacts, but failing to integrate a broad range of perspectives into the "regular" curriculum. We were hopeful that Enid could help us surmount the many perceived obstacles to achieving a multicultural curriculum.

Prior to Enid's arrival, the faculty had assembled a list of nearly 100 questions to which we expected her to provide answers. Instead, Enid made it clear that her job was to help our faculty develop the capacity to discover their own answers. She also shifted our attention to the "hidden curriculum," the subtle yet powerful patterns of interactions which shape the environment of every school. Her final exercise for the day was to have us reframe those original questions.

In November, Enid returned for the first in a series of three-to-four-day visits in each section of the school. She observed classes, met with teachers individually and collectively, and held informal meetings with parents. Many of her observations have been simple yet profound, as have been her persistent questions: Why do we want or need anti-racist curriculum? Our answers have gradually shifted from an emphasis on the moral imperative to an understanding that racism limits and debilitates all our children.

What does an anti-racist curriculum look like? This is the question which CFS teachers struggle with daily. Our experiences seem to indicate that the answer is dynamic, that both the content of the curriculum and the strategies which teachers employ must be continually reexamined in light of new research and insights. In broad terms, an anti-racist curriculum recognizes that no act is neutral, that everything we do in the classroom is either anti-racist or supports and perpetuates racism; an anti-racist curriculum embraces content, perspective, and delivery.

Most white children have spent their academic lives looking into distorted mirrors of their history and culture which only reflected people like themselves; most children of color have been pointed toward a narrow window, which offered an obstructed view of the world and their place in it. We have come to understand, at times imperfectly, that the curriculum must offer all of our children windows as well as mirrors. Our task as responsible educators is to smooth out the distortions and remove the obstructions.

In June, each faculty member writes a curriculum report which summarizes the triumphs, failures, frustrations, and lessons to be learned from the previous year's teaching experiences. The reports which follow here offer vivid, moving, and deeply personal accounts of how three very different teachers grapple with the question of what it means to teach in an anti-racist school.

Berit "Bisse" Bowman has taught for three decades, the last two at CFS. As a Swedish immigrant, as the senior faculty member at CFS, and as a CFS parent, Bisse has both witnessed and taken part in the school's 30-year evolution. In her quest for authentic curriculum resources, Bisse has amassed an impressive range and depth of both materials and personal knowledge, and she herself has become an invaluable resource.

Laraine Morin's arrival at CFS coincided with the first academic year following MAP. During her first three years at CFS, from 1988 to 1991, Laraine was the only full-time permanent faculty member of color. As a result of her training, her years of teaching experience, and her clarity of insight, Laraine has played a critical role in the articulation of the school's vision for curriculum reform.

As an extended-maternity-leave replacement, Susan Benett was thrust into the CFS scene two-and-a-half years after the MAP report, one year after her colleagues had undergone racism-awareness training—by which time the commitment to multicultural, anti-racist education had become part of the fabric of the school—and was able to view the school's efforts from a different perspective.

The strength of any school lies in the capacity of its faculty and staff to grasp, articulate, and continually develop its vision. We offer Cambridge Friends School not as a *successful* model of an anti-racist school—for our struggles are ongoing and our successes are sometimes outnumbered by our failures—but as an example of an institution earnestly committed to engaging in the process of long-term, fundamental change.

Susan

My first year at CFS and my first experience with multicultural education left me uncomfortably straddling the fence, and regularly out of place—some days falling into one neighbor's yard and some days into the other's. One year has wrought confusion, discomfort, anger, openness, conflict, and challenge.

On my first day at CFS, the day I was being interviewed, I stood in the back of a seventh-grade history class. *Who were some of the first people to come to the Americas?* the teacher questioned. I wondered at the answer myself. Some Viking perhaps, Eric the Somebody?

The teacher began with an African king whom some anthropologists and historians believe may have come to South America years before Columbus, who may have influenced native art and folklore. I nodded to myself that this was a new piece of information, and perhaps this was what my interviewers meant by multicultural education. I listened more: "*And the people there thought that this African king was a god.*"

Alright! a young black man in the class called out. That must be the reason multicultural education is good, I thought. And I figured I'd seen and heard what it was all about.

Then the teacher asked about Columbus, and so began 15 minutes of Columbus bashing. He was a mercenary, a businessman, the bringer of imperialism, colonialism, slavery. He ruined and destroyed.

Now multiculturalism seemed a bit more dangerous to me, a lot more confusing. What had happened to Columbus as a hero? I thought, standing in the room, that if a multicultural education is to teach from different points of view, what had happened to Columbus's point of view. Had it become worthless, even meaningless, in light of the destruction which had followed him, his accomplishments without any heroism at all? I certainly would not have gotten on a wooden ship and headed off into the unknown on a hunch.

I slipped out of the room somewhat angry, definitely confused, and wondering what it would mean to teach at this school.

I began teaching. The meaning of multicultural education soon was washed over by the daily concerns of learning names, assigning reading, checking homework, and keeping things semi-orderly. I was reminded of the idea again, when a co-teacher and I had a short talk about *To Kill A Mockingbird*. We had just finished reading it and seeing the movie. As we were pushing the VCR cart back to storage, she mentioned that we might not teach it again. She explained that it contained no powerful black characters and that the great white Atticus father figure, is the savior of the black Tom. It perpetuated stereotypes. Yet, at the same time, I said, we had kids reading the book with enthusiasm, remembering lines, and quoting them directly. Important lines about understanding others and walking in their shoes before judging them. Wasn't that a good way of getting at perspective, at point of view?

And what happens to Shylock and Huck Finn? I'd heard about this debate, read articles about it in papers and magazines, but here it was in my classroom. I thought about that same young man who had shouted "Alright!" to the thought of an African king explorer, and wondered what he felt when he read the word "nigger" or saw Tom die.

As a Jewish woman, I thought about what I felt when I read Shakespeare, not even *Merchant of Venice* but other plays in which a comment here or line there would denigrate Jews. I would feel angry, sometimes afraid that the stereotypes might be true. Yet would I ask that Shakespeare not be taught? We locked up the VCR and let the issue rest.

Multiculturalism was coming home. I was talking about it with my husband, my family, my friends. Newspaper articles and editorials on the topic suddenly seemed everywhere: from "political correctness" to power over the content of the classroom. Parts of me sighed in sadness. I had come to teaching for love of literature, for enthusiasm in words, and somehow that seemed to be less important than picking stories, poems, and novels that "fit." I flipped from one side of the fence to the other. Loving my favorite novels, knowing that teaching required enthusiasm from me, yet also believing that there was a world of literature not being taught that I could love as deeply and as well.

Therefore, for my elective English course, I decided to teach *Betsey Brown* by Ntozake Shange and *Women Warrior* by Maxine Hong Kingston. I'd call the course "Ethnic Literature," which seemed a bit weird a title, but I wasn't sure what else to call it. I read *Betsey Brown* a few weeks before the class began, and I was astonished at all I did not know about black history. Who were these poets, scientists, and musicians mentioned in the book?

Embarrassed and a bit shamefaced, I asked our head of development and resident black history expert, Linda Mizell. She talked and talked, and then gave me two books to read: a history book called *Before the Mayflower* and *Black Voices*, an anthology of poetry and essays. I began to think of my own limited knowledge of African American history. As I listened to Linda, taking in what she was saying about W.E.B. Du Bois, I suddenly, shockingly realized that not only had I never taken a black history or black literature course, I had only had one black teacher and that was in graduate school. So was multicultural education adding more to the curriculum, including more people of color among the faculty?

Our music teacher, with whom I had spent one lunch hour a week in a new teacher support group, was fired. I had felt from the first that she was different from the average CFS teacher in demeanor, in temperament, even in her accent and clothing. She was definitely not Cambridgey. I wondered if these outward appearances hadn't influenced the decision to ask her to leave. She somehow hadn't grasped the multicultural, anti-racist policies of the school and had openly crossed them—openly, because she was the music teacher, publicly producing schoolwide programs of song and dance. My reaction to her leaving was a hunkering down and a sense of relief that my classroom seemed less public, and therefore provided me space to make mistakes, mistakes that I believed would not be far different than the music teacher's, just more private and confined.

A month or so later I attended a racism-awareness workshop. It was a three-day, intensive exploration of racism in America, in myself, in history. We started the workshop by thinking of a person, not a twentieth century person, whom we admired. I thought for a while. I couldn't come up with one person. But I thought about the immigrants who left familiar homes, terrain, language, to come to the United States. I had just moved to Boston, and that was hard enough. I couldn't imagine what bravery it took to do what they had done. When it was my turn, I gave my answer. I felt a cold chill. Somehow it had been a "bad" answer. Was it because the immigrants had been settlers, usurpers of land already owned? I started the workshop thinking it was an indoctrination.

As the days built, there were moments of revelation, moments of debate, times of stiff-necked refusal, times of openness. We watched slides of racist consumer packaging, discussed our first experiences with someone of another race, shared in games that made the issues of power and control more concrete. I began to wonder if multiculturalism and anti-racism were not so much about "sharing cultures" but about power and control.

A few weeks later I came into my eighth-grade English elective and found a heated discussion going on. Linda had worn a Howard University sweatshirt to school that said *Black by nature, proud by choice* on the front and *It's a black thing you wouldn't understand* on the back. Some of the white girls in the class were upset by the shirt; they felt put off by it. *Why does it say "you wouldn't understand?" "We want to understand,"* they said, *"so why aren't we allowed to understand?"* The two black students in the class, a boy and a girl, on the spot to defend and explain, defended and explained. It wasn't about understanding, they said, it was about experience. "It is about what it is to be black," said the boy. "And you can't know 'cause you aren't black."

"Why is it that when we celebrate Kwanzaa, Linda only calls up black kids to do the stuff, but when we do Chanukah anybody who wants to take part, Jewish or not, can?" asked a girl.

"Because, our ceremonies have been taken over by you for years. Our music and everything. This ceremony is ours. Oh, forget it." The black girl gave up in frustration.

I tried to straddle that fence, to help the white students understand what they were angry at, to help the black students understand what they were angry at; but somehow, maybe because of the music teacher's firing, or my own confusion, I knew this was more than I could handle. I didn't want to shut it down and say "let's all turn to page 82 now." It seemed that this sorting out was what it was really all about. I asked a student to see if Linda was free to help us.

She came and talked with the class and led their discussion for over an hour. We bled into other class time, and barely stopped for lunch.

A lot of what she said was blurry to me: issues of race being self-qualified— you are what you believe you are—yet society defines you whether you ask for their definition or not. As a Jew, I thought of my baseline fear of race definition by society. A mixed race girl in the class, who looks white, said that she was defined as white, even by black people, when she felt equally a part of her black heritage. There were tears, and those are colorless.

Enid Lee, an anti-racist consultant, came to my class. She observed and we talked. "Why do you call it "Ethnic Literature?" she asked. "I don't know," I said. I had picked books about growing up in America in which the characters have to contend with the dominant society and their own ethnicity. They feel conflicted, I explained.

"Yes, but by calling it Ethnic Literature, you take it out of the mainstream. It is not Literature then, but a qualified type of literature. Why not call it 'Literature About Growing Up' or 'Coming of Age Novels?' "

Finally, an easy change to make. And a relieving one, too. Then we talked about a project a group in that class was working on. They had found all the different words for African American used in *Betsey Brown*. Then they were going to ask teachers and children from all age levels what reactions they had to the different words, from "black" to "colored" to "nigger."

"What do you think of them going to the lower grades to ask these questions?" Enid asked me.

"I'm uncomfortable about it. But I don't know what to think really." We sat for a moment, and I did what I always try to do when an issue is bugging me and I can't find the center. I put it into my own world. "If they were doing a paper on women and they were going to ask kindergartners what they thought when they heard the word 'cunt,' I wouldn't allow it."

Enid smiled.

Finally we approached the end of the year. Quietly, a black student support group had begun. The one black boy from my seventh-grade class and the few in the eighth-grade attended. The group ended the year with a small party for the eighth-grade graduates. They served cake and ice cream and each member of the group invited a white friend from their classroom to attend. Although it seemed somewhat exclusive, it seemed okay at the same time.

I remembered getting a note explaining it in my mailbox and asking for suggestions or questions. I'd wondered about it being during school hours and not during lunch times or after school. But somehow, even though I had been asked, I didn't feel the right to complain. Honestly, I don't know why. It wasn't a problem in my classroom for it to be scheduled when it was. I counted on my black student to go when he wanted, and not go when he didn't want to. I didn't discuss it with the other students, for I felt it was like taking an art class or going to the library: a personal option, not a classroom decision.

One morning, soon after the cake and ice cream, I found a heated debate going on in my math class, again about Kwanzaa and being excluded. These were different white students, but the same black students. The discussion veered into the black student support group. "Why can't I come to it?" asked a white girl. "I want to help, I want to understand."

"Cause you're not black, idiot," said the black boy. He was angry and tired of explaining. The black girl had given up, her head resting on her arms.

I explained using the one technique I had acquired to understand something out of my ken. "Look, if it were a girl's support group, would you want boys to be there on a regular basis? What if we wanted to talk about getting our periods or cramps or boys? Some things are easier to talk about with people who've experienced it and understand what you mean."

"No, if a boy wanted to come, I would let him come." She was crying. I had the feeling that in her mind the separation was not about talking about feelings and experiences, but about talking about white people. Her friend became her black friend, who might be talking about her white girlfriends, or more specifically, about *her,* and who would share those secrets only with other black friends.

I think that feeling of exclusion and secretiveness overwhelmed these adolescents. It had even begun to overwhelm me. We talked all period, dropping math for the day. But the tears didn't end.

When class was over, I sought out Bill, the eighth-grade homeroom teacher. We talked. The resentment and anger were widespread, not only in my math class but pervasive in our seventh and eighth grades. We decided to call an upper school meeting in the library. We asked Linda to join us. And so began over three hours of talking: Black kids feeling put upon and angry; white kids feeling left out and confused; Asian and mixed race kids wondering how they fit into this; friends defending friends and not listening beyond loyalties.

And then, some listening and some breaking through.

We talked until lunch, and they still wanted more. We broke into small groups. In my group, everyone wanted healing. "What makes us one as well as makes us different?" they wanted to know. We didn't have an answer. Some kids complained that the school divided rather than unified, while they all agreed it was important to recognize differences. Kids felt loss, and we had no easy answers to give them.

At year's end, I sat down with Mary, the Head, to talk about the future. I had been on a one-year contract filling in for a woman on maternity leave. She had asked for a second year.

"The school has made a commitment to hire faculty of color," Mary told me. "We'd like you to come back next year, but after that we will open the job up and anyone can apply. The woman you filled in for, you, and of course outside resumes. But our commitment is to hiring faculty of color."

I listened. Did she mean I would not be considered at all? That my color was being judged above my ability to teach? After a year I had seen and heard and learned enough to know that multiculturalism was more than teaching that an African set foot in South America before Columbus. I knew that the school had only one black faculty member and two staff members. Not a fair ratio in a school that is working to be multicultural. In the abstract, I agreed.

But in reality, I sat on the other side of that fence, seeing the school's commitment, remembering my own ignorance of black history, recalling my singular experience of having a black teacher in over 18 years of education, yet refusing to sacrifice myself and fall into agreement, because I could still see, clearly, that other side—the side that I had learned as a danger from my own people's history—racial classification.

My first year introduced me to ideas I had never considered before, challenged beliefs I did not realize were even there, stirred angers that had lain unexpressed. It was and remains a trying, tiring process. For me, it raised more questions than it answered, yet I am grateful that I have engaged in the questioning and the struggle. Philosophy has leapt out of the articles in magazines and actively into my life. I know that no matter what happens, whether I am hired back at Cambridge Friends School or go on somewhere else, I shall never be the same teacher again.

Bisse

1968 was quite a year to arrive in the United States. Not long after my first, tentative week as a teacher at Cambridge Friends School, Martin Luther King, Jr., was assassinated. The following morning a special Meeting for Worship convened at school. To this day, it remains one of the most moving and meaningful experiences I have had. Several African American CFS alumni joined us, later telling us, "We just knew there would be Meeting, and we needed to be there." That Meeting, with all the strong emotions, seeing people reaching out to each other, and hearing "We Shall Overcome" sung softly, made me aware of how very little I knew and how much I had to learn—not just as a teacher, but as a person.

I was trained as a teacher in Sweden and had taught a mixed first–second grade there in a little country school since 1962. Although much is universal when it comes to working with young children, there is also a world of difference in basic techniques between teaching reading/writing in Swedish and English, and, even more so, to teach in a vastly different, and richer, multifaceted culture.

As I grew and learned, I began to reflect on Sweden and on the education I had received there. While many Swedes pride themselves on lack of prejudice and have made it their business to point out problems in other countries, there are many attitudes which need work. I became more aware of the holes in my education. What had I learned of the Sami ("Lapps" as non-Sami call them), the oldest population of the northern reaches of Scandinavia? Not much. They "raised reindeer" and sang in a style called "jojk."

As I began to learn about some of the American Indian nations, I realized how woefully little I knew of the Sami, and soon began to find striking parallels in their histories: forced conversion to Christianity, the children being carted off to boarding schools and forbidden to use their native language, land taken away for farming, logging, mining, and hydroelectric power, etc. I also began to remember incidents from my childhood, when a neighbor had chastised my mother for "letting her play with those dirty Gypsy children," and disparaging comments being made about Finnish immigrants, "they all fight with knives, you know."

All this was humbling, and eye-opening. Although my parents, my mother in particular, had quietly tried to counteract some of those attitudes, it is clear that all of us who grew up in Sweden then were insulated, ignorant, and deprived of learning about the richness of the cultures of the people already there in our small country. I've often heard it said that Sweden is a homogeneous society. It was a myth then, and is even more so now. One out of eight people living in Sweden now is an immigrant!

One question which comes to mind is: How can you even begin to learn about and understand people in other countries and of other cultures, if you don't understand, know, and appreciate the one you are living in? I feel very fortunate to live, learn, and teach here. Although there are struggles to be fought, prejudices to overcome, and much to be learned, there is also a truly fantastic richness, a mosaic if you will, of people, cultures, languages, and beliefs surrounding us and making up the communities in which we live. And as a teacher, to be not only allowed, but encouraged, to draw from all of this is very special, indeed.

I believe a multicultural curriculum is one which is truly integrated in all aspects of the school day and school year. Broadly, this means to have "antennas out" in listening to the conversation among children and observing them on the playground, having plenty of time for small group and class discussions; a varied selection of books for the class library, for reading in groups, and for reading aloud; making sure that curriculum is "presented" in such a way that it is accessible to children's varied learning styles; choosing music to sing and listen to; thinking about what is displayed on the classroom walls; including a diversity of cultures in all subjects; choosing games to play in P.E.; teaching art techniques and learning about the work of different artists, and so on. It isn't really all that different in "subject matter" from what has been done before—but the *focus* is. Do the children find themselves reflected (and validated) in the curriculum? Whose voices and perspectives are represented? Who is missing? Are materials translated into English authentic? To me a successful multicultural curriculum is one which is almost hard to point to. It should be the basic fabric of all we do, ready to be embellished in many different ways, but still the base.

I have mixed feelings about ideas such as "Native American Day/Week" and "Black History Month." All too often, these may be the only times of the school year students hear the voices of people of color. The Martin Luther King Jr. Holiday and Black History Month have certainly had the effect of raising awareness through specials on T.V., article series in newspapers, and art exhibits, and therefore enriched the curriculum of many schools, CFS included. Ideally, though, I would like to see the day come when such special days, weeks, or months were no longer needed anywhere.

It feels a little strange to try to tease out what is "multicultural" from the class curriculum since it is, in a way, counter to how I feel about it as a whole. It is a way, though, to take a closer look at some of the things we worked on, to evaluate, and to think about where to go on to. What follows are some excerpts from a curriculum report written at the end of the school year a couple of years ago.

Fall Theme: From Sheep to Shirt

It is always nice to have a hands-on, multidisciplinary theme for the class to begin the year with. It is a way to help integrate new students into the class, and a wide range in reading/writing skills are easily accommodated.

We began by spending some time learning about wool: shearing, carding and spinning. We found photos of people in many different parts of the world engaged in the yarn-making process, and we compared the tools and techniques being used. A parent in the school brought fleece, carding combs, drop spindles, and a spinning wheel into the room, and not only demonstrated how to card and spin wool, but encouraged all the children to try.

Later we collected a variety of plants, ranging from onion skins to goldenrod flowers to black walnut hulls, prepared dye baths, and dyed yarn samples. The only tools we needed were a hot plate, a stainless steel pot, and water! In the end, we had over 30 different colors of yarn to work with.

As the children began using the yarns to weave their own miniature rugs, we read books based in different cultures, such as *The Goat in the Rug* (Dineh) by Charles L. Blood and Martin Link and *Pelle's New Coat* (Sweden) by Elsa Beskow.

We looked at weaving patterns from different parts of the world and learned about different kinds of looms. We located pictures, patterns, books, and tools on a world map, and kept written and/or illustrated records of all the activities. A weaver came to visit the class, bringing a wonderful array of weaving samples and a harness loom on which the children were allowed to weave!

Books

Since about 1986, there has been a wonderful increase in the publication of books written and illustrated by people of color. The CFS library collection has benefitted tremendously, and hence the reading corner in the classroom. It has also meant being able to find multiple copies of "trade books" to use in the reading groups. Recent favorites are Ann Cameron's books about *Julian* and Mildred Taylor's *Song of the Trees.*

The reading corner has had a great variety of picture books all year. We have discussed each book as we read it aloud, talking not just about the story but also about the author and illustrator. The books have portrayed a variety of ethnic and economic backgrounds, as well as myths, fairy tales, and legends from around the world. We have asked questions such as: "What do you think about that?" "How would you have acted?" "Do you agree with that?"

It is important to help children read critically and to take from each book what they like, what makes them think twice, what moves them, and of what they disapprove. The children have learned about differences, but they have also discovered commonalities: "I feel like that too, sometimes!"; "That reminds me of . . ." It is a pretty great experience to realize that you know three different stories about why the north star stands still, that you know a European, a Chinese, and an Iroquois "Cinderella" story, and that children the world over laugh and cry over similar things.

The fun and challenging part about reading groups is finding good materials to extend the book you are reading. For instance: Reading *Indian Hill* by Clyde Robert Bulla, we found some National Geographic articles about the Dineh, and a couple of books written in both Dineh and English, such as *Tonibah and the Rainbow* by Jack L. Crowder. The children in the group also cooked an American Indian cornmeal desert for the whole class to enjoy as a snack. We live in New England, yet the majority of us know very little about the First People of this area beyond some vague notions about the "first" Thanksgiving. Looking for tales from the Eastern Woodlands people during the summer proved frustrating. While beginning to understand some of the reasons for the paucity of materials in bookstores, my determination to learn more grew.

This year I read more biographies/autobiographies aloud to the class than in earlier years. I think this was in part triggered by having the children write "autobiographies" at the beginning of the year. In any case, the first one we read was *A Grain of Wheat* by Clyde Robert Bulla. He is one of the children's favorite writers, and they really enjoyed hearing how he got started writing. One of the more inspiring biographies was about Langston Hughes. Reading it carried us on to reading a lot of his poetry. The children brought in collections of his poems, and they wrote some wonderful poems themselves.

We found a good biography of Martin Luther King, Jr., and one about Mahalia Jackson was read in connection to listening to gospel music during rest time. One of those great classroom moments happened when suddenly the children began making connections between Mahalia Jackson and Martin Luther King: "You mean she sang at a fund-raising thing for *the* bus boycott? The one that Martin Luther King helped organize?"

Paying close attention to the illustrations in the books we read aloud, and learning a little about the artists, helped enrich the class experience. Some examples: Comparing the illustrations in two books about the Dineh—one illustrated by a Dineh artist, one by an artist of a different background; looking at pictures by a Finnish and a Swedish artist to try to figure out the technique for painting winter scenes, and then using a similar technique to illustrate stories and poems about winter; noticing that the clothing in the illustrations for a Vietnamese fairy tale look more Chinese than Vietnamese, and finding out that the artist is Chinese American; noticing the borders carefully painted around each page of a West African tale, and then seeing several children design their own borders for their writing paper; discussing illustrations which depict people in a stereotypical fashion.

Math and Science

Dispersed throughout the year in the classroom science groups were some sessions spent learning about scientists of different backgrounds, with special emphasis on Black and female scientists. While learning about the wildflowers found in a city landscape, we looked at children's books with particularly good illustrations of plants and wildflowers, and talked about who the illustrators were.

It was fun to listen to the children who knew how to count to 10 in another language and to learn from them. This gave these children a chance to share something special from their own family background.

The children also learned that the wonderful Tangram puzzles were developed in China a long time ago, and, when playing trading games in various number bases, that the number base is 20 in both a West African culture and an Inuit culture.

Art in the Classroom/Wall Displays

Art is a natural mode of self-expression for children, and we keep a variety of art materials near at hand all the time. The children are encouraged, and taught, to explore different techniques, such as drawing, painting, modeling in clay, sewing, and weaving. To be able to "report" on something you learned with an observational drawing or a clay model is important to many children who are not yet comfortable expressing themselves by speaking or in writing— or who just *are* more visual in their orientation. It has happened, many a time, that a child can tell volumes about what she/he learned in a drawing, and, when compared to lengthy, written efforts by another child, you find the drawing to be the more informative!

The walls in the classroom are always filled with creative efforts by the children, be they paintings, collages, stories and poems, or colorful patterns generated in math groups. We avoid the premade bulletin board materials available in school catalogues, since we feel the classroom walls ought to reflect the children in the room.

We paint a new alphabet for the room every year, and last year's alphabet moves to the library. We list the letters in the alphabet, then each child picks a letter to paint and generates ideas for what to depict. There are some things I've kept an eye on during past years, such as talking to the children about why not to paint a Ninja for the letter N, or an Indian for I.

But I is a tricky letter. There are not many "paintable" words which begin with the short i sound. So, until some years ago, I compromised (maybe that is too nice a word) and agreed to have children paint an igloo, while explaining that the word really means "dwelling," and that not all igloos are (or were) made of snow blocks. After a seminar at the Children's Museum ("Through Indian Eyes: Whose Vision Is It, Anyway?"), I couldn't live with that "easy" way out of the short i problem any more. I talked to the children about what I felt, we got out a dictionary, decided on "ink" and "iguana," took down the igloo pictures in both the library and the classroom, and two eager volunteers painted new "i-posters." It was humbling.

Class Discussions

Group and class discussion times are wonderful opportunities for taking a look at how we perceive the world around us. We begin and end each school day with a meeting: the first one to set the tone for the day, to plan activities, to read aloud, and to give the children a chance to share their thoughts and ideas; the last one to "wrap up" the day. In addition, we often meet right after morning recess and just before lunch—and other times as needed.

If you take the time to talk, to give the children and the teachers a chance to get to know each other as people, the atmosphere in the classroom gradually becomes one where it is safe to bring up issues for discussion. Not long ago we took the time to sort out a playground situation where one child had felt excluded from a game. After thinking of strategies to help someone be included, one of the girls began talking about something that had happened outside of school.

"I was over at my friend's house, and we were playing on the sidewalk. Two big, White boys came up to us and said I couldn't play with her, because she's Black, and I'm not. I told them they didn't have the right to talk to us that way."

Her friend reached over, took the first girl's hand, and said, "It made us feel really bad." "That's racism!!" said one of the boys in the class, indignantly.

We talked for a while longer, even though we all realized the time for math groups was getting shorter by the minute. When we finally broke up, one of the children said, "Well, how can you have math anyway, if you have all that on your mind?"

Stray Thoughts

I wonder if we sometimes, in our eagerness to improve and diversify our community and curriculum, overlook the "invisible" diversity, such as economic differences, the diversity of culture, language, and religion among our White community members, and the questions of identity among adopted children who do *not* look different from their parents.

There are times during the school year that some of this diversity lets itself be noticed: holiday times ("Do you celebrate some Christian holidays, too?" "Do you have to be White to be Jewish?"), clothing drives ("I remember getting my clothes out of boxes, just like these. It felt nice that someone had thought enough to share with us," from a mother who arrived in the United States as a war refugee from Eastern Europe), and comments like "My grandmother speaks hardly any English."

Let's not overlook this—acknowledging this less noticeable diversity can't but help enrich all our lives. And just maybe, if these "smaller" differences (or someone's uniqueness) are not denied, one can become more open toward the "bigger" ones. The more open we all become, and the more we learn, the richer we will all be as people. When we celebrate diversity, we really celebrate life.

Laraine

No teaching is neutral; it is professional and personal, intellectually challenging and emotionally satisfying, an individual undertaking and a communal action. I am an African American woman, a Roman Catholic, and a native Bostonian. I carry into the classroom my own early experiences, my curiosity, fears, preferences, culture, and race. It is this personal history, shaped by and shaping the learning process, which gives meaning to the lessons I teach.

I think the one factor that has most influenced who I am as a teacher is that I'm the mother of three kids who were all evaluated as special needs, and all of whom have very *different* learning issues. Invariably, I've had to do battle with teachers who couldn't see that there were learning issues there which had nothing to do with race, and so we had to wade through the race stuff before they could even begin to look at my children's needs.

Those experiences have made me more sensitive and aware of everyone's learning issues. Very few teachers truly understand that there are as many ways of learning as there are kids. If a kid doesn't "get it," we usually don't assume that it's a matter of teaching style, but rather that there's something wrong with the kid, particularly in the case of kids of color—because she's black or he's ESL. As a result, the kids themselves have internalized the perception that race is the predominant factor in their learning.

Although I have been a "successful" student for most of my academic life, it was not until graduate school that I had any pride in myself as a learner.

Very early in elementary school I received the message that being Black was not commensurate with academic success. The positive parts of my studying were flukes, incidences to be taken on faith but not explained through ability or hard work. No matter what the affirmations from home and the community, the message from school was that I was not valued. In the world of my childhood, the world of school, studying, playing, and peer acceptability, "success" was not an expectation for African Americans.

What I now know is that in school I had no voice. My preferences for learning were, for the most part, strongly discouraged. The pleasure I derived from color and patterns and my need for humor as I work were dismissed as unimportant. The ease with which I could access the content once I understood how relationships worked—relationships among groups of people, communication systems, geographical features—was viewed as topsy-turvy. All this contributed to a sense of never being quite right, of doing well in spite of myself. Even my left-handedness contributed to the teachers' views of me. But at the base of it all was the deafening silence on race and culture, the total exclusion of Africans and African Americans—of me—in any valued part of the curriculum.

In one of my graduate school courses, there were 24 of us, all of us experienced teachers, most of us in our thirties. I was the only Black person in the course, in fact the only one in my program. One day we did an exercise in which everyone had to point out on a map where their families had come from. I was the only one out of that group whose grandparents, all four of them, had been born in the United States. I realized then that if anyone had roots in this country, it was me; I was "All-American," a claim that nobody else in that room could make. At the same time, we all knew who was the most marginalized, who would be viewed in most circumstances with the most suspicion, whose capability and competency would be most questioned.

I don't know what it is specifically about that incident that makes it so significant to me, or if it has any connection with anything else. I do know that it often comes to mind as I reflect on, reconcile, and reframe my understanding of what it means to be "multicultural," and of what that means in the classroom for me as a teacher and the students as learners.

I taught for six years at a Catholic school in the South End, where virtually all the students were African American or Latino. For those kids, race was never an issue in terms of *how* they learned, although it was certainly the major issue in why they needed to learn, because once they left that building, race would be the major determinant in how the world defined their possibilities. In the classroom, they were safe and free to be themselves as learners. I didn't have to worry about kids hiding because they needed to protect themselves. Of the three principals I had there, only one understood that paradigm, even though one of the others had a graduate degree in multicultural education.

There are so many places outside of the classroom where white kids can be themselves, and so few outside of their homes and community structures where kids of color can be themselves. If we're serious about anti-racist education, we have to make our classrooms places where kids' learning styles and strengths and skills are observed and validated and valued. As Enid Lee has said so clearly, we must stop asking what we can do to build the self-esteem of children of color, and instead ask ourselves what we do that erodes their self-esteem.

The four years that I've been at CFS have been challenging and satisfying. The work that the school is doing allows me a personal and professional honesty which I deeply value, which urges me to learn more about content and its implementation so that I might take more risks with my craft.

For the last two years, I've used Africa as the central theme in my fifth–sixth grade homeroom. Once I knew that CFS was serious about trying to become an anti-racist school, using Africa as the focus of my curriculum was the only possible decision I could make. Unlike teaching about Medieval England or Ancient Mesopotamia or even Nineteenth-Century New England, I knew that using themes concerning Africa and African life would bring up with much more power the issues of race and inclusion and personal style and intellectual honesty.

The size, diversity, complexity, and richness of Africa and African life have left me overwhelmed. Even though I had the relative luxury of having Africa as a central theme for the entire school year, there were questions about where to begin and what to include. There was, and is, so much that I don't know.

I do know, with certainty, that the dearth of age-appropriate materials isn't an excuse for not teaching about Africa; in fact, it helps make the case for why we *should* teach about Africa. The kids have picked up on the fact that there's so little information available. They look at an atlas, and the questions begin to roll out. "Look, Laraine," they say, with a mix of indignation and anger, "there are 12 pages of maps devoted to the United States, and 4 to tiny little Australia, but only 2 to Africa. Only 2 maps for that whole big giant continent! Why?"

Those questions become a valuable lesson that I never could have planned by myself. It allows the kids to be thinkers, to come up with their own answers, to develop perspective. If they can't figure out for themselves that there is a reason why they can't find maps and information on Africa or on ancient African civilizations, then I haven't done my job.

What follows is the language arts section of a curriculum report which I wrote two years ago, at the end of my second year at Cambridge Friends. There is so much that I would do differently now. I've realized since then that I have to let go of content for content's sake. I've always understood that intellectually, but the kids have given me a much more immediate, visceral understanding of why it's important.

When we challenge kids to think, when we open up the curriculum to perspective as well as content, then questions of power get raised. It is intellectually and emotionally dishonest to avoid teaching certain subjects, or to teach them in a vacuum, simply because we might be uncomfortable with the issues that are raised or our inability to authoritatively address them. One of the risks of letting go of content is that kids sometimes ask questions for which we don't have answers. Letting go of content means letting go of the power and control that we have as teachers.

Clinging to the gospel of content can be a way of preserving racist practices. Many of us perpetuate the myth among our students and their parents that content makes for a good education—that the ability to answer jeopardy questions and score high on the SAT defines a well-educated person—and because we control the content, we have the power.

That's a very dangerous situation for kids of color and for our collective future. Unless our kids learn to think for themselves, to know and monitor their own social and intellectual strengths in changing situations, they run the risk of never learning how to change those situations for themselves and others. They have to become independent learners, and that's hard to do. As a teacher, I have to help them develop tools for evaluating what they're doing and how they're doing it—and then, I have to get out of the way.

Teaching language arts this year has been an exciting experience for me. One of the best parts has been working with Merryl Pisha, our learning specialist: watching how she approaches the writing process, listening as she suggests different ways to teach about writing, trying out new ideas with her, and feeling free to complain or rejoice about how the ideas have been received by the kids. Merryl has helped me so much to think about what I see as some important aspects of writing and to communicate them in a way that is beneficial to the children.

What we did this year was different for the students. I saw a lot of growth in them; everyone benefitted in some way. The kids who made the most progress were the ones for whom writing is not easy. Using graphic organizers to plan structure and paragraphs, webbing ideas, writing drafts on the computer, and using the Spell Checker were all things that helped.

There were two good examples of kids who struggle with their writing and who were very successful this year. The first one started the year with good ideas and an active imagination, but he limited himself in how much he would write; he struggled both with his handwriting and with his organization. One of the first things we did was to have him think and write at the computer. He went from three-sentence stories to stories that were much longer, but still poorly organized. Once we introduced webbing and planning from the web, his organizing really took off. What was really exciting was that he could see a connection between what was in his head and what he was able to put on paper once he could view it all in front of him and plan from the web.

The second student, on the other hand, is very methodical, precise, and concrete. It is difficult for him to generate ideas, especially with creative writing assignments. His writing improved because the webbing allowed him to look at his ideas and fill in what he didn't have. The improvement for him also came as he practiced webbing and planning his written work (in both language arts and in social studies); the more he used the tool, the more extended his thinking became.

I could probably think of at least one positive outcome of using graphic plans for everyone in the class who was willing to use the tools. (About three kids weren't open to trying what we were doing in language arts. They "did the thing," but clearly only under duress.) For kids who were good writers already, planning and webbing gave them a try at some things new and a way to stretch their ideas and organization.

I enjoyed the approach we took in reading according to genre. Starting with mysteries was a very good idea. The kids connected easily with this category, and it was possible for every level of reader to find a good book within his/her ability.

Next year, I would like to start again with mysteries. I think that I will include an Imanmu Jones novel (by Rosa Guy) so that we can think and talk about the ways in which a mystery that has a Black protagonist and is written by a Black author might be different from mysteries which are written by Whites with White heroes. I would like to include an opportunity for everyone to read a mystery where the hero is a woman/girl. Too many times the boys tend to stick with strong male characters, and a little diversity would be good.

The activities in the biography section of language arts were much more structured than those in the mystery genre. Students were required to read three biographies. One had to be about a person born before the twentieth century and one about a person who was the opposite sex of the reader. Both of these restrictions were good.

Biography is another genre in which language arts and social studies can be combined. I was impressed with how readily the children picked up biographies about people of color, and I think the next step is to extend their connection with diversity from the points of view of life-style, overcoming obstacles, and values (both individual and communal).

One of the most powerful things that Merryl said to me this year was that she saw the opportunity for kids to try something new and not only to practice what they already know. The more I have reflected on this, the more it seems to have ramifications in lots of areas—*particularly* that ability to approach problems, situations, and experiences from a positive position. Next year, I would like to be more articulate with the kids about learning something new, understanding themselves better, and becoming more independent learners.

The biggest disappointment for me in language arts this year came when we read *The Legend of Tarik*. I really enjoyed reading this book: it is set in Medieval times, it takes place in Africa, includes a woman who acts independently as one of the main characters, and really shows that as Tarik matures not everything is resolved in him. What I tried to do was to connect this novel with our social studies activities on ancient Africa. What I ended up doing was sacrificing the novel to do social studies. Because the social studies unit was so big, I dragged the reading of this book out too long.

I think the book needs to stand either in the reading section of the curriculum as part of the adventure genre, where we can look at the struggle between good and evil, the conflicts of growing up, the idea of taking a journey, etc. Or it needs to be in the social studies curriculum as part of what enriches the study of African kingdoms and brings out the flavor of the fourteenth and fifteenth century African villages along the trade routes. I tried to do too much with this book and the kids didn't get as much out of it as they could have.

Two positive things did come from this reading. The boys got to see an African hero in a novel. This was a connection that was made in reading this book and in studying about Africa at the same time—one more window on the world in a section of literature that is popular with boys in this age group. The second outcome was brought about from an Ann Landers (or Dear Abby) column which listed eight or nine signs of maturity in young adults. These included self-confidence, decisionmaking, restraint, planning ahead, empathy, etc. Everyone enjoyed choosing three signs of maturity and then looking for examples of their choices as the book progressed. It was interesting to see the choices. We could almost tell where people were in their own maturation by their ability to choose and to observe the growing maturity in Tarik and Stria.

For the last extensive language arts activity the students were required to compare and contrast material on one topic from two different sources. Topics included: comparing sibling rivalry in two different novels; Malcolm X before and after prison from his speeches and his autobiography; a comparison of Louis Armstrong and Charlie Parker; a look at two different views of Charlie Parker, one from a biography and the other from a movie; how Jews were treated in *The Devil's Arithmetic* and how Blacks were treated in *To Kill a Mockingbird;* a comparison between Bo Jackson as a football player and as a baseball player.

It was exciting to watch kids pick topics. It was not the kids who have the most facility with writing who necessarily found this assignment the most fun. Merryl provided a wonderful structure for the kids to work within. I really want to use it next year for much more of our expository writing. Two or three of the kids found the structure so helpful that they wrote not only the two required paragraphs using this method, but used the structure for their whole report.

This assignment provided lots of room for choice for the kids, of range to pull interest and thinking together, and of organizational structure for clear writing. I loved watching the kids think and try to put it into order, and see what it was they were actually doing. That's what made it so rewarding: knowing that the kids were conscious of what they were doing. I really believe that by the end of the year, almost all of the kids understood having a structure for writing, whether or not they wanted to follow it. We could actually have a conversation about the writing that was conversation, and not just "What do you want me to fix, and how should I fix it?" It was a great project on which to end the year.

3

Classroom Tapestry

A Practitioner's Perspective on Multicultural Education

Judith J. Richards

Throughout the past quarter century (my own time as both a college student and urban educator), I have been aware of both increasing support and renewed opposition toward multicultural education.

In the late 1960s and early 1970s racism in both society at large and its educational institutions was acknowledged. My first teaching placement was at the Gibson School in Dorchester, Massachusetts. Jonathan Kozol had just written *Death at an Early Age,* as an indictment of the Boston Public School System, following his own time as a teacher at the Gibson School. Many educators voiced the belief that a monocultural curriculum needed to be abandoned to make room for a more multicultural approach. College curriculums (for example the emergence of African American Studies Departments) as well as the position statements of professional education organizations (for example, ASCD in 1977 and AACTE in 1979) reflected the recognition of multicultural education as a cornerstone of quality education.

However, the 1980s brought a new conservative climate to the United States. Hakim Rashid of Howard University observed that "from a public policy perspective, multicultural education was not an educational priority." The back-to-basics movement took hold and multicultural education was seen as an obstacle, not an enabler to the "three R's."

We cannot allow multicultural education to be viewed as vague policies and curricular add-ons (the first cuts during economic recession) or relegated to ethnic potluck dinners in the schools and communities. Nor can we allow multicultural education to be misrepresented or distorted simply because it is politically safe to do so. Today's educators have the opportunities to be the agents of change and multicultural education can address "the structures of inequity and challenge the status quo."[1]

The purpose of this chapter will be to examine these structures, to look at some of the new scaffolding for change, and finally to bring the reader in touch with the fabric of a multicultural curricula.

Clarity of the structural issues might be best served by establishing common understanding of the vocabulary inherent in this topic. Asa Hilliard notes that

47

"in education we frequently do not enjoy common terminology. We use the same words some of the time but we do not have common meaning for some of these words."[2] Toward this end, this chapter highlights some of the relevant terminology that is used frequently in current literature and offers some *possible* "working definitions" in the context of classroom implementation so that we might begin a shared basis of understanding.

Culture and Multicultural Education

Paulo Freire defined culture as anything that human beings make and Spradley and McCurdy[3] suggest that culture is like a recipe for producing behavior and artifacts as well as the "acquired knowledge that people use to interpret experiences and generate social behavior." These basic foundations allow us to identify the shared ways that a human group does things.

In our third- and fourth-grade interaged classroom, we often talk about the ways in which older children share the classroom culture with incoming third graders. In this sense we are using the word culture to represent a shared set of behaviors, expectations, and vocabulary common to our classroom family. Freire's definition also permits me to be specific and concise when I describe the cultural learning component of each project that I assign in a Teaching Mathematics to Children Course at Wheelock College. For these projects, undergraduate students are to design a set of manipulatives that will encourage a child's understanding of a particular math concept. The materials must be age-appropriate, promote cooperative learning, and be culturally significant. For example, students may use a set of symbols or artifact replicas to introduce classification, seriation, and conservation. The culture represented may be the student's own heritage, or a culture of interest. The student is expected to move well beyond a "tourist approach" and to provide accurate cultural information with the project.

Multicultural education is the *process* that honors the multicultural nature of the society in which we live and, as an agent of change, examines the connections between power and knowledge. We need to make a major paradigm shift in our thinking and begin to uncover deceit and omission in our present knowledge base. As part of their Theoretical Framework for Whole Learning, Sheli Wortis and Lynn Hall [Literacy/Curriculum Connections in Cambridge Public Schools] share the following statement about how children learn in interrelated fields:

> Multicultural education is inclusive rather than exclusive. It encompasses many dimensions of human differences. . . . It affirms and validates each child's culture and background. It provides for the growth of positive self-esteem among all children and guarantees that each child will feel successful. By providing all children equal opportunity to learn, multicultural education gives each child a chance to reach her/his full potential. The ultimate goal of multicultural education is to develop children's ability to function competently within multiple cultures.[4]

Ethnicity and Multiethnic Education

Family members "teach culture" through a complex network of verbal and nonverbal socializations. In this sense, culture is learned and is a factor of where and when you were born and raised. Therefore, members of any ethnic group *may* share common cultural traditions, interpretations of events, and knowledge, but the teacher must be careful not to make any assumptions about cultural understanding based on ethnic designations. As part of federal, state, and municipal desegregation guidelines, students are often assigned "ethnic codes." For example, in the instances when a "4" is used to denote a "white Hispanic" child and a "5" represents a "black Hispanic child," the classification codes may actually separate siblings raised in the same family who certainly share cultural understanding. Some federal desegregation documents also use the terms "white" and "nonwhite" to designate children. To be defined as nonanything implies a missing attribute and has perhaps led to the blatant designations of "culturally deprived" that have not left the vocabulary of some educators.

It is curious to listen to speakers from Eurocentric cultures denounce other ethnocentric schools and curricula. It seems to be an argument akin to the "English-only" platform; one should only learn to read and write in your native language, if your native language is English. Many families who belong to the loosely defined macrocultural group accepted the "melting pot theory" which required giving away their own ethnic identity. When curricula have included ethnic studies, ethnicity is often seen as "other than white." Joanne Rizzi, developer of "The Kid's Bridge" exhibit on multicultural diversity at the Boston Children's Museum, suggests that all children need to find answers for the question "Where do I fit in?" She reminds us that we need to make sure *all* children need to feel that they have ethnicity. Stephen Rose further suggests that knowing you have a culture of your own helps to work out how to go about understanding other people's cultures.

It is ethnic group membership that often identifies or distinguishes people. Most references define ethnic groups as distinguishable, or set apart one from another. When cultures or ethnic identity is raised as a school issue, it is often used interchangeably with race. The concept of race was an effort to divide humans into broad categories and it began as part of an eighteenth-century trend by many European scientists to classify all living things. Montagu[5] called race a dangerous myth and notes that "it is not possible to make the sort of racial classifications which some anthropologists and others have attempted. The fact is that all human beings are so mixed with regard to origin that between different groups of individuals, overlapping physical traits is the rule."

While outsiders may view a group as distinguishable [exclusive], ethnic groups must be inclusive and allow for intragroup diversity. "Broad categories are artificial and lack the traditions, morals, and values that are attached to origins such as Ghanian, Lithuanian, Irish or Haitian."[6]

For purposes of clarity, I have used only the terms multi*cultural* education in this chapter. Both multi*cultural* and multi*ethnic* education are used in the literature to describe similar strategies. For example, James Banks refers to multiethnic education as the *reform movement* designed to make some major changes in the education of children.[7] The concepts and practices of multicultural education are beneficial to all classrooms regardless of the ethnic diversity of the student body. However, the reverse is not true. All too often, teachers assume that their practice and curricula need not change if their classroom community is ethnically diverse. The claim that "I don't notice color" or "I teach every child in the same way" is a dangerous trench hold. Consider the following differences in the 1987 high school drop-out rates:

Native North Americans—42 percent

Hispanics—39.9 percent

Blacks—24.7 percent

Whites—14.3 percent

Asians/Pacific Islanders—9.6 percent

These stark differences point out that we have achieved neither excellence nor equity[8] in our schools. More than 50 years ago, Dr. W.E.B. Du Bois wrote:

> A mixed school with poor unsympathetic teachers, with hostile public opinion and no teaching of truth concerning black folk is bad. A segregated school with ignorant placeholders, inadequate equipment, poor salaries, and wretched housing is equally bad. Other things being equal, the mixed school is the broader more natural basis for the education of its youth. It gives wider contacts, it inspires greater self confidence, and suppresses the inferiority complex. But other things seldom are equal, and in that case, sympathy, knowledge and truth outweigh all that the mixed school can offer.[9]

Minority Group

The term minority group is also often used interchangeably with ethnic group. From a numerical perspective this is an absurd substitution. By the year 2020, one-half of the school-age children in the United States will be children of color.

Minority group is also used to identify those ethnic groups that have an "underrepresented"[10] status in the society. In educational curricula, one major effect of this status has been to ignore or distort the contributions of people of color. While inclusion does not guarantee increased self-esteem, I have watched many children and adults reclaim knowledge when they saw themselves reflected in the curriculum. While most ethnic groups in the United States have experienced underrepresented status at some point in their history; others have remained in this position for generation upon generation. In this respect, a minority group suffers common *discrimination* and subordination along with their more positive common identity. Discrimination and one of its insidious educational manifestations, lowered expectations and "down-teaching," is a fact in many American educational settings.

The majority status group or macroculture has a vague identity. Anglo-European language, tradition, and social values determine many aspects of life in the United States and whereas Anglo and other western European Americans are "born into a relative position of power, it has no real meaning for the vast majority of self-perceived whites and gives only artificial powers."[11]

The Ultimate Obstacle: Racism

Racism in the United States operates on several levels: individual as well as institutional. On all levels, racism is racial prejudice in practice and is related to power and status. Racism is perpetuated in our schools through textbooks and other materials that either omit or portray false information about certain racial groups. Many educators and academics from Eurocentric cultures have not had to share the power of knowledge before. Unfortunately some still belong to the "If it's knowledge, I know it, and if I don't know it, then it's not knowledge" school. Enid Lee, an internationally renowned expert on race relations, sees evidence of racism in a teacher's expectations that students from given racial groups are not naturally as good at certain subjects (academic) and good in others (music and athletics, for example). Teachers may not always be conscious of the malice in this practice; however, as Lee suggests, racism is measured by effect as well as intent. The long-term effect of racism in our society and educational institutions has been devastating. One only has to read the news throughout the United States (Dubuque, Michigan, Bensonhurst, etc.) to see the results of students who have been given an inaccurate, distorted view of themselves and other cultural groups. More than one-half of the tenth through twelfth graders surveyed in a recent Harris poll had knowledge of violent racial incidents and one-fourth of these students responded that they had been the target of a racial or ethnic attack. Enid Lee concluded an interview with the following observation:

> By and large, education is further on in addressing racism than most other institutions. That's my assessment when I look at Health or Policing for example. Teachers are beginning to show the rest of society how to deal with racism in a progressive and responsible way. At least we have begun to name the issue. Now we must continue to eradicate racism in all its forms.[12]

Whereas it was important to have shared understanding of relevant vocabulary, multicultural education must move beyond the rhetoric. This is not a movement designed by experts in "ivory towers," but a grass-roots effort on all levels of the educational community.

51

A 1991 California report, *Embracing Diversity,* "concludes that all California teachers should be proficient in four major areas: language development, knowledge of cultures and backgrounds of their students, the building and teaching of student-centered curriculum that integrates diverse cultures of the students, and the establishment of a classroom and school climate that actively combats prejudice and builds respect among racial, ethnic, and national groups."[13] California is not alone in developing state-level scaffolding. In 1990, the New York Board of Regents directed the Commissioner of Education (Thomas Sobol) and his staff to develop a detailed plan for increasing understanding of the history and cultures of diverse groups both in the United States and throughout the world. Two of Sobol's considerations were to operationalize the idea that a multicultural curriculum is appropriate for all children ("All children in our society should learn about the society as a whole, in its diversity as well as its unity") and to acknowledge that curriculum restructuring is not enough ("We must also attend to instructional material, teaching method, teacher education and support, the composition of school staff, school organization and operation, assessment practices and all the rest").[14]

All educators must make a commitment to fight racism. As Spike Lee might tell us, it is time to "do the right thing!" The policy transformations in states like New York and California must now be followed by operationalization in every school and classroom. Teachers often use the quantity of topics they presently cover in their curricula as an excuse for not embracing a new vision. As we abandon the falsehoods, we have the room to increase our knowledge of the cultures and rich ethnic traditions of our students. Sheli Wortis and Lynn Hall point out that "children and adults alike gain awareness and appreciation of diversity when offered interaction in a meaningful context."[15] In this light, our own classroom motto is "Nou aprann ansanm, yon aprann lot" [We learn from each other]. Wortis and Hall urge us to remember that in a world "where people of color are in the majority, we need to build classroom environments and curricula that daily reflect and respect the full range of cultural diversity."[16] I believe that the key word in this statement is *daily*. Process-based multicultural education is not limited to monthly ethnic events, to the "holiday syndrome,"[17] or to posters on the wall. During a recent panel discussion of educational pluralism, a young African American high school student from the audience asked why she was denied the opportunity to learn about the contributions of African Americans in history class. The school district where she lives has moved toward a "time-share" structure due to financial constraints. Students attend classes in shifts throughout the calendar year. This student's shift assignment did not include the month of February, when "black history" was taught as an isolated topic. As Dell Hymes wrote in 1981, "One can honor cultural pride on the wall of a room, yet inhibit learning within them."

"Designing curriculum appropriate for diverse learners is an exercise in translation, integration and synchronization."[18] Throughout the remainder of this chapter I will use a weaving metaphor to bring the reader a visual and tactile image of life in our classroom community. Many metaphors are often used for this purpose, from musical to culinary images. In choosing a weaving metaphor, I wished to emphasize the *active* nature of the curriculum. "To become meaningful, a curriculum has to be enacted by pupils as well as teachers, all of whom have their private lives outside of school. . . . A curriculum as soon as it becomes more than intentions is embodied in the communicative life of an institution, the talk and gestures by which pupils and teachers exchange meaning."[19] Imagine, if you will, both child and adult learners as active *weavers*. Through the weaving metaphor, we can visualize multicultural learning as an infusive part of the children's school day when we allow teachers to make use of their current understanding of a child's developmental learning, and the appropriate scope and sequence of skill acquisition as the *warp*. The diverse cultures of all classroom family members are the *weft* threads. The intricate designs we weave through our intercultural contacts enrich us all. The knowledge fabric belongs to us all. It is our new shared cognition. At the same time, we continue to see our unique selves in the patterns of the cloth. In this respect, beginning to implement a multicultural curriculum means working with current classroom strengths. It does not mean starting over or adding on. A teacher need not be overwhelmed by the thought of yet another curriculum to fit into their classroom day and another set of lessons to plan.

In the following pages I offer a schematic weaving of one of the thematic units of study from our third- and fourth-grade classroom; a detailed description of some of these activities and examples of children's writing.

Just as a tapestry becomes more valuable as the number of threads and knots increase, the strength of classroom learning becomes more meaningful when it is inclusive of many cultural perspectives.

"A Sense of Place"

This thematic unit of study was developed in our ethnically, linguistically, and economically diverse classroom community during the 1991 fall semester. Nancy Childs (a graduate student intern) and I began the development process during the previous summer. Nancy's interest and experience as a naturalist was the catalyst for this study, and our co-construction of the thematic framework was the beginning of a wonderful partnership.

"A Sense of Place" has been a successful unit of study for an integrated day classroom because of the strong connections to all areas of the curricula and classroom environments. In building the framework (*loom*) Nancy and I used two sets of guidelines. The first (Appendix A) was from the work of Mari E. Endreweit and Kay Sardo at Bank Street Graduate School of Education. It was part of the "Teacher Notebook" to support enactment of the Bank Street model in Follow Through classes in the 1970s. My copy is well worn, and continues to provide clear criteria for choosing a "piece of the world for closer study." The second (Appendix B) is based on a set of critical review questions written by Geneva Gay at Purdue University. Affirmative responses to these questions

A SENSE OF PLACE

Mathematics
- Problem solving in the context of folktales
- Alternative algorithms, e.g., ancient Egyptian multiplication algorithm
- Closed shapes: polygons angles lines, line segments in Babylonian history
- Ancient number systems and evolution of place value
- Hindu and Arabic numbers
- Bob Moses's work: number line and algebra; articles on the real line of the MBTA
- Sense of place surveys in Central Square

Learning Environments
- Classroom guest speakers with a special sense of place
- Minitrips to:
  1. Walden Pond
  2. Central Square
  3. Mr. Thompson's farm
  4. The Black Heritage Trail
  5. A night hike at Habitat
  6. Overnight trip to Martha's Vineyard to meet with the Wampanoag tribal council members

Writing
- Intergenerational interviews
- Sense of place writing trip reflections
- Documenting all experiences and reflections during theme

Literature
- *A Jar of Dreams*
- *The Banza*
- *Song of the Trees*
- *Island of the Blue Dolphins*
- *The Cartoonist*
- *Bridge to Terebithia*
- *My Side of the Mountain*
- *Julie of the Wolves*
- *Toto-Chan, A Girl at the Window*
- Moshup stories (Wampanoag)
- Haitian folk tales

The Arts
- Landscape painting in the style of Haitian artists
- Weaving with yard dyed with natural dyes
- Musical appreciation, patterning Haitian drumming
- Learn Ayiti Cheri song
- Instruments from natural materials
- Basketing with natural materials

Science
- Planting beans, corn, and squash
- A closer look at natural habitats
- Natural dyes
- Medicinal and edible plants
- Rainforest ecology, deforestation and reforestation projects in Haiti

History and Map Making
- Reinvestigating the explorers, particularly Columbus's voyages
- Map work with Chicago city maps (Jean Baptise Point du Sable) and Washington, DC, maps (Banneker)
- Building models of the Citadel in the block area

Games
- The travels and cultural borrowing of games: three-in-a-row games
- Oware/Wani/Mancala/Kay (stone games)
- Wosle

"assure that ethnic and cultural diversity permeates all their component parts and has informed the entire decision making process that produced the designs."[20]

I have chosen a few of the curricular strands to describe in some detail, in the hopes that this will give the reader a sense of the texture of this theme.

Literature

Our working definition of literacy, and by extension literature, is inclusive of the rich oral storytelling tradition found throughout the African Diaspora. Since one-third of the children at the Saundra Graham and Rosa Parks School are Haitian American, we make particular effort to include Haitian folktales and storytelling in our curriculum. The traditions of oral storytelling are part of other cultures as well, and also have status in our literature curriculum during all thematic studies.

A focus on "A Sense of Place" offered a wealth of children's literature that was both relevant and culturally significant. We were able to find a wide selection of books both to read aloud and to use in novel groups. This year we chose to read aloud E. B. White's *Triumpet of the Swan* and Jean Craighead George's *My Side of the Mountain,* since characters in both books had a protective sense of natural places. We noted that the *Oz* series by Frank Baum, *Toto-Chan, A Girl at the Window* by Tetsuko Kuroyanagi, *The Wheel on the School* by Meindert de Jong, and *Roll of Thunder, Hear My Cry* by Mildred Taylor are but a few of the classics that might be read to 8, 9, and 10 year olds during this theme.

As in all third- and fourth-grade classrooms, children in our class have made (or are making) the transition from learning to read, to reading to learn. Our first round of novel groups during this theme were heterogeneously grouped. Children in each of the four groups read one of the following novels: *Bridge to Terebithia* by Katherine Paterson, *Island of the Blue Dolphins* by Scott Odell, *Song of the Trees* by Mildred Taylor, and *The Cartoonist* by Betsy Byars. The characters of these novels represent cultural and linguistic diversity, and all have a special sense of place. One of the settings is urban and the rest are rural or remote. All of these novels evoke empathy and involvement from their readers. Children met biweekly to discuss common strands (character dilemmas, setting descriptions, etc.) and to read aloud favorite passages. In a second round of novel groups, some children read *A Jar of Dreams* by Yoshiko Uchido, the story of a Japanese American girl's sense of self and place in California during the Depression. Readers experience the discrimination and eventual Japanese encampment through Rinko's eyes. (I believe that this was a timely choice given the large media coverage of the anniversary of the bombing of Pearl Harbor. While I am sympathetic to the families who lost fathers and sons, mothers and daughters at Pearl Harbor, I am fearful of the resurgence of bigotry toward all Asians. I believe that a balanced perspective in classrooms is an important step toward preventing this fall out.) Other children read *The Banza,* a Haitian story retold by Diane Wolkstein. *The Banza* like many other Haitian folktales has characters that are animals not indigenous to Haiti. This prompted many discussions and follow-up research to learn about indigenous and endangered animals of Haiti, North America, and other world regions. It gave us a chance to think about a place from the animal's perspective. *The Banza* also offers the subtle inclusion of names in Kreyol. This allowed Haitian children to have teaching roles in the group, and for all children to learn additional vocabulary in Kreyol. A third set of children read *Julie of the Wolves* by Jean Craighead George. This is the story of Miyax, a native Alaskan girl who journeys alone onto the tundra in her determination not to loose her sense of self as an Inuit. The author's powerful descriptions of the environment, coupled with the main character's thoughts and narrative, bring the reader a strong sense belonging to this place.

Writing About a Sense of Place

Through the eyes of the characters in all of these books, we all realized how much our sense of who we are is related to the special places that we hold in our hearts. Never was this more clear to me than when a child, who was trying to decide who to call on during a classroom meeting said, "Anthony, you *know* that I'll always be there for you. We're both from Potoprins, so this time I'll call on somebody else." This camaraderie and sense of community is a cornerstone of our classroom discourse practice. It also prompted our writings about our own personal sense of place. Children wrote about a wide range of memories and special places. The example on p. 57 is representative of classroom writings.

In addition, children interviewed their parents about their own sense of place, both as children and as adults. This brought parents into our community of learners. The pieces of writing on p. 58 are excerpts from these interviews.

Just as master weavers are able to change the pattern in their weaving by sometimes passing the weft under and over more than one warp thread at a time, dynamic classrooms nurture the interrelatedness of curricula, and often the lines between them are not clearly drawn. In this same fashion, the strand that I have labeled learning environments provided fertile ground for additional writing and reading to learn experiences.

Learning Environments

We had several wonderful classroom visitors, including Aliyah Mahoud, another Graham and Parks teacher. Aliyah spent the afternoon with us to share her thoughts, as a Muslim woman, about Mecca. Her joy in talking about Mecca, and family members who had made the Hajj, gave us all a sense of this special place. In addition to bringing community resources into the class-

My favorite place is in Haiti
My favorite place is outside
is the yard. I used to play with
my friend Wisli. We used to throw
rocks at birds. There was a big
tree. The tree was growing
knips We picked some and
ate them. Knips are little green
balls and they have orange
inside the shell. Some times
they taste good and some times
they taste awful. The inside
looks slimmy. there are not
many houses around the yard.
There lots of trees. They are all
different. Sometimes my brother
and sister eat the birds We
catch. They cook them in a
pan over a fire. I ate
Some too. It tastes good.

room, we took small groups of children out into the community, thus eliminating the four walls that often constrain learning. During this theme, some children visited a man who has lived on the same farm for over 90 years. He shared the wisdom of his years and his well-established sense of his land. Children saw his gardens and his root cellar with both canned and dried provisions. The children who visited Mr. Thompson returned to the classroom with a new sense of patience and perseverance. Another group went to Boston's Beacon Hill neighborhood for a guided tour of the Black Heritage Trail. We saw and heard about the homes, schools, businesses, and churches of Boston's African American community during the 1800s. Children walked through Holmes Alley with a new *sense* of what a *safe place* might be. They saw some of the homes that were stops on the underground railroad. A third group of children went to neighboring Central Square to gather data for a mathematics project. Their task was to look for evidence of people bringing their own sense of place with them when they moved to Cambridge.

A Sense of Place in Mathematics

The survey team came back to the classroom with great confidence. They had found the empirical evidence! In a four-block length of Massachusetts

When my Dad was my age, he had two favorite places.
One of the places was the top of an avocado tree in his
back yard near the wall. The other one was a little way from
his house at the edge of Mexico City in the hills. It had
rocks and hills and valleys. That's what he liked about it. He also.
liked it because it was peaceful.
                              by Ben

My Dad's special place now
is where he lives now
He has only been through
Three different places. IF
My Dad could go any where
In the world he would
go to the place where his
ancestors are. in El Salvador
          by Noemi

Avenue, children counted six East Indian stores or restaurants. One Eritrean restaurant, two Chinese businesses, two Middle Eastern restaurants, one Japanese store, and two Greek stores. They designed graphs and wrote about their experiences in their math journals.

In addition to the data-collection bridge to other areas of the curricula, we found many thematic connections in mathematics. I always begin the school year with geometry, as a way of broadening children's narrow sense of mathematics as mostly arithmetic. This year we started with two-dimensional, or planar geometry. Students explored spaces that were bordered by line segments. They reinvented rules for predicting the number of bisectors and the number of diagonals that a polygon will have. These reinvented rules are now part of our shared knowledge base. They belong to us as part of our new spatial sense. During our study of lines and line segments, we used many of the three-in-a-row games collected by Claudia Zaslavsky. While most children living in the United States are familiar with Tic-Tac-Toe, a similar game is called Tapatan in the Philippines and is known as Achi in Ghana. I have also seen it played by children on the Caribbean island of St. Vincent.

The notion that games and other knowledge might have traveled throughout the world was reinforced when we began a study of numbers. We looked at our 10 digit *place* value number system and read about its Hindu and Arabic origins. This system had been used for over 1000 years before it was adopted in northern Europe. "This cultural borrowing is typical of the way in which ideas spread from one region to another."[21]

Our senses of the number line and of algebraic thinking, as well as our familiarity with the transit system, were developed through a process designed by Robert Moses.[22] Children rode the MBTA red line from one end point to the other, using Park Street station as 0 (zero). After a day of riding the train, we came back to the classroom to talk and write about the experience. Our talk and writing have moved from intuitive language to language that includes more and more vocabulary from the mathematical register. I am convinced that this process will bring an increasing number of students to the "algebra table" when they reach middle school. Algebra is now part of our sense of place.

As with most of our activities, problem-solving is a cooperative learning activity. The practice of weaving arithmetic and problem-solving situations into the cultural folktales of the children in the classroom has allowed children of color to assume leadership roles in diverse (in terms of ethnicity, gender, language, and arithmetic skill) groups. For example, I took a well-known problem concerning the sequence of fillings and pouring with a 3- and a 7-liter container to achieve exactly 5 liters of water and weaved it into the Haitian story of Teyzen.

"Krik [krak]. Do you remember the story of Teyzen? Well, one day Asefi and her brother Dyesel were going to the river to get water. Their mother gave them each a calabash. Asefi's calabash held 7 liters when it was full. Dyesel's calabash held 3 liters when it was full. Their mother told them to bring home exactly 5 liters of water. Tell about the fillings and pouring that the timoun [children] must do in order to bring home 5 liters of water."

The concept of culture and knowledge as movable, connected to but not dependent on a single place was not distant for the many children in our classroom who could remember their own move to the United States. This brings us the last wrap thread that I will detail in a narrative form.

A Sense of Place in History and Mapmaking

The media deluge concerning the quincentenial anniversary of Christopher Columbus's arrival in the Americas has prompted many classroom meetings to discuss the event through the eyes of indigenous people. We looked critically at the truths and "untruths" surrounding the voyages of Columbus. When Columbus arrived in Haiti (Ayiti is from the original name for the island that Columbus insisted on calling Hispaniola) in 1492, there were perhaps a million Arawak people living on one of the most beautiful tropical islands in the world. Forty years later there were less than 200. "The discovery of the island began the genocide of its people."[23] Classroom children questioned why we would celebrate Columbus claim to "discovery" when none of us celebrate the day our homes were robbed or our families assaulted. Fortunately, there are an increasing amount of resources to replace the falsehoods surrounding Christopher Columbus with truths.

The word discovery is rarely used in our classroom now. Places are visited, respected, and admired, but not claimed. We have a collective "sense of place" that is in harmony with the earth and with each other.

We find closure for each of our theme studies in a different way. For the "sense of place" theme, we chose to collect all of our writings, photographs, and illustrations in books. We invited families and school friends to join us for a celebration of our work. It was the day to take the weaving down from the loom!

"A Sense of Place" is an example of a theme that provides opportunities to view the curriculum through many cultural lenses. We have also developed all classroom curricula through ethnocentric themes of study. We have identified activities, developed lessons, chosen literature, etc., to give central status to several cultures previously underrepresented in school curricula, for example, Haiti, a Native American Nation, or one of the cultures of Africa. In addition, we have developed intense focus studies through Japanese, Greek, and Latin American perspectives. These ethnocentric curricula have been the fruit of lengthy studies and investigations by staff and parents. They often began with the expertise and contributions of one adult member of the community of learners and were developed over time. When there is little published curriculum, it is the responsibility of the teacher to model active learning. "The role of the teacher is to make the student's world and the classroom congruent. . . . The teacher must read information from the cultures of their students."[24]

An ethnocentric curriculum must also be woven thoroughly into the fabric of the classroom. In an ethnocentric curriculum, our weaving might look more like the Mexican *Ojos de Dio*

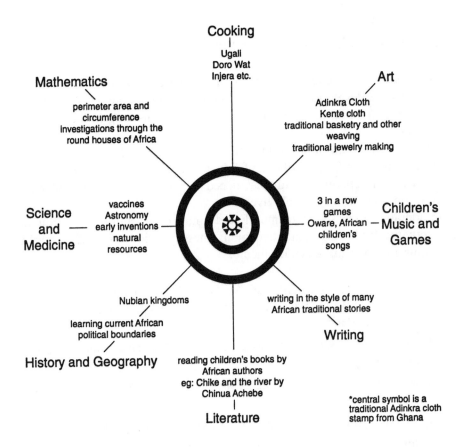

The multicultural cornerstones of our school environment are a daily part of classroom life. They exist not only in the curriculum but in the daily language and practice of our community of learners. Toward this end, we have borrowed many words from languages other than English that best met our needs. For example we use "Ago" and "Ame" (from the Twi language of West Africa) as the call and response for sharing information with the whole group. Any member of the classroom may say "Ago" if (s)he has something to say to the rest of us. By responding "Ame," we acknowledge the speaker and are ready to listen respectfully.

As teachers, we have the opportunity to begin the change toward a more pluralistic curriculum at the "grass roots" classroom level. As Asa Hilliard noted, "A wealth of old multidisciplinary international, and multiracial literature exists that would allow us to find the true stories of the roles of all groups in human history so that we could include them in the school curriculums." To enter this process is to be prepared to say, "**Ame**" . . . I am ready to listen and to learn about all cultures respectfully. "Ultimately if the curriculum is centered in truth, it will be pluralistic."

Appendix A
"Getting Started: Teacher Planning"

"The view of learning as a dynamic and integrative process in which the basic skills are developed as tools for achieving more significant knowledge about humankind and the world is a thread which runs long in the history of education."

The following scaffolding is adapted from the work of Mari Endreweit and Kay Sardo at Bank Street College of Education. The teacher must accept the task of choosing a theme of study that indeed helps children to better understand their world and the way people live in it.

In addition, a classroom theme of study must offer multiple opportunities and activities for learning and interaction. These questions may offer an initial screening for choosing a central theme.

1. Is this theme of personal interest? Am I already knowledgeable and enthusiastic about it? Will I take time to increase my own knowledge base outside of the classroom?

2. What is the accessibility of resources within the school, and the greater community?

3. What is the relevance of this central theme to the lives of classroom children?

4. Does this theme offer the potential for conceptual learning?

5. Is this theme suitable for the age level of the children in this classroom?

6. Does this theme offer the potential for independent learning?

7. Is there adequate, and uninterrupted time in the school calendar for planning and implementing this core curriculum?

Appendix B
"A Critical Review"

The following questions, adapted from "Designing Relevant Curriculum for Diverse Learners" by Geneva Gay; provide a solid foundation for developing new classroom themes of study.

"To assure that ethnic and cultural diversity permeates all the component parts, and has informed the entire decision making process that produced the designs; several specific questions can be used."[25]

1. *Does* the curriculum goal reflect sensitivity to, and celebration of the cultural diversity of the students?

2. *How* will the content and learning activities affirm the cultures of diverse students?

3. *Does* diversity permeate the entirety of the curriculum?

4. *Does* the pluralistic content used as the context for major skill development, and not merely as an add-on feature?

5. *Will* students from many ethnic groups find the instructional materials meaningful to their own life experiences?

6. *Will* a wide variety of culturally different examples and situations be used throughout the curriculum design to illustrate major concepts?

7. *Are* these examples and experiences comparable in kind, significance, magnitude and function, to those selected from the 'macro-culture'?

8. *Are* the performance expectations (goals and objectives) similar for all learners?

9. *Do* the suggested methods for teaching, and the proposed student activities respond to the learning styles and preferences of diverse students?

10. *Do* the evaluation techniques allow different ways for students to demonstrate achievement?

11. *Will* the self esteem and confidence of diverse learners be improved by the proposed curriculum?

Notes

1. Enid Lee, in Charlotte Morgan, "Speaking Out on Racism. An Interview With Enid Lee," *OPSTF NEWS* April 1989, 6–9. See also Hakim Rashid, "Teacher Perceptions of the Multicultural Orientation of Their Preservice Education and Current Occupational Settings," *Educational Research Quarterly* 14, No. 1 (1990).

2. Asa Hilliard, "Teachers and Cultural Styles in a Pluralistic Society," *National Education Association Journal* (January 1989), 7(6), 65–69.

3. J. P. Spradley and W. McCurdy, *Anthropology: The Cultural Perspective* (New York: John Wiley and Sons, 1975).

4. Sheli Wortis and Lynn Hall, "Infusing Multiculturalism in a Whole Language Classroom," *The Whole Language Teacher's Association Newsletter* 3, No. 2 (1990).

5. A. Montagu, *Man's Most Dangerous Myth: The Fallicy of Race* (New York: Oxford University Press, 1974).

6. Stephen D. Rose, as quoted by Charles A. Radin, "Whites Must Find Identity in a World of Color," *The Boston Globe*, July 29, 1990.

7. James Banks, *Multiethnic Education: Theory and Practice,* 2nd ed. (Boston, MA: Allyn and Bacon, 1988).

8. Christine L. Bennett, *Comprehensive Multicultural Education Theory and Practice,* 2nd ed. (Needham, MA: Allyn and Bacon, 1990).

9. W.E.B. DuBois, "Does the Negro Need Separate Schools?" *Journal of Negro Education* as quoted by Derrick Bell (1987), *And We Are Not Saved: The Elusive Quest for Racial Justice* N.Y: Basic Books and by Christine Bennett, *Comprehensive Multicultural Education Theory and Practice,* 2nd ed. (Needham, MA: Allyn and Bacon, 1990).

10. Martha Montero-Sieburth, "Conceptualizing Multicultural Education: From Theoretical Approaches to Classroom Practice," *Equity and Choice,* 4, No. 3 (1988), 3–12.

11. Rose, op. cit. (Ref. 6).

12. Lee, op. cit. (Ref. 1).

13. "Embracing Diversity," (San Francisco: California Tomorrow, 1990).

14. Thomas Sobol, "Understanding Diversity," *Educational Leadership* 48, No. 3 (1990), 29–30.

15. Wortis and Hall, op. cit. (Ref. 4).

16. *Ibid.*

17. Valerie Hinderlie, et al., "Caring for Children in a Social Context: Eliminating Racism, Sexism and other Patterns of Discrimination," Child Care Resource Center, 1981.

18. Geneva Gay, "Designing Relevant Curriculum for Diverse Learners," 20, No. 4 (1988).

19. Douglass Barnes, *From Communication to Curriculum* (London: Peguin Books, 1976).

20. Gay, op. cit. (Ref. 18).

21. Claudia Zaslavsky, "Bringing the World into the Math Class," Curriculum Review, 24, No. 3 (1985), 62–64.

22. Cynthia Silva and Robert Moses, "The Algebra Project: Making Middle School Mathematics Count," *The Journal of Negro Education* 59, No. 3 (1990).

23. Wenda Parkinson, *This Gilded African Toussaint L'Overture* (London: Quartet Books, 1980).

24. Molefi Kete Asante, "Afrocentric Curriculum," *Education Leadership* 49, No. 4 (1991), 28–31; See also Asa Hilliard, "Why We Must Pluralize the Curriculum," *Educational Leadership* 49, No. 4 (1991).

25. Gay, op. cit. (Ref. 18).

The Blind Men (Women) and the Elephant

A Case for a Comprehensive Multicultural Education Program at the Cambridge Rindge and Latin School*

Sandra Dickerson

I began teaching at the Cambridge Rindge and Latin School in 1974. I was assigned to what was then the Cambridge High and Latin School—a college preparatory school whose curriculum philosophy was homogeneous grouping, tracking. As I commenced teaching at the Cambridge High and Latin School, I received my assignment—three basic level, senior English classes and an elective English course entitled "Minority" Literature. I do recall feeling strange, alienated, a singleton working in a void or a chasm, for I was the only "minority" English teacher at the high school level. This dilemma has prevailed for half of my years of employment at the high school.

Albeit, this was my accustomed predicament—an African American woman having been born in Wisconsin, graduated from all white secondary schools where White teachers tolerated my presence. I grated my way to honor roll status in the English Department of the University of Wisconsin among chilling stares that said I was not supposed to be there.

At the Cambridge High and Latin School, no "new teacher's orientation" eased the transition into a new environment, a new profession. No support system would provide direction. No closet for my coat. No desk. I floated. I carried materials, in arm, to three or four different classrooms. My coat and preparation materials were left on a table in the teacher's lounge where I spent my preparation time. In that first year, I remember vividly sitting in the teacher's lounge preparing for my classes and a woman asked me "Are you a part of that new bilingual thing?" I replied "no," and told her that I worked in the English Department. She then said in an indignant tone, "Not Mr. ———'s English Department." I told her that was correct. Her next statement was, "Oh my God, how'd that happen?" Years later whenever our paths would cross, "Oh my God, how'd that happen" would swell silently in my throat and make it warm.

I would become only the second African American teacher to be tenured in the English Department at the High and Latin School. The first had been

*This paper is dedicated to the work of the Onesimus Project.

promoted to the Guidance Department the same year that I started. To maintain my balance, I rely on her heavily especially since I had inherited her schedule. The department could not be left without "one."

The following year, another African American woman was hired in the English Department. In 1981 she became the Chairperson of the English Department. Thus, again, I became Cambridge's only "minority" English teacher at the high school level. This situation lasted until approximately 1983, when an African American male was hired.

Since that time, the school has undergone tremendous change—some of which threatened its stability as an urban educational institution. In 1974, our school consisted of approximately 2700 students who were served by two schools—The Rindge Technical School, a technical and vocational school, and the Cambridge High and Latin School—a college preparatory school. In 1974 the Cambridge schools were headed by an African American superintendent. A black principal headed the Cambridge High and Latin School. This phenomenal situation existed because in 1969 the High and Latin school had been overcome with racial strife. This included sit-ins, strikes, and protests by Black students, who demanded more Black faculty and Black History and Literature courses. The protests erupted into violence, which was controlled by police in riot gear and police dogs. On the surface, it would appear that this should have been a supportive environment. It was. I enjoyed a warm personal relationship with the principal, however, I never got to know the superintendent. Both men worked in an atmosphere that was tainted with nonsupport. The black superintendent resigned in 1975. In 1980, a new high school complex was completed and the two schools merged. The principal of the Rindge Technical school retired. Everyone felt that the black headmaster of the Latin School would become principal of the newly combined Cambridge Rindge and Latin School. Not so. Much waving of fists and gnashing of teeth commenced at the School Committee level. Suddenly, the headmaster was no longer principal of any school, for he was tenured to the old Cambridge High and Latin. That school no longer existed and, therefore, neither did he—a mere technicality to be sure; but it held. In 1980, the current principal, who is white, was appointed as headmaster of the new school complex—the Cambridge Rindge and Latin School.

Today the Cambridge Rindge and Latin School is a comprehensive urban high school which consists of 2095 students who matriculate in six different programs or houses. The concept is frequently referred to as "schools within a school."

The Pilot School

This school is an alternative high school program, which was founded in 1969, and it emphasizes cross-grade curriculum and democratic decision-making. The pilot school is located on the topmost floor of the building—the fifth floor. The building comes to an apex on the fifth floor like the top of a pyramid. The students who gain entrance into the Pilot School generally come from professional families. In fact, a recent study reported that approximately 50% of the Pilot School students reported that their parents were professionals. The mean scores on standardized tests of the Pilot School students tend to be significantly higher than those students in all other programs. Also, there is a kind of language that is associated with the Pilot School. Whenever, one inquires after a staff member, one says, "is so and so on the 'floor'?" Or she/ he left the "floor" to go downstairs to lunch. Students who take classes elsewhere in the building speak, with some consternation in tone, of taking classes "downstairs." Pilot School students intend to take the majority of their classes in the Pilot School, on the "floor." The English and social studies classes in the Pilot school are nonleveled and heterogeneously grouped. Freshmen sit in these classes beside seniors. This system works well. The Pilot School reported having no students who could be classified as requiring special education or Title I services. Pilot School teachers teach only four classes. All other teachers at CRLS teach five courses, except for English teachers who teach four. The Pilot school has 251 students.

"Fundy"

The Fundamental School was founded in 1976 and it is a self-contained school, which is housed on the fourth floor of the building. The fourth floor of the building is larger than the fifth floor, but it is not as large as the third and second floors. The philosophy of the Fundamental School is couched in its strict discipline and academic standards, which include a dress code and a homework policy. The Fundamental School has the "floor" vocabulary also. Fundamental faculty and students also speak of being on and off of the "floor." Moreover, the staff of the Fundamental School readily recognize their students. It has been reported to me by several African American students, not enrolled in the Fundamental school, that they are not allowed on the fourth "floor." And whenever they go up there seeking to talk with another student during the lunch hour, they are promptly asked to "go back downstairs."

House "A"

Although House "A" has no stated or recognizable philosophy, it has garnered the reputation of the "college preparatory house." Most of the courses that are taught in House "A" are classes which are homogeneously grouped by ability level—House "A" has tracking deeply ingrained in its academic philosophy. This is combined with the fact the House "A" is known to have guidance counselors who are zealous about their duties. They advocate for their couselees in disputes with teachers, they make sure that they meet the necessary college

requirements, and place them in the "right" courses. They stand out conspicu-
ously in their endeavors. In short, they do their jobs. The administrator of
House "A" is an African American woman who has been in an acting capacity
in her position for three years. House "A" ranks third after the Pilot School and
the Fundamental School as the "school of choice" for incoming freshmen and/
or their parents. There is an unofficial anthem in the building which is "if you
want to go to college, go to House "A." Students in House "A" are frequently
called "preppies." House "A" has a total of 373 students.

The Bilingual House

The Academy is located in the "Arts" Building of CRLS. The Academy
occupies all three floors. The Arts building is connected to the "main" or Rindge
building by breezeways on the second and third floors. Cooperative learning,
team teaching, and democratic decisionmaking are the major components of
the Academy's philosophy. The Academy houses most of the bilingual students
who are new immigrants to the city.

The House has striven, with only marginal success, to overcome its reputation
as the "Bilingual House." However, by virtue of its staff and its curriculum it
involves itself with a preponderance of bilingual activities. A sizable number
of the faculty are bilingual or trilingual. Additionally, the largest concentration
of faculty of color are concentrated in the House. All of the ESL teachers belong
to the Academy. A new administrative team of the Academy consists of three
Whites and one Black female.

The student body consists of a large contingency of French Haitian students
who are counted, for statistical purposes, as Black. Moreover, Chinese, Ethiopian, Erithrean, Portuguese, and Hispanic students dominate the Academy.
Additionally, for the majority of these students, English is their second language. Because of its geographical location and the constituency of the faculty
and student body, the Academy has been referred to as "another country" by
both other students and staff outside of its parameters. The Academy is the
largest house. There are 452 students enrolled in the House.

Occupational Education

The Rindge School of the Technical Arts is located on the first floor of the
main or Rindge Building. Established in 1990, with ties to the original Rindge
Technical School established in 1888, RTA is a separate school within the
CRLS complex. It offers vocational courses such as carpentry, electricity, and
automotive. These vocational courses merge with other academic courses and
with fine arts. However, RTA students spend 50 percent of their school day in
vocational shops. The standardized test scores of the RTA students tend to be

the lowest among the houses/programs. Two hundred twenty students are enrolled in the Rindge School of the Technical Arts.

Enterprise Co-op

This program is the smallest among the alternative, self-contained programs at CRLS. It is housed in a complex across the street from the main campus in a building that referred to as "the garage." The main goal of the program is to facilitate students who are experiencing problems with academic performance or attendance in the traditional setting. As an alternative solution to a traditional classroom setting, the Enterprise Co-op offers smaller classes, more flexible scheduling, and an activity-centered environment which involves outdoor adventures, weekend camping trips, and a rowing program on the Charles River. The students in the Enterprise Co-op also run their own nonprofit businesses which are a wood shop and a commissary kitchen that prepares food for the teacher's cafeteria. There are 21 students enrolled in the Enterprise Co-op program.

The Leadership School

The Leadership School was established in 1990 (the Leadership School was known formerly as House "C"). It is housed on the second floor of the Rindge Building. The Leadership School emphasizes leadership training, just conflict resolution, and community service. The academic focus of the Leadership School is college preparatory. The presumption is that all students will be prepared to go to college. In addition to guidance counselors, students are assigned to mentors during their freshman year who will oversee their academic progress until graduation. Although the Leadership School faculty teaches a wide variety of upper level and/or advanced placement courses, it is not perceived by the larger school environment as a college-bound program. Two years ago the administrator of the Leadership School developed heterogeneously grouped freshman English and social studies classes. A few very vocal and affluent parents protested loudly and organized a letter-writing program against the philosophy. They were successful in obtaining a reversal of the practice. The Leadership School was selected fourth as a school of choice after the Pilot School, the Fundamental School, and House "A" by parents and students. The Leadership School is not a self-contained program. The Leadership School appears to have no identifiable space to call its own. The sense of community as defined by space is lost. Students from all other programs regularly traverse its corridors throughout the day, moving up to House "A," Fundamental School, Pilot School, the Academy, or the gymnasium. Its corridors are the most congested of the entire complex during the passing time between periods.

Also, it is often the case that students from other programs and houses such as Fundamental or Pilot are involuntarily transferred to the Leadership School when they do not adhere to the principles (often this means failing or being disruptive) of the alternative schools. Additionally, once the school year begins, Leadership School is most likely to receive incoming students from throughout the greater Boston area, except those who are bilingual, who are usually placed in the Academy. Leadership School then tends to receive students who are in academic difficulty and who pose a larger proportion of behavioral problems because they may have "failed" somewhere else. The result of all of this is that the Leadership School is perceived by some staff and students as a "dumping ground." It is also perceived as the "Black House."

The administrator of the Leadership School is an African American woman. She is the only tenured Black administrator at CRLS as of this writing. She resigned at the end of the school year. The student enrollment of the leadership school is 350. I am a faculty member of the Leadership School.

Calling the Question: What is Multicultural Education?— Defining the Elephant

Definition

Multicultural education is a complex system of education which includes promoting cultural pluralism and social equality; programs that reflect diversity in all areas of the school environment; staffing patterns that reflect the diversity of American society; teaching an unbiased, inclusive curriculum; ensuring equity of resources and programs for all students as well equitable academic excellence (outcomes) for all students.[1]

In my own teaching philosophy, I incorporate the above definitions by being ever conscious of designing curriculum that (1) promotes cultural sharing and mutual respect; (2) develops skills such as knowledge building, the ability to compare and make extrapolations; (3) promotes creativity and critical thinking skills; and (4) develops leadership abilities in all students. Above all, my teaching philosophy is tempered with the belief that *all children can learn,* and that all children have gifts. It is my job to help students facilitate their own giftedness.

Historically, multicultural education meant teaching the culturally different. Thus, the goal was to assimilate students of color and students from diverse language groups into the "cultural mainstream" and into the existing social structure by offering transitional bridges within the existing school programs. This approach spawned the birth of bilingual education.

The human relation's approach was used to help students from different backgrounds "get along" better and appreciate each other. This approach stressed human relation's activities and integration. The major fault in this approach was that it was not oriented toward a goal. Student exchanges and visitations fit this category.

The ethnic studies or single-group studies was also not oriented toward a goal beyond expounding on the activities of a single group. Generally, these kinds of single-group or ethnic studies take the form of separate or segregated courses or "add-ons" to existing courses. These courses always lack integration into the mainstream courses. Likewise, they lack the goal of social change—eliminating prejudice. In these courses, groups are sensitized to each other's contributions as well as to each other's victimization. Such courses as "Black History" or "Black Literature" or "Minority Literature" are prime examples of an environment that promotes and sustains a segregated curriculum.

Whenever anyone asks if there is multicultural education at the Cambridge Rindge and Latin School, the answer usually includes expounding upon the rich diversity of the student population. It is true that there are over 130 different cultures represented at CRLS. In some classrooms, if there are 30 students present, often there may be 27 distinctly different cultures present. The principal celebrates these differences by prominently displaying 30 or 40 flags from different countries around the world in the cafeteria. Nonetheless, flags and warm brown, black, and yellow bodies do not a multicultural curriculum make.

Some will allude to the six segregated sections of Black History that are taught by the social studies department or to the "Literature of Groups in Conflict" course that I teach as proof positive that multicultural education is taking place. Still others will hold up the single examples of books and supplemental material that they "add on" to the "regular" course content.

The Cambridge Rindge and Latin School is a majority "minority" school (oxymoron used for clarification). In fact, this is true systemwide. Exactly 58.9 percent of the High School schools consist of students from diverse cultures. To me, these glaring statistics mean that 58.9 percent of everything in the CRLS environment should involve color. However, this is not the current condition or philosophy.

Programs

The schoolwide student ethnic codes are reflected in Table 1.1. The House and program student ethnic code distribution is reflected in Table 1.2. The

TABLE 1
Schoolwide Student Ethnic Codes by Percentage ($N=2095$)

Native American	Black	Asian	Hispanic	Total Diverse	Whites	Totals
0.3	39.5	6.0	13.1	58.9	41.1	100.0

TABLE 2

Student Ethnic Distribution by Program and House at the
Cambridge Rindge and Latin School

House/ Program # totals	Black	Asian	Hispanic	Total Diverse (%)	White (%)	Total
Pilot	33.5	6.0	9.2	48.7	51.3	100.0
Fundamental	36.2	4.9	14.3	56.0	44.1	100.0
House "A"	39.4	4.0	8.3	51.7	48.0	99.7*
Academy	47.8	12.4	15.7	75.9	24.1	100.0
RSTA	29.1	0.5	21.4	51.0	48.6	99.6
Enterprise Co-op	38.1	0.0	14.3	52.4	47.6	100.0
Leadership	45.1	4.6	11.4	61.1	38.3	99.4*

*All of the percentages may not equal 100.00% due to the omission of one or two native American students in the count. Data accurate as of 3 February, 1992

Department faculty ethnic code distribution is reflected in Table 3. Some of the programs at CRLS reflect proportional ethnic code distribution and others do not. The data indicate that the Pilot School is underrepresented with Blacks and Hispanics. This is troublesome because the Pilot School is the number one school of choice among the programs at CRLS. It could be argued that since the Pilot School receives the abundance of applications, then it should be able to balance its student populations to parallel those in the larger environment. If the defense of the Pilot School is that Blacks and Hispanics do not apply in the same proportions as Asians and Whites, then one might question the perception of the Pilot School by Blacks and Hispanics. This should be addressed forthwith, since the diverse student population in Pilot School totals only 48.7 percent and the schoolwide figure is 58.9 percent.

The ethnic representations of students in the Fundamental School approximate those in the general population. The slightly lower populations of Blacks and Asians might be corrected by drawing from the excess of applications, since the Fundamental School is the number two choice among students and parents.

The Academy is underrepresented with White students. Perhaps this is because the majority of the House's curriculum addresses the needs of a bilingual population. This may also account for the glaring overrepresentation of students of diverse cultures.

It is difficult to understand why the Rindge School of the Technical Arts—a program that stresses vocational training and the building trades—is so underrepresented with black students. This is despite the fact that RSTA offers majors in computer education, culinary arts, drafting, and career options in

TABLE 3

Schoolwide Ethnic Percentages of Teachers by Department (*N*=227)

Department	Black (%)	Asian (%)	Hispanic (%)	Diverse (% total)	White (%)	Total (%)
Bilingual (*T* = 17)	23.5	5.8	11.7	41.0	59	100.0
English (*T* = 28)	10.7	0	0	10.7	89.3	100.0
Mathematics (*T* = 25)	8	0	0	8	92	100.0
Social Studies (*T* = 21)	4.7	0	0	4.7	95.3	100.0
Science (*T* = 20)	5	0	0	5	95	100.0
Business (*T* = 7)	28.5	0	0	28.5	71.5	100.0
Drama (*T* = 4)	0	0	0	0	100.0	100.0
Library Media (*T* = 3)	0	0	0	0	100.0	100.0
Modern Languages (*T* = 13)	0	0	0	0	100.0	100.0
Music (*T* = 17)	14.7	0	0	0	85.3	100.0
Reading (*T* = 3)	0	0	0	0	100.0	100.0
Physical Education (*T* = 10)	10	0	0	0	90.0	100.0
Guidance (*T* = 15)	13.5	6.6	6.6	26.5	73.5	100.0
Bureau of Pupil Services (*T* = 38)	7.8	0	0	7.8	92.2	100.0
Title I (*T* = 6)	16.0	16.0	0	32.0	68	100.0

*Data from the 1991–92 CRLS Course Catalog.

cooperation with Lesley College. The only explanation is that the applications for the RSTA program have been steadily declining in recent years. Moreover, the decision to go into a program at the High School is made at the end of the eighth grade, and many Black and Hispanic students may erroneously view the RSTA program as a program that does not lead to the pursuit of a college degree.

The Leadership School is overrepresented with black students by more than five percentage points. It has already been stated that some in the CRLS environment see the Leadership School as a "dumping ground," whereas others see it as the "Black House." The latter reputation may have been earned because the Leadership School is run by two Black administrators.

Other student activities such as the drama productions, the science club, the math and science teams, and the debate team are dominated by Whites and Asians. Generally, these teams consist of no more than approximately 5% Blacks. Rarely do they contain Hispanic students. Of course, the basketball and football teams are predominantly Black. Additionally, the school dances tend to be predominantly Black.

"Like Flies in the Buttermilk"

Staffing

At the present time there is a critical shortage of teachers of color at CRLS. The greatest concentration of staff of color (classroom teachers) is in the Bilingual Department. There are 7 classroom teachers—three French Haitian, one Ethiopian, one Chinese, and 2 Spanish bilingual teachers. The Bilingual Department consists of 18 teachers. (See Table 3)

The largest departments are English, math, social studies, and science. These are the subjects that every student must take to graduate. Each of these departments consists of approximately 28 persons. If you combine the professional staff of color (who are all African American) in the above-mentioned departments, you are speaking of seven individuals. Among the seven teachers, there are three in the English Department—one who is a 20-year veteran teacher who works in the Rindge School of the Technical Arts on grant funds. So, theoretically, he could disappear when the funds dry up. Another Black male works in the Pilot School and is generally not accessible to students outside of the Pilot School. I am the only African American teacher who is accessible to students who are not in alternative programs. (However, my classes tend to include students from all houses and programs.)

The Math Department, consisting of 25 members, has *one* Black female who teaches basic math classes. Another Black male teacher is a part-time staff developer who teaches three math classes. (All other staff developers are White and teach two classes.) One Black man works in the Social Studies Department amid 21 other White staff members. In the Science Department, one Black woman who holds a Ph.D. in biology, teaches basic and intermediate level science classes in a department with 20 other White staff members. The Business Education Department is a seven-member department and two of its members are Black. They also teach lower level business education courses.

In other special areas, the situation is even worse. In the Dramatic Arts Department, there are four staff members, none of color. In the Home Economics Department, there is *one* in a 10-person department. In the Library and Media Department, there are none among three. In the Modern Languages department, there are none. The Music Department consists of seven persons. There is one Black man who is full time in the building, and another Black woman who is a traveling music teacher who alternates between the high school and several elementary schools. Additionally there is another Black man, a teacher's aide, who teaches drums in the Music Department. The Physical Education Department is a 10-member department. The diverse staff consists of *one* African American man. The Reading Department is a three-person department. None are persons of color. Guidance counselors are assigned to each house or program. Additionally, guidance counselors are assigned to the Career Resource Center—a center that serves as a clearinghouse for college and scholarship information—and to the Student Service Center—a point of impact for many students who arrive to register at CRLS after the year has commenced.

The collective guidance department consists of 15 persons. Among these, four are diverse staff members. One Asian woman works in the Pilot School. One African American male works in House "A." One French Haitian counselor and a Hispanic counselor work in the Academy. No guidance counselor of color works in the Career Resource Center or in the Leadership School (an African American male was hired as an extended term substitute in guidance during the course of this writing), the Rindge School of the Technical Arts, the Fundamental School, or the Student Service Center.

The Bureau of Pupil Services provides services to students with special needs to help meet the requirements of most academic programs. The Bureau derives a large portion of its funds from Chapter 766 state funds. The Bureau has 35 staff members; two of this number are African American. No other racial group is represented.

The Title I program is an instructional support program that provides individualized instruction to students who may need help with the basic fundamentals in math or reading. Title I also derives a large portion of its funding from state and federal sources. Title I consists of six professionals. Two are Black and one is Asian. The overwhelming majority of the students who receive services in the Title I program are Black and Hispanic.

Since 1981, the Cambridge School Department has been under a Court-ordered settlement agreement to hire minority staff and administrators until such time that the numbers reach 25%.

The lack of more diversity among the CRLS staff has a profound influence in the total school environment and in the way that curriculum is influenced.

For the most part the curriculum development reflects the narrow scholarship of Western Europe or White Anglo-Saxonism of American scholarship. It is reflected in the kinds of plays produced by the Drama Department and in the music that is played for the bell changes where one is more likely to hear Broadway show tunes rather than a variety of music which is reflective of the student population. It is reflected in the sponsorship of annual trips to Japan, Russia, and Paris. It is reflected in the abundant study of Europe throughout the curricula in all departments. It is apparent when Black students and faculty are not allowed to hold Black history programs in the school's auditorium, thus leaving us to scurry for other nooks and crannies in the school, which are unsuitable. This in effect devalues our cultural contributions and devalues us as teachers and learners in the CRLS environment. This devaluing is reflected in the frustration levels of diverse groups of students and in their low self-esteem as learners and achievers in the CRLS environment. Recently, a group of students calling themselves "the Concerned Black Students" wrote some of their concerns in an open letter to the entire school. At first the letter was handed to selected teachers with whom the students felt safe; and then it spread like chicken feathers on the wind around the entire school. Excerpts from the letter stated:

> We are upset because this school is supposed to be so multi-cultural! If this is so, then why isn't everyone given the same rights and privileges? Why are the needs of so many people, especially people of color ignored? When information comes in that could benefit so many, why is it only given to a few handpicked students and kept away from the majority? . . . This letter was written for the purpose that the feelings of many students who are otherwise too afraid to express them could be made known. Also, it was written in the hope that it would inspire those who have their own problems with this school to rise up and voice their opinions. We see a lot of problems in this school and we are demanding that they be addressed.[2]

"Teachin Your Own Thang"

The Curriculum

I believe that the "curriculum" is everything that teachers do from the time they enter their classrooms until they leave it. It is the books and materials, the homework assignments, and what gets tested and what does not. It is what is placed on the walls and what is not. I know of an English and a French teacher who have a variety of pictures on their walls of famous people and their accomplishments. However the only pictures which contains a person of color is a picture of a famous NBA basketball star who graduated from our school. I am sure they are not aware of the message that this sends.

Additionally, the hidden curriculum is who gets called upon and who does not. It is who receives a smile and who does not. It is who receives profuse comments on their papers and who does not. It is who receives encouragement to go on to college and who does not.

The truly multicultural education environment is a totally inclusive and equitable teaching/learning environment for students as well as staff.

> Inclusive teaching/learning is an educational process that includes the experiences of multiple cultures, religions, classes, both women and men, and preferred sexual identities as necessary and central to the total teaching and learning environment.
>
> It creates a tolerant environment for all students and staff where everyone feels invested, safe, and where everyone has the same sense of educational outcomes, access to policy implementation, to power, to organizations, and to opportunity. Additionally, all staff whether professional or support staff have equal access to professional growth and development.[3]

In the CRLS environment, it is the fact that all teachers of upper level subjects are White. It is the politics of power in which all curriculum decision about who will teach what subjects are in the hands of Whites.

Teachers are completely autonomous in creating courses and course content at CRLS. This is both a blessing and a curse. It has been a blessing for me personally. I have been able to do my own "thang." I gradually liberated myself from teaching the lowest track "Business English" courses by teaching all elective English courses which are offered to juniors and seniors. Basically, these courses are nonleveled. The only course which I have taught continually since 1974 has been a course entitled: Literature of Groups in Conflict (formerly Minority Literature). Within this course I believe that I have created a multicultural, gender-balanced curriculum—teaching literature by and about Native Americans, Asians, Jews, Blacks, and Hispanics. Among some of the titles that are staples for the course are *Tell Me a Riddle* by Tillie Olsen, *The Storyteller* by Leslie Marmon Silko, *Farewell to Manzanar* by Jeanne Wakatsuki and James D. Houston, *The Margarita Poems* by Luz Maria Umpierre, *Alien Turf* by Piri Thomas, *Autobiography of Malcolm X* by Alex Haley, and *Sula* by Toni Morrison. Additionally, I am a "cutter and a paster"—continually gathering short selections from periodicals of every description to undergird and supplement the groups that are studied in the class.

More significantly, I use the students' own experiences and cultures to generate curriculum. These have been among my most rewarding teaching experiences. After a recent multicultural poetry unit, I asked students to generate their own poems. I simply provided them with themes such as "The Homeless," "Adolescent Life," etc. Two male students and one female student burst from their seats and confessed that they wrote poetry profusely and shared their poetry journals openly with the class. Another student, who had recently lost his father to cancer, spoke of it for the first time in a poem. It was at times such as these that my teaching career equaled pure joy. At the end of the semester, I collated the student-written poems and published a booklet entitled: *Rising*

Stars: A Collection of Original Poetry from a Literature Class. With their permission I have reproduced a couple of examples. An East Indian student, Dharmesh, wrote:

Am I Homeless?

Am I Homeless?
Because I live on every street?
Because I have nothing to eat?
Because I have enough to wear?
Or because I ask for change?
  Yes, I am a homeless
I don't have my future
But I had big dreams, when I was young
But I am too old now, to make a big dream

Let me tell you one more thing
Because I'm homeless Earth's My mattress
And Sky my Blanket
Just because I am homeless.

Jared, a White student wrote,

Racism

Racism inflicts emotional scars in
Minds like a blade does to flesh
Leaving forever the burns of racial slurs which do not heal
with time.

Why are Africans in their own land forced
To live in townships. If we could only unite,
We could help them fight this
Hardship
We could end this fight and live at peace.

In another student-centered project which I originated, students interview each other to find out about their cultures. Then they take another set of questions home to parents and obtain information about the family's history. The questions involve very personal aspects such as: under what circumstances the family came to America, information about grandparents' and parents' occupations, and recipes for traditional foods. The project ends with an "Ethnic Food Fair" where students bring in a dish that is traditional for her/his culture to share with the class. The stories and recipes are then collated and published in booklet form. Often parents, grandparents, and aunts and uncles send word for copies of the stories. This curriculum project won a proclamation from Governor Michael Dukakis in 1987, and a prize and recognition from "World of Difference Teacher Incentive Awards Contest" which was sponsored by The Anti-Defamation League of B'Nai Brith in 1992.

I cannot take the space it would require to elaborate upon the richness of these stories. One student wrote about her father's demise in the Jonestown Guyana massacre. Another, Jewish, student wrote about her grandmother who lived in Worcester, Massachusetts in the early 1900s and "played down her Jewishness" because the Ku Klux Klan was active in Worcester at that time.

Often at the beginning of the year, students try to camouflage their cultural identities. Many times this changes by the end of the project. I witnessed two Jamaican female students who suddenly began to communicate openly in the Jamaican Patois at the conclusion of this unit. Another student who was of Cuban and Arab ancestry found her voice. She had begun the semester barely speaking above a whisper whenever she spoke in class. A fifth-grade teacher had silenced her by telling her that her Spanish accent made her speech incoherent. Once during an oral report on Vietnam the same student held the entire class spellbound as she relayed to the class a unique story about her father's being the captain of a Cuban ship that was docked just off the Vietnam coast during an attack by the Americans. As she read in a wee voice, we were all mesmerized by the information and the point of view of the war from her father's ship. At the close of her presentation, we all gave her a standing ovation. Soon after that her voice grew stronger.

In my written composition classes, I use writing models that are multiculturally based. This serves a twofold purpose. It teaches writing models and it exposes students to writing by authors which they might otherwise not come to know. The shorter pieces of Toni Morrison, Eudora Welty, Langston Hughes, and Victor Hernandez Cruz are among those included.

The policy of teacher autonomy over curriculum design has given me a tremendous sense of power and professional satisfaction. However, just as it has given me the power to be inclusive, it has given others the right to be exclusive. In the English Department, many teachers include some works by women and authors of color—mostly African American. However, there are many courses which do not. I know of a Science Fiction course in the department in which all of the selections are by White male authors. Courses which traditionally have been associated erroneously with Western European culture include few works, if any, by women and almost no works by authors of color. These include Myths, Legends, and Folklore, Nineteenth-Century British Fiction, Reading in English Literature and Literary Hero.

It would be fair to say that among the 28 English teachers in the English department, there are those who are standing guard over the Anglo-Saxon canon, there are those who realize that the canon needs to be expanded, and there are those few who are consciously working to expand it. There are three segregated courses in the department. They are Black Literature which is taught by a Black man, Women in Literature which is taught by two White females, and there is Literature of Groups in Conflict which I teach.

I have brought up the subject of multicultural education to the English depar ent many times. The department has been without a coordinator for thre ars. Last year, the Teacher-in-Charge (TIC) of the department asked faculty to vote on the topics which they wanted to address in the current school year. I wrote a lengthy plea for the department to address the topic of multicultural education. Of course, the democratic process ensured that my topic would not be heard. My response was to write a rather substantial letter to the TIC detailing my concerns for the constant evasion of the topic of making the English curriculum more inclusive. I sent copies of the letter to the Assistant Superintendent of Curriculum, to the Assistant Principal of Curriculum, to the principal, and to the Leadership School Administrator. The principal and assistant principal did not respond. The Leadership School Administrator and the Assistant Superintendent of Curriculum are the only two persons who responded.

During the next school year, 1991–92, the TIC of English set forth several committees. The committee which I joined was the "Issues" committee. In the first committee session, I stated that my issue was multicultural education. The reply from one of the staff members was "we know that's your issue." Then it was as if I had not spoken. They proceeded to the next "issue" which, I believe, was the current disarray of the book room. The meeting ended with my volunteering to supply an annotated list of books which were located in the Teacher's Resource Center on multicultural education. At the second meeting of the "Issues" committee, I broached the subject again. And again, I was skimmed over as if I had not spoken. I said, "Excuse me please. I would like to know how people in the department address multicultural education?" One person said, "I teach *The Women of Brewster Place*." Another stated that she taught *Annie John*. Still another said he taught *Invisible Man* in Advanced Placement English. I was reminded that I had promised to deliver some kind of reading list. And as quickly as it had begun, the conversation was closed. Without a coordinator in the English Department, my battle for more inclusive teaching has taken on the tact of persuading person by person. This is draining. It feels sometimes as if I am trying to cultivate flowers in the desert. However, sometimes I do look back over my shoulder and see a cactus flower in bloom—someone else has added something diverse, rich, and wonderful to her/his reading list. At times like these, I am rewarded and smile inwardly.

My perception of the current status of multicultural education in the English Department at CRLS is one of "add-on" or separate, segregated courses. In terms of the larger school curriculum, there has never been a time when a department chairperson or an administrator has dealt comprehensively with the broad scope of multicultural education which I have outlined in this paper.

A former chairperson of the Social Studies Department made a valiant effort at reform. Throughout her tenure, she conducted workshops on racism and sexism awareness. I spoke to her and in a recent interview she said,

> I was trying to get them to reflect on who they were teaching and get them to
> realize how they were going to teach; rather than blame, categorize or label their

students. If I could get them to do this, then I could get them to do more inclusive teaching.

However, I was doing this in isolation and I was not being supported. In fact I felt somewhat ridiculed. This was not a priority of the High School nor of the system.[4]

My perceptions concerning the other academic departments are about the same. I frequently ask math or science teachers what they do to address multicultural education. Their replies often go something like this. "Oh, I don't have to bother with that, I teach math." On the other hand, I know of a White science teacher who teaches biology and she actively affirms diversity in her curriculum and in all of her endeavors. I feel that the other academic departments are a "mixed bag." Last year, a group of students demanded that more than *one* Black History course be taught. This year there are five, segregated sections of Black History being offered at CRLS. Two sections are being taught by White teachers, one who has had no previous training in the subject, and three are being taught by the *one* Black teacher in the department. Some of the teachers in the department view the teaching of Black history negatively.

Notwithstanding, there are some extremely conscientious White educators in my building who are aware of the curriculum and staff deficits. There are media and library personnel who continually ask me and other teachers of color for book and video titles. Another special education teacher works diligently to be inclusive. A photography teacher teaches the photography of the renowned Black photographer James Vanderzee. However, these few positive efforts represent pearls in the sea. They are the exception rather than the rule. Nevertheless, a comprehensive systematic approach that affirms diversity is lacking at the Cambridge Rindge and Latin School.

"A Tale of Two Cities"

Equity of Resources, Access to Programs, and Academic Excellence

In 1986, after 14 years of witnessing mostly White and Asian students receive the top academic awards, recognition and prizes, I started to ask some questions. I called a meeting of the collective Black staff (we have an organization called The Concerned Black Staff) on June 10, 1986. The consensus was that most of the academic awards went to students who matriculated in the upper level classes. Next, the Black staff commissioned another Black staff member and me to write a report which detailed the numbers of Black, Hispanic, and Asian students who were enrolled in upper level English, science, social studies, and math classes. What we found was that only 8.37 percent of all Black students, 2.22 percent of all Hispanic students, 17 percent of all Asian students, and 16.45 percent of all White students took upper level English courses. In mathematics, 3.7 percent of all Black students, 1.1 percent of all Hispanic students,

45.3 percent of all Asians, and 11 percent of White students took upper level math courses. In science, 7.5 percent of all Black students, 2.8 percent of all Hispanic students, 39.3 percent of all Asian students, and 19.0 percent of all White students were enrolled in upper level science classes.

The report concluded that academic achievement, as defined by enrollment in upper-level courses, was like a "Tale of Two Cities"—one pursuing the higher level academic track which consisted of White and Asian students and another lower level which consisted of predominantly Black and Hispanic students.[5] The precipitating factors were multifaceted and too numerous to detail here. However, among the more glaring factors were inconsistent delivery of guidance services, teacher expectations, and prior elementary school attendance. Black students from the more affluent neighborhood schools were more likely to end up in upper level classes.

In a follow-up study in 1989, I interviewed 36 Black and Hispanic students to obtain their first-hand impressions about taking upper level classes. Their answers covered a wide range. Generally, the findings demonstrated that Black and Hispanic students were not being counseled into upper level classes. Many said that they were not aware that there was such a thing as upper level classes. However, those Black and Hispanic students who enrolled in upper level classes faced some difficulties in those classes. These difficulties took the form of trouble mastering the subject matter, enduring racial harassment, or experiencing feelings of alienation and isolation. One Black male student said that a teacher told him openly that he did not belong in a trigonometry class because he once asked for help on a problem that the teacher had deemed as "simple." Another Hispanic student felt overburdened with the work in her Intensive Biology Class. An African American student felt external pressures from her peer group for taking all upper level classes.

During the course of this writing, the enrollment study of minorities in upper level classes has been replicated. Although the report has not been released officially, preliminary findings indicate that the same low patterns of enrollment of students of color are about the same as they were in 1986. According to an assistant principal, science classes have shown some noticeable improvement. However, English, social studies, and mathematics are about the same.

A casual stroll through the corridors making surface observations reveals that there have not been dynamic changes. One classroom will be predominantly Black and Hispanic, whereas another one next door will be predominantly White and Asian. The students themselves are very aware of the situation. Very often students judge the level of a class by the race of the majority of the students who are in it.

On the first day of my Written Composition class this semester, I had a White female student ask me as she peered around the room and observed only one other White student, "What level class is this?" When I replied "Intermediate to Advanced," she sighed questioningly. The next day, she withdrew.

"Black Teachers: Where They At?"

Student Perceptions

The Black students are acutely aware of the inequities of staff of color at CRLS. We are seven in number and serve a diverse population of 58.9 percent of the entire student body of 2095. The students are not blind. They feel the deficits in every aspect of the school environment. As has already been stated, there are seven of us in the major academic subject areas which are required for graduation. There is not one Hispanic teacher in the classroom; not even in the Modern Language Department. A White teacher teaches Spanish, German, and Latin. No Black teacher teaches an upper level class. So not only is the student body segregated into academic ghettos and barrios-tracks, the faculty is too. The academic assumptions at CRLS are that higher level knowledge attainment is claimed by the White and Asian student population and it is taught by the White staff. Conversely, lower level knowledge attainment is perceived as the venue of Black and Hispanic students and taught to them by the Black staff and some of the White staff.

Black students feel the sting of this discrepancy acutely. My class, Literature of Groups in Conflict, is an elective English course for juniors and seniors. Frequently, in class discussion, it is revealed to me by students who have spent their entire high school career at CRLS that the readings in my class represent the first time that they have read any works by authors of color or that having me as a teacher often represents their first experience with a teacher of color.

All of the Black teachers in the building are utilized beyond our capacity to mentor Black students—to write college recommendations; advise them about college, life, and the future; to coach them. We often hear their complaints. We listen to them constantly as they relay to us their experiences of benign and blatant racism, about all sorts of double standards in the curriculum, about their sense of unfairness in the enforcement of the school rules and regulations. Almost every day, a student who is not in one of my classes, will approach me in the hallway requesting information on Black book titles, help with college essays, and information on Black colleges. Or, on some occasions these requests take on the form of a question such as, "Ms. Dickerson, do you know Mr. or Mrs. ———? Do you think he or she is a racist?" Recently, on one such instance, a student told me of a White teacher who demanded to be called "Mam" (as in "Yes Mam and No Mam") while insisting on referring to students by their first names. Another student told me about a time when the teacher went around the class and, student by student, tried to predict who would go to college and who would not. The end result was that all of the White students had been prophesied upon as becoming successful and the majority of the Black students had not. My advice is often along the lines of encouraging students to challenge racist remarks openly in hopes that they will cause personal reflection. These obligations are overwhelming at times. However, what I am more concerned with is the latent effects which encircle students—the stigma of being devalued as learners and the deteriorating self-esteem which may be faced by some students in some classes.

In January, a group of students produced a film entitled: "Black Teachers: Where They At"; this film is a half-hour documentary in which several students and six Black teachers were interviewed. The questions centered on exploring the reasons behind the scarce numbers of Black teachers at CRLS and how this has impacted upon the Black student population of the school.

The narrator of the film began with this statement:

> It's a question that remains unanswered, but it's always on my mind. Where are our Black teachers? Although this school is supposed to be multicultural diverse, why is there a lack of Black teachers?
>
> We feel that the absence of Black teachers is robbing Black students of caring, cultural understanding, and academic encouragement.

Another Black female student said,

> We have some White teachers teaching Black history. And, I think that's a problem. I think they should hire more Black teachers. The majority of this school is, you know, minority. There should be more Black teachers at least teaching Black history.

A black male student said, "I have no black teachers this year or last year." When asked "Why do you think that is?" by the interviewer, He replied,

> I think the system is prejudice. We don't have any Black teachers in Fundamental School. We don't have any Black counselors. No Black anything in Fundamental School that I am aware of. And I think we should have some hired.

Although there is *one* Black teacher in the Fundamental School, the student obviously had not come in contact with her.

The film received mixed reviews throughout the city. Some White teachers in the building have the impression that the Black teachers are highly visible. This is probably due to the fact that many of us are highly involved with large number of students outside of our classes in a myriad of cultural and academic activities. However, high visibility does not ensure the multiplication of our numbers like amoeba. The Black students have said, "Where They At?" During the writing of this paper the film was screened before a group of students and teachers. In the ensuing discussion, a Black female student said,

> When you have a Black teacher, they make you do your work. They get to know you, they talk to you. The White teachers teach you and tell you to do your work and that's it.

This past school year, 1991–92, was a dynamic year for student activism and student demand in terms of the curriculum and staffing patterns. One of the more potent student movements which took shape at CRLS during the course of this writing is the Onesimus Project. The project consists of a group of thirty people who are both alumni and current students. For the most part they are middle-class, bright, and articulate. What binds them together is the realization that they are or have been short-changed in their high school education with regards to multicultural education.

In May of 1992, members of the project went before the School Committee and sternly requested money for the project. It is not clear if they received the funds from the School Committee. However, within 60 days they raised at least $26,000 and began to work eight hours a day to organize a curriculum reform movement. In their initial project description they stated:

> We believe that our society, and our schools in particular, must help bring people together in ways that respect and celebrate diversity. Schools have a special role in educating a new generation of young people—so that they can share values of respect, and a vision of a society committed to equity and social justice. School curriculum will play a central role in this work. Curriculum is the "common ground" for teachers, students, parents, and community members. . . . Current curricula need revision: curriculum must be taught from many perspectives, rather than a single one; curriculum must include the contributions of many cultures, not just the dominant one; curriculum must look honestly and constructively at the injustices as well as the accomplishments of the past.[6]

The Onesimus project hopes to develop a three-year implementation plan which will culminate with the creation of a multicultural English and social studies curricula.

"Taking Off the Blindfold: Doin The Right Thing"

Recommendations

There are many impediments in the CRLS environment that must be overcome before any comprehensive multicultural antibias educational plan can be undertaken. First, we need a schoolwide, anti-racist sensitivity program. Other Massachusetts school systems which were faced with similar kinds of change mandates have undergone racism awareness programs. This was the case at the Cambridge Friends School and the Brookline Public Schools. Teachers need to be aware that all of their actions, whether conscious or not, have an impact upon students.

The Curriculum

Many teachers ignore the rapidly swelling enrollment of our diverse student body, which is, as of this writing, 58.9 percent. Many teachers consciously profess a "business as usual" curriculum philosophy in which they guard what they consider to be the "best," high quality of scholarship. This usually unconsciously and consciously include a Western European approach to the subject matter which is male-centered. These curricula approaches oftentimes hide under the labels of "classic" or "advanced." These curricula approaches have the effect of silencing those who are different because of culture or gender. A new curriculum philosophy should be espoused which does the following: (1) promotes cultural sharing and mutual respect; (2) develops skills such as knowledge building, the ability to compare and make extrapolations; (3) promotes creativity and critical thinking skills; and (4) develops leadership abilities in all students. This should undergirded with the belief that *all children can learn.*

Tracking

At the present time, most of the courses, outside of a few elective English and social studies courses and the courses in the Pilot School, are homogeneously grouped by ability level. The result is that we have in our school academic ghettos and barrios that are acutely segregated by race and by economics. I realize that there are many faculty who know no other approach and who feel that suddenly abolishing this system would place a hardship on their usual methods of instruction. Therefore, first there needs to be a comprehensive, multiyear, staff development process that sensitizes teachers to the cultural contributions of diverse groups represented in our student body; that retrains teachers in the art of cooperative learning; that illustrates effective tutoring; that demonstrates approaches to the nonbias curriculum; and that espouses a philosophy that all children can learn.

Staff Development

Although the present staff development workshop format allows for staff to design and lead their own workshops, there is no requirement that multicultural education must be addressed. A new staff development model should be designed that includes themes which concentrate on demonstrating the multicultural, gender-appropriate approach for every workshop. The philosophy that permeates these workshops should be that the multicultural curriculum is good for all students. It helps us to achieve a truly pluralistic society in which all people accept and respect each other. It helps all students to see themselves reflected in the curriculum, and this helps to make all students more accepting learners. It assists teachers in freeing themselves from the perpetuation of a narrow, one-dimensional scholarship. Teachers who implement multicultural approaches, regardless of the subject areas, should be encouraged and *rewarded* to share their outcomes, to share what forms the inclusive curriculum takes, and to disclose how barriers were encountered. Most of all, the goals of the multicultural gender-inclusive curriculum should be espoused as one which "equips students, parents, and teachers with the tools needed to combat racism, ethnic discrimination, sexism; and one which seeks to find ways to build a society placing all people on an equal footing."[7] Ending discrimination through curriculum change at our school is imperative. There is no neutral ground. One of the ways that discrimination works in the CRLS environment is that it treats some people's experiences, namely, students from diverse cultures, as though they don't count, as though they are less valuable than other peoples'. This attitude also affects teachers of color. Many times the faculty of color are left out of the decision-making process either by a democratic vote of the majority or by virtue of the subjects we teach which are not in the pipeline for grants, high level exposures, and other opportunities. This is done consciously and unconsciously through exclusion in the curriculum and in staffing. Teachers, staff, and administrators must realize that equity and excellence are not in conflict. The new workshop format should be expansive enough to allow a substantial selection of multicultural workshops in all subject areas; and attendance should be mandatory not voluntary as in the current model. Additionally, the new model must also be permeated with the philosophy that all children can learn and achieve academic success at the highest levels.

Staffing

All of the indicators for education into the year 2015 indicate that the proportion of educators from diverse cultures will decrease. However, this does not mean that we should not try. There is a critical shortage of culturally diverse staff at CRLS. The students feel it and we, the Black staff, feel it. New and innovative efforts must be utilized to recruit more teachers of color into the profession. First, schools of education should recruit students from urban school districts with large diverse populations within their areas. In return, school districts such as ours could affirm a policy that provides easy access for colleges and universities to perform research and that places student teachers in our classrooms. Schools of education could provide career minicourses at CRLS, conducted by students of color, which detail all of the elements of the teaching profession, thus encouraging high school students into the teaching profession.

We need more color in our school. The faculty is basically White with sprinkles of Black. A resume bank should be established which includes a resume of all student teachers who complete their practicum in our school. The average age of teachers in our building is about 45. This process would ensure us a constant reservoir of younger teachers of all races. We will need them soon.

Gate Keepers: Policy and Power

At the present, teachers have complete autonomy for designing courses at the Cambridge Rindge and Latin School. This is a strength of the School. However, it is also its weakness. Presently, there is no mandate for multicultural education. This must change. Leadership at all levels must be aggressive and clear. Evaluation should include assessment of all of the components of multicultural education that have been outlined in this paper. Teachers must design curriculum which does the following: (1) promotes cultural sharing and mutual respect; (2) develops skills such as knowledge building, the ability to compare and make extrapolations by all students in a classroom; (3) promotes creativity and critical thinking skills among all students; and (4) develops leadership abilities in all students. Above all, teachers should exemplify a belief that *all children can learn*. If teachers expect students to dance to their music, it must have many different beats—drums must be heard from around the world.

Currently, we have no person of color at the High School who is in charge of an academic department. This must change. All administrators of color at CRLS are Black. All Black administrators at the High School deal primarily with discipline—police work. All people who have policy and power over the curriculum are White. This must change. At the current time the Social Studies Department and English Department are without leadership. These vacancies should create an opportunity to hire persons of color to fill both of them.

Additionally, opportunities for professional growth and development should be extended to the staff of color. The majority of sabbaticals over the last 10 years have been awarded to White males. Many opportunities for large grant-funded projects for staff to work outside of the building have gone to White males. Many incentives for release time to work on special projects have also gone to White males. This must stop. Black faculty should be encouraged and be offered the opportunity to teach upper level classes. Equity of resources and opportunities must be the battle cry of the leadership of the Cambridge Rindge and Latin School so that we can have completely multicultural, gender-inclusive environment—an environment where all cultural experiences are treated respectfully. This includes enrichment to the point where all students and staff have equal access to policy-making, programs, opportunity, information, power, and outcomes for those who learn and for those of us who teach.

Notes

1. C. E. Sleeter and C. A. Grant, "An Analysis of Multicultural Education in the United States," in *Facing Racism in Education*, ed. N. M. Hidalgo, C. L. McDowell, and E. V. Siddle (Cambridge, MA: Harvard Education Review, 1991), 138–161.

2. J. Youte, M. Robinson, and C. Sneed, from "An Open Letter from the Concerned Black Students," 28 February 1992.

3. S. A. Dickerson, "Eating in the Kitchen Equal and Separate: A Theoretical Framework for an Inclusive Teaching/Learning Educational Environment" (working paper in progress), 1992.

4. C. Chaet, from a telephone conversation, 21 March 1992.

5. S. A. Dickerson and W. McLaurin, "An Enrollment Study of Minority Achievement at the Cambridge Rindge and Latin School (report to the Cambridge School Department), 1986.

6. The Onesimus Project, "Healing Education through Multicultural Perspectives," Cambridge Rindge and Latin School, Background and Need for the Project, 1992.

7. E. Lee: Taking Multicultural, Anti-racist Education Seriously," *Rethinking Schools: An Urban Educational Journal*, 6, No. 1 (1991), 6.

Bibliography

Cole, B. (1991). "The School Reform of the Eighties and its Implications for the Restructuring of the Nineties," *Crisis*, 98, No. 8, 23.

Dickerson, S. A. (1992). "All about Us: Portrait of a Literature Class (unpublished curriculum project).

Gay, G. (1988). "Designing Relevant Curricula for Diverse Learners," *Education and Urban Society*, 20, No. 4, 327ff.

Richards, S. (Producer, and Goodridge, C. and Williams, D. (Directors) (1992). *Black Teachers: Where They At?* Cambridge, MA: Cambridge Cablesystems (film).

Saxe, J. G. (1876). "The Blind Men and the Elephant," in *The Poems of John Godfrey Saxe* (Boston, MA: James R. Osgood and Company).

Transformative Pedagogy and Multiculturalism

bell hooks

Despite the contemporary focus on multiculturalism in our society, particularly in education, there is not nearly enough practical discussion of ways classroom settings can be transformed so that the learning experience is inclusive. If the effort to respect and honor the social reality and experiences of groups in this society who are non-White is to be reflected in a pedagogical process, then as teachers on all levels, from elementary to university settings, we must acknowledge that our styles of teaching may need to change. Let's face it. Most of us were taught in classrooms where styles of teaching reflected the notion of a single norm of thought and experience, which we were encouraged to believe was a universal norm. This has been just as true for non-White teachers as for White teachers. Most of us learned to teach emulating this model. As a consequence many teachers are disturbed by the political implications of a multicultural education because they fear losing control in a classroom where there is no one way to approach a subject but multiple ways with multiple references.

Among educators, there has to be an acknowledgment that any effort to transform institutions so that they reflect a multicultural standpoint must take into consideration the fears teachers have when asked to shift their paradigms. There must be training sites where teachers have the opportunity to express those concerns while also learning ways to creatively approach the multicultural classroom and/or curriculum. When I first came to Oberlin a few years ago, I was disturbed by what I felt was a lack of understanding on the part of many professors of what the multicultural classroom might be like. Chandra Mohanty, my colleague in women's studies, shared these concerns. Though we were both untenured, our strong belief that the Oberlin campus was not fully facing the issue of changing curriculum and teaching practices in ways that were progressive and promoting of inclusion led us to consider how we might intervene on this process. We proceeded from the standpoint that the vast majority of Oberlin professors, who are overwhelming White, were basically well-meaning, concerned about the quality of education students receive on our campus, and were therefore likely to be supportive of any effort at education for critical consciousness. Together, we decided to have a group of seminars focusing on transformative pedagogy that would be open to all professors. Initially, students were also welcome but we found that their presence inhibited honest discussion. For example, on the first night, several White professors made comments that could be viewed as horribly racist. The students present left the group and shared what was said around the college. Since our intent was to educate for critical consciousness, we did not want the seminar setting to be a space where any one would feel attacked or their reputation as a teacher sullied. We did, however, want it to be a space for constructive confrontation and critical interrogation. To ensure that this could happen, we had to exclude students.

At the first meeting, Chandra (whose background is in education) and I talked about the factors that had influenced our pedagogical practices. I emphasized the impact of Brazilian educator Paulo Freire's work on my thinking. Since my formative education took place in racially segregated schools, I spoke about the experience of learning when one's experience is recognized as central and significant and how that changed with desegregation, when black children were forced to attend schools where we were regarded as objects and not subjects. Many of the professors present at the first meeting were disturbed by our overt discussion of political standpoints. Again and again, it was necessary to remind everyone that no education is politically neutral. Emphasizing that a White male professor in an English department who teaches only work by "great White men" is making a political decision, we had to consistently work against and through the overwhelming will on the part of folks to deny the politics of racism, sexism, heterosexism, etc., that inform how and what we teach. We found again and again that almost everyone, especially the old guard, were more disturbed by the overt recognition of the role our political perspectives play in shaping pedagogy than by their passive acceptance of ways of teaching and learning that reflect biases, particularly the White supremacist standpoint.

To share in our efforts at intervention, we invited professors from universities around the country to come and talk both formally and informally about the kind of work they were doing and observing that was aimed at transforming teaching and learning so that a multicultural education would be possible. We invited Princeton professor of religion and philosophy Cornel West to give a talk on "decentering Western civilization." It was our hope that his very traditional training and his progressive practice as a scholar would give everyone a sense of optimism about our ability to change. In the informal session, a few White male professors were courageously outspoken in their efforts to state that they could accept the need for change but were simply uncertain about the implications of the changes. This reminded us of the reality that it is difficult for individuals to shift paradigms and that there must be a setting for folks to voice fears, to talk about what they are doing, how they are doing it, and why. One of our most useful meetings was one in which we asked professors from different disciplines (math, science, literature, etc.) to talk informally about how their teaching had been changed by a desire to be more inclusive. Hearing individuals describe concrete strategies was an approach that helped dispel fears. It was crucial that more traditional and/or conservative professors who had been willing to make changes talk about motivations and strategies.

When the meetings concluded, Chandra and I initially felt a tremendous sense of disappointment. We had not realized how much the faculty would need to undergo a process of unlearning racism, learning about colonization and decolonization, to fully appreciate the necessity for creating a democratic liberal arts learning experience. All too often we found a will to include those considered "marginal" without a willingness to accord their work the same respect and consideration given other work. For example, in women's studies, individuals will often focus on women of color at the very end of the semester or lump everything about race and difference together in one section. This kind of tokenism is not multicultural transformation but it is most familiar to us as that change individuals are more likely to make. Let me give another example. What does it mean when a White female English professor is eager to include a work by Toni Morrison on the syllabus of her course but then teaches that work without ever making reference to race or ethnicity. I have heard individual White women "boast" about how they have shown students that Black writers are "as good" as the White male canon when they do not call attention to race. Clearly, such pedagogy is not an interrogation of the biases conventional canons (if not all canons) establish but yet another form of tokenism.

The unwillingness to approach teaching from a standpoint that includes awareness of race, sex, class, etc., is often rooted in the fear that classrooms will be uncontrollable, that emotions and passions will not be contained. To some extent we all know that whenever we address subjects in the classroom that students are passionate about, there is always a possibility that there will be confrontation, forceful expression of ideas, and, at times, conflict. In much of my writing about pedagogy, particularly in classroom settings with great diversity, I have talked about the need to critically examine the way we as teachers conceptualize what the space for learning should be like. Many professors have conveyed to me their feeling that the classroom should be a "safe" place; that usually translates to mean that the professor lectures to a group of quiet students who respond only when they are called on. The experience of professors who educate for critical consciousness indicates that many students, especially students of color, may not feel at all "safe" in what appears to be a neutral setting. And that it is the absence of a feeling of safety that often promotes prolonged silence or absence of student engagement.

Making the classroom a democratic setting where everyone feels a responsibility to contribute is a central goal of transformative pedagogy. Throughout my teaching career, White professors have often voiced concern to me about non-White students who do not talk. As the classroom becomes more diverse, teachers are faced with the way the politics of domination like racism or sexism often are reproduced in the educational setting. For example, White male students continue to be the most vocal in our classes. Students of color and some White women express fear that they will be judged as intellectually inadequate by these peers. I have taught brilliant students of color, many of them seniors, who have skillfully managed to never speak in classroom settings. Some express the feeling that they are less likely to suffer any kind of assault if they simply do not assert their subjectivity. They have told me that many professors never showed any interest in hearing their voices. Accepting the decentering of the West globally, embracing multiculturalism, compels educators to focus attention on the issue of voice. Who speaks? Who listens? And why? Caring about whether all students fulfill their responsibility to contribute to learning in the classroom is not a common approach in what Freire has called the "banking system of education" where students are regarded merely as passive consumers. Since so many professors teach from that standpoint, it is difficult to create the kind of learning community that can fully embrace multiculturalism. Students are much more willing to surrender their dependency on the banking system of education than teachers. Concurrently, they are much more willing to face the challenge of multiculturalism.

It has been as a teacher in the classroom setting that I have witnessed the power of a transformative pedagogy that is rooted in a respect for multiculturalism. Working with a critical pedagogy based on my understanding of Freire's teaching, I enter the classroom with the assumption that we must build "community" in order to create a climate of openness and intellectual rigor. Rather than focusing on issues of safety, I think that a feeling of community creates a sense that there is shared commitment and a common good that binds us. What we all ideally share is the desire to learn—to actively receive knowledge that enhances our intellectual development and our capacity to live more fully in the world. It has been my experience that one way to build community in the classroom is to recognize the value of each individual voice. In my classes, students keep journals and often write paragraphs during class which they read to one another. This happens at least once, irrespective of class size. Most of the classes I teach are not small. They range anywhere from 30 to 60 students. And at times I have taught more than 100. To hear each other (the sound of different voices), to listen to one another, is an exercise in recognition. It also ensures that no student remains invisible in the classroom. Some students resent having to make a verbal contribution, and so I have had to make it clear from the onset that this is a requirement in my classes. Even if there is a student present whose voice cannot be heard in spoken words, by "signing," even if we cannot read the signs, they make their presence felt.

When I first entered the multicultural, multiethnic classroom setting, I was unprepared. I did not know how to cope effectively with so much "difference." Despite progressive politics, my deep engagement with the feminist movement, I had not really been compelled to work within an inclusive setting—one that is truly diverse—and I lacked the necessary skills. This is the case with most educators. It is difficult for many educators in the United States to conceptualize how the classroom will look when they are confronted with the demographics which indicate that "whiteness" may cease to be the norm ethnicity in classroom settings on all levels. Hence, educators are poorly prepared when we actually confront diversity. This is why so many of us stubbornly cling to old patterns. As I worked to create teaching strategies that would make a space for multicultural learning, I found it necessary to recognize what I have called, in other writings on pedagogy, different "cultural codes." To teach effectively a diverse student body, I have to learn these codes. And so do students. This act alone transforms the classroom. The sharing of ideas and information does not always progress with the same quickness that it may be transmitted in the more homogeneous setting. Often professors and students have to learn how to accept different ways of knowing, new epistemologies, in a multicultural setting.

Just as it may be difficult for professors to shift their paradigms, it is equally difficult for students. I have always believed that students should "enjoy" learning. Yet, I found that there was much more tension in the diverse classroom setting where the philosophy of teaching is rooted in critical pedagogy and, in my case, feminist critical pedagogy. The presence of tension and at times conflict often meant that students did not "enjoy" my classes or "love" me their professor as I secretly wanted them to do. Teaching in a traditional discipline from the perspective of critical pedagogy means that I often encounter students who make complaints like: "I thought this was supposed to be an English class, why are we talking so much about feminism." Or, they might add race or class. In the transformed classroom, there is often a much greater need to explain philosophy, strategy, and intent than in the "norm" setting. I have found through the years that many of my students who "bitch" endlessly while they are taking my classes contact me at a later date to talk about how much that experience meant to them, how much they learned. In my professorial role I had to surrender my need for immediate affirmation of successful teaching (even though some reward is immediate) and accept that students may not appreciate the value of a certain standpoint or process straightaway. The exciting aspect of creating a classroom community where there is respect for individual voices is that there is infinitely more feedback because students do feel free to talk and talk back. And, yes, often this feedback is critical. Moving away from the need for immediate affirmation was crucial to my growth as a teacher. I learned to respect that shifting paradigms or sharing knowledge in new ways challenges and it takes time for students to experience that challenge as positive.

Students have taught me that it is necessary to practice compassion in these new learning settings where individuals may be confronting shifts in paradigms that seem to them completely and utterly threatening. I have not forgotten the day a student came to class and told me: "We take your class. We learn to look at the world from a critical standpoint, one that considers race, sex, and class. And we can't enjoy life anymore." Cross race, sexual preferences, ethnicities, I saw students nodding their heads. And I saw for the first time that there can be, and usually is, some degree of pain involved in giving up old ways of thinking and knowing and learning new approaches. I respect that pain. And include recognition of it now when I teach, that is to say I teach about shifting paradigms and talk about the discomfort it can cause. A White student learning to think more critically about questions of race and racism may go home for the holidays and suddenly see their parents in a different light. They may recognize nonprogressive thinking, racism, etc., and it hurts them that new ways of knowing may create estrangement where there was none. Often when students return from breaks, I ask them to share with us what ways information, ideas, etc., they have learned and/or worked on in the classroom impacted on their experience outside the classroom. This gives them both the opportunity to know that difficult experiences may be common and it gives them practice at integrating theory and practice, ways of knowing with habits of being. We practice interrogating habits of being as well as ideas. Through this process, we build community. In the diverse setting, it often takes longer for folks to feel comfortable engaging one another rigorously, critically, and we often have to learn how to practice compassion. Many of us, students and professors, have to learn how to act in community.

Despite focus on diversity, our desires for inclusion, many professors still teach in classrooms that are predominantly White. Often a spirit of tokenism prevails in those settings. This is why it is so crucial that "whiteness" be studied, understood, discussed, so that everyone learns that affirmation of multiculturalism, and an unbiased inclusive perspective, can and should be present whether or not people of color are present. Transforming these class-rooms is as great a challenge as learning how to teach well in the setting of diversity. Often if there is one lone person of color in the classroom, they are objectified by others and forced to assume the role of "native informant." For example, a novel is read by a Korean American author. White students turn to the one student from a Korean background to explain what they do not under-stand. This places an unfair responsibility on a student. Professors can intervene on the process by making it clear from that onset that experience does not make one an expert, by perhaps even explaining what it means to place someone in the role of "native informant." It must be stated that professors cannot intervene if they also see students as "native informants." Often students have come to my office complaining about the lack of inclusion in another professor's class. For example, a course on social and political thought in the United States includes no work by women. When students complain to the teacher about the lack of inclusion, they are told to make suggestions of material that can be used. Often this places an unfair burden on a student. It also makes it seem that it is only important to address a bias if there is someone complaining. Increasingly, students are making complaints because they want a democratic, unbiased, liberal arts education.

Multiculturalism compels educators to recognize the narrow boundaries that have shaped the way knowledge is shared in the classroom. It forces us all to recognize our complicity in accepting and perpetuating biases whether it be sexism, racism, or homophobia. Students seem most eager to break through barriers to knowing. They seem most willing to surrender to the wonder of relearning and learning ways of knowing that go against the grain. When we (educators) allow our pedagogy to be radically changed by our recognition of a multicultural world, we can give them the education they desire and deserve. We can teach in ways that transform consciousness, creating a climate of free expression that is the essence of a "truly" liberatory liberal arts education.

6

Multicultural Teacher Introspection

Nitza M. Hidalgo

Many educators around the country are interested in developing a multicultural approach in their teaching. They find themselves in classrooms with 25 children of varying racial and cultural backgrounds and are looking for ways to connect what they do in the classroom to the cultures represented by their students. Before we can begin to understand others, however, we need to understand ourselves and what we bring to our interactions with others. For this reason, it is important for teachers interested in learning more about other cultural groups to first look inward.

The initial step in the process involves introspection. Teachers need to ask themselves some fundamental questions: What framework do we bring into the classroom? How does our cultural perspective color our view of the world? Posing these questions helps teachers analyze the deep-rooted cultural features of their backgrounds. Teachers may thus begin the process of understanding how our beliefs and behaviors are culturally based and how our system of beliefs is similar to or different from our students' beliefs.

Many teachers may not be accustomed to thinking of ourselves as cultural or ethnic. This experience is likely rooted in our training and socialization, both direct and indirect, which have been monocultural in nature. The mainstream perspective presented through schooling is really an Anglo-European perspective. Thus, becoming an educated "American" implicitly means becoming Anglicized.[1]

Until recently, schooling in general did not include much information about the experiences of racial and ethnic groups in the United States. Different perspectives were marginalized, often presented as attachments to the main orientation, especially in the area of curriculum. Most practicing teachers have not been exposed to a multicultural knowledge base.[2] When teachers were presented information about racial or ethnic groups, the mainstream perspective was typically used to evaluate the information. It was the filter through which information about diverse populations was interpreted.

Not only has the framework for interpretation of knowledge been monocultural—that is, Anglo-European—but variations have been judged to be less valuable. When African Americans, Latinos, Native Americans, and Asian Americans were mentioned, the deficit model came into play. That model viewed racial and ethnic differences as deficient, or lacking. Children of color were implicitly judged deficient because they did not bring to school the same majority culture represented in the school and classrooms. Without realizing it, teachers learned mainstream or "whiteness" to be the norm by which all knowledge about others was measured within schooling.

Adoption of this mainstream perspective reinforces a lack of ethnic consciousness among a good many classroom teachers. Thus, schooling does not require us to think of ourselves as ethnic and may, in fact, minimize ethnic awareness in favor of Americanization.

The irony is that each of us has been socialized in some culture, and often more than one culture. Our culture provides a lens through which we view the world and interpret our everyday experiences.[3] Culture informs what we see and understand, as well as what we omit and misconstrue. Many components make up our view of the world: our ethnic and racial identification, the region of the country we come from, the type of neighborhood we live in, our socioeconomic background, our gender, the language(s) we speak, our disabilities, our past experiences, and our life-style. We need to think about the ways in which these parts of us define our perspectives.

We may think about culture as existing on at least three levels: the symbolic, the behavioral, and the concrete.[4] Our values and beliefs lie on the symbolic level. How we ascribe meaning to our experiences depends on the values we hold and the beliefs that we may have. This level is the most abstract and difficult to articulate, yet it is essential to our interpretation of the world.

This level of culture is implicit and shared by others within our reference group. Our values and beliefs help us to interpret our experiences and shape socially appropriate behavior. For example, the definition of family may vary from one cultural group to another, depending on the importance the group places on family cohesiveness. The Puerto Rican concept of family may go beyond the extended family to kinlike relations with friends (compadres/comadres), while the U.S. American definition of family may include only the nuclear family living at home.[5]

The behavioral level refers to how we define our social roles, the language(s) we speak, the rituals we practice, and the form taken by our nonverbal communication. Our behavior reflects our values. The roles we ascribe to women and men within U.S. culture are different from the gender roles of other cultures. Even within our culture, for instance, the role of women has undergone subtle modifications because of the women's movement. These role ascriptions are based on our beliefs, as a society, about the importance of women's work and their contribution to the household. In response, men have also had to redefine their roles within various situations as evidenced by the development of parenting, rather than solely maternity, leave policies. Thus, it is evident that culture is a dynamic, not static, process.

Also on the behavioral level, language mirrors thought; our language reflects our beliefs and values. Think about the associations we make with simple words like black and white. Is it sheer coincidence that we can generate many negative connotations for the word black and many positive connotations for the word white? Regarding language, the feminist movement has worked to eliminate commonplace correlations such as men and girls (versus men and women) because of the inequality inherent in this type of comparison. These are subtle distinctions that have profound effects on our thinking.

Educators often begin to think about multiculturalism at the concrete level, yet movement to a more abstract understanding is needed. The concrete culture is the most visible and tangible level. The products of culture, such as our cultural artifacts, exist at this level. Technology, music, foods, and artistic works and materials are the concrete, visible elements of culture. This is what is most often interpreted as "the culture" of ethnic groups. School festivals highlighting ethnic foods, flag displays from different countries, performance of ethnic music, and playing international games tend to result in a superficial and exotic impression of multiculturalism. This would be comparable to French students expecting to learn about U.S. culture by studying our ritual practices on the Fourth of July. Knowing about barbecues and fireworks displays tells French students little about the meaning Independence Day has in our nation. Foods, holidays, games, and artifacts reveal little about how ethnic groups experience and make meaning of the world.

Given this definition of culture, we can begin to explore how our own cultural perspectives shape our thinking and actions. In order to answer eventually the broad question of how our cultural perspective influences our work in the classroom, we begin with specific introspective information gathering. A preliminary exercise in staff development work with teacher groups requires that we locate ourselves by region, ethnicity, and family system. The exercise requires teachers to respond to the following questions.[6] Where were you born? What language(s) or dialect(s) were spoken in your home? Where did you grow up? Describe your neighborhood. What is your ethnic or racial heritage? Was religion important during your upbringing? If yes, how? Who makes up your family? What traditions does your family follow? What values does your family hold dear? How do the members of your family relate to each other? How is love expressed? How is your culture expressed in your family? These preliminary questions can help teachers begin their introspection by locating themselves in a framework familiar to them—their family background.

The processing of answers derived from this exercise allows us to become located in our personal social constructions. Teachers can thereby reflect on our conceptualization of family and the definition of social roles and behavior within different families. Becoming aware of our definitions may help with the understanding of alternative definitions of family. Meaningful insight comes from having to think about our backgrounds and then sharing this information with others. From sharing, we gain an awareness of the similarities and differences between the various definitions. Derman Sparks[7] recommends that teachers form a support group of colleagues to facilitate the introspection process. In most instances, we learn that despite diversity of meaning, family and community provide us with social safety nets that we can return to when needed for security and connection to others. This kind of exercise, which explores differences and similarities between ethnic and racial groups presents insightful alternative ethnic and cultural interpretations for teachers. We begin to understand our similarities within our diversity.

Once we have thought about the preliminary questions, a deeper level of introspection can occur. After locating ourselves within a particular family and neighborhood, questions related to the individual should be considered. The questions to think about may include: What is our cultural heritage? How does our cultural background influence how we perceive and understand others? What are our values and beliefs? How do our values influence our behavior toward children? How does our socioeconomic class frame our view about children in poverty? What is our definition of normal? How do we think about differences in children, and do we implicitly relate difference to deficiency? Do we believe there are gender differences in certain types of cognitive or physical abilities? Do we think all children can learn?

These questions do not have simple answers. They touch upon many issues that we may not even be able to talk about, specifically, our values. The aforementioned questions are not related to value clarification, but will reveal our implicit cultural and social constructions. Because some aspects of culture are so ingrained, introspection is required to discover how our attitudes, behavior, and interactions are affected.

For example, through introspection, a teacher may discover she believes, like many U.S.-born Americans, that individuals are the basic building blocks of society. As a society, U.S. families rear children to be independent individuals. We hold individualism in high esteem. In contrast, many Puerto Rican parents believe that the family's welfare comes before that of any individual member; the Puerto Rican definition of individualism takes a different form. Puerto Rican children are reared to value interdependency and to hold family obligation in high esteem. These conflicting beliefs may surface in a classroom when a student (especially a female) is absent from school for an extended period to care for younger siblings. Uninformed about the cultural value of interdependency, the teacher may think the child's parents do not value education. In fact, Puerto Rican parents highly value education and encourage their children to succeed academically.[8] The teacher's reaction to this situation may be based on how the ingrained nature of our cultural beliefs interrelate with our learned societal conceptions.

A number of outcomes may result from the introspection process: teachers may sense a lack of true cultural understanding, or they may feel disadvantaged. When asked to define themselves ethnically and culturally, some educators have a very difficult time. Many lack an ethnic consciousness. The difficulty often stems from previous schooling and socialization since the Anglo-European perspective in schools defines the average "American" as one who is White. Although ethnicity and race are distinct social constructions and ethnicity is an essential part of culture, being ethnic in the United States is implicitly defined by some educators today as being non-White. This belies the experiences of

many U.S. citizens, such as those of Italian and Irish heritage who are White ethnics.

Being "American" seems to be cast as a denial of ethnicity; ethnicity is generalized as an exotic, cultural trait. It often seems that to be "American" is to be nonethnic, when in fact it is closer to being a-ethnic, a consciousness related to the melting-pot myth that requires a loss of ethnicity in return for membership in mainstream U.S. society.

A melting-pot formulation leading to Americanization can be seen as the result of combined ethnicities cancelling each other over the generations into "Americans." The melting-pot theory is not equally accepting of all ethnic and racial groups. While the contributions of ethnic groups are supposed to compose the common core, when one examines the "common culture," the core is primarily Anglo-European values, beliefs, and achievements. For example, as Americans we commemorate holidays such as Thanksgiving, a celebration of ancestral survival (and its underlying values of determination and hard work), but the reduction of Native Americans to second-class status which facilitated ancestral survival is not acknowledged. The subtle message is to become "American" is to be nonethnic.

On occasion, introspective teachers communicate a sense of disadvantage from our own schooling. We sense that past knowledge presented to us has offered only a partial picture of our multicultural heritage. We have received only a partial education because our schooling was monocultural in nature. We feel the loss of a significant part of our history, a loss which denies us a fuller sense of humanity and citizenship because it has distorted the importance of Anglo-European traditions by omitting diverse contributions to our society. We realize that exposure to alternative interpretations of reality may dispel the sense of superiority implicitly taught to mainstream citizenry and may better promote egalitarian social relations between people from different backgrounds. Some teachers decide this blockage to our true humanity is something we, as adults wishing to gain a multicultural awareness, have to break down.

Introspection also creates cognitive dissonance for teachers when we must reconcile differing versions of reality. This experience can be so powerful because teachers realize that the information we trusted and believed in may be only partially true and that varying cultural interpretations demand we accustom ourselves to more ambiguity. The dissonance can cause us to adjust our existing framework of knowledge and certainty. We can no longer be satisfied with easy answers because through introspection and sharing come deeper insights into the complexities of a multicultural society.

Understanding and facing the complexity of a multicultural society, where there is no one way to do things, promotes critical thinking capacity. We begin to think critically about ourselves, our beliefs, and our histories, and, consequently, about how our beliefs are framed by societal constructions. We begin to recognize the implicit power attributions unequally assigned to cultural groups in the United States. We have to move beyond ourselves as individuals because we have been socialized within a particular society that shares a common history. The process of examining our assumptions and beliefs results in a critical awareness of past and present U.S. contexts.

Asking introspective questions can lead to an intellectual awareness of the functions of culture. Teachers need to go beyond a cognitive awareness of the influence of culture to an affective understanding. Knowing something in the abstract is insufficient to the awareness we seek; we have to be able to empathize with the experiences of others. Knowing about inequality in the abstract, believing in the principle of equality, is only a first step toward the multicultural awareness needed in classrooms. We need, for example, to put ourselves "in the shoes" of new immigrants facing institutionalized prejudices to feel their reality. The goal is to complement our intellectual introspections with affective understanding. We need to transcend thinking about differences to achieve an emotional connection. Although we can never know another's cultural experiences in the same way as the person who undergoes those experiences, we can achieve an emotional empathy along with an intellectual awareness.

The understanding we seek goes far beyond learning about traditional holidays and ethnic foods, which are the more concrete levels of culture. Once we understand how culture shapes our perspective, our inquiry shifts to the classroom to examine how our beliefs influence our behavior. The questions to pose can be general, or directed toward a particular topic which arises in classrooms daily, such as discipline or teacher/student interactions.

A general question would be: How are our values expressed in classroom dynamics with children? More specific questions related to the areas of authority and discipline are: How do we perceive authority? Does authority come with an ascribed role? For example, does the role of teacher automatically give teachers respect, as in the U.S. American culture, or must respect be earned through the behavior of the person fulfilling that role? What do we consider appropriate behavior for children when interacting with adults? For example, when being reprimanded, do we expect children to look an adult in the eyes or to look down to show respect, as in many Latino cultures? These classroom dynamics inherently shape teachers' expectations of children, but are rarely examined from a cultural perspective. Having clear definitions of appropriate behavior facilitates problem-solving when differing behavior is encountered because we have information on our cultural interpretations to compare and contrast to other interpretations. A critical awareness of how culture functions in the classroom demands, as a first step, teachers' insight into our own culture.

Teachers' sustained interactions with children affect how children feel about school. To understand how cultural background designates particular forms of verbal and nonverbal interaction teachers may ask: What kinds of verbal and nonverbal interactions would we consider appropriate between children and the teacher? Specifically, how do we use touching behavior in the classroom? For Puerto Ricans, touching behavior exists within most interpersonal communications.[9] Puerto Rican children expect a lot of touching and hugging behavior from adults they trust; touching behavior is interpreted as an expression of liking for children. Each of these questions invites a comparison to the cultural perspective the teacher brings to the classroom. If we begin with our own perspectives and what shapes them, we then have a basis for comparing differences and similarities between our perspectives and those of our students.

The teacher introspective process occurs in different phases; completing each phase moves teachers closer to the next phase. The first phase examines cultural and social values, both on an individual and societal basis. The second phase situates awareness on an affective level. The third phase transposes teachers' values and behavior into the classroom context. Each phase is interactive with the preceding and following phase. At each phase, teachers should work not in isolation, as we do in so many other professional processes, but in support groups or teams. Within the safety of a supportive environment, teachers can more productively examine our cultural values, beliefs and assumptions. We can share our findings with each other and gain wisdom about the power of cultural diversity.

Efforts to infuse multicultural awareness into a professional development program for teachers have expanded in recent years, largely due to the increase of immigrant children and children of color in public schools and to a growing awareness of the significance of multicultural education reform. School should create the environment which fosters teacher development for teachers to be able to replicate multicultural awareness with their students.[10]

Teachers need to become introspective ethnographers in our own classrooms to decipher the cultural meanings that we and our students bring to the group. Once teachers understand our assumptions and beliefs and can appreciate and accept the unique cultural contributions of our students, we can use this knowledge to mediate effectively between the children's culture and the other cultures represented in the school.

Acknowledgment

The author wishes to thank the National Coalition of Advocates for Students, Boston, for their support of the initial version of this paper.

Notes

1. J. Banks and C. McGee Banks, *Multicultural Education: Issues and Perspectives* (Boston, MA: Allyn and Bacon, 1989). See also J. Banks, *Teaching Strategies of Ethnic Studies* 5th ed. (Boston, MA: Allyn and Bacon, 1991).

2. C. Grant, "Urban Teachers: Their New Colleagues and Curriculum," *Phi Delta Kappan* (June, 1989) : 764–770.

3. J. Spradley, *The Ethnographic Interview* (New York, NY: Holt, Rinehart & Winston, 1979).

4. M. McGoldrick, J. Pearce, and J. Giodano, eds., *Ethnicity and Family Therapy* (New York, NY: The Guilford Press, 1982).

5. R. Salgado, "The Puerto Rican Family," in *Puerto Ricans in the Mid '80s: An American Challenge* (Alexandria, VA: National Puerto Rican Coalition, Inc, 1985).

6. H. Sheldon and D. Burden-Patmon, *Odyssey Exercise* (Boston, MA: Community Change, Inc., n.d.).

7. L. Derman-Sparks and the A.B.C. Task Force, *Anti-Bias Curriculum* (Washington, DC: National Association for the Education of Young Children, 1990).

8. N. Hidalgo, "*i saw puerto rico once:*" *A Review of the Literature on Puerto Rican Families and School Achievement in the United States*, technical report (Boston, MA: Center on Families, Communities, Schools & Children's Learning, 1992).

9. J. Nine-Curt, *Puerto Rican Non-Verbal Communication* (Cambridge, MA: National Assessment and Dissemination Center for Bilingual Education, 1978).

10. S. Sarason, *The Predictable Failure of Educational Reform* (San Francisco, CA: Jossey Bass Publishers, 1990).

Part III

Developing the Curriculum of Multicultural Education

Revisioning the Canon and Curriculum of the Schools

7

Promises, Pitfalls, and Principles of Text Selection in Curricular Diversification

The Asian-American Case

Sau-ling C. Wong

In recent years, multicultural education has been coming under increasingly virulent public attack as left-wing thought-policing to enforce "PC-ness" or "political correctness."[1] As Dinesh D'Souza suggests by the catchy title of his assault on post-civil rights university policies and curricula, multicultural education is "illiberal education."[2] In one sense, the backlash might be considered an overreaction: it reflects an exaggerated sense of cultural beleaguerment on the part of the majority and targets something which, far from being a full-fledged ogre displacing Western Civilization, is still struggling to come into its own.[3] In another sense, though, the reaction is perfectly proportionate to the threat *as perceived* by those who stand to lose in the reordering of cultural priorities; it is thus a part of our current sociopolitical reality and not to be dismissed as mere paranoia. For as the detractors of multiculturalism rightly grasp, the idea of a multicultural education entails a radical rethinking of what America means, of what being American means.

For the educator committed to multiculturalism, constructing an inclusive literature curriculum represents one of the readiest and most effective means to realize its vision: in Stimpson's words, "to bring dignity to the dispossessed and self-empowerment to the disempowered, to recuperate the texts and traditions of ignored groups, to broaden cultural history."[4] Yet the process of curriculum diversification is fraught with potential problems that good intentions alone cannot resolve. In the following discussion, I will use the incorporation of Asian-American literature as a focus, to bring out certain general issues—the promises, pitfalls, and principles of textual selection—involved in expanding a college or high school literature curriculum.

In a short poem[5] entitled "Chinese Hot Pot," Chinese-Hawaiian poet Wing Tek Lum expounds:

> *My dream of America*
> *is like* da bin louh
> *with people of all persuasions and tastes*

109

> *sitting down around a common pot*
> *chopsticks and basket scoops here and there*
> *some cooking squid and others beef*
> *some tofu or watercress*
> *all in one broth*
> *like a stew that really isn't*
> *as each one chooses what he wishes to eat*
> *only that the pot and fire are shared*
> *and the sweet soup*
> *spooned out at the end of the meal.*

This poem represents a version of the promise of multiculturalism from which a curriculum designer could easily draw inspiration. The melting pot, which is a piece of metallurgical equipment, is often confused in the popular imagination with a stew pot or soup pot. Lum plays upon this common misunderstanding to create a revisionist definition of multicultural America. Israel Zangwill's 1909 play *The Melting-Pot*,[6] which popularized the term as a metaphor for American nationhood, presents a concept of acculturation modeled on the rigors of alchemy. In distinguishing between gold and dross, and in stressing the Biblical, purifying powers of the fire, the process of Americanization assumes a discriminatory and destructive aspect: the immigrant or ethnic minority is to be improved, through necessary ordeals, until he or she is worthy to become a "true American." Lum, on the other hand, proposes a secularized, hierarchy-free, and decentralized vision of America, in which constituent peoples are friends and equals, voluntary participants in cultural transformation and mutual enrichment. Everyone is equidistant from a center whose only function is to facilitate nourishment and fellowship. There isn't even a preconceived notion about the end product of such interaction—the resulting soup is not a stew in the proper sense of the word, because there is no recipe to guide its creation.

I cite Lum's poem not only to affirm the multicultural vision it embodies, but also to underscore two important general observations about translating it into curricular inclusiveness. These points need to be made before I proceed to the specific Asian-American examples. First, it is not so much the act of inclusion as the spirit in which it is conducted that matters most. Nobody can deny that the melting pot is inclusive too: it takes in one and all. That is precisely why the image has had such a strong hold on the national consciousness—it speaks to a certain aspect of the reality of a nation built largely, though by no means exclusively, by immigrants and their descendants, In this sense, it is no different from the Chinese hot pot. However, the inclusiveness of the melting pot is typically informed by a zealous sense of mission to mold others to a predetermined standard of desirability: difference is tolerated only to the extent that it can be "corrected," proving the superiority of the improver. Thus inclusiveness can be manipulated to curtail rather then encourage diversity.

What this means in educational practice is that the inclusion of a "minority" work of literature in a hitherto Eurocentric curriculum is no guarantee that the voices it represents will be respected. Conversely, a curriculum that, whether from bureaucratic impediments, time constraints, or some other factor, cannot be as inclusive as one would hope is not automatically incapable of fostering intercultural understanding. A great deal depends on how the classroom teacher implements the revision. A reading list or a syllabus is an inanimate document; as such, it satisfies institutional demands for explicitness and stability of form, for citation and dissemination. But as such, too, it needs activation by a teacher and can therefore be subverted by insensitive handling. Thus how chosen works are actually taught is as important as, sometimes even more important than, which works are listed.

The second general observation I wish to bring out with the poem on the Chinese hot pot concerns power. Wing Tek Lum suggests that the distinctness of American culture consists not in what it is but what it *enables*. There is no authority, no judge, at the center of the table to decide whether squid is better than beef, or tofu better than watercress. Even though the melting pot image has been in disrepute for a while now, the notion of complete decentralization of cultural authority, rather than a reshuffling in the pecking order, is really quite startling—its very radicalness is a suitable provocation for our collective soul-searching. In educational practice, however, such an ideal is extremely difficult to attain. At the same time that we strive for it, therefore, it is imperative, given the imperfections of our world, our human nature, and our institutions, that we be conscious of the operations of power that unavoidably go into any curricular or pedagogical decision.

A brief digression on the etymology of the word *include* may give us a useful reminder on this point. The word *include* is made up of two parts, the prefix *in* and a Latin root meaning *shut* or *close*. This structure hints a certain complexities in the vision of inclusiveness which at first sight seems so straightforwardly innocuous. Inclusion and exclusion are always simultaneously implicated. Whereas *inclusiveness* connotes openness and acceptance, the etymology of the term suggests a necessary act marking the distinction between inside and outside. Furthermore, since a curriculum is not just a theoretical construct but a framework for practical action, it is not infinitely expandable; at some point, inclusiveness has to stop. Such acts of boundary-drawing requires an arbiter and presupposes a position of power.

There is thus a constant tension between a decentralized, egalitarian cultural ideal and the tendency for actual power to express itself in terms that encode an implicit positioning. One indicator of this tension is how difficult it is to even name the literatures that are under discussion here, as well as the ones that they are posed against. Whether we say "minority literatures" or "marginal literatures" or even "marginalized literatures," as opposed to "mainstream literature," each term already betrays a certain alignment with power, a certain center of gravity. For example, although the term "marginalized" emphasizes the process of disenfranchisement, to call upon the concept of marginality at all is, to some extent, to have conceded that the center of one group is somehow more real, more deserving of recognition, than the center of another group. Using the term "mainstream," as Lauter notes in his "The Literatures of

America: A Comparative Discipline,"[7] implies subscription to a "Great River theory of American letters" that reduces other works to tributaries (48). Yet such terms have become so entrenched, and so convenient, as to be difficult if not impossible to avoid in practice.[8] Even terms like "multicultural literatures" or "multiethnic literatures" are hardly genuine solutions to the problem of nomenclature. In current usage, the Euro-American "classics," though indubitably a part of American cultural reality, are understood *not* to be covered by these terms—which are, in fact, euphemisms for works by people of color. Appearance notwithstanding, the *multi* prefix in these terms does not signal thorough decentralization or full "cultural democracy."

We, as educators pondering inclusiveness, are already positioned on the inside of the establishment and are invested with at least some power; moreover, this power may have become so natural-seeming to us that we may exercise it without awareness. I emphasize this point because terminological, interpretive, and pedagogical choices have to be constantly made as we teach a course involving multicultural literature. A key instructional means of eliciting insight being comparison and contrast, at every turn we need to decide what to compare a marginalized literature to, and to what end. If this is done from a fallacious assumption of one's impartiality, however well-intentioned, the purpose of broadening the curriculum, namely, to honor the articulation of previously suppressed subjectivities, will be seriously undermined.

Keeping these two observations about spirit and about power in mind, I will turn now to Asian-American literature for illustrations of the process of curriculum diversification. On what bases does one decide on which works to include, and what does one do with them once they are selected? What are some problems and pitfalls that the curriculum designer is likely to encounter?

Since few institutions are inclined, or, if inclined, equipped, to offer courses devoted exclusively to marginalized literatures, I will assume a situation where Asian-American works form only a part of a more general course, and where the teacher is trained in either "mainstream" American literature or another marginalized literatures. Institutional reluctance to study literatures of domestic minorities is usually justified in terms of scarcity of campus resources, maintenance of standards of scholarship, or resistance to extraneous political pressure that infringes on academic freedom. But these criteria are not applied even-handedly: departments and programs on European cultures are typically not subjected to criticisms of esoterism or special interest partisanship. The discrepancy in treatment results from an automatic attribution of intellectual respectability to European and Euro-American topics. It also stems from a variation of the NIMBY syndrome—"not in my backyard." It would be noble and humanitarian to have a homeless shelter, but "not in my backyard." Likewise, to learn about another people and another culture would be wonderful for one's education, but if this people or culture happens to be a domestic minority from one's backyard, and alive and kicking and making noise to boot, then the humanistic ideal be damned—let us stick to exotic peoples, preferably safely dead, in faraway lands! In terms of institutional policy-making, this means favoring the study of Tang Dynasty poetry or *The Tales of Genjii* over the study of English-language works by Asians about life in America; after all, who knows what volatile social and political issues might come up in the latter?

Indeed the particular bane of Asian-American literary studies is that its scope and nature are perpetually misunderstood. Because of the West's Orientalist fascination with the high cultures of Asia, as well as its long history of colonialist involvement in the continent, Asians in the United States have been customarily linked to Asians in Asia, with scant regard for the role they have played in the building of this nation and the dynamic cultural transformations they have undergone as immigrants and settlers. In fact, often under the pretext of cultural sensitivity, Asian Americans, in life or in art, are expected to play the role of exotic no matter how long they and their families have been in the United States.

The assumption of terminal alienness, of ineradicable difference, takes many forms; two anecdotes from my academic life will hint at its rampancy. Once, at an interdepartmental faculty reception, when I described my field as Asian-American literature, the listener immediately asked whether I specialized in China or Japan. The word *American* was simply not heard, even though I produced, at close range, sound waves that came into contact with my colleague's eardrums. In another instance, I was asked by a state educational agency to help with a supplementary booklist on non-Western literature. When I pointed out that it would defeat the purpose of furthering cultural sensitivity to code both Chinese and Chinese American titles with a single letter C—when I protested that it made little sense to mix *The Dream of the Red Chamber*, a Qing Dynasty classical novel, with Frank Chin's play[9] about Chinatown in the 1960s, *The Year of the Dragon*—I was politely told that it would be too troublesome and confusing to add *CA* for "Chinese American" to the code. My only recourse was to register my protest by refusing to have myself listed as a volunteer consultant.

Given such persistent "Othering" of Asian Americans, then, the first cardinal principle in selecting texts for a diversified curriculum should be to stress *the Americanness of the group's cultural expressions*. By "Americanness" I do not mean unexamined allegiance to hegemonic myths of nationhood, but the condition of being an integral part of America's history and contemporary life. According to standard usage in the field, the term *Asian-American literature* refers to literature written by Asians permanently residing in the United States and thus covers a bewildering array of works. They differ widely in geographical setting, explicitness of ethnic markers, preoccupation with identity issues, handling of Asian cultural influences, and many other aspects. Although it is often tempting, especially for teachers who have admired or studied Asian languages and cultures, to select Asian American works with the most novelty appeal, works that seem the most intriguingly foreign. I would strongly urge the opposite practice, in order to maintain the focus steadily on Asian Americans as a people of color with a long history in this country.

This brings me to a second principle of text selection: *historical/informational value*, which raises the specter of ideological interference but must be taken into account if the goals of curriculum diversification are to be honored. Bearing in mind the interrelatedness of inclusion and exclusion, given limited class time, I would always give priority to works that introduce students to some key aspects of the Asian-American historical experience of which their schooling has kept them ignorant. This would mean, for example, preferring John Okada's *No-No Boy*[10] or Joy Kogawa's *Obasan*[11] over other Japanese American works, to ensure that students learn about the forcible relocation of Japanese in the United States and Canada during World War II. As long as one does not simplistically equate literature with historical accounts, but rather recognizes the traces of history in their myriad and often veiled forms, I have no qualms about making historical/ informational value a legitimate factor in the choice of texts.

Weighing a literary work's potential for historical education unavoidably brings up the issue of "political correctness." Yet in my approach, *literary interest* ranks high on the list of criteria to be considered in text selection, for I believe our students, even those with little previous exposure to literature, to be far more perceptive and sophisticated than they are usually given credit for, and not in dire need of ideological inoculation.

Works such as Joy Kogawa's *Obasan* are rich both in political insights and formal pleasures. (Indeed, such works exist in greater abundance in "minority" literatures than most people realize.) However, if faced with a decision between a so-called "PC" text of limited literary interest, on the one hand, and, on the other hand, an "un-PC" work informed by a vivid sensibility and written in language affording many interpretive opportunities, I would unhesitatingly choose the latter. For instance, Yoshiko Uchida's 1982 autobiography *Desert Exile: The Uprooting of a Japanese American Family* provides not only a comprehensive, factually accurate account of Japanese American internment, but also a measured assessment of the experience that would be virtually invulnerable to community criticism on ideological grounds.[12] In contrast, Monica Sone's autobiography, *Nisei Daughter*, first published in 1953, expresses many assimilationist sentiments now regarded as outmoded.[13] A mechanical application of the historical/informational principle might point to Uchida's book as superior. Nevertheless, *Nisei Daughter* records the traumatic contradictions of the times in such a compelling and revealing manner that it never fails to generate profitable discussions; in comparison with Sone's spirited prose, Uchida's even, dignified writing appears somewhat bland. If skillfully taught, *Nisei Daughter* can probably disabuse students of naive notions about the Japanese American experience much more effectively than *Desert Exile*. I surmise that disregard of literary interest often does far more damage to the students' engagement with "minority" literature than alleged lack of "PC-ness."

In the foregoing discussion, my preferred term is *literary interest* rather than *literary merit*. The word *merit*, much favored by anti-multiculturalists, reifies historically constructed standards and obscures its consensual, power-imbued nature. Often it refers to a certain type of intricate design, beloved of Ph. D. students and professors, whose superiority has been generalized into universal applicability. My handy if somewhat ad hoc distinction between literary interest and literary merit is intended to unsettle the received definitions of what makes worthwhile reading. Granting the idea of literary merit for the sake of the argument, I maintain that there is actually a broader, more fruitful concept, literary interest, which allows for the investigation of telltale lacunae, ruptures, inconsistencies, what traditional meritocrats would call structural or stylistic "flaws" in a work of literature, as part of an overall close reading. Much can be learned from these so-called flaws about the meaning of the work and its situation in multiple discourses. Thus it is possible to have a work that is short on literary merit but long on literary interest, and worthy of inclusion in an expanded curriculum for that reason.

For example, Carlos Bulosan's *America is in the Heart*,[14] about the lives of migrant Filipino farmworkers in California during the Depression, is disjointed, sloppily written in places, and often frustrating to read. Yet the book can be profitably taught not only because of the raw power of Bulosan's prose, but also because the structural fracturing reflect ideological contradictions to which Filipino Americans were subjected during that historical period.[15] Prior to Philippine independence in 1946, Filipinos in America were "nationals" holding American passports; unlike other Asians such as the Chinese or the Japanese, they were exempt from exclusionary laws and deportation threats. At the same time, however, they were also a despised and exploited minority lacking the rights of citizenship. Employing the genre of the patriotic narrative of immigration and Americanization, invoking images of mobility over the American landscape, Bulosan cannot but come up against historical contradictions that constantly threaten to "derail" his story and generate startling mixtures of events and sentiments. From this perspective, *America Is in the Heart* is a key Asian-American text and should not be shunned on a narrow consideration of what makes "good writing."

A final principle to be considered in curriculum revision is what I call *intertextual compatibility*, by which I mean a work's potential for resonating with other texts chosen for the course—I refer here to a nonspecialist course. Certainly, one of the most recognized purposes of curriculum diversification is to understand the historical and cultural distinctiveness of marginalized groups. Yet no less important (though less frequently discussed) is the study of commonalities between ethnic groups. Only through a fine-grained comparison and contrast of diverse literary works can a new understanding of American identity emerge. There is thus a place for thematically organized nonspecialist courses in which the literary productions of more than one group are examined. For example, Kogawa's *Obasan* may be paired with Alice Walker's *The Color Purple*[16] to study the themes of damage and healing, of silence and the need for voice; Bulosan's *America Is in the Heart* may be studied alongside Tomás Rivera's . . . *Y No Se Lo Tragó la Tierra (And the Earth Did Not Devour Him)*,[17] to reveal the similarities and differences in migrant farmworkers' lives from two ethnic groups and two historical periods. The combinations are limited only by one's purpose and resourcefulness.

A word of caution is in order regarding intertextual considerations. Comparison is never merely a matter of intellectual curiosity: What catches one's eye as belonging together, and what one notices in the juxtaposition as interesting parallels and contrasts, are socially determined. As touched on earlier, comparative literary studies have the potential to subvert, rather than promote, the goals of multicultural education, by prematurely demonstrating how "we are all the same under the skin." A truly inclusive literature curriculum is one that does not automatically anoint the Euro-American tradition as the reference point for comparison, or use it as a stamp of approval to validate the experiences of disenfranchised groups. Intertextual compatibility is not a neutral quality but is, by nature, ideologically informed, produced by the commitment, discernment, and vigilance of the curriculum designer.

Once the curriculum is revised, it has to be implemented. What are some pitfalls to guard against in teaching Asian-American literature? Several varieties of what I call "reductive reading" can be identified here. The term "misreading" is avoided in this discussion because it suggests deviation from a single authoritative, putatively objective interpretation. The concept of "reductive reading" acknowledges that readers are positioned differently, by race or ethnicity, gender, social class, and so forth, but maintains that some perspectives do tend to simplify. Reductive reading refers to the failure to do justice to a work's interacting layers of meaning, some of which are consciously articulated by the author while others are unconsciously revealed.

The first common type of reductive reading is *decontextualization*, stemming from inadequate sociohistorical knowledge about Asian Americans. For example, Louis Chu's *Eat a Bowl of Tea*,[18] a novel set in post-World War II New York Chinatown, is superficially about a young husband who becomes impotent from parental and community pressure to produce an heir. However, beyond the level of individual psychology, the novel is really a comedy of community renewal reversing the effects of discriminatory immigration policies. Prior to the repeal of the Chinese Exclusion Act in 1943 and the enactment of the War Brides Act in 1945, which allowed Chinese American GI's like Ben Loy, the protagonist, to bring in their wives, the Chinese American population was largely male and in danger of dying out. Hence the emphasis on the pregnancy of Mei Qi, Ben Loy's young wife, and the offended elders' eventual acceptance of an illegitimate child, which at first glance goes against patriarchal values. But since the author was apparently writing for an "insider" audience of fellow Chinese Americans, he did not include any historical explication in the novel. An unsuspecting reader might end up seeing *Eat a Bowl of Tea* as an indictment against the tyranny of Chinese patriarchal values. (It is interesting to note that when director Wayne Wang made a film from the novel for a crossover audience, he found it necessary to supply the information about immigration history through a speech at Ben Loy's wedding banquet.)

As the *Eat a Bowl of Tea* example shows, closely related to decontextualization is the imposition of cultural stereotypes onto the text. Decontextualization alone is relatively easy to remedy through appropriate research—once the problem is identified. The greater harm is done when cultural stereotypes prevent one from realizing one's blind spot in the first place, so that one fails to note how the actual text contradicts or problematizes the familiar expectations. This pitfall, which takes several interrelated forms, I call *culturalism*, that is, the tendency to exaggerate exoticism and the determining role of culture in Asian-American life, allowing a facile concept of cultural difference to arrest inquiry into the complexities of the Other, and thus inadvertently perpetuating Otherness.

One manifestation of culturalism is to assume some mystical pipeline of authenticity from Asian Americans to their "heritage culture," ignoring the fact that their American experience has had a transforming influence. Consequently, one tends to detect unusual (by one's own standards) cultural attitudes and practices at the slightest provocation; misses ironies and other subtle meanings; and takes at face value the mediated pronouncements made by American-born Asians about Asia, fellow Asians, or their parents. Maxine Hong Kingston's *The Woman Warrior*[19] offers a sobering paradigm of this process. In the fourth chapter of the book, "At the Western Palace," the American-born narrator's aunt comes from China to reclaim her husband after decades of separation. When the attempt fails, the aunt goes crazy and starts drawing curtains in the daytime against invisible enemies. The narrator and her siblings, having to extrapolate a concept of Chinese culture from scanty data, say to each other, "Chinese people are very weird" (183). This is precisely what many a reader (including professional critics) have done with the rest of *The Woman Warrior*. When the second-generation narrator makes half-baked generalizations about Chinese culture to make sense of her confusing life, many readers mentally squirrel away her statements as nuggets of valuable anthropological information—the Chinese love the number six, the Chinese don't smile when they have their photographs taken. In the process, they end up missing the most crucial point that Kingston is trying to dramatize, namely, the need for American-born Asians, already distanced from their ancestral culture, to invent a viable selfhood.

Another related source of culturalist reading arises from the reification of cultural conflict, as if Asian ethnicity were some congenital defect, as inevitable as chicken pox and as stigmatizing as harelip, of which Asian Americans have to somehow cure themselves. In Monica Sone's terms, being Japanese American is like being a circus freak with two heads; at the end of *Nisei Daughter*,[20] after the humiliations of interment, she claims to have come to terms with this condition and is now glad she gets "a real bargain in life, two (cultures) for the price of one" (236). But the last time in the book she mentions anything Japanese without apology is when she describes having to burn family mementos to avoid suspicions of loyalty to Japan, which gives the lie to her claim of cultural integration. This is a point often overlooked by teachers and students alike, who tend to consider the trajectory from cultural conflict to assimilation as a given, seeing no unconscious irony in Sone's cheerful account.

While cultural conflicts no doubt exist, the central place they are made to assume in Asian-American life is really the result of a cultural script having been imposed by the dominant society on immigrants and especially their descendants, socializing them into "mainstream" codes through varying degrees of self-rejection. Reification of the cultural script is so prevalent that, especially in combination with lack of historical knowledge about Asian Americans, it prevents readers from seeing the way American-born characters misconstrue their parents' motives and misinterpret their behavior. In John Okada's *No-No Boy*,[21] a novel about a Nisei man who goes to jail for refusing to serve in the American army during World War II, the protagonist Ichiro rants about the misfortune of having parents who, after years in the United States, still think of Japan as home and force him to make a choice between the two countries. This account of his suffering conforms so well with the script of intergenerational cultural conflict that readers typically read it straight. An informed, nonculturalist reader, however, would be able to see how American ideology has distorted his framework of interpretation: American-educated Ichiro is unaware of the Alien Land Laws, in force since the 1920s, prohibiting "aliens ineligible to citizenship" (Issei or first-generation Japanese included) from owning land. The parents' sojourner mentality, the target of Ichiro's bitterness about his "cultural conflict," is at least partly imposed and embodies sociopolitical constraints as much as cultural preferences.

Because of the pull of culturalism, social class factors often get left out of the picture in interpretations of Asian American literature; in other words, readings can suffer from *depoliticization*. For example, non-Asian reviewers of Amy Tan's bestselling *The Joy Luck Club*[22] are quick to focus on the mothers' exotic ways and on intergenerational cultural misunderstanding, as a result often ignoring textual complexities that point toward alternative readings. In truth, as Lisa Lowe puts it,[23] *The Joy Luck Club* "represents antagonisms that are not exclusively generational but are due to different conceptions of class and gender among Chinese-Americans" (36). In his enthusiastic review of the novel, Orville Schell,[24] a well-known China-watcher, poses the Joy Luck mothers in their embroidered silk gowns against the Americanized daughters with their suburban life-style, to stress the centrality of cultural conflict in Chinese American existence. But what Schell has omitted to mention—must have failed to even notice—is that his juxtaposition involves an anachronism: the "funny Chinese dresses with stiff stand-up collars" were worn by the women when they first arrived in the United States as refugees, some three decades ago. As they are described in the fictional present of the 1980s, the Joy Luck aunties wear Western "slacks, bright print blouses, and different versions of sturdy walking shoes": "tonight, there's no mystery" (28). Melani McAlister, who detects Schell's revealing error, goes on to point out in her insightful paper that the affluent daughters' embarrassment at their mothers is more class- than culture-based.[25] When upwardly mobile Waverly Jong feels resentment against her mother's color-mismatched outfits or drab hairdo, she blames her predicament on the older generation's stubborn refusal to assimilate. And yet the mother's sartorial sins are due less to Chineseness than to a habit of frugality acquired through years of hardship as an impoverished immigrant: in China, before the flight from war and deprivation, the Joy Luck aunties did not use to be so fashion-blind. What appears to be a classic example of cultural conflict, then, turns out to be a mask for the fear of being déclassé; only a careful reading approach, respectful of the complexities of the Chinese American experience, can counteract the depoliticizing pressures of culturalism.

A final pitfall I wish to address is *universalizing appropriation*, the tendency (already alluded to earlier) to level differences and obscure Asian-American uniqueness in the process of comparison and contrast with other literatures, especially "mainstream" literature. The possibility of revealing intertextual resonances is what makes a multicultural literature curriculum exciting; nevertheless, a comparative approach risks privileging categories from the dominant culture and eclipsing the endeavors at self-definition made by the "minority" writers. A prime example of this tendency is provided by *The Woman Warrior*, a favorite reading in courses on feminist literature. If one simply extracted instances of misogyny from the book to prove the ubiquity of sexism, and antisexist statements to prove the importance of feminist resistance, much would be lost. The oppression experienced by white women is certainly comparable to that experienced by Asian American women in some aspects; to that extent one might speak of a common female condition. On the other hand, people of color are acutely aware that in the United States, ethnicity tends to be gendered and gender ethnicized. The ultra-feminization of Asian American women and the effeminization of Asian American men, both corollaries of the group's marginal status as the "good minority," are two sides of the same coin. *The Woman Warrior* has generated a long-standing controversy within the Asian American community because many readers perceive a conflict between feminism and cultural nationalism (Cheung[26]); the issues raised by this debate must be addressed even in a course "just on gender." The same goes for courses that purport to deal with genres alone, such as American autobiography or the postmodernist novel; or else with "universal" themes such as the mother–daughter relationship, the quest for spiritual transcendence, and the power of storytelling, all of which are present in *The Woman Warrior* but take peculiarly Asian American forms.

The issues discussed above all have analogs in other marginalized literatures, although specific situations vary, calling for appropriate reorientations in the curriculum designer's sensitivities. For example, while exoticization plagues all people of color to some extent, African American literature has a more assured, less contested place than its Asian American counterpart as a component of *American* literature; consequently, curricular decisions may be made to emphasize African-origin elements in the tradition, such as the role of the griot. This thrust appears opposite to that argued for Asian American literature, yet the underlying issue—how to promote understanding of a group's cultural distinctiveness within a pluralistic context—remains unchanged. Hopefully, as curriculum diversification proceeds, patterns of sameness and difference between the literatures of people of color, as well as between them and "mainstream" literature, will emerge with increasing clarity, to foster a true spirit of cultural catholicity.

Notes

1. Catharine R. Stimpson ["Presidential Address 1990: On Differences," *PMLA* 106, No. 3 (1991), 410, n. 6] provides references to the "political correctness" debate in the press. For a recent example of backlash rhetoric, see the 18 February 1991 issue of *The New Republic*. For refutations of anti-multiculturalist views as represented by William Bennett, E. D. Hirsch, and Allan Bloom, see Paul Lauter, *Canons and Contexts* (New York: Oxford University Press), especially chapters titled "Looking a Gift Horse in the Mouth," "Whose Culture? Whose Literacy?," and "The Book of Bloom and the Discourse of Difference," pp. 243–286.

2. Dinesh D'Souza, *Illiberal Education* (New York: Free Press, 1991).

3. For example, a 1984–1985 Modern Language Association survey of English departments found 34 percent of the departments adding courses on women writers and 25 percent adding course on ethnic minority literatures; however, the requirements of the major had remained stable. [See Phyllis Franklin, "Waiting for the Barbarians," *Modern Language Studies* 20, No. 1 (1990), 8, cited in Stimpson, op. cit., p. 410, n. 6.]

4. Stimpson, op. cit., p. 404.

5. Wing Tek Lum, "Chinese Hot Pot," *Expounding the Doubtful Points* (Honolulu, HI: Bamboo Ridge Press, 1987), p. 105.

6. Israel Zangwill, *The Melting-Pot*, 1909 (New York: Macmillan, 1910).

7. Lauter, op. cit.

8. In this essay, I will continue to use some of them, but with quotation marks to show qualification when necessary.

9. Frank Chin, *The Year of the Dragon, Chickencoop Chinamen and the Year of the Dragon* (Seattle, WA: University of Washington, 1981).

10. John Okada, *No-No Boy* (1957: reprint, Seattle, WA: University of Washington Press, 1979).

11. Joy Kogawa, *Obasan* (Boston: Godine: 1982).

12. Yoshiko Uchida, *Desert Exile: The Uprooting of a Japanese-American Family* (1982; reprint Seattle, WA: University of Washington Press, 1984).

13. Monica Some, *Nisei Daughter* (1953; reprint Seattle, WA: University of Washington Press, 1979).

14. Carlos Bulosan, *America Is in the Heart* (1943; reprint, Seattle, WA: University of Washington Press, 1973).

15. Another factor is biographical: the ailing Bulosan was pressured by impatient editors to finish the book quickly; see Elaine H. Kim, *Asian American Literature: An Introduction to the Writings and their Social Context* (Philadelphia, PA: Temple University Press, 1982).

16. Alice Walker, *The Color Purple* (1982; reprint, New York: Washington Square Press, 1983).

17. Tomás Rivera, . . . *Y No Se Lo Tragó la Tierra*, 1971 [And the Earth Did Not Devour Him], trans. Evangelina Vigil-Pinon (Houston, TX: Arte Publico Press, 1987).

18. Louis Chu, *Eat a Bowl of Tea* (1961; reprint, Seattle, WA: University of Washington Press, 1979).

19. Maxine Hong Kingston, *The Women Warrior: Memoirs of a Girlhood among Ghosts* (New York: Knopf, 1982).

20. Sone, op. cit.

21. Okada, op. cit.

22. Amy Tan, *The Joy Luck Club* (New York: Putnam, 1989).

23. Lisa Lowe, "Heterogeneity, Hybridity, Multiplicity: Marking Asian American Differences," *Diaspora* 1, No. 1 (1991), 24–44.

24. Orville Schell, "Your Mother Is in Your Bones," *New York Times Book Review*, 19 March 1989, 3.

25. Melani McAlister, "(Mis)reading the *The Joy Luck Club*," paper presented at the "Asian American Cultural Transformations: A Literature of One's Own" conference, University of California, Santa Barbara, 27 April 1991.

26. King-kok Cheung, "The Woman Warrior versus the Chinamen Pacific: Must a Chinese American Critic Choose between Feminism and Heroism?," in *Conflicts in Feminism*, ed. Marianne Hirsch and Evelyn Fox Keller (New York: Routledge, 1990), 234–251.

8

Beyond Island Boundaries

Ethnicity, Gender, and Cultural Revitalization in U.S. Puerto Rican Literature

Edna Acosta-Belén

Introduction

One of the most common concerns among those who study the Puerto Rican reality is the extent of the alleged Americanization or cultural assimilation resulting from almost a century of U.S. colonial domination of the island. This cultural aggression, a process endemic to the colonial relationship between Puerto Rico and the United States, which began in 1898, has been the subject of numerous studies and debates over the preservation and deterioration of Puerto Rican national identity and culture, and its inexorable connection with the political status of Puerto Rico. In recent years, for example, several aspects of this debate have resurfaced and captured public attention as a result of congressional hearings on the possible holding of a plebiscite to decide the future political status of Puerto Rico.

The focus of this cultural predicament often fails to transcend the political context of the status question or tends toward the fervent protectionism of an immutable Puerto Rican cultural tradition, or the denunciation of an alleged transculturation in which all cultural change is attributed to U.S. influence. A more fruitful analysis, as has been well-demonstrated by the new Puerto Rican historiography of the past two decades, is the detailed study of cultural processes in reference to the economic structures and social classes that engender them, and the conflicts that result from the dynamic interaction of those who share the social and historical scene. From this perspective, a great deal has been learned about those sectors historically marginalized and excluded from cultural processes, and of their struggles and strategies for self-affirmation and cultural survival within the context of colonial subordination and dependency in which they are inserted.

Within the complex and diverse ramifications of this national debate, the question of the cultural identity of those Puerto Ricans living in the United States (or, for that matter, the identity in question, frequently referred to by critics), has been generally relegated to a secondary status or left to a handful of scholars who live in the U.S. metropolis. In this chapter I would like to examine some of the most significant aspects of how this identity is configured, the ways in which it is articulated and mediated in the literary expressions of the Puerto Rican migrant community, and, at the same time, highlight those elements that bring coherence to this body of literature, and the diverse meanings and functions that it imparts to the building of a Puerto Rican identity in U.S. society. As a secondary aim, I will attempt to link the analysis of how and with what means groups placed in positions of internal colonialism within U.S. society formulate and affirm their own identity with the problematic issue of identity and anticolonial struggle in Puerto Rico.

The Myth of a Puerto Rican Poverty of Culture

In a previous study about the literature of the Puerto Rican minority in the United States, published in the late 1970s,[1] I pointed out how, at that time, the importance of the literary works by Puerto Rican writers born or raised in the United States was being underestimated or overlooked by island writers and critics. I also stressed the need to view these cultural expressions in regard to the Puerto Rican national question and the subordinate socioeconomic position occupied by Puerto Ricans within U.S. society. With all the limitations of that seminal study, one of the aspects I most wanted to emphasize was the way in which this literature provided to the Puerto Ricans born or raised in the United States, a means of cultural validation and affirmation of a collective sense of identity that served to counteract the detrimental effects of the socioeconomic and racial marginalization that Puerto Ricans have experienced in the metropolis. I further pointed out that this cultural effervescence among Puerto Ricans of the diaspora was part of a burgeoning consciousness among ethnoracial minorities in the United States, a process that began during the 1960s, an era of intense social and political activism and upheaval in favor of civil rights, equal opportunity among the races and sexes, and opposition to the Vietnam War. Finally, I underscored the "anti-Establishment" character of this literature and its commitment to denouncing inequality and injustice in U.S. society and as a consciousness-raising tool for promoting social change among the writers' respective communities. At the time, my analysis was based on an emerging literary output from only a handful of authors. By comparison, there is now an abundant and better defined body of literature that is increasingly receiving critical attention.

In this essay, I would like to expand some of these initial ideas within a broader theoretical framework and provide a more integrated and nuanced view of the formative and developmental processes of this literature, commonly identified as *nuyorican* or *neorican*, terms which originally had negative connotations particularly in the way that it was used on the island. Regardless of its implied geographic limitations, since not all U.S. Puerto Rican writers are from New York, the label is not generally accepted by many writers themselves (especially the poets), as a word that defines a collective Puerto Rican identity stemming from the migrant experience and thus differentiated from that of the island.[2]

When the discussion around the issue of cultural identity surpasses national borders and extends to the Puerto Rican migrant community, island intellectuals frequently tend to underrate or to be critical about the work of writers who persist in identifying themselves as Puerto Ricans, but do not necessarily speak or write Spanish fluently, a sign they view as an unquestionable indication of assimilation into U.S. society. These critics view the work of Nuyorican authors, who write primarily, although not exclusively, in English, as a mere extension of American literature. They are generally reluctant to acknowledge any substantial relationship of this literary experience to the island's cultural patrimony. Other times, appreciation of this literature is limited to conceiving of it as an example of the "nuyorican identity crisis," as if this particular identity issue was in no way related to the island's cultural experience or was totally detached from its colonial reality. Paradoxically, because of the U.S. presence in Puerto Rico, identity has been an ardent issue of intellectual and political debate on the island throughout most of this century.

In turn, U.S. society tends to blame Puerto Ricans ("the blaming the victim syndrome") for their failure to ascend the slippery ladder of socioeconomic mobility and for their ostensibly limited cultural development; factors attributed to the fact that they are not sufficiently assimilated into the U.S. mainstream culture, refusing to follow the assimilation patterns established in the past by other white European immigrant groups.

Scholars like Glazer and Moynihan,[3] among many others, contributed to the notion of the "cultural deficiency" of Puerto Ricans based on an alleged weakness in the cultural and linguistic aspects of the Hispanic heritage of Puerto Rico that migrants bring with them. They concluded that these cultural deficiencies are transferred to the U.S. Puerto Rican community and thus generate their relative weakness in the areas of cultural development, community organization, and leadership when compared to other minority groups. For many of these scholars, Puerto Rican migrants have lived in a cultural desert sharing as much the culture of poverty as a poverty of culture.

The subsequent publication of works such as *Memoirs of Bernardo Vega* by César Andrew Iglesias[4] and Jesús Colón's *A Puerto Rican in New York and Other Sketches*[5] have helped to dispel some of these opinions. These writings have revealed the political activism, cultural effervescence, and communal spirit that prevailed in the early Puerto Rican community and represent a significant step in overcoming the cultural invisibility of Puerto Ricans in U.S. society. Despite the fact that the cultural invisibility of Puerto Ricans has been gradually overcome in recent years, the literature produced by these authors still occupies a marginal place in U.S. society and is known even less in Puerto Rico.

The emergence and development of a literature written in English or which bilingually integrates the use of English and Spanish in the same text, produced by second-generation Puerto Rican writers in the United States, has awakened among some island intellectuals old concerns about the preservation and deterioration of the *puertorriqueñidad* (the essence of being Puerto Rican) that includes fruitless attempts to define who is a true Puerto Rican.[6] This compelling concern is grounded in the fact that, for almost a century, Puerto Ricans on the island have had to wage their own battles against U.S. colonialism and cultural assimilation policies intended to *denationalize* the Puerto Rican people, policies which have impeded to varying degrees the process of development of a strong sense of national identity and consciousness that might threaten U.S. control over the island. A more promising analysis, in my opinion, is to try to understand the various functions of the affirmation of a Puerto Rican identity within U.S. society among the various generations of migrants, and the specific ways in which this identity is articulated and revitalized in their cultural expressions.

Culture, Ethnicity, and Identity

To avoid any possible semantic confusion, I wish to establish that, within the context of this chapter, culture, is not conceptualized as an immutable monolithic entity composed of an essence or intrinsic characteristics, but rather we subscribe to the definition advanced in the work of García Canclini[7] which defines culture as "the production of phenomena which contribute, through the symbolic representation and reelaboration of material structures to the understanding, reproduction or transformation of the social system. . . ." (p. 41). It is by means of a process of symbolic reproduction that the structures of reality are built, transformed or invented, giving meaning to the ideas and experiences of social groups. The forging of a culture is, therefore, a dialectical process inseparable from class relations and antagonisms.

On the other hand, when we refer to the concept of ethnicity within the context of U.S. society, we do not confine ourselves to the preservation of specific cultural traditions or national characteristics by a given ethnic group, but to the process by which this group sees itself as separate from the dominant group in that society, and by which each group tends to place itself in dynamic interaction within the dichotomy them/us.[8] Therefore, ethnicity is also seen as a function of class differences.

For most groups that come to the United States, the transition or separation that transforms them from immigrants/migrants to ethnics is an immediate one. This separation, based on prevailing ethnocentric and racial prejudices, makes ethnicity an invention, a cultural construction that while providing a sense of belonging to a collectivity for the ethnic group, it also segregates it from the mainstream society (see Hobsbaum[9] and Sollors[10]).

Identity, on the other hand, is the way in which culture becomes significant to individuals and the way they define themselves. Identity is also distinguished by its changeable and variable nature, especially in contact situations where there is more than one culture flowing together and interpenetrating one another.[11] It takes its configuration from the many perceptions and ideas that the individuals internalize about themselves and their surroundings. In multicultural environments such as the United States, the identity of an ethnic group cannot be reduced to the internalization of the features of only one culture or in exclusive relation to the elements of a specific immutable cultural tradition with which a common language is shared.

Many studies have highlighted how, in recent decades in the United States, the multicultural or ethnic revitalization movement has represented a response from ethnoracial minorities to their structural and cultural marginalization and to the assimilation pressures from the dominant Anglo-American society, thereby challenging its cultural hegemony. This multicultural revitalization has also engendered, within U.S. academic circles, an intellectual reevaluation and redefinition of the ethnocentric Euro-American cultural theories and canons. In the case of the American literary canon, it has been quite obvious that until recently the artistic works of minority groups and their cultural and historical presence had been covered with an invisible veil. Consequently, these groups are now engaged in appraising and defining their diversity in a country which, from its formative stages as a nation, excluded the native cultures that occupied its territory as well as those cultures later introduced by the enslavement of the African people and through immigration.

Puerto Ricans Between Two Worlds

The limited scope of this chapter does not allow a more detailed analysis of all the complex ramifications of the debate over the cultural authenticity of the artistic expressions of second-generation Puerto Ricans in the United States. Most of the arguments are already well-known and this discussion tends to lead to an ideological impasse. A more promising approach is to focus on the structural conditions which promote the process of cultural revitalization among U.S. Puerto Ricans. Deserving particular attention are those elements of cultural resistence that arise from this process and the instrumental nature of these literary expressions which instead of weakening or tarnishing Puerto Rican national culture, draw upon its vitality, producing *alternative* cultural forms of the migrant experience. These artistic expressions reflect elements of continuity and change with regard to the island's traditions. They are cultural forms which also reflect, both on an individual and collective level, the awakening of a consciousness of a Puerto Rican nationality or a national consciousness in the United States.[12] This process, in turn, provides a sense of historical continuity to the presence of a Puerto Rican cultural tradition in the U.S. metropolis—a process initiated during the last decades of the nineteenth century when figures such as Ramón Emeterio Betances, Eugenio María de Hostos, Francisco "Pachín " Marín, and Lola Rodríguez de Tió, among others, shared the experience of exile in New York City—and adds a new phase to this tradition (see Flores[13]).

Any analysis of the Puerto Rican reality in the United States must begin with an understanding of the colonial conditions of the island that provoked the migratory process which has resulted in at least 40 percent of the population presently residing outside the island national boundaries and inside the continental United States. Contact between the island and the metropolis is maintained by a commuter or circular migration facilitated by geographic proximity and the so-called "air bridge" between these two worlds. This situation is also facilitated by the fact that Puerto Ricans hold U.S. citizenship.

Of all the Puerto Ricans in New York City, 48.1 percent are first-generation migrants.[14] The other half of the population is composed of those generations born or raised in the United States. As a result, it can be expected that cultural continuity from one generation of Puerto Ricans to another will always be accompanied by substantial changes and transformations. These generational differences define a cultural context in the United States where we find the presence of Puerto Rican writers whose works are studied as an extension of the island literature because they write in Spanish and were born and raised in Puerto Rico, along with Nuyorican writers. I am referring to writers such as Iris Zavala, Manuel Ramos Otero, Iván Silén, Etna Iris Rivera, and Edgardo Sanabria, among many others, who have resided for extended periods of time in the United States. This reality points to the necessity to also reevaluate the Puerto Rican literary canon which so far has refused entry to Nuyorican literature. This rejection is something which has captured the insight of many Nuyorican writers (see Mohr[15]) and is exemplified by the following verses of Tato Laviera:

> yo peleo por ti, puerto rico, ¿sabes?
> yo me defiendo por tu nombre, ¿sabes?
> entro a tu isla, me siento extraño, ¿sabes?
>
> pero tu con tus calumnias, me niegas tu sonrisa. . .
> me desprecias, me miras mal, me atacas mi hablar,
> mientras comes mcdonalds en las discotecas americanas,

(Tato Laviera,[16] "nuyorican," p. 53)

Note that the poet questions the reason for the rejection by his fellow compatriots on the island when they, themselves, from his point of view, have also adopted "Americanized" ways represented here by McDonald's and discoteques.

Puerto Rico, cradle of the ancestors, becomes in the following verses of Miguel Piñero[17]: "the slave-blessed land / where nuyoricans come in search of spiritual identity / and are greeted with profanity." It is this generation of Puerto Ricans, born or raised in the metropolis, who have taken a libation from that fountain of "spiritual identity" mentioned by Piñero, but when they visit the island are confronted with the cultural prejudices that divide Puerto Ricans into *los de aquí y los de allá* (those from here, meaning the island; and those from over there, meaning the United States). This rejection is compounded by the prejudice and marginalization they already face in U.S. society. Another clear indication of this rejection is the scant interest among island intellectuals for the reading, study, or translation into Spanish of the writings of Nuyorican authors. (Among the few translation efforts are *Herejes y mitificadores*, edited by Efraín Barradas and Rafael Rodríguez[18] and the translations[19] of *Puerto Rican Obituary* and other works of Pedro Pietri by Alfredo Matilla). Thus, we wish to stress the need to incorporate the Nuyorican cultural experience into the general discourse on Puerto Rican national culture, acknowledging the connections between U.S. colonial domination of the island and the migrant experience.

A New Cultural Discourse

If we consider that one of the main consequences of colonialism is the translocation of workers from the colony to the metropolis where colonial conditions are reproduced by means of what has been described as *internal colonialism*,[20] for colonial minorities such as the Puerto Ricans, affirming a separate identity from the society in which they occupy a subordinate position produces cultural expressions that reflect their marginal life conditions and their conflicting interactions with the privileged sectors of U.S. society. It is from this interaction and interpenetration with an antagonistic social order that mediating cultural forms emerge.

A more holistic understanding of the processes of acculturation or assimilation can be achieved by considering the nature of the power relationship behind the socioeconomic contact between two cultural entities. In the case of Puerto Ricans, this implies a recognition of their subordinate position as a colonial minority. These processes entail the presupposition that there is a loss of the culture of origin which is gradually replaced by the adoption of the dominant culture of the nation to which a group immigrates. Contradictorily, many studies confirm that the presence of immigrant groups and their potential assimilation into U.S. society always has been selective in nature, depending on the fluctuating needs of the U.S. labor force which has given preference to white European groups and on the prevailing "filias y fobias"[21] (preferences and fears) of U.S. society at a given historical moment. If Puerto Ricans and other ethnoracial minorities had assimilated, the barrios or enclaves of New York would not exist, nor would Puerto Ricans still be relegated as a group to the the lowest end of the spectrum among all minority groups on many socioeconomic indicators.

Some scholars have argued that although assimilation of U.S. ethnoracial minorities has not occurred at a structural level, it has otherwise occurred in cultural terms. This assumption is indicative of the fact that not enough attention has been paid to the alternative ways of cultural adaptation, innovation, and resistance found among these groups; nor to the process of inventing new traditions or the cultural syncretism that emerges from settings where there is contact and diffusion of cultures under conditions of domination and subordination. The changeable nature of identity allows every cultural minority, depending on its historical specificities and structural position, to activate its own mechanisms of adaptation and accommodation, self-preservation or resistance to the pressures it endures from the dominant society.

Also ignored is the role that academics and other professional members of these minority groups have played in the process of exposing the myths and stereotypes of their respective groups perpetuated by the dominant society. Minority scholars have subjected the various disciplines to a rigorous examination of their theoretical and interpretive bases and have attempted to develop new cultural paradigms in which the differentiation and validation of ethnoracial identity are at the forefront of the social struggles of these groups. They are challenging the hegemonic notions and exclusionary tendencies of the prevailing Western theoretical constructs and representational modes that have excluded, distorted, or diminished the presence and contributions of subaltern groups to the making of history and society. This does not imply, however, that the cultural revitalization process described herein is a mere political strategy to advance individual socioeconomic interests as some scholars have argued.[22] The cultural and psychosocial impact of this ethnic revitalization on the formation of a self-concept, on the development of a collective sense of identity, on the articulation of resistance toward various forms of oppression, and on the cultural enrichment of the community itself as it recovers and takes possession of its own history, has left an indelible imprint and shed new light on any future analysis of the minority experience in U.S. society.

The affirmation of a Puerto Rican identity in the United States, a process similar to that undergone by other ethnoracial minorities such as the Chicano, African American, and Native American communities, is part of the broader process of multicultural revitalization carried out among oppressed peoples in many parts of the world which had its most sparkling moments during the 1960s and 1970s. This movement, which some have considered one of pseudo-ethnicity[23] or a temporary symbolic ethnicity [24] and for which others have predicted a premature decline,[25] continues redefining the true nature of the American experience on several fronts. Mostly it has demonstrated that the core of this purported experience is not the mythical "melting pot" or fusion of other cultures with a mainstream Anglo-American cultural current as many theorists had predicted, but rather the negation of this false and static universalist model of cultural homogeneity and the affirmation of a U.S. society in which diversity and multiethnic interaction constitute its true cultural nucleus.

At a global level, Smith,[26] in his book *The Ethnic Revival*, argues that ethnic revitalization movements, which reached their peak in recent decades in the Western industrialized nations including the United States, represent a concerted response on the part of marginalized minorities to the inequitable conditions created by modernization, the uneven economic development and wealth distribution inherent in industrial capitalism, and an international division of labor which intensifies antagonisms between the class interests of those who control the means of production and the workers they exploit. Smith also shows how these internal movements within the metropolitan centers of the advanced capitalist nations have been invigorated by their solidarity with the self-determination and decolonization movements of Third World nations and other progressive struggles around the world.

From this global theoretical framework, it can be concluded that the forces which produce and sustain the international division in labor are those that, in turn, generate and maintain a segregated labor force in societies like the United States.[27] These conditions also foster a *cultural* division of labor in which ethnic, racial, and gender distinctions are superimposed on class differences. These structures, which historically have reflected inequities among ethnic groups, races, and sexes, tend to reproduce and manifest themselves with greatest intensity in the large urban centers of world capitalism.

Yancey, Eriksen, and Juliani[28] corroborate that the extreme conditions of inequality, racial segregation, and dependency upon social institutions faced by ethnoracial minorities have served as catalysts to the visibility of ethnicity in recent decades. They also predict that as long as those inequitable structural parameters exist for the working class of U.S. urban centers, the cultural vitality of these groups will persist.

Within this framework, the cultural expressions of Puerto Ricans and other ethnoracial groups are a creative way of critically looking at the inequalities and conflicts that arise from their interaction with the Anglo-American mainstream society and recording their struggle to overcome them. While these groups challenge the cultural and socioeconomic hegemony that promotes an unfulfilled American dream, they affirm a distinctive collective identity which preserves, rejects, modifies, or transforms elements taken from the culture of origin, from the surrounding world of the oppressor, and from their interaction with other subordinate groups with whom they share cultural and racial affinities or a similar structural position. These new cultural expressions are manifestations of an encounter that produces reciprocal conditioning and the articulation of a social and cultural consciousness. Besides maintaining a link with the past, "a tradition is invented" (to use a term coined by Hobsbaum[29]) that asserts some cultural configurations of its own, with social, political, and psychological functions of great significance, and which adds new shadings to the cultural legacy of Puerto Ricans in the United States and on the island for future generations.

The perpetuation of inequality and racism within the Western nations has maintained ethnoracial minorities on the lowest rung of the social hierarchy. For these sectors, diversity based on ethnic and racial differentiation has become a fundamental instrument of the class struggle within U.S. society: being Puerto Rican (or Hispanic/Latino, according to the prevailing collective bureaucratic label) implies a separation from the dominant society, a recognition of the lack of privileges, and falaciousness of the myths of equality, prosperity, and democracy that U.S. society promotes and which they do not share.

The subordinate-class experience that Puerto Ricans share with other ethnoracial groups, and the contacts and cultural convergences among them, accounts for the popular character of their cultural expressions which reflects the working-class origins of many of their creators. For instance, in the case of Nuyorican poetry, there is a creative intention to transmit it, whether in oral or written form, to the people; or, as Miguel Algarín would say,[30] "to tell tales of the streets to the streets" (p. 11). The concept of "street poetry," introduced by these writers, is illustrative of a consciousness among its creators of the aspects of production, circulation, and reception of their work.[31]

For these authors, Puerto Rico provides a frame of reference for continuity with ancestral "roots" (to use Alex Hailey's famous metaphor), although, in the case of the Puerto Ricans, these roots are not hidden in the memory of ancestors on a distant continent, but possess the vitality of a present time because of the geographic proximity and continual migratory flow to and from the island. Barradas' critical analysis of Nuyorican poetry[32] established that for these writers Puerto Rico is the mythical fountain from which gushes the images and symbols of searching, self-definition, struggle, and survival. The content of these symbols and images is accepted, rejected, or modified by the cultural and linguistic contact with Anglo-American society and with the surrounding communities within which these groups evolve. In Nuyorican cultural expressions, we can see the influence of the African-American culture, particularly in the music (see Aparicio[33]), as well as from other Latino groups with whom they share the urban enclaves. If we consider, for example, the Chicano experience, we see a greater affinity with the Native American experience. The extent of these affinities or influences is related to the racial and historical background of each one of these groups.

Anglo-American ethnocentricism and racism reject cultural and linguistic differences that go beyond those that are folkloric, picturesque, or culinary. Proponents of the U.S. "English Only Movement," for instance, are a reprehensible example of the entrenched collective paranoia about ethnolinguistic groups ingrained in the mainstream culture. The loss of the immigrant's vernacular language and the acquisition of English are valued by the dominant society as a fundamental step in the path toward complete assimilation. Contradicting this notion is the fact that assimilation or the total integration into U.S. society has not taken place among ethnoracial groups. On the other hand, the emphasis on the adoption of English as the sole language of schooling is a way of denying immigrants a complete validation of their identity, while it facilitates their functioning in the labor force of the dominant society and as consumers.[34]

The configuration of ethnic identity is not based exclusively in reference to features of a specific traditional culture of origin, or maintaining its corresponding language. The historical experience of many nationalities that have evolved within a context of colonial oppression has demonstrated that the survival and affirmation of certain colonial cultures do not depend exclusively on the preservation of a native language. For example, the Irish, Phillipinos, and Jamaicans, for a diversity of reasons, were not assimilated into the nationality of the colonizer, even though they have adopted to a large degree the use of an imposed language. Thus, we cannot engage in the study of the formation of

Puerto Rican identity in the United States based solely upon deterministic cultural and linguistic preconceptions.

Minority cultures evolve from a context dominated by capitalist power structures and relations with all their homogenizing tendencies. Although contact with these structures produces a tempering of cultural resistance, especially with regard to language (Spanish in the case of Puerto Ricans), the separation or differentiation from the dominant Anglo-American culture is maintained by means of a creative bilingualism, characterized by the use of everyday, street, or coarse language and code switching, where English and Spanish linguistic codes are alternated. Spanglish or "broken English" become effective means for communicating different social and cultural experiences.[35] For Puerto Rican minority writers, what some have described as "alingualism" or "chronic illness,"[36] becomes "creative interlingualism,"[37] an essential element of a bilingual poetics that combines two linguistic codes and takes advantage of the idiomatic resources of both languages, thereby broadening meaning and communicative possibilities. The two languages, Spanish and English, serve as vehicles for poetic discovery and experimentation and, in turn, lend coherence to a fragmented world turning it into what Nuyorican poet Víctor Hernández Cruz[38] identifies as "bylingual wholes"; a bilingual and bicultural totality that incorporates into the communal "enclave," as the poet Tato Laviera suggests, the codes and messages, which are encoded in the culture and music. It is a bilingualism that nurtures itself from its interaction with jive, Black English, and, most recently, the rap phenomenon; and a biculturalism that connects jazz and soul music with the *bomba* and *plena* to produce musical hybrids such as *salsa* (see Aparicio[39]). Many sociolinguistic studies corroborate the communicative expansion that arises from this bilingualism and confirm that most Latinos in the United States speak some degree of Spanish in their own homes and communities,[40] suggesting that language still is a vital cultural force within the community. One of the astonishing realities which I was unable to anticipate two decades ago, was the bilingual vitality that has endured in Nuyorican literature.

The Multiple Levels of Consciousness

In looking at the structuring and transformation of Puerto Rican identity in the United States, the works of Juan Flores[41] have been indispensable. He reaffirms the notion that[42] "any interpretation of this cultural process presupposes a coherent analysis of the conditionings of the political and economic reality, in this case, colonialism, the migration of the work force and racial inequality" (p. 57). In the evolution of the Nuyorican cultural consciousness, Flores discerns four definitive moments "which intersect and coexist simultaneously. These include (1) the immediate perception of the surrounding reality which isolates and excludes Puerto Ricans from the prevailing society and culture and which places them in what he terms a "state of abandonment"; (2) the contrast between what Flores describes as "the state of enchantment" of the Nuyorican with respect to the island culture in contrast with the "cultural sterility" (p. 58) of the city of steel; (3) the transposition of the underlying island culture in which "looking at New York, the Nuyorican sees Puerto Rico" and reinserts himself/herself into the world of the big city; and (4) "the selective connection and interaction with the surrounding U.S. society" and the "cultural coalitions with other colonial minorities" (pp. 57–61). Flores concludes his analysis by pointing out that this literature reflects the process of "awakening of a national consciousness or the consciousness of nationality" and the consciousness of an emergent class that arises from the validation that is given to popular culture.

With regard to the presence and formation of a class consciousness and a consciousness of nationality in the identity-structuring process formulated by Flores, I would like to add other levels of consciousness which, in my opinion, also merit attention since they contribute to a more integrated and nuanced vision of cultural revitalization in Nuyorican literature. I first refer to the development among women writers, of a feminine consciousness, which encompasses multiple aspects of womanhood, and a feminist consciousness which expresses varying levels of awareness of the oppression and subordination that characterize the structural position of women. Another form of consciousness that deserves to be emphasized as a derivative of this revitalization movement, which will be discussed later, is the formation of a shared consciousness among the various Latino groups that transcends the specific national and cultural specificities of each group in favor of embracing a broader collective identity.

With regard to forms of feminine and feminist consciousness, I would first like to stress the importance of considering gender, a basic principle of social classification, as a factor that together with the differences in class, race, and ethnicity already discussed, also interacts simultaneously in the structuring of identity. As a result, in the process of forging an identity, we must distinguish between dimensions of oppression and subordination that women share with men—in this case, those based upon socioeconomic, racial, and ethnic factors—and those which are unique because they depend entirely on their gender. The recognition of this *other* dimension of subalterity is what has led women writers to establish and define their own literary tradition.

While men, who tend to be conceived of or conceive of themselves as universal beings devoid of gender, perceive their oppression in U.S. society on the basis of ethnic, racial, or class differences, women additionally endure all the elements of negation and marginalization that come from sexism. Therefore, for women writers, gender will be an essential factor in the search for expression and articulation of their own identity. This process also entails a confrontation with the caprices or vagaries of a patriarchal ideology within the culture of their own group, as well as in the culture of the broader society. As a result, their responses to and strategies against oppression are going to differ from those formulated by men.

This consciousness of the multiple forms of oppression that confront women has become an integral part of the work of Latina writers in recent decades, and is a process not exempt from contradictions. While women writers attempt to demythify the cultural roles, values, and icons manufactured by a patriarchal ideology and subvert those cultural beliefs about family, sexual relationships, and behavior in general which are presented as universal, but which, in reality, are grounded on the subordination of women, they are also trying to validate that same cultural heritage. The poem "Latin Women Pray" by Judith Ortiz Cofer[43] dramatizes this dilemma:

> Latin women pray
> in incense sweet churches,
> they pray in Spanish to an Anglo God
> with a Jewish heritage.
>
> And this Great White Father,
> imperturbable on His marble pedestal,
> looks down upon his brown daughters,
> votive candles shining like lust in
> His all-seeing eyes,
> unmoved by their persistent prayers.
>
> Yet year after year before
> His image they kneel
> Margarita, Josefina, María and Isabel
> all fervently hoping
> that if not omnipotent,
> at least He be bilingual. (p. 89)

What the poet recognizes here with ironic tone is the submission and marginalization of women in a world that is culturally, socially, and racially differentiated, but also dominated by a male God.

The growing literature by women writers was limited, for a long time, to the recognized talents of Nicholas Mohr and Sandra María Esteves, but now includes other names such as Judith Ortiz Cofer, the mother–daughter duo of Rosario Morales and Aurora Levins Morales, and Carmen de Monteflores, among others. These writers are creating a new sphere of activity which requires the adoption of criteria which incorporate gender as an analytical category that is as valid as class, race, and ethnicity aimed at dismantling the patriarchal and pseudouniversal definitions of being a woman and substitutes them with a new epistemology conceived by women themselves. The African American sociologist Elizabeth Higginbotham[44] has emphasized the necessity of breaking out of those frameworks that limit our knowledge and understanding of the privileged position of being white in a racist society, being wealthy in a class society, being part of the dominant culture in an ethnocentric society, and being male in a sexist society. In a context which gives a multiplicity of meanings and shadings to identity and in which differences are reaffirmed, it is to be expected, then, that gender be a prominent factor. This does not mean that the question of nationality or ethnicity is necessarily subordinated to the problems or oppressive experiences endured by women. On the contrary, this remains a simultaneous component of the broader problematic of identity.

The valuable work of Sánchez Korrol[45] and of the research task forces at the Center for Puerto Rican Studies in New York City[46] have extensively documented the recent development of a Latino consciousness in the United States as an expression of a wider sense of identity and spirit of solidarity among the different Latino groups, and their presence in earlier periods of development of the Puerto Rican community in the United States. In recent times, the revitalization of a Latino consciousness often functions like a double-edged sword. Bypassing the conceptual imprecision of the term Latino we must be mindful of the ways in which the U.S. government has imbued the bureaucratic label "Hispanic" with a false sense of uniformity that hides the different socioeconomic and cultural experiences of each of these groups. On the other hand, at a political level, an increased Latino consciousness has facilitated collective struggles and the formation of coalitions on problems related to inequality and discrimination in areas such as employment, education, housing, and other social services. These alliances facilitate obtaining government resources and the acquisition of political power, but they can also increase competition and create strong rivalries among the various groups.

In his study of Puerto Ricans and Mexicans in Chicago, Padilla[47] argues that this broader category of Latino identity is oriented toward social action, political change, and cooperative mobilization resulting from specific needs and priorities of the different groups. It is on this level that ethnicity becomes a strategy or instrument that facilitates and enhances the possibilities of negotiation with the power structures.

There are other factors that demonstrate that this Latino consciousness in the United States goes beyond being a social or political strategy utilized by different groups only as the need arises. A Latino consciousness also serves to strengthen the individual struggles of each group. A patent example is found in the convergence of the forms of feminine/feminist consciousness with Latino consciousness. Horno-Delgado et al.[48] underscored the ways in which *latinismo* among women writers constitutes a unifying element that incorporates other elements of solidarity with other women's liberation movements in the United States and Latin America. This process is consolidated by adopting the term "women of color" which reflects a symbolic of identification with the working class and with other Third World women's struggles. The collections *This Bridge Called My Back*,[49] *Cuentos: Stories by Latinas*,[50] (1983), and *Compañeras: Latina Lesbians*,[51] and, more recently, the book of criticism, *Breaking Boundaries*,[52] attest to the emergence of a literary discourse based upon a cultural subjectivity of being a Latina, which recognizes the shared experiences both at an individual and interethnic levels, but also that transcends national origins in its spirit of solidarity and identification with the liberation movements of all women and other groups oppressed because of class position, race, ethnicity, or sexual preference.

To the old argument that the struggle against sexist oppression should be subordinated to the class struggle, women have responded with their own creative forms of resistance. The image of women as "the last colony," developed in the theoretical works of the German feminists Maria Mies, Veronika Bennholdt-Thomson, and Claudia von Werholf,[53] stresses the necessity to continue the dialogue over the *decolonization* of women and gender by formulating alternative theoretical frameworks based on a feminist epistemology and validates a consciousness that rejects the notion that women are passive victims or deliberate accomplices to their own subordination.[54]

Of course, I am not suggesting that these forms of consciousness discussed above exist in isolation from one another. On the contrary, as I have already argued, they constitute overlapping spheres which intersect and interact simultaneously in the configuration of identity.

In conclusion, we have been able to appreciate that U.S. Puerto Rican literature reveals multiple levels of consciousness molded by racial, class, and ethnic subordination and to which much be added, in the case of women writers, the dimension of gender. These artistic expressions recreate the encounter and conflictive struggle with the dominant society in which the mechanisms of oppression are generated: the imposition of Anglo-American culture and language and devaluation of the culture and language of the minority; segregation and institutionalized racism that have marginalized these groups within the school system and forced them to survive in urban decay; the exploitation shared in factories, migrant camps, and other servile occupations; and dependency on public assistance programs. The antagonistic encounter between these respective dominant and minority cultural worlds does not necessarily manifest itself in clear-cut oppositions, but, rather, as a mixture of life experiences and representations that recreate the ambiguities and dualities corresponding to the unresolved nature of the contradictions of two social groups in conflictive interaction. This encounter involves attitudes of contestation, rejection, and resistance, but also of integration, interpenetration, and mythification or lessening of these contradictions.[55]

For U.S. Puerto Rican writers the dialectic tension between two different cultural worlds is expressed through dichotomized interpretations of the surrounding reality. The most prevalent dualities in Puerto Rican literature include:

(1) The fragmentation of identity produced by marginalization and oscillation between the two cultural and linguistic contexts (boricua versus spic; Spanish versus English; white people versus people of color):

> *I am two parts/ a person boricua/spic*
> *past and present*
> *alive and oppressed*
> *given a cultural beauty*
> *. . . and robbed of a cultural identity.*
>
> *I speak the alien tongue*
> *in sweet boriqueño thoughts*
>
> (Sandra María Esteves,[56] p. 20)

Being Puertorriqueña
Americana
Born in the Bronx, not really jibara
Not really hablando bien
But yet, not Gringa either
Pero ni portorra, pero si portorra too
Pero ni qué what am I?

Y que soy, pero con what voices do my lips move?

(Sandra María Esteves,[57] "Not neither")

I think in spanish/i
write in english
abraham in español
abraham in english
tato in spanish
"taro" in english

(Tato Laviera,[58] "my graduation speech," p. 7)

(2)   The geographical "separation" between the island and the metropolis
where Puerto Rico provides the biological genesis and the mythical roots
of historical continuity with the present, in contrast with the crude reality
of the "mean streets" of New York City:

There are people dying in the streets
in houses suspended in cockraoch nightmares
waging chemical warfare with their own brains
in factories chained leg to leg
waiting for their lunch bell to existence
a key to unlock the castrated tension
of broken backs whipped in slavery

(Sandra María Esteves,[59] "Improvisando," p. 16)

(3)   The distance produced by social and cultural differences between the
contexts of island and metropolis, and the rejection and alienation perceived by the Nuyorican in both contexts:

the slave blessed land
where nuyoricans come in search of spiritual identity
and are greeted with profanity . . .

(Miguel Piñero,[60] "This is Not the Place Where I Was Born," p. 14)

(4)   The clash between the values of a materialistic society and the spiritual
values attributed to the oppressed class:

turn off the stereo
this country gave you
it is out of order
your breath
is your promised land
if you want
to feel very rich
look at your hands
that is where the definition of magic is located at

(Pedro Pietri,[61] "Love Poem for my People," p. 78)

These conflictive encounters, illustrated by the quoted texts, also generate conciliatory responses that capture the "tropicalization" of New York and the recreation of Puerto Rico in the enclaves of El Barrio (Spanish Harlem), Loisaida (New York's Lower East Side), Los sures (Williamsburg, Brooklyn) or the Bronx:

My Home/el barrio
where people rest their feet;
outside on the fire escapes, . . .
yes, this is home/our paradise
and you're always welcomed
as long as you're poor

(Jesús Papoleto Meléndez,[62] "of a butterfly in el barrio," p. 22)

Pienso en mi tierra
los barrios de Nueva York
mi madre calle
adonde se crió un tipo nuevo de este mundo
el Puertorriqueño que no habla el español.

(Sandra María Esteves,[63] "Esclavitud," p. 19)

This was the inheritance
of your son, born in New York:
that years before
I saw Puerto Rico,
I saw the mountains
looming above the projects,
overwhelming Brooklyn,
living by what I saw at night,
with my eyes closed

(Martín Espada,[64] "We Live By What We See At Night," p. 17).

Finally, the affirmation of differentiality is contained in a unique cultural synthesis which redefines identity and replaces Anglo-American ethnocentrism with a syncretic multiculturalism rooted in popular culture and the working-class experience that serves to reaffirm individual and collective liberation:

> *I am what I am and I am U.S. American I haven't wanted to say it because if I did you'd take away the Puerto Rican but now I say go to hell . . . I am what I am I am Puerto Rican I am U.S. American I am New York Manhattan and the Bronx . . . I am what I am I am Boricua as Boricua come from the isle of Manhattan . . .*

(Rosario Morales,[65] "I Am What I Am," p. 138)

> *assimilated? que assimilited,*
> *brother, yo soy asimilao,*
> *asi mi la o sí es verdad*
> *tengo un lado asimilao,*

(Tato Laviera,[66] p. 54).

> *we gave birth*
> *to a new generation,*
> *AmeRícan salutes all folklores,*
> *european, indian, black, spanish,*
> *and anything else compatible:*
> *. . . AmeRícan, defining myself my own way any way many*
> *ways Am e Rícan, with the big R and*
> *the accent on the í*

(Tato Laviera,[67] "AmeRícan," p. 94)

On a theoretical level, these diverse elements that characterize Nuyorican literature can be related to the general outline elaborated by García Canclini in his prominent essay *Las culturales populares en el capitalismo*,[68] in which the cultural production of the subordinate classes is viewed as playing three major functions: (1) an economic instrument which reproduces the social reality; (2) a weapon in the political struggle for hegemony; and, lastly, (3) the psychosocial role of building a consensus and identity and symbolically neutralizing or elaborating contradictions (p. 74).

In recent years, as the quincentennial commemoration of the encounter between the Old and New Worlds approaches, many scholars have explored and reflected on the reciprocal images that have emanated over the centuries from this contact among cultures. I would like to suggest that the application of the theoretical frameworks that have dominated the dialogue over culture contact and racial amalgamation in the Americas could be useful in the analysis of the phenomena of cultural convergence and syncretism which are being produced in the bosom of U.S. society and may lead to a better appreciation of the nuances and complexities of cultural pluralism, and of the diverse forms that emerge from cultural revindication struggles.

From a quick glance at the literature of Puerto Rico, it becomes immediately apparent that a great majority of island authors of different generations have played a fundamental role in the anticolonial struggle. One of the most notable characteristics of Puerto Rico's intellectual elite has been their position at the forefront of the resistance against U.S. colonialism and cultural aggression, and their support of the ideal of national independence and self-determination for the Puerto Rican people. Nonetheless, it has not been as easy to recognize that Puerto Rican writers and intellectuals in the United States are also contributing in their own ways to the process of affirming a distinct Puerto Rican national identity as part of their own struggles for equality and social justice.

Notes

1. Edna Acosta-Belén, "The Literature of the Puerto Rican Minority in the United States," *Bilingual Review* 5 (1–2) (1978): 107–116.

2. Miguel Algarín and Miguel Piñero, eds., *Nuyorican Poetry: An Anthology of Words and Feelings* (New York: Morrow, 1975).

3. Nathan Glazer and Daniel Patrick Moynihan, *Beyond the Melting Pot* (Cambridge, MA: Harvard University Press, 1974).

4. César Andreu Iglesias, ed., *Memorias de Bernardo Vega* (Río Piedras, P.R.: Ediciones Huracán, (1977). *Memoirs of Bernardo Vega* trans. by Juan Flores (New York: Monthly Review, 1984).

5. Jesús Colón, *A Puerto Rican in New York and Other Sketches*. 2nd ed. (New York: International Publishers, 1982).

6. Eduardo Seda Bonilla, "Who is a Puerto Rican?: Problems of Socio-Cultural Identity in Puerto Rico," *Caribbean Studies* 17 (1–2) (1977): 105–121.

7. Néstor García Canclini, *Las culturas populares en el capitalismo* (México: Editorial Nueva Imagen, 1982).

8. Margarita B. Melville, "Los hispanos: ¿clase, raza o etnicidad?" in *Hispanos en los Estados Unidos*, eds. Rodolfo Cortina and Alberto Moncada (Madrid: Ediciones de Cultura Hispánica, 1988), 131–145.

9. Eric J. Hobsbaum and Terence Ranger, eds., *The Invention of Tradition* (Cambridge: Cambridge University Press, 1983).

10. Werner Sollors, ed., *The Invention of Ethnicity* (New York: Oxford University Press, 1989).

11. María Jesús Buxó Rey, "A nuevos significados, nuevas realidades culturales." in *Hispanos en los Estados Unidos*, eds. Rodolfo Cortino and Alberto Moncada (Madrid: Ediciones de Cultura Hispánica, 1988).

12. Juan Flores, " 'Qué assimilated, brother, yo soy asimilao': La estructuración de la identidad puertorriqueña en los Estados Unidos," *Casa de las Américas 26* (1985):54–63.

13. Juan Flores, "Puerto Rican Literature in the United States: Stages and Perspectives," *ADE Bulletin* 91 (1988): 39–44.

14. Clara Rodríguez, *Puerto Ricans Born in the U.S.A.* (Boston: Unwyn Hyman, 1989).

15. Nicholosa Mohr, "The Journey Toward a Common Ground: Struggle and Identity of Hispanics in the U.S.A." *The Americas Review* 18 (1) (1990): 81–85.

16. Tato Laviera, *AmeRícan* (Houston: Arte Público Press, 1985).

17. Miguel Piñero, *La Bodega Sold Dreams* (Houston, TX: Arte Público Press, 1980).

18. Efraín Barradas and Rafael Rodríguez, eds., *Herejes y mitificadores: Muestra de poesía puertorriqueña en los Estados Unidos* (Río Piedras, P.R.: Ediciones Huracán, 1984).

19. Pedro Pietri, *Puerto Rican Obituary* (New York: Monthly Review Press, 1973), *Obituario Puertorriqueño* trans. Alfredo Matilla (San Juan, P.R.: Instituto de Cultura, 1981).

20. Robert Blauner, *Racial Oppression in America* (New York: Harper & Row, 1972); James M. Blaut, "Americanization versus Ghettoization," *Antipode* 15(1) (1983): 35–41.

21. Alberto Moncada, "Americanización frente a hispanización," in *Hispanos en los Estados Unidos*, eds. Rodolfo Cortina and Alberto Moncada (Madrid: Ediciones de Cultura Hispánica, 1988), 120–129.

22. Orlando Patterson, "Context and Choice in Ethnic Allegiance: A Theoretical Framework and Caribbean Case Study" in *Ethnicity: Theory and Experience*, eds. Nathan Glazer and Daniel Patrick Moynihan (Cambridge, MA: Harvard University Press, 1974), 305–349.

23. Seda Bonilla, op. cit. (Ref. 6).

24. Herbert J. Gans, "Symbolic Ethnicity: The Future of Ethnic Groups and Cultures in America," *Ethnic and Racial Studies* 2(1) (1979): 1–20.

25. Joshua Fishman, et al. *The Rise and Fall of the Ethnic Revival* (Berlin: Mouton, 1985).

26. Anthony Smith, *The Ethnic Revival* (Cambridge: Cambridge University Press, 1981).

27. Frank Bonilla and Ricardo Campos, "A Wealth of Poor: Puerto Ricans and the New Economic Order," *Daedalus* 110(2) (1981): 133–176.

28. William L. Yancey, Eugene P. Eriksen, and Richard N. Juliani, "Emergent Ethnicity: A Review and Reformulation," *American Sociological Review* 41(3) (1976): 391–402.

29. Hobsbaum and Ranger, op. cit. (Ref. 9).

30. Algarín and Piñero, op. cit. (Ref. 2).

31. Canclini, op. cit. (Ref. 7).

32. Efraín Barradas, "De lejos en sueños verla: Visión mítica de Puerto Rico en la poesía neoyorrican," *Revista Chicano-Riqueña* 7(3) (1979): 46–56; see also Ref. 18.

33. Frances Aparicio, "La música popular en la poesía neorriqueña," paper presented at the LASA International Congress, Miami, Florida, 1989.

34. Blaut, op. cit. (Ref. 20).

35. Edna Acosta-Belén, " 'Spanglish': A Case of Languages in Contact," in *New Directions in Language Learning, Teaching, and Bilingual Education*, eds. Heidi Dulay and Marina Burt (Washington, D.C.: TESOL, 1975), 151–158.

36. Carlos Varo, *Consideraciones antropólogicas en torno a la enseñanza del Spanglish* (Río Piedras, P.R.: Librería Internacional, 1971).

37. Juan Bruce-Novoa, "Introduction," *Chicano Authors: Inquiry by Interview* (Austin, TX: University of Texas Press, 1980); Guadalupe Valdés-Fallis, "Code-Switching in Bilingual Chicano Poetry," *Hispania* 59(4) (1976): 887–886.

38. Víctor Hernández Cruz, *By Lingual Wholes* (San Francisco: Momo's, 1982).

39. Frances Aparicio, "La vida es un Spanglish disparatero: Bilingualism in Nuyorican Poetry," in *European Perspectives on Hispanic Literature of the United States*, ed. Genvieve Fabré (Houston, TX: Arte Público Press, 1988), 147–160.

40. Leobardo Estrada, "Understanding Demographics: The Case of Hispanics in the United States," in *Sociocultural and Service Issues in Working with Hispanic American Clients*, eds.

Lester B. Brown, John Oliver, and J. Jorge Klor de Alva (Albany, NY: Rockefeller College Press, 1985), 1–15; see also Rodrígues, op. cit., Ref. 14.

41. Flores, op. cit. (Refs. 12 and 13).

42. Flores, op. cit. (Ref. 12).

43. Judith Ortiz Cofer, *Reaching for the Mainland,* in *Triple Crown: Poems by Roberto Durán, Judith Ortiz Cofer, and Gustavo Pérez Firmat* (Tempe, AZ: Bilingual Press, 1987), 63–120.

44. Elizabeth Higginbotham, "It's Time to Talk About Privilege: Developing an Inclusive Curriculum in Sociology," paper presented at the 84th Annual Meeting of the American Sociological Association, San Francisco, California, 1989.

45. Virginia Sánchez Korrol, *From Colonia to Community: The History of Puerto Ricans in New York City,* 1917–1948 (Westport, CT: Greenwood Press 1983).

46. Centro de Estudios Puertorriquénos. 1979. *Labor Migration Under Capitalism: The Puerto Rican Experience.* New York: Monthly Review Press; Felilx Cortés, Angel Falcón, and Juan Flores, "The Cultural Expression of Puerto Ricans in New York City," *Latin American Perspectives* 3(3) (1976) 117–150; Juan Flores, John Attinasi, and Pedro Pedraza, "La Carreta Made a U-Turn: Puerto Rican Language and Culture in the United States," *Daedalus* 110(2) (1982): 193–213.

47. Félix Padilla, *Latino Ethnic Consciousness: The Case of Mexican-Americans and Puerto Ricans in Chicago* (Notre Dame, IN: University of Notre Dame Press, 1985).

48. Asunción Horno-Delgado, Eliana Ortega, Nina M. Scott, and Nancy Saporta Sternback, eds., *Breaking Boundaries: Latina Writings and Critical Readings,* (Amherst, MA: University of Massachusetts Press, 1989).

49. Cherríe Moraga and Gloria Anzaldúa, eds., *This Bridge Called My Back,* (New York: Kitchen Table Press, 1981).

50. Alma Gómez, Cherríe Moraga, and Mariana Romo-Carmona, eds., *Cuentos: Stories by Latinas* (New York: Kitchen Table Press, 1983).

51. Juanita Ramos, ed., *Compañeras: Latina Lesbians* (New York: Latina Lesbian History Project, 1987).

52. Horno-Delgado et al., op. cit. (Ref. 48).

53. Maria Mies, Veronika Bennholdt-Thomsen, and Claudia von Werlhof, *Women: The Last Colony* (London: Zed Books, 1988).

54. Edna Acosta-Belén and Christine E. Bose, "From Structural Subordination to Empowerment: Women and Development in Third World Contexts," *Gender & Society* 4(3) (1990): 299–320.

55. Canclini, op. cit. (Ref. 7).

56. Sandra María Esteves, *Yerba Buena* (Greenfield: Greenfield Press, 1980).

57. Sandra María Esteves, *Tropical Rains,* 1984, African Caribbean Poetry Theater.

58. Tato Laviera, *La Carreta Made a U-Turn* (Houston, TX: Arte Público Press, 1981.

59. Esteves, op. cit. (Ref. 56).

60. Piñero, op. cit. (Ref. 17).

61. Pietri, op. cit. (Ref. 19).

62. Jesús Papoleto Meléndez, *Street Poetry and Other Poems* (New York: Barlenmir House, 1972).

63. Esteves, op. cit. (Ref. 56).

64. Martín Espada, *Trumpets for the Islands of Their Eviction* (Tempe, AZ: Bilingual Press, 1988).

65. Aurora Levins Morales, and Rosario Morales, *Getting Home Alive* (Ithaca, NY: Firebrand Books, 1986.).

66. Laviera, op. cit. (Ref. 16).

67. Ibid.

68. Canclini, op. cit. (Ref. 7).

In Search of Asia through Music
Guidelines and Ideas for Teaching Asian Music
Susan Asai

Introduction

Music-making is a wonderful way for people to express themselves. Do you play a musical instrument or sing in a community chorus, church choir, or informally in the shower? Do you think music is a unique way to communicate what is beautiful, sacred, sad, or wondrous? Music-making is a creative activity that can tell us a lot about people of other cultures. As a Japanese music specialist, I have always admired the reverence Japanese people have for nature. In the repertoire of the *koto* (13-string zither), musical pieces have titles like "Autumn in Saga," "Spring Music," and "Music of the Plovers" in referring to the cycle of seasons or natural settings.

The ever-increasing involvement of Asia in world politics and the global economy demands greater knowledge of this part of the world. The expanding Asian population in the United States, particularly with the recent influx of Southeast Asians, also prescribes being more informed about Asian cultures.

In some communities, especially urban ones, students are exposed to other cultures within the growing diversity of their classrooms. Such diversity can be positive if students are given opportunities (1) to explore the similarities and differences they share, (2) to analyze and question stereotypes, and (3) to learn to appreciate and respect different viewpoints and perspectives.

Historically, art has played an important role in human development as cultures evolved among people who shared the same language, worldview, and aesthetics. The study of the musical arts, thus, can serve as an important introduction to Asia. This chapter intends to provide a hands-on approach to teaching about Asian music. Some strategies and guidelines for organizing teaching materials will be discussed, including suggestions for integrating the study of Asian music into the general curriculum. A bibliography and discography at the end of the chapter will undoubtedly be of great value in becoming acquainted with this area of study.

Where Does One Begin?

What sources to use and how to structure the material is our first concern. The field of ethnomusicology provides both sources and a framework in which to organize information on Asian music. Ethnomusicology is an approach to the study of music, not only as an expressive art form, but in relation to human life. The value music has within a culture is revealed by its use—when, where, and by whom it is performed. The question of how music functions in a society is considered from a number of different angles, making this field of study an interdisciplinary one. As an interdisciplinary field, related studies in history, ethnography, folklore, literature, dance, religion, theater, archeology, etymology, iconography, and other fields concerned with cultural expressions can serve as a basis for investigating a particular music.[1] Such a broad approach to music offers an opportunity to learn much about a culture as a whole.[2]

Ideally, a collaboration between instructors of music and social studies would facilitate organizing this interdisciplinary subject. Collecting the necessary musical examples and possible songs for students to learn is a task in itself, especially since there is a scarcity of such materials on Asia. Music teachers would have more knowledge of and better access to music texts that have only recently begun to include a variety of music from Asian countries other than Japan. Working with a music teacher would also facilitate the search for sound recordings from which to make class listening tapes. A social studies teacher would be the most qualified for collecting the cultural information, such as geography, history, language, customs, and other areas which will frame the study of the music. Bibliographies and discographies for Asian countries accompanying this chapter will help to begin the search. Team teaching, in general, generates more innovative ways of presenting the information.

Students can also be responsible for collecting information. If teachers provide clues to various research headings, students will certainly lighten the load for teachers and improve their research techniques. Another suggestion is to have teachers provide sources for study units in the classroom and hold students accountable for finding the information needed.

The Road Map to Asia

Asian countries can be subdivided into three basic groups: (1) East and Far East Asia, (2) Southeast Asia, and (3) South Asia. East and Far East Asia includes the countries of Tibet, China, Korea, and Japan. Southeast Asia covers Thailand, Laos, Vietnam, Cambodia, Burma, Indonesia, Malaysia, and the Philippines, whereas the subcontinent of India is South Asia.

If the plan is to cover all Asian countries, lessons can be organized according to the three groups given above. Another plan is to form balanced groupings by choosing two or three countries from each of the above categories and rotate teaching each of these groupings. If there are any students in the class from an Asian country, it would be instructive to include it. Asian students could make the music and culture of their country come alive for the other students with personal accounts and information.

When it has been decided what countries to include, the next step is to make an outline for each. Initially, it is important to know the geographical location and brief history of a country in setting the context for studying its music. Often its geographical location places it within a larger cultural grouping, e.g., the gong and chime cultural sphere that covers most of the Southeast Asian countries.

Next, introduction of the general characteristics of a country, such as food, clothing, currency, customs, festivals, rituals, religion, social structure, and type of government, all provide clues to the subsequent study of its music. For countries consisting of many cultural subgroups, such as Laos where there are numerous peoples living in the mountains (Hmong, Kmhmu, Lue, etc.), it would be best not to gloss over these groups. If time is restricted, at least distinguish the minority groups while introducing the dominant culture.

When presenting the music and musical instruments, one way to organize the material is according to genre, i.e., classical music, folk music, theatre music, sacred music, secular music, instrumental music, vocal music, or popular music. Describe music as having structure; of being created from the interweaving of melody, rhythm, and dynamics into a specified form. Also include aspects of style, such as tempo, tone color of musical instruments, vocal quality, or the influence of the spoken language on singing. Talking about musical style involves a discussion of what a culture deems beautiful or pleasing since musical style is determined by a culture's aesthetic. Instrument-making traditions could be a source of interest as in Indonesia, where metaphysical and ritualistic meanings are associated with the manufacture of gongs. A brainstorming session with students about music they like and relating it to definitions of melody or rhythm may facilitate their understanding of these concepts.

The question of who plays music and the status afforded musicians ties into discussing the social fabric of a particular culture. It might be of interest to distinguish musical styles associated with women or men or those of a certain occupation. Again, brainstorming with students about music associated with certain occupations, age groups, ethnic backgrounds, or socioeconomic status here in the United States will provide some base of comparison for them.

Often dance is integral to the study of music. In Asia, much of the music cannot be studied without some reference to the accompanying dance. Discussion of the accompanying dance could include the types of movements featured or the rhythmic or melodic coordination between the music and dance. Other interrelated art forms worth exploring are theater, poetry reading, and storytelling.

Musical examples should accompany the discussion of the different genres or styles that are central to a culture. For each country or culture, one or two examples of at least two different genres or styles should be the minimum. Possible couplings of genres are (1) instrumental and vocal music, (2) classical and folk music, (3) traditional and contemporary music, or (4) sacred and secular music. Further additions could include music for theater, dance, and festivals. The available recordings for each country or culture may dictate the musical genres presented in class and the number of examples included on the listening tape. A discography is provided at the end of this chapter to assist in identifying sources for collecting music. Recordings of music may be available at a public library, a nearby university or college, or buying them at stores or through record houses or catalogs.

Music tapes created for the classroom are to be used as a tool for directed listening. Choose specific music styles or genres to study according to the musical examples available; then use musical examples to illustrate the music genre or style presented in class. Teachers and students should strive to develop their listening skills together by learning to distinguish different musical instruments, specifying sound qualities (nasal, shrill, bright, dark, etc.), determining volume levels (loudness or softness), and identifying the main melody or distinct rhythms. Teachers can create listening guide charts for students to use in the directed listening sessions and to fill in the appropriate information.

Live performances in the classroom, at a concert, or a festival is ideal for experiencing the process of music-making. Ways to find musicians to invite into the classroom are discussed under the upcoming section on community resources. Active participation on the part of the teacher in presenting the artist is imperative. A teacher's positive and enthusiastic response to the guest artist is important since students take cues from their teacher in such learning situations.

Historical, social, and cultural background material can be gleaned from a number of written sources. Besides encyclopedias, there is a series of books published by the Human Relations Area Files Press in New Haven, Connecticut. *Laos: Its People, its Society, its Culture* and *Cambodia: Its People, its Society, its Culture* are two books from this series that include similar volumes of other Asian countries. These books are outdated, but they provide some important in-depth information. Area handbooks originally written for military personnel and printed by the Superintendent of Documents, U.S. Government Printing Office are also invaluable, although outdated. This series includes: *Area Handbook for Vietnam, Area Handbook for the People's Republic of China, Area Handbook for the Republic of Korea, Area Handbook for South Korea,* and *Area Handbook for Laos,* and other countries.

For information about Asian music, *The New Grove's Dictionary of Music and Musicians* is the most authoritative encyclopedia. Material can be found under the name of a country, culture, genre, or musical instrument. One asset of using this source is the bibliographic listings given at the end of sections or the entire article. These listings can serve as a starting point in creating an Asian music bibliography. A second encyclopedic source is *The New Harvard Dictionary of Music.* Other written sources appear in the bibliography that accompanies this article. Other avenues that lead to sources include selective bibliographies and reviews from Asian studies and educational journals.

Possible Prototypes

There is a paucity of sources for teaching Asian music on the K–12 level. A recent publication, however, can serve as a simple model for organizing one's material. The book, *From Rice Paddies and Temple Yards: Traditional Music of Vietnam,* is a collaborative work by Phong Thuyet Nguyen and Patricia Shehan Campbell. Nguyen, an ethnomusicologist, educator, and performer specializing in his native Vietnamese music, works as a perfect complement to Shehan-Campbell, a music educator and consultant on music in early and middle childhood, multicultural music education, and the use of movement as a pedagogical tool. Together they have created a very workable format for the classroom.

A summary of the historical and cultural background of Vietnam opens the book. The first chapter includes information about climate, food, early history, French rule, U.S. involvement, customs and traditions, festivals, traditional clothing, and ethnic makeup. A map of Southeast Asia displays the geographical location of Vietnam and the countries with which it shares borders. Maps are instructive tools for students who are first learning about a country. It places the country in a tangible context and is also useful in tracking cultural influences of countries that are contiguous to it.

After setting the cultural and historical stage, Vietnamese musical forms and instruments are introduced. The authors point out the influence of the highly tonal spoken language in Vietnam on both vocal and instrumental music. General characteristics of traditional Vietnamese music—melody, dynamics, rhythm, and tonality—are all introduced before musical instruments are presented. This section ends with a brief summary of traditional musical forms performed in Vietnamese communities here in the United States.

Information about the retention of traditional music forms brought by different ethnic groups in the United States is available in *The New Grove Dictionary of American Music,* edited by H. Wiley Hitchcock and Stanley Sadie. Learning about native traditions that have been kept alive by immigrant populations in the United States would give students some idea of the cultural continuity that serve as a tie between two continents for certain groups.

The final section of *Rice Paddies and Temple Yards* is the interactive part of the text consisting of Vietnamese songs. Background information about each song is given along with a translation of the song text followed by a guide to the pronunciation of the Vietnamese words. The accompanying study guide gives step-by-step suggestions to how to teach the songs, including body movements for the rhythm. The methodology provided in this book is invaluable and is transferable to the teaching of songs and music from other Asian cultures.

A valuable asset to the book is the accompanying cassette tape that includes a performance of each of the songs presented in part 2.

For the high school level, a second model for organizing learning material is found in Chapter 1 in *Worlds of Music: An Introduction to the Music of the World's Peoples* by Jeff Todd Titon (general editor), James T. Koetting, David P. McAllester, David B. Reck, and Mark Slobin. This text is ordinarily used on a college level, but the framework of ideas can be modified to suit the level of your students. Four main components serve to explore a music-culture, a term that refers to "a group of people's total involvement with music."[3] This model is more music specific. The first component sets out to define the what and when of music in a particular culture by posing questions about its meaning, sense of aesthetics, and the occasions and frequency in which it is performed. Musical subcultures defined by region, ethnicity, religion, age, or socioeconomic status are also investigated.

The second component to this model addresses the question of who plays music. The study of a culture's social organization will provide clues to the musical roles of people according to age, gender, or occupation. The social status and prestige accorded music-makers in a culture is also examined. This area of inquiry might best be understood by students if they analyze the relationship between social structure and music-making in the United States first, before surveying such relationships in other cultures.

Studying details of the music itself forms the third component. Determining the structure of a particular music by examining its musical scales, tuning systems, rhythms, sound qualities, and dynamics informs students of how a music achieves a recognizable style. Surveying various musical genres, studying the relationship between language and music in song texts, the composing process, the passage of music from one generation to the next, and the accompanying dance or physical activity associated with a music are all areas of inquiry in this section.[4]

The final component of studying music-culture takes into account tangible objects associated with music-making, such as musical instruments, sheet music, and the impact of the electronic media—radio, stereo systems, tape recorders, television, and video recordings. The study of musical instruments includes a discussion of what types are used, who makes them, how they are distributed, and their transformation according to changes in musical taste and style.[5]

This second more advanced model also requires listening to musical examples that illustrate the various genres, structural elements, musical instruments, and sense of aesthetics. *Worlds of Music: An Introduction to the Music of the World's Peoples* is accompanied by two cassette tapes containing examples from music-cultures presented in the book—native American, South Indian, East European, and West African. It is possible to simplify this model for less technical coverage.

Both models are only guidelines for organizing lesson plans. Once the material becomes more familiar, formats should be designed according to the level of the students in a class, the amount of time there is to cover the material, whether the subject is taught by two teachers or one, or how much this study is integrated with other subjects in the curriculum.

For further strategies consult the book *Asia—Teaching About/Learning From* by Seymour Fersh. Fersh proposes differentiating approaches according to age. He outlines three levels and describes teaching concepts for each. For the elementary grades, he suggests organizing material around the student, i.e., "helping students develop skills, positive attitudes, understandings, appreciations, and actions concerning Asian peoples and cultures."[6] One study unit proposed for this level is to compare a holiday or celebration students are familiar with to an equivalent event in an Asian culture. Examples of such events include a marriage ceremony, a funeral, or a New Year's celebration.

The strategy for junior high level continuing to the tenth grade emphasizes process, i.e., to set up the study in a way that will help students to understand and appreciate the ways in which culture functions as a whole. This is similar to the ethnomusicological approach presented earlier in this chapter. Fersh mentions that the main goal is for students to realize the interrelationships between different components of a culture (social, historical, artistic, linguistic, etc.).

Next, for grades eleven and twelve and continuing on to post-secondary education, the strategy changes to an emphasis on the content of the study. The model outlined earlier from the text *Worlds of Music* best exemplifies this approach.

Begin with the Students

Students will be better prepared to learn about diverse cultures if they are first certain of their own identity. An important initial step is to help students identify and reinforce their own "personal culture" from which to build their self-esteem. Once this has been established, students are better equipped to extend their learning to include knowledge of diverse cultures.[7]

Pamela and Iris Tiedt and other educators suggest having students research and construct their family trees as one activity for affirming students' identities. The research process requires students to conduct interviews with older members of the family to piece together the family genealogy; find and study old photos of the family; and if information is incomplete, read records in courthouses or libraries. With this information, students would then draw their family tree. A starting point for students can be identifying the ethnic origin of their surname.[8]

Autobiographies of students is also one way to integrate family information into the classroom. Students would research their family history, as well as stories that have been passed down from one generation to the next. Customs and traditions of the family should be included, such as the food they eat, their religious or cultural observances or celebrations, or any keepsakes in the family. As part of their autobiography, students could bring in some artifact or object representative or symbolic of their cultural or family background and present it to the class. Autobiographies of any Asian students in the class can also serve as a starting point for lessons in Asian music.

It is important to have students share information about their family backgrounds, histories, and stories. Emphases should be placed on the fact that (1) people have feelings that are more alike than different, (2) different customs and attitudes can be an asset to society, (3) people of all groups have a contribution to make, (4) prejudice and stereotyping is usually based on lack of information, and (5) understanding others will enrich our own lives.[9] For further exploration of cultural tolerance, the following sources contain lessons and/or activities toward greater understanding and cooperation in the classroom: (1) *Elementary Perspectives 1: Teaching Concepts of Peace and Conflict* by William J. Kreidler, (2) *Open Minds to Equality: A Sourcebook of Learning Activities to Promote Race, Sex, Class, and Age Equity* by Nancy Schniedewind and Ellen Davidson, and (3) *The Cooperative Sports and Games Book: Challenge Without Competition* by Terry Orlick.

For greater diversity within the classroom community, have students do a survey of ethnic groups living in their town or neighborhood and choose one group to research by obtaining demographic information from town hall and interviewing, if possible, at least two people from that community. Interviews should function to find out why people moved or chose to live where they are, when they came, and if they maintain any cultural celebrations or activities. This information should be written into reports and also shared with the class.

The above activities will help students develop a sense of belonging. Developing a community within the classroom would be the next step in building on the students' heightened sense of who they are. Such a classroom community would allow every student to contribute in some way. Also, a communal setting provides security for students as they ready themselves to learn about other cultures.

Integrating Asian Music into the General Curriculum

Music as viewed within the field of ethnomusicology is not an isolated phenomenon. Music, particularly in non-Western cultures, functions more actively in people's everyday life. It is natural, therefore, to combine the study of Asian music with art, history, literature, and geography.

The study of an Asian country's geography and history is, as stated in the previous section, important in providing a framework for the study of its music. Art study units can feature the interrelationship of music to other art forms, such as wood carving, mask-making, or textile dyeing techniques in the making of masks, costumes, or ritual items used in relation to music-making. The literary arts offer a rich entry into a culture in terms of their language, philosophy, aesthetics, and worldview. The musical connection to the literary arts are very strong in Asian cultures since many of the songs are musical settings to poetry. Also, a look at the political conditions in a country can lead to an understanding of the state of its arts. Importantly, a well-integrated study program illustrates relationships between all elements of a culture and presents cultures as whole entities.

There are teachers now who specialize in multicultural education and create area studies programs for public schools. The following activities are suggestions of such a teacher who served as a consultant for this chapter, Berta Berriz, a specialist in Caribbean culture. Creative activities for Asian music can be learning a well-known song or dance of a country or culture. A more challenging activity could be the writing of song texts to a given melody that the students know well. Themes for song texts could be based on ideas, objects, or people characteristically found in a specific culture such as (1) food, (2) clothing, (3) musical instruments, (4) dances, (5) flora and fauna of that country, or (6) occupations, or (7) games.

Other ideas are to talk about music as a form of social expression and have students write about their favorite music and discuss the "message of the music" and the targeted audience for the message. Then, study could be directed toward how a certain music in Asia functions as an expression of a distinct social group.

Students can also be taught sensitivity to tone quality deemed aesthetically pleasing in a culture, such as raspy, clear, bright, dark, etc. A preferred tone quality relates to whether string, wind, or percussion instruments predominate in a culture's music. The study of tone quality can also serve as a lesson about the science of sound, an aspect of the physical sciences. Other musical connections to the physical sciences could include the study of whale songs as music, computer programs that are capable of printing out music represented in graphs or notation, and experiments with sound in liquid as opposed to air.

A goal might also be to have the students learn some musical skill, such as a popular rhythm that can be played on drums or other instruments or hand-clapped to accompany either singing or dancing in the classroom. In addition, rhythmic patterns found in music could serve as a basis for studying basic concept of patterns and predictability in math. Another possibility is to borrow musical instruments or cultural artifacts associated with music-making from a nearby museum or university and have the students create a play using these items.

Artists are vehicles of culture. Bringing in artists and performers into the classroom create a lasting impact on students. Experiencing music live, actually seeing and talking with performers, makes a culture come alive. I remember the tremendous impact that two older Hmong musicians had on students in one of my Music of Asia classes. The students were silently attentive when these musicians relayed stories of having to flee their country and expressed their lament over the loss of Hmong culture in the Americanization of their young people. Of great interest to students were stories of how music played a role in the courtship between young Hmong men and women.

Lecture demonstrations, particularly ones involving students, are also effective formats. Demonstrations by instrument-makers and dancers are valuable. Dance is especially suitable due its universal appeal and because body movement is an important activity for all ages. Workshops and artist-in-residence programs that are demanding in terms of process or involve learning to master a particular skill are ideal.

Field trips to museums, artists' studios, library programs, plays, and music and dance performances all contribute toward a diverse learning experience. A visit to a Japanese garden or a Cambodian Buddhist temple provides a setting that traditionally holds value for people of Japan or Cambodia.

Films, videotapes, and slides of the performing arts borrowed from libraries, music schools, or museums can supplement lessons. In Boston, the Museum of Fine Arts has a slide library that teachers can use free of charge. Videotapes are valuable for visually oriented dance and theater, as well as discovering the artistic interdependence of music and dance. *World Music and Dance* is an excellent videotape series by JVC, with accompanying materials providing informative background information and descriptions of the music and dance. Costumes, instrument-playing techniques, and contexts for music are all effectively conveyed in this video series.

Many schools, however, face budget cuts that drastically reduce their ability to bring in outside artists, purchase musical instruments or materials, or do any of the above activities. Teachers today are advised to collaborate with other local schools in organizing performances, artists-in-residence programs, and resources. School-based management in some schools are another opportunity for teachers to have some say in the spending of school budgets. Also, teachers are learning now to write grants to local funding agencies, collaborate with community centers, as well as research trust funds or any sources of funding in the community.

Any and all of the above activities and experiences can be valuable for language arts study if students are required to keep a journal for many of the activities and lessons.

The Community as a Resource

With dwindling resources in the schools, many teachers are turning to their communities. People, institutions, and organizations in the local community can prove to be a rich reservoir; initially, however, it requires a little digging.

State and local arts agencies are places to begin the search for performers, craftpeople, and guest speakers to bring into the class. If the agency has a resident folklorist, he or she would be the one to contact. Other sources for identifying artists might be the local public library, museums, or community art galleries and centers. Ethnic studies departments or programs, student organizations of different ethnic backgrounds, course catalogs, and professors are all resources that might exist in a local community college or university.

The city of Boston is well-endowed culturally, and a list of some of the cultural and educational organizations listed at the end of the chapter might spark an idea of what is available elsewhere. Multicultural festivals in the local area featuring performances could be a substitute for bringing in musicians and dancers into the classroom. Boston has a number of multicultural festivals annually, such as the Cambridge River Festival (sponsored by the Cambridge Arts Council); Lowell Folk Festival (sponsored by the Lowell National Historical Park); Bread and Roses Heritage Festival in Lawrence; Massachusetts Maritime Festival in Salem (sponsored by Folklorists in New England); and First Night, which takes place on New Year's eve. Festivals featuring specific communities include the Las Posadas Festival which presents bilingual (Spanish–English) children's theater and the Celtic Festival sponsored by the Boston Scottish Fiddle Club. All of the institutions and organizations mentioned in the list at the end of the chapter and in this paragraph were found in an incredible directory called the *Folk Directory,* published by the Folk Arts Network in Cambridge, Massachusetts. The *Folk Directory* contains sections on Festivals; Crafts and Art Making; Folk Arts in Education; Folklife and Ethnic Arts; Organizations and Resources; Events and Concerts; Performers; Poetry; Puppetry; Radio, TV, and Theatre; Storytelling; and Teaching Aids, which is only a partial list to illustrate the breadth of this publication. Similar organizations in local communities might also have directories they have compiled.

In large cities, consulates of different countries are also an important source for books, films, and videotapes containing general information. Some lend their materials if they have proof that it is being used for educational purposes. The Children's Museum in Boston not only has multicultural exhibits, events, performances, and workshops, but a Resource Center that has a rich variety of books and teaching materials on many countries and cultures. It would be worthwhile to locate museums, in the community or within driving distance, that have more international holdings in their collection or perhaps a specialist in a particular country or culture.

There are also multicultural programs offered to public schools by organizations like the New England Folklife Center of Lowell in Massachusetts. This organization is a resource for identifying and locating performers, as well as craftspeople. The New England Folklife Center's "Partners in Education" program trained eighth graders to act as folklorists and journalists in interviewing traditional craftspeople. The program had seventh graders collect folklore on their family's holiday traditions, keepsakes, naming traditions, and stories. There may be similar organizations in the community or state that offer such programs.

There are also a number of publication services that have sprung up in the wake of Asian studies curriculum development. The catalog of the Boston company, Cheng & Tsui Company [(617) 426-6074] is worth obtaining. This company distributes books on a wide range of topics on Chinese culture, including an affordable paperback series consisting of high-quality translations of Chinese literature, both classical and modern. Cheng & Tsui also advertise a Japan Film Collection, in addition to reference works and movies and TV programs from China. SSEC Publications in Boulder, Colorado [(303) 492-8143] has teaching materials for K–12 teachers that can be integrated into a range of social studies units. These teaching materials are entitled *Japan in the Classroom* and *Teaching about Korea*. Also, a set of slides on Oriental painting and sculpture from China, Japan, and India are available from Sandak, a division of G. K. Hall & Co. in Boston [1 (800) 343-2806].

Final Comments

Studying Asian music provides a palette of musical tastes, sounds, and contexts that contrast with that of the West. Subjects like this open doors in the minds of young people who are maturing in a world made smaller by the ever-growing technological strides in communication. The phenomenon of the global village demands an open-mindedness that can only be achieved with an education that is challenging, creative, and humanistic. Art is a powerful tool that traverses deeper meanings in life and expresses all that is human about us.

Hopefully, this chapter will assuage teacher's apprehensions of teaching about an area of the world that is perhaps less familiar. All that is needed is an eagerness to learn and a willingness to put aside biases and preconceived notions. Teaching about cultures other than one's own is a two-way street; one that presses for a creative dialogue with students as you set out on a musical journey of Asia together.

Notes

1. Mantle Hood, *The Ethnomusicologist* (Kent, OH: Kent State University Press, 1982), 3.

2. For a more detailed definition of ethnomusicology as a field of study, please read the entry in the *Harvard Dictionary of Music*, 2nd ed. Willi Ape.

3. Jeff Todd Titon, James T. Koetting, David P. McAllester, David B. Reck, and Mark Slobin, eds., *Worlds of Music: An Introduction to the Music of the World's Peoples* (New York: Schirmer Books, 1984), 1.

4. Titon et al., *Worlds of Music*, pp. 5–7.

5. Titon et al., *Worlds of Music*, pp. 7–8.

6. Seymour Fersh, *Asia—Teaching About/Learning From* (New York: Columbia University Press, 1978), 9.

7. Pamela Tiedt and Iris Tiedt, *Multicultural Teaching: A Handbook of Activities, Information and Resources*, 3rd ed. (Boston: Allyn and Bacon, 1990).

8. Tiedt and Tiedt, *Multicultural Teaching*, pp. 59–62.

9. Tiedt and Tiedt, *Multicultural Teaching*, p. 62.

Teaching Sources

Jo Ann Hymes, ed., *Asia Through Film* (An Annotated Guide to Films on Asia in the University of Michigan Audio-Visual Education Center) (Ann Arbor, MI: Center for Japanese Studies, University of Michigan).

Seymour Fersh, *Asia: Teaching About/Learning From* (New York: Teachers College Press, Columbia University, 1978).

Lynne Jessup, *World Music: A Source for Teaching* (Danbury, CT: World Music Press, 1988).

William Anderson and Patricia Shehan-Campbell, eds. *Multicultural Perspectives in Music Education* (Reston, VA: Music Educators National Conference, 1989).

The Diagram Group, *Musical Instruments of the World, An Illustrated Encyclopedia* (New York: Facts on File Publications, 1976).

Pamela L. Tiedt and Iris M. Tiedt, *Multicultural Teaching. A Handbook of Activities, Information, and Resources* (Boston: Allyn and Bacon, 1990).

East and Far East Asia

Bibliography

Far East Asia

Essays on Asian Music and Theater (New York: Performing Arts Program of the Asia Society, 1971).

Malm, William P., *Music Cultures of the Pacific, the Near East, and Asia*, 2nd ed. (Englewood Cliffs, NJ: Prentice-Hall, Inc., 1977).

Malm, William P., "Music, East Asian," in *Encyclopedia Britannica*, 15th ed. Vol., XII (1974), 669–691.

Picken, Laurence, *The New Oxford History of Music: The Music of Far Eastern Asia 1*. (London: Oxford University Press, 1957).

Tibet

Crossley-Holland, Peter, "Annotated Bibliography of Western Studies of Tibetan Music," *Ethnomusicology* XI/2 (1967).

Lhalungpa, Lobsang P., "Tibetan music: Secular and Sacred," *Asian Music*, 1/2 (1969).

Kaufmann, Walter, *Tibetan Buddhist Chant*. (Bloomington, IN: Indiana University Press, 1975).

China

"China," *New Oxford History of Music*, Vol. I (1957).

Crump, James and William Malm, eds., *Chinese and Japanese Music-Dramas*. Michigan Papers in Chinese Studies, No. 19 (1975).

Galk See Chew, *Dragon Boat—20 Chinese Folk Songs for Voices and Instruments* (London: Chester Music, 1986).

Kishibe, Shigeo, "On the Origin of the P'ip'a" *The Transactions of the Asiatic Society of Japan,* Second Series, XIX (1940).

Kuttner, Fritz, "The Music of China," *Ethnomusicology,* VIII/2 (1964).

Lai, T. C. and Robert Mok, *The Jade Flute* (New York: Schocken Books, 1985).

Liang, David, *Music of the Chinese Ch'in* (Taiwan: Chinese National Music Association, 1972).

Liang Mingyue, *Music of the Billion. An Introduction to Chinese Musical Culture* (New York: Heinrichshofen Edition, 1985).

Liu, Tsun-yuen (Article on practical details of ch'in performance). *Selected Reports* I/1,2 (Los Angeles: UCLA Institute of Ethnomusicology, 1968).

Lieberman, Frederic, *Chinese Music* (Annotated Bibliography) (New York: Society for Asian Music, 1970).

Moser, Leo J., *The Chinese Mosaic: The Peoples and Provinces of China* (Boulder, CO: Westview Press, 1985).

Picken, L. and Peter Crossley-Holland, "China," *Grove's Dictionary of Music,* 5th ed. (1954).

Schafer, Edward, *The Golden Peaches of Samarkand* (Berkeley: University of California Press, 1963).

Schafer, Edward, *The Vermillion Bird* (Berkeley: University of California Press, 1971).

Van Gulik, R. H., *The Lore of the Chinese Lute* (Tokyo: Sophia University, 1940).

Yeh Yung-Ching, ed., *Chinese Folk Songs* (New York: ARTS, Inc., 1972).

Korea

Bang-Song Song, *Korean Music* (Providence, RI: Asian Music Publications, 1971).

Heyman, Alan, "Pansori," *Essays on Asian Music and Theater* (New York: Asia Society, 1971).

Heyman, Alan, "Comparative Critical Study of Korean Traditional Music Today," *Korea Journal,* II/9 (1962).

Pratt, Keith, *Korean Music: Its History and Its Performance* (Seoul, Republic of Korea: Jung Eum Sa Publishing Corp. and London: Faber Music Ltd., 1987).

Provine, Robert C. "The Treatise on Ceremonial Music (1430) in the Annals of the Korean King Sejong," *Ethnomusicology,* XVIII/1 (1974).

Rockwell, Coralie, *Kagok* (Providence, RI: Asian Music Publications, 1972).

Korean National Commission for UNESCO, ed. *Traditional Korean Music* (Korea: Si-sa-yong-o-sa Publishers, Inc. and U.S.A.: Pace International Research, Inc., 1983).

Japan

Adriaansz, Willem, *The Danmono of Japanese Koto Music* (Berkeley: University of California Press, 1973).

Bauer, Helen, and Sherwin Carlquist, *Japanese Festivals* (Rutland, VT/Tokyo: Charles E. Tuttle Co., 1965).

Befu, Harumi, *Japan: An Anthropological Introduction* (New York: Harper & Row Publishers, 1971).

Berger, Donald Paul, *Folk Songs of Japan* (New York: Oak Publications, 1972).

Bock, Felicia C., "Elements in the Development of Japanese Folk Song," *Western Folklore* 7 (1948): 356–369.

Brandon, James, et al., *Studies in Kabuki. Its Acting, Music, and Historical Context*. A Culture Learning Institute Monograph, East-West Center (Honolulu: University of Hawaii Press, 1978).

Crump, James, and William Malm, eds., *Chinese and Japanese Music-Dramas*. Michigan Papers in Chinese Studies, No. 19 (1975) (University of Michigan Press).

Yuki, Minegishi, comp., *Discography of Japanese Traditional Music* (Tokyo: Japan Foundation, 1980).

Fukuda, Hanako, *Favorite Songs of Japanese Children* (Hollywood, CA: Highland Music Co. (avail. World Music Press), 1965).

Garfias, Robert, *The Music of a Thousand Autumns, The Togaku Style of Japanese Court Music* (Berkeley: University of California Press, 1975).

Hall, John Whitney, *Japan: From Prehistory to Modern Times* (Rutland, VT/Tokyo: Charles E. Tuttle Co. 1974).

Harich-Schneider, Eta, *A History of Japanese Music* (London: Oxford University Press, 1973).

Harich-Schneider, Eta., *Roei: The Medieval Court Songs of Japan* (Tokyo: Sophia University, 1965).

Hattori, Ryutaro, *Japanese Folk Songs* (Tokyo: The Japan Times, 1974).

Inoura, Yoshinobu, and Toshio Kawatake. *The Traditional Theater of Japan* (New York/Tokyo: John Weatherhill, Inc., 1981).

Komiya, Toyotaka, ed., *Japanese Music and Drama in the Meiji Era, transl. and adapted by Donald Keene (Tokyo: Toyo Bunko, 1969).*

Kato, Shuichi, A History of Japanese Literature—The First Thousand Years (Tokyo/New York/ San Francisco: Kodansha International Ltd., 1979).

Keene, Donald, *Bunraku. The Art of the Japanese Puppet Theatre* (Tokyo: Kodansha International Ltd., 1973).

Kishibe, Shigeo, *The Traditional Music of Japan* (Tokyo: Kokusai Bunka Shinkokai, 1969).

Komparu, Kunio, *The Noh Theater: Principles and Perspectives* (New York/Tokyo/Kyoto: Weatherhill/Tankosha, 1983).

Lieberman, F., "Music in *Tale of Genji*," *Asian Music* 2, No. 1 (1971), 39–42.

Malm, William P., *Japanese Music and Musical Instruments* (Rutland, VT: Charles E. Tuttle, 1959).

Malm, William P., "Practical Approaches to Japanese Music," *Readings in Ethnomusicology* (New York: Johnson Reprint, 1971).

Matsumiya, S., "Traditional Music and Dance in Japan Today: its Stability and Evolution," *International Folk Music Council Journal* 11 (1959): 65–66.

Nakamura, Yasuo, *Noh: The Classical Theater* (New York: Weatherhill, 1971).

Tsunoda, Ryusaku, et al.; comp., *Sources of Japanese Tradition, Vol. 1 & 2* (New York/London: Columbia University Press, 1969).

Tamba, Akira, "Aesthetics in the Traditional Music of Japan," *World Music* 18, No. 2 (1976): pp. 3–10.

Togi, Masataro, *Gagaku. Court Music and Dance,* trans. Don Kenny (New York/Tokyo/Kyoto: Weatherhill/Tankosha, 1971).

Tsuge, Gen'ichi, *Japanese Music: An Annotated Bibliography* (New York: Garland Publishers, 1986).

157

Wade, Bonnie, C., *Tegotomono: Music for the Japanese Koto*. Contributions in Interculture and Comparative Studies, No. 2 (Westport, CT: Greenwood Press).

White, F. and K. Akiyama, *Children's Songs from Japan* (New York: Marks Music Corp., 1960).

Yokomichi, Mario, *The Life Structure of Noh* transl. Frank Hoff and Willi Flindt (Tokyo: Nogaku shorin, n.d.).

Discography

Tibet

Le Chant du Monde, *Mongolie Sin-Kiang*, LDY 4039.

Songs and Music of Tibet, Folkways FE 4486.

Musique tibetaine du Sikkim, Contrepoint MC 20.119.

The Music of Tibet: The Tantric Rituals, Anthology AST 4005.

Tibet, UNESCO Musicaphon series. Musicaphon BM 30 L 2009-2011.

China

Beating the Dragon Robe—A Traditional Peking Opera, Folkways FW 8883.

China, Capitol T 10087 (Popular music).

China's Instrumental Heritage, Lyrichord LL 92.

Chinese Classical Masterpieces for the P'ip'a and Ch'in, Lyrichord LL 82.

Chinese Classical Music, Lyrichord LL 72.

Chinese Drums and Gongs, Lyrichord LL 102.

China Today, Bruno 50115.

The Music of China, ed. Frederic Lieberman, Anthology AST 4000 and 4002.

Music of Confucius' Homeland. Lyrichord LL 112.

The Ruse of the Empty City, Folkways FW 882.

Korea

Korean Court Music, LLST 7206.

Music from Korea. Volume 1: The Kayakeum, East-West Center Press EWS-1001 (1965).

Musique bouddhique de coree. (Musee de l'Homme), Vogue LVLX 253.

Pansori, Nonesuch H 72049.

Japan

Eighteenth Century Traditional Music of Japan (Keiko Matsuo and Her Ensemble), Los Angeles, CA: Everest 3306.

Japan. The Ryukyus, Formosa, and Korea, The Columbia World Library of Folk and Primitive Music, Volume 11, collected and edited by Alan Lomax, Columbia Masterworks, 91A 02019.

Japanese Koto Music with Shamisen & Shakuhachi, New York: Lyrichord Discs Inc. LLST 7131.

Japanese Koto Classics (Shinichi Yuize, *Koto*Master), New York: Nonesuch Records. H-72008.

Shakuhachi: The Japanese Flute (Kohachiro Miyata, *Shakuhachi*), New York: Nonesuch Records (Explorer Series). H-72076.

Music From the Kabuki—Leading Soloists of Japan, New York: Nonesuch Records (International Series). H-72012.

Joruri: Music of the Great Japanese Bunraku Puppet Theater, New York: Lyrichord Discs Inc. LLST 7197.

Ningyo Fudoki [Doll Topography Suite], RCA. CR-10039.

Suwa Daiko, Japan: King Record Co., Ltd. KR(H) 5053(s), 1968.

O-Suwa-Daiko: Japanese Drums, GREM G 1029.

Kodo—Heartbeat Drummers of Japan, Sheffield Lab. CD-KODO (CD only).

Tsugaru Jamisen: Takahashi Takeyama, Japan: Crown Record Co. SW-5037.

So Meikyoku Shirabe [Koto. Survey of Famous Pieces]. Tokyo: Victor Musical Industries, Inc. SJL-2055.

Koto and Flute: The Music of Kinichi Nakanoshima, Los Angeles, CA: Liberty Records, Inc. (World Pacific Records). WPS-21443 or WP-1443.

The Azuma Kabuki Musicians Columbia Masterworks. Columbia Records, Inc. ML 4925 (1954).

The Koto Music of Japan, New York: Elektra Records (Explorer Series). HS-72005.

A Bell Ringing in the Empty Sky (Goro Yamaguchi, *Shakuhachi,* New York: Nonesuch Records (Explorer Series). H-72025.

The Traditional Music of Japan, Tokyo: Japanese Victor JL 32-4.

Classical Music of Japan, Elektra EKL 268.

Zen, Goeika et Shomyo Chants, Lyrichord LL 116.

Japanese Temple Music, Lyrichord LL 117.

Gagaku. The Imperial Court Music of Japan, Lyrichord LLST 7126.

Japanese Noh Music, Lyrichord LLST 7137.

Japanese Kabuki Nagauta Music, Lyrichord LLST 7134.

Japon 3—Gagaku, Ocora 558 551 (1980).

The Music of Japan II: Gagaku. A Musical Anthology of the Orient. UNESCO Collection. Edited for the International Music Council by the International Institute for Comparative Commentary in English, French, German. Notes by Hans Eckardt. Kassel, Basel, Paris, New York: Barenreiter Musicaphon, BM 30 L 2013.

The Music of Japan V: Shinto Music [A Musical Anthology of the Orient. UNESCO Collection]. Edited for the International Music Council by the International Institute for Comparative Commentary in English, French, German. Recordings and notes by Eta Harich-Schneider. Kassel, Basel, Paris, New York: Barenreiter Musicaphon.

Films and Videos

China

A Night at the Peking Opera. Radim Films. Format: 16 mm color (20 min.).

Korea:

Korean Folk Dances. University of Washington Press. Format: 16 mm (25 min.).

Japan

Discovering the Music of Japan. Arthur Barr Productions. Format: 16 mm. Video (21 min.).

Kodo: Heartbeat Drummers of Japan. Kinetic Film and Video. Format: 16 mm. VHS, Beta (28 min.).

Films or videos available through Japanese Consulates in the United States:

1. *An Invitation to Traditional Music*

2. *Bunraku: Puppet Theater of Japan*

3. *Kabuki: The Classic Theater of Japan*

Southeast Asia

Bibliography

Southeast Asia—General

Asian Music, vii/1 (1975) (Southeast Asia issue).

Becker, Judith, "Percussion Patterns in the Music of Mainland Southeast Asia," *Ethnomusicology* XII/2 (1968).

Brandon, J., *Theatre in Southeast Asia* (Cambridge, MA: Harvard University Press, 1967).

Embree, J. F., and L. O. Dotson, *Bibliography of the Peoples and Cultures of Mainland Southeast Asia* (New Haven, 1950).

Groslier, Bernard, *The Art of Indochina*, transl. George Lawrence (New York: Crown Press, 1962).

Keyes, Charles, *The Golden Peninsula* (New York: Macmillan Press, 1977).

LeBar, Frank, *Ethnic Groups of Insular Southeast Asia* (New Haven, CT: Human Relations Area Files, 1972–75).

LeBar, Frank, Gerald Hickey, and John Musgrave, *Ethnic Groups of Mainland Southeast Asia* (New Haven, CT: Human Relations Area Files, 1964).

Maceda, Jose, "A Search for an Old and a New Music in Southeast Asia," *Asian Music* 51 (1979): 160–168.

Maceda, Jose, "III: Arts of Southeast Asian Peoples," *Encyclopedia Britannica*, 15/1974.

Selected Reports, 2/2 (Southeast Asia issue), ed. David Morton (Los Angeles: Institute of Ethnomusicology, 1975).

Traditional Drama and Music of Southeast Asia, ed. Mohd, Taib, and Osman ((Kuala Lumpur, Malaysia: Dewan Bahasa dan Pustaka, 1974).

Wolters, Oliver W., *History, Culture, and Region in Southeast Asian Perspectives* (Singapore: Institute of Southeast Asian Studies, 1982).

Vietnam

Tran Van Khe, *La Musique Vietnamienne Traditionelle* (Paris: Presses Universitaires de France, 1962).

Tran Van Khe, "Musicians in North and South Vietnam," *World of Music,* xi/2 (1969): 42ff.

Pham Duy, *Musics of Vietnam* (Carbondale, IL: Southern Illinois University Press, 1975).

Phong Thuyet Nguyen and Patricia Shehan-Campbell, *From Rice Paddies and Temple Yards: Traditional Music of Vietnam* (Danbury, CT: World Music Press, 1989).

Thailand

Becker, Judith, "Music of the Pwo Karen of Northern Thailand," *Ethnomusicology* VIII/2 (1964).

Morton, David, "The Music of Thailand," in *Music of Many Cultures: An Introduction,* ed. by Elizabeth May (Berkeley/Los Angeles, University of California Press, 1980).

Morton, David, *The Traditional Music of Thailand* (Los Angeles: University of California Press, 1968).

Malaysia

Malm, William P., "Music in Kelantan, Malaysia, and Some of its Cultural Implications," *Studies in Malaysian Oral and Musical Traditions* Michigan Papers on South and Southeast Asia No. 8 (Ann Arbor, MI: Center for South and Southeast Asian Studies, University of Michigan, 1974).

Burma

Williamson, R. C., "The Construction and Decoration of the Burmese Harp," *Selected Reports* I/2 (1968): 45–77.

Laos

Miller, Terry, *Traditional Music of the Lao. Kaen Playing and Mawlum Singing in Northeastern Thailand,* Contributions in Intercultural and Comparative Studies No. 13 (Westport, CT: Greenwood Press, 1985).

Indonesia

Anderson, William M., *Teaching Asian Musics in Elementary and Secondary Schools: An Introduction to the Musics of India and Indonesia* (Adrian, MI: Leland Press, 1975).

Brandon, James, *On Thrones of Gold: Three Javanese Shadow Puppet Plays* (Cambridge, MA: Harvard University Press, 1970).

Hood, Mantle, and Hardja Susilo, *Music of the Venerable Dark Cloud: The Javanese Gamelan Khjai Mendung* (Los Angeles: Institute of Ethnomusicology, UCLA, 1967).

Kunst, Jaap, *Music in Java* (The Hague: Martinus Nijhoff, 1949).

Lindsay, Jennifer, *Javanese Gamelan* (New York: Oxford University Press, 1979).

McPhee, Colin, *The Balinese Wajang Koelit and Its Music* (New York: AMS Press, 1981).

McPhee, Colin, *Music in Bali; A Study in Form and Instrumental Organization in Balinese Orchestral Music* (New Haven, CT: Yale University Press, 1966).

Kartoumi, Margaret J., ed., *Studies in Indonesian Music* (Clayton, Victoria: Centre of Southeast Asian Studies, Monash University, 1978).

Discography

Southeast Asia

Music of Southeast Asia, comp. Harold Courlander/Notes by Henry Cowell, Folkways Records RE 4423.

Sounds of the World: Music of Southeast Asia, Music Educators National Conference (1982).

Laos

Laos, UNESCO Musicaphon series, ed. by Alain Danielou. BM 30 L 2001.

Laos—Musique pour le khene, Lam Saravane, Ocora 558.537.8 (1982).

Thailand—Lao Music of the Northeast, Lyrichord LLST 7357 (1973).

Cambodia

Anthologie de la musique du Cambodge, ed. Jacques Brunet, Ducrete-Thomson DUC 20-22.

Cambodge, ed. J. Brunet, Galloway GB 600520 (1974).

Cambodge: musique instrumentale, ed. J. Brunet, CBS 65522 (1973) [disc notes].

Cambodia: Folk and Ceremonial Music, ed. J. Brunet, EMI-Odeon CO64-17841, 1973 [disc notes].

Cambodia, UNESCO Musicaphon series, ed. Alain Danielou. BM 30 L 2002.

Music of Cambodia—Musical Anthology of the Orient, Barenreiter BM 30 L 2002.

Royal Music of Cambodia, ed. J. Brunet, Phillips 2, 1971 [disc notes].

Traditional Music of Cambodia, compiled, performed, and edited by Sam-Ang Sam, Center for the Study of Khmer Culture, 1987. TMC-SS-NR001.

Vietnam

From Rice Paddies and Temple Yards: Traditional Music of Vietnam. (Accomp. tape to textbook of same name), ed. by Phong Thuyet Nguyen and Patricia Shehan-Campbell, World Music Press, 1990.

Folk Songs of Viet Nam, ed. Stephen Addiss, Folkways FTS 31303 (1968).

Music from North and South Vietnam, ed. Stephen Addiss, Folkways AHM 4219.

Music of Viet Nam (Tribal music of the Highland People, Traditional Music, Folksongs), ed. Pham Duy, Stephen Addiss, and Bill Crofut, Ethnic Folkways Library FE 4352 (1965).

Musique Du Viet-nam, Tradition Du Sud, Ocora OCR 68.

Vietnam, UNESCO Musicaphon series, ed. Alain Danielou. BM 30 L 2022.

Malaysia

Malaysia, UNESCO Musicaphon series, ed. Alain Danielou. BM 30 L 2026.

The Music of Malaysia, ed. William P. Malm, Anthology AST 4006.

Temiar Dream Music, Folkways FE 4460.

Burma

Folk and Traditional Music of Burma, Folkways FE 4436.

Thailand

Les Mons De Thailande (Music of Hmong people), CBS (France) 81389 (1976).

Music of Thailand, ed. Harold Courlander, Folkways FE 4463.

The Traditional Music of Thailand (2 vols.), IER 7502 (1968).

Indonesia

Bali [folk music], EMI Odeon 3C 064 17858.

Bali. Les Celebres Gamelans, Arion 3OU 130.

Bali South [Compositions of Wajan Gandera, Gamelan Master, Peliatan, Bali], IE Records, IER-7503.

Dancers of Bali, Columbia ML 4618.

Gamelans de Bali, Disques BAM 5.096 (1963).

Golden Rain, Nonesuch H-72028.

The Jasmine Isle (Central Java and Sunda music), Nonesuch H-72031.

Javanese Court Gamelan Nonesuch H-72044 (1971).

Music from the Morning of the World, Nonesuch H-72015.

Music of Indonesia 2. Indonesian Popular Music, Smithsonian/Folkways SF 40056.

The Polyphony of South-East Asia; Bali: Court Music and Banjar Music, Philips 6586 008.

Street Music of Java [Popular music idioms], Original Music, OMO 701.

The Sultan's Pleasure. Javanese Gamelan & Vocal Music, Music of the World, T-116.

163

Videos and Films

Indonesia

Indonesian Dance Drama, University of California, Los Angeles. Available from UCLA or Original Music.

Serama's Mask, Coronet Films and Video (1979).

Shadowmaster, C. L. Reed and John Knoop, producers (San Francisco: Highland Laboratories Foundry Films, 1981).

Topeng: The Masked Dance Theater of Bali (New York: Asia Society, 198-.

South Asia (India)

Bibliography

India—General

Basham, A. L., *The Wonder That Was India* (New York: Grove Press, 1959).

Dowson, John, *A Classical Dictionary of Hindu Mythology* (London: Routledge & Kegan Paul, 1961).

Edwardes, Michael, *A History of India* (New York: Universal Library, 1970).

Lanmoy, Richard, *The Speaking Tree: A Study of Indian Culture and Society.* (New York: Oxford University Press, 1971).

Zimmer, Heinrich, *Philosophies of India* (New York: Meridian Press, 1961).

Indian Music

Anderson, William M., *Teaching Asian Musics in Elementary and Secondary Schools: An Introduction to the Musics of India and Indonesia* (Adrian, MI: Leland Press, 1975).

Brown, Robert E., "India's Music," *Readings in Ethnomusicology,* ed. David P. McAllester (New York: Johnson Reprint, 1971), 293–329.

Deva, B. Chaitanya, *An Introduction to Indian Music* (New Delhi: Publications Division, Ministry of Information and Broadcasting, Government of India, 1973).

Kinnear, Michael S., comp., *A Discography of Hindustani and Karnatic Music* (Westport, CT: Greenwood Press, 1985).

Gosvami, O., *The Story of Indian Music: Its Growth and Synthesis* (Bombay/New York: Asia Publishing House, 1961).

Holroyde, Peggy, *The Music of India* (New York: Praeger, 1972).

Krishnaswamy, S., *Musical Instruments of India* (Boston: Crescendo Publishing Co., 1971).

Massey, Reginald, and Jamila Massey, *The Music of India* (New York: Crescendo-Taplinger, 1976).

Nijenhuis, Emmie te, *Indian Music: History and Structure* (Leiden: Brill, 1974).

Popley, Herbert A., *The Music of India* (Boston: Crescendo Publishing Co., 1971). (Originally published in New Delhi, 1966).

Shankar, Ravi, *My Music, My Life* (New York: Simon and Schuster, 1968).

Wade, Bonnie C., *Music in India: The Classical Traditions* (Englewood Cliffs, N.J.: Prentice-Hall, 1979).

White, Emmons E., *Appreciating India's Music: An Introduction, with an Emphasis on the Music of South India* (Boston: Crescendo Publishing Co., 1971).

Indian Dance

Devi, Ragini, *Dances of India* (New York: Books for Libraries, 1980).

Discography

Bhavalu—Impressions (South Indian music), Nonesuch H-72019.

Carnatic Music—The Music of South India, World Pacific WPS 21450.

Classical Indian Music, Odeon (India) MOAE 147.

Classical Music of India, Nonesuch [Explorer Series] H-72014.

Concerto for Sitar and Orchestra [Ravi Shankar], Angel S-36806.

Devotional Songs. EMI (India).

Dhyanam (Meditation): South Indian Vocal Music, Nonesuch H 72018.

Drums of North and South India, World Pacific WPS-21437.

Evening Ragas from Benares, MHS Stereo 737BL.

Folk Music of India (Orissa), Lyrichord LLST 7183.

Folk Music of India (Uttar Pradesh), Lyrichord LLST 7271.

Folk Songs and Dances of Northern India, Olympic 6108.

Hariprasad Chaurasia Flute Sound Recording, Nimbus Records p 1987.

Master of the Sarangi, Nonesuch 72062.

Music of India, Keyboard Jr. Recordings KPL-32.

Music of India—Sharan Rani, World Pacific WP 1418 (1962).

Music of India: Three Classical Ragas, Angel 35468.

Music of Southern India, Nonesuch H-72003.

A Musical Journey Through India (Los Angeles: Department of Ethnomusicology, UCLA, 1988).

Pallavi—South Indian Flute Music, Nonesuch 72052 (1973).

Predawn to Sunrise Ragas, Connoisseur 1967.

Ragas, Songs of India, Folkways FG 3530.

Ramnad Krishnan: Kaocheri: A Concert of South India Classical Music, Nonesuch H 72040.

Sarangi, The Voice of a Hundred Colors, Nonesuch 72030.

Shehnai Recital by Bismillah Khan, Odeon (India) MOAE 113.

The Sounds of India: Ravi Shankar, Sitar, Columbia CL 2496.

Suryanarayana Playing the South Indian Vina, Philips 6586 023.

165

Tamil Devotional Hymns, EMI (India) ECLP 2445.

Ten Graces Played on the Vina, Nonesuch H-72027 (1968).

Vidwan: Carnatic Tradition, Nonesuch 72023.

Violin Solos of Carnatic Music, Odeon (India) ECSD 2435.

Films and Videos

Discovering the Music of India, Arthur Barr Productions. Format: 16 mm. Video (21 min.).

Famous Musicians: Ravi Shankar, Warren Scholat Productions. Format: Film strip.

Folk Musicians of Rajasthan, UCLA. Format: VHS, Beta (45 min.).

Folk Performers of India, UCLA. Format: VHS, Beta (45 min.).

God with a Green Face, American Society for Eastern Arts. Format: 16 mm. (*Kathakali* dance drama).

10

African American Children's Literature
The First One Hundred Years
*Violet J. Harris**

Introduction

African Americans have been depicted in general literature since the seventeenth century. Essentially, the depictions are stereotyped, pejorative, and unauthentic.[1] Literature created by African Americans for children first appeared in the late nineteenth century. This literature has never been a central component of schooling. Not unlike that of African American literature written for adults, African American children's literature has had a tumultuous past. That past included limited awareness among readers; circumscribed publication and distribution; omission from libraries, school, and bookstores; and uninformed criticism. Several factors contribute to this state of affairs but one important factor is the existence of literary canons.

Canons, or sanctioned lists of works perpetuated by critics, educators, and cultural guardians, constitute the literature many students read. For example, in primary school, students read "classics" such as *The Tale of Peter Rabbit* (Potter, 1902; 1989); *The Little Engine That Could* (Piper, 1954; 1980), and *Make Way for Ducklings* (McCloskey, 1941). Elementary school students tend to read classics such as *Little House on the Prairie* (Wilder, 1953), *Bridge to Terebithia* (Paterson, 1977), and *Charlotte's Web* (White, 1952; 1975). By the time most students have graduated from high school they will have read books from a canon which includes *The Scarlet Letter* (Hawthorne, 1983), *Lord of the Flies* (Golding, 1962), and other works deemed necessary for cultural literacy. Unfortunately, literary canons tend to include a preponderance of books that reflect the experiences, values, perspectives, knowledge, and interpretations of Whites, particularly Anglo-Saxons. Few texts written by African Americans or other people of color are designated classics, even though many exhibit extraordinary literary merit, expand or reinterpret literary forms, or

*My colleague, Jane Mason, provided invaluable critical commentary during the preparation of this manuscript.

provide a forum for voices silenced or ignored in mainstream literature. The vast majority of students do not read African American classics such as *Roll of Thunder, Hear My Cry* (Taylor, 1976), or *M. C. Higgins, The Great* (Hamilton, 1974) because literary canons perpetuated in schools have become a part of a selective tradition. The same cultural processes that have led to the development of selective traditions have tended to ignore the contributions of African Americans to children's literature.

The purposes of this article are to examine, broadly, the historical development of literature written for African American children from the late nineteenth century to the present, to discuss possible trends in African American children's literature, and to assess the value of that literature to literacy education. Explanation of and justification for the development of African American children's literature is evident when one examines the selective tradition in children's literature and the depiction of African Americans within that tradition.

The Selective Tradition in Children's Literature

Because literature is a valued cultural commodity, traditions evolve around its definitions, functions, and value.[2] The same holds true for children's literature, which is indeed a valuable and valued cultural commodity. Children's literature serves the important role of mediator between children, cultural knowledge, and socialization by adults. Moreover, because children's literature has long maintained this traditional role in society, it possesses both symbolic and real power. However, when a tradition is selective or, worse, when it sets up inaccurate and damaging stereotypes, the meanings and knowledge shaped by it become significant because they shape individuals' perceptions of the world and their roles in it.

The selective tradition in children's literature regarding African Americans has been replete with stereotypes. Critic Sterling Brown[3] analyzed the images of African Americans in American literature and determined that the literary depictions of African Americans entertained Whites and, when combined with prevailing theological arguments and "scientific" data from the social sciences, provided literary justification for institutionalized racism. As Brown concluded: "[T]he Negro has met with as great injustice in American literature as he has in American life. The majority of books about Negroes merely stereotype Negro character" (p. 180). Brown identified seven prevalent stereotypes of African Americans in literature and in the works of the literary canon: "the contented slave," "the wretched freeman," "the comic Negro," "the brute Negro," "the tragic mulatto," "the local-color Negro," and "the exotic primitive."

Each of these stereotypes existed in children's literature as well. For instance, *Elsie Dinsmore* (Finley, 1868–1893), a tale of a pious planter's daughter, abounds with contented slaves, one of whom is Elsie's faithful "Mammy," Aunt Chloe. Aunt Chloe epitomizes endurance, strong religious convictions, and loyalty to the slave system. The following excerpt captures the relationship between Aunt Chloe and Elsie and the attributes of the contented slave:

> [Aunt Chloe:] My precious pet, my darlin' chile, your ole mammy loves you better dan life; an did my darlin forget de almighty Friend dat says, "I have loved thee with an everlasting love, an' I will never leave thee, nor forsake thee"? (pp. 64–65)

Indeed, most early literary texts which depict slavery present it in this manner or as an idyllic institution; few portray the horrors of slavery. Another example of a stereotype in children's literature is the comic Negro. African American males are usually the victims of that stereotype, whereupon they are depicted as dim-witted children who constantly grin, eat, misunderstand simple directions, and scratch their heads. For example, in *Epaminondas and his Auntie* (Bryant, 1907; 1938), the male slave Epaminondas is depicted as inherently stupid:

> O' Epaminondas, Epaminondas, you ain't got the sense you was born with; you never will have the sense you was born with! Now I ain't gonna tell you any more ways to bring truck home. (p. 14)

Such texts were not aberrations or exceptions, they were typical of their time. Many remain in circulation today as reprints or they are available in libraries. Other copies are passed down within families as treasured artifacts. For example, a graduate student of mine recently refused to sell me her copy of *Little Brown Koko* (Hunt, 1951), a book similar to *Epaminondas and his Auntie*, because the former was one of her favorite books as a child and one which she recently shared with her own children.

Perhaps the one book which cemented stereotyped images of African Americans in popular culture is Helen Bannerman's *The Story of Little Black Sambo* (1899; 1923). For many, primarily Whites, the title engenders fond memories. While some will admit their embarrassment for liking the story, a few still defend their childhood reactions and admit they do not understand the negative reactions of African Americans to the story. By contrast, some African Americans conjure up images of discrimination, name calling, and grotesque caricatures of their race's physical features when references to the book are made. Many also remember their own acute embarrassment when the story was read, or they recall their intense anger when they themselves might have been referred to as "Sambo." An examination of the text, particularly the illustrations, demonstrates the validity of African Americans' responses. In some of the editions, the illustrations show Black people as simian-like or with protruding eyes and large, red lips, extremely dark skin, and, in the case of males, long, gangly arms.

Again, one cannot label a book such as *Little Black Sambo* atypical; rather, it is a typical depiction. Stereotypes of African Americans are pervasive in all aspects of American culture. For example, businesses adopted the "mammy" and "uncle" stereotypes to sell pancakes, hot cereal, and other commodities. Further, movies such as *The Birth of a Nation* (1915) aided in the entrenchment of stereotypes, and the literary images were reinforced in school texts from elementary schooling through university training. For example, Elson[4] notes that African Americans are portrayed in social studies and science texts as intellectually and physically inferior to all other racial groups. The very pervasiveness of the stereotypes in all aspects of life suggests that African American children have difficulty encountering literature or other cultural artifacts that portray them truthfully. Additionally, the sociocultural milieu of the early periods did not bode well for the creation and distribution of authentic literature. Those who desired to offer alternative images had to battle against the institutions and processes involved in the development of popular culture.

The Beginnings of a New Tradition: 1890–1900

Recent research suggests that literature for African American children did not appear until the 1890s.[5] Nonetheless, it is probable that some African American religious, social, fraternal, or economic organization created literature for children prior to this period. Quite possibly, those works languish in attics, rare bookstores, or archives. Many extant copies no longer exist; they survive only as references noted in equally obscure texts. For example, in *The Horizon,* an early twentieth-century periodical published by W. E. B. DuBois, an advertisement appeared for a periodical for African American children entitled *The Young Set.* However, a search of periodical catalogs and archival holdings reveals no evidence that the magazine was ever published.

Thus far, early writers and contemporary researchers cite the work of Mrs. A. E. Johnson in the 1890s as the beginnings of African American children's literature.[6] Johnson's first novel, *Clarence and Corinne, or, God's Way* (1890) usually is cited as the first work by an African American writing in this genre. Johnson's novel parallels similar didactic and moral tracts published for children in the nineteenth century. The implicit purpose of the novel was not necessarily to entertain but to promote piety, obedience, refinement, and morality among children and convince them of the virtues of achieving stable middle-class status and sensibility. As in other texts of this type, the central characters are members of the working poor who achieve middle-class status through perseverance and hard work. Clarence and Corinne are energetic, intelligent, hopeful, and ambitious. Clarence wants to attend school and his adoring sister shares his desire. Like other heroes and heroines, Clarence and Corinne do not abandon their dreams. They experience a series of vicissitudes and victories and ultimately overcome their poverty-stricken beginnings to achieve respect, education, marriage, and middle-class status.

Despite its designation as the first African American children's novel, *Clarence and Corinne* is not strictly for African American children nor is it strictly a novel of African American experiences even though the author was African American. Johnson's novel features White characters. For whatever reasons, she chose not to portray African American experiences. Perhaps she was trying to write a "color-blind" novel, yet the sociocultural milieu of her time may have dictated the presentation of White characters.

A more suitable candidate for the designation of first African American children's book is Paul Laurence Drunbar's *Little Brown Baby,* a collection of dialect poems first published in 1895. The poetry is generally of good quality but difficult reading for children because of the orthographic representation of the dialect. An excerpt from the work demonstrates the linguistic facility needed to recite the title poem:

> Little brown baby wif spa'klin' eyes
> Come to yo' pappy an' set on his knee.
> What you been doin', suh—makin' san' pies?
> Look at dat bib—you's ez du'ty ez me. (p. 3)

To his credit, Dunbar's dialect does not resemble the inaccurate language evident in other stories such as Page's *Two Little Confederates* (1888; 1932). On the whole, Dunbar's poetry is humorous, nonpolitical, nonreligious, and generally concerned with mundane topics. The collection seems more an appreciation of African American folk culture than an attempt to garner or inspire racial pride, solidarity, or uplift in an overt manner. For some, Dunbar's dialect poetry, with its comical situations and whimsical characters, harkens to the stereotype of the comic Negro. For others, *Little Brown Baby* is a celebration of, or at least a homage to, African American folk culture and a subtle celebration of racial pride.

Arguably, one hesitates to discuss themes and motifs in the African American children's literature of the nineteenth century for the simple fact that only two works qualify.[7] Nevertheless, some themes and motifs appear consistently in both. For example, perseverance, love of family, goodness, and kindness are emphasized. Simple pleasures such as dances, church activities, and picnics rather than elaborate, expensive activities are those deemed to bring joy. However, *Clarence and Corinne,* a text in which religious didacticism dominates, does not radiate the ebullient tone of *Little Brown Baby.*

Dunbar's and Johnson's books both have entertainment, socialization, educational, and aesthetic value; yet, to a certain extent that value was limited by the historical period during which the books were published. The majority of African American children during that time were illiterate; few could have encountered the texts in their schooling because major strictures were placed on the funding, curricula, and type of schooling provided for African Americans.[8] Given the immense popularity he enjoyed and the secular nature of his works, it is likely that more African American children were introduced to Dunbar's work. Nevertheless, both Johnson's and Dunbar's works are notable as antecedents of an alternative literary tradition. The expansion of that tradition occurred as more African Americans became literate and came to view literature as an important element of schooling.

An Emergent Tradition: 1900–1920s

The expansion of the new literary tradition awaited the development of an educated African American middle class which demanded culturally authentic literature for African American children. Enhancement of the new tradition also necessitated the emergence of an educated group of persons interested in writing as a vocation of avocation. It also depended on the further development of African American publishers and changes in attitudes among White publishers. These necessary preconditions emerged during the early 1900s. In comparison to the previous period, a veritable flood of texts appeared. Some were readers (books used for literacy instruction) such as *Floyd's Flowers* (Floyd, 1905) and *The Upward Path* (Pritchard & Ovington, 1920). Others were traditional works of fiction.

Many of the texts published during this period can be labeled oppositional texts; that is, they are works that contradict a theme, motif, or stereotype. For instance, Mary White Ovington, a White radical who was associated with the National Association for the Advancement of Colored People (NAACP) for a number of years, wrote two significant oppositional texts: *Hazel* (1913) and *Zeke* (1931). Her books were published by The Crisis Publishing Company, an enterprise of the NAACP, and advertised in *The Crisis,* the NAACP's official publication, and in *The Brownies' Book,* a periodical for children published by DuBois in 1920 and 1921.

Hazel details the activities of a middle-class African American child who is pretty, intelligent, cultured, and kind. Hazel, the protagonist, experiences few racial strictures growing up in Boston. She does not encounter racial prejudice until she visits her grandmother in rural Alabama; however, following her grandmother's wisdom, she handles it in a thoughtful manner and decides to dedicate her life to the eradication of prejudice. By contrast, *Zeke* focuses on rural African Americans in the South. Zeke is a poor boy from Alabama who rises to middle-class status and respectability after attending a Tuskegee-like school. A few of the characters from *Hazel* appear in *Zeke* (i.e., Hazel reappears as the refined colored benefactress who aids Zeke and motivates him to achieve).

As forerunners of an emerging tradition, *Hazel* and *Zeke* provide more authentic depictions of African Americans but they also contain a few stereo-types, some more positive than others. For example, colorism is an aspect of *Hazel*. While Hazel is depicted as light skinned with straight hair, her best friend Charity is portrayed as a "pickaninny": dark skinned, plain, mischievous, and poor. Refinement, restraint, beauty, and moderation are embodied within the character most resembling Whites; and indolence, passion, lack of restraint, and physical plainness are embodied within the darker character. As Brown[9] argues, this dichotomous stereotype was quite extensive in American literature, as evidenced by the number of novels featuring "tragic" mulattoes.

Nonetheless, Ovington attempted to provide African American children with truthful cultural images, entertain them, imbue them with racial pride, and inform them of the achievements of their race. Like earlier writers, she often included didactic asides and vignettes in her novels, and they contain frank discussions about lynching and negative racial attitudes. Quite clearly, Ovington created her work specifically for African American children. She tried to apprise them of the sociocultural realities they faced and attempted to offer them a model of social interaction. The value of Ovington's works is apparent: her books were among a few alternatives to the stereotyped images of African Americans, and they represent the continued development of an emergent tradition.

Refinement and expansion of the new tradition in the 1920s evolved from the work of W. E. B. DuBois. As evidenced in his powerful essays in *The Souls of Black Folk*[10] and *Dusk of Dawn*[11] DuBois long held a special interest in children. In the realm of children's literature, DuBois's most important contribution was the formation of the DuBois and Dill Publishing Company with Augustus G. Dill. DuBois and Dill were responsible for three endeavors: *The Brownies' Book* and the publication of two biographies, Elizabeth Ross Haynes's *Unsung Heroes* (1921) and Julia Henderson's *A Child's Story of Dunbar* (1921).

The Brownies' Book deserves special note because it was the premier periodical for African American children until the appearance of *Ebony, Jr.!* in the 1960s.[12] Under the direction of DuBois and literary editor Jessie R. Fauset, *The Brownies' Book* became a beacon of hope, featuring fiction, folktales, biographies, poetry, drama, news pieces, and five monthly columns designed to inform, educate, and politicize children and their parents and to showcase the achievements of people of color. Through *The Brownies' Book,* DuBois and Fauset sought to achieve seven goals: to "make colored children realize that being 'colored' is a normal, beautiful thing"; to inform them of the achievements of their race; to teach them a code of honor; to entertain them; to provide them with a model for interacting with Whites; to instill pride in home and family; and to inspire them toward racial uplift and sacrifice. The attainment of these goals, DuBois believed, would result in the creation of a personality Harris[13] refers to as "refined colored youth"—young African American counterparts of the "race men" and "race women" of the early years of the twentieth century. Such youngsters revered education, exhibited personal and racial pride, and were committed to social solidarity and uplift. Several letters published in *The Brownies' Book* from young readers are evidence that some children assimilated the magazine's goals:

> I think colored people are the most wonderful people in the world and when I'm a man, I'm going to write about it, too, so that all people will know the terrible struggles we've had. I don't pay any attention any more to the discouraging things

I see in the newspapers. Something just tells me we are no worse than anybody else. (1920, October, p. 308)

Similarly, Haynes sought to inform African American children of their race's achievements, to inspire racial pride, and to imbue her young readers with a specific ideological view. In the 22 biographies of now well-known persons, among them Frederick Douglass, Harriet Tubman, Alexander Pushkin, and Paul Cuffee, she introduced children to African Americans rarely depicted in the school texts of her day. As Haynes writes in the Introduction to *Unsung Heroes:*

> This story and the other stories in "Unsung Heroes," telling of the victories in spite of the hardships and struggles of Negroes whom the world has failed to sing about, have so inspired me, even after I am grown, that I pass them on to you, my little friends. . . . May you with all of your years ahead of you be so inspired by them that you will succeed in spite of all odds. (unnumbered pages)

DuBois, his editors, and authors quite unabashedly attempted to imbue children with an ideology that was quite radical in children's literature. Their explicit appeals for racial solidarity, pride, and uplift, and their authentic representations of African American life contrasted sharply with the images in general children's literature. The success of DuBois and his associates, however, is difficult to determine. At least 5,000 subscribers received *The Brownies' Book* monthly; however, 12,000 subscribers were needed to sustain continuous publication.[14] The number of copies of Haynes's and Henderson's books sold is as yet undetermined. It is quite conceivable that the imprimatur of DuBois and his association with the NAACP, both considered radical during the period, resulted in reduced sales and distribution. Nonetheless, some children read the texts and the magazines, and it is quite probable that the desired effects were achieved.

The bold objectives and literature developed by DuBois and others were refined further in the period that followed the 1920s. Some changes and advances occurred between 1930 and 1940 which suggested that African American children's literature would have a more promising future. Evidence for that assertion is found in the numbers of books published, the publication of books by major White publishers, and the appearance of many titles in journals or guides directed to librarians.

Strengthening of the Tradition: 1930–1940

While many people contributed to the strengthening of the tradition, the literary efforts of Carter G. Woodson deserve special recognition. Woodson and the authors he published created materials which further expanded the tradition nurtured by DuBois and his associates. Woodson's legacy, at least in children's literature, is as influential as that of DuBois. He established Negro History Week, and founded the Associated Publishers and the Association for the Study of Negro Life and History. These three endeavors continue to have direct influences on the education of African American children and on the literature created for them. In his *The Mis-Education of the Negro*,[15] Woodson articulated a philosophy of education similar to DuBois's, arguing that the education African Americans received in his day had not been devised for, nor did it serve to the benefit of, African Americans. Rather, Woodson claimed, that education was suited mainly for the purpose of maintaining the lowly caste status of African Americans. To ameliorate those conditions, he contended that African American schooling needed to undergo a complete metamorphosis resulting in new texts, new pedagogical techniques, new purposes and goals, and a new kind of teacher unfettered by the internalization of racist ideology. Consequently, Woodson hypothesized, those changes would result in the molding of African American youth educated for individual advancement, skillful in critical thinking, and personally committed to the advancement of their race.

Woodson achieved some of his objectives through the Associated Publishers. This enterprise published a significant number of folklore collections, biographies, poetry anthologies, and histories explicitly designed to educate, entertain, and emancipate. In *African Myths* (1928), for example, Woodson sought to provide children with authentic African folktales. Similarly, the publication of poetry anthologies by Helen Whiting and a reader by Jane D. Schackleford (which depicted the activities of a middle-class African American family) ensured that African American children would have literary choices other than *The Story of Doctor Dolittle* (Lofting, 1948), or *Little Brown Keko*.

As evidence of Woodson's successes, Associated Publishers continues to exist. During the 1970s many of the titles first published in the 1930s were reissued, most likely as a result of increased demand for authentic African American literature and the general lack of availability of this type of literature from White publishers. Literature published subsequently maintained the gains achieved by Woodson, but a subtle shift in tone and ideology occurred as African American children's literature garnered greater mass acceptance.

The Shift to Assimilation: 1940–1970

Certainly, no one person was responsible for the literature of this period, but Arna Bontemps created an extensive body of work over two generations which no doubt helped propel African American children's literature into the mainstream. Bontemps could be characterized as the contemporary "father" of African American children's literature. His body of work—16 novels, biographies, poetry anthologies, histories, and folktales—represents the acceptance of African American children's literature among White publishers and readers and the continued expansion of the literature for African American children. Bontemps's *Popo and Fifina* (1932), written with poet Langston Hughes, remained in print for more than 20 years and was translated into several languages.[16] Another text Bontemps edited, the poetry anthology *Golden Slippers* (1941), is notable because it includes poetry by well-regarded and renowned poets such as Dunbar, Countee Cullen, Claude McKay, Langston Hughes, and James Weldon Johnson. *Golden Slippers* deviates from the conventional children's poetry anthology format by not emphasizing didactic poetry, traditional poetic forms, or poetry written especially for children. Moreover, it, like most of Bontemps's other work, was published not by an African American publishing company but by a major White publisher.

The tradition of providing literary models for children to emulate continued with Bontemps, who early expressed concern about the dearth of biographies for African American children.[17] Bontemps himself altered the situation considerably by writing six collective and individual biographies including *The Story of George Washington Carver* (1954) and *Frederick Douglass: Slave, Fighter, Freeman* (1959).Bontemps's fiction is notable as well. In addition to his collaboration with Hughes, he collaborated with illustrator and author Jack Conroy on several picture books for children. These books are important because of their genre (tall tales) and because the characters within them are White. Additionally, a tone, albeit a subtle one, celebrating the working class and the working-class perspective runs throughout the books. In his noteworthy singularly composed fiction, books such as *Lonesome Boy* (1955; 1987) and *You Can't Pet a Possum* (1934), Bontemps celebrates African American folk culture and language patterns. Aside from its literary quality, Bontemps's work is significant because it represents the integration of African American children's literature into the mainstream as well as the shift from explicit racial themes to the more subtle use of race and emphasis on the authentic depiction of African Americans as they engage in typical activities such as attending picnics, hopping trains to the big city, and playing with friends.

Overall, that shift from an emphasis on explicit racial themes and consciousness in literature to a more assimilationist posture utilizing only subtle racial undertones probably corresponds with the changes in the status of African Americans and the increased push for integration that occurred during the period. Bontemps and his contemporaries, writers such as Jessie Jackson (*Call Me Charlie*, 1945) and Lorenzo Graham (*North Town*, 1965) created works about African American experiences for children of all races. The publication of their work by White publishers resulted in increased sales to schools and libraries as well as increased readership for children's literature by African American authors.

The literature of this period is important because many of the works fall within the category labeled "social conscience literature" by Sims.[18] As Sims notes, the authors of this literature deliberately attempted to develop a "social conscience—mainly in non-Afro-American readers, to encourage them to develop empathy, sympathy, and tolerance for Afro-American children and their problems" (p. 17). She further argues that these books "were created from an ethnocentric, non-Afro-American perspective" (p. 18). Some of the literature fits into another of Sims's categories: "melting pot" books. These books "ignore all differences except physical ones: skin color and other racially related physical features. The result is that the majority of them are picture books" (p. 33). The guiding principles underlying the creation of such melting pot books are assimilation, universal experiences, and integration, principles that cloak the emphasis on cultural diversity which earlier authors acknowledged, highlighted, and celebrated.

The social conscience and melting pot books served important functions: the amelioration of ignorance about African Americans, the portrayal of African Americans as possessing universal values and sharing universal experiences, and the provision of aesthetic experiences. Although these books were deemed vital during their historical period, the reality of African American life and the continued racial discrimination and retrenchment of the era belied the books' attempts to present a rosier picture. This leads one to question whether the cloaking of cultural differences results in negative or positive consequences.

In the period that followed, several sociocultural factors led to the emergence of a cadre of writers whose avowed purposes for writing and illustrating children's books harkened back to those of DuBois and Woodson. Another category devised by Sims, "culturally conscious" literature, explains the function of this emerging literature and details some of its recurring themes and motifs.

Culturally Conscious Literature: The 1970s and Beyond

Culturally conscious literature, according to Sims, comes nearer to "constituting a body of Afro-American literature for children. They are books that reflect, with varying degrees of success, the social and cultural traditions associated with growing up Black in the United States" (p. 49). Sims argues that the primary intent of these books is "to speak to Afro-American children about themselves and their lives" (p. 49). The elements that distinguish culturally conscious books are: major characters who are Afro-American, "a story told from the perspective of Afro-Americans, a setting in an Afro-American community or home, and texts which include some means of identifying the characters as Black—physical descriptions, language, cultural traditions and so forth" (p. 49).

The list of writers who have created culturally conscious literature in this period surpasses the total number of writers in all the previous periods. That list includes Lucille Clifton, Tom Feelings, Eloise Greenfield, Rosa Guy, Virginia Hamilton, Sharon Bell Mathis, Walter Dean Myers, the late John Steptoe, Mildred Taylor, and Brenda Wilkinson. It also includes the newer writers of the 1980s such as Angela Johnson, Patricia McKissack, Emily Moore, Joyce Carol Thomas, and Camille Yarbrough. These writers have distinguished themselves because their works are decidedly African American in tone and range of content and because the literary quality of the works equals and in many cases, surpasses the quality of general children's literature. Some of the writers have received numerous prestigious awards such as the Newbery or Caldecott medals.

Several of these authors have written statements about their aesthetic philosophies reminiscent of Langston Hughes's 1926 manifesto, "The Negro Writer and the Racial Mountain."[19] Virginia Hamilton, arguably the best writer in children's literature today, has written extensively on her craft. Her views are crucial because she has received more awards than any other children's writer (with the possible exception of Katherine Paterson) and because she has written in a variety of genres.[20] Hamilton[21] capsulates her aesthetic philosophy thusly:

> I want my books to be read. I want an audience. I struggle daily with literary integrity, black cultural integrity, intellectual honesty, my desire for simplicity in the storytelling, and the wish for strong, original characterization, exceptional concepts for plots. . . . But when I sit down to write a story, I don't say to myself, now I'm going to write a black story. (pp. 12–13)

Other African American writers echo Hamilton's thoughts. Author/illustrator Tom Feelings[22] articulates his opinions on the aesthetic and ideological functions of art in children's books as follows:

> Books are wonderful tools, and art for children can affect and has the ability to intensify children's perceptions of reality and stimulate their imagination in a certain way. They can also teach racism and reinforce self-hatred and stereotypes. (p. 73)

The works these culturally conscious authors create are not monolithic; they present the range of African American experiences. The images portrayed in their works are culturally and historically authentic. Further, many of the writers capture the orality of Black vernacular English without resorting to inaccurate dialect. The illustrations in many of the books are extraordinary in terms of their artistry and their rendering of the immense variations in physical features among African Americans. An excerpt from the folktale *Mirandy and Brother Wind* (1988) demonstrates this fidelity to both truthful portrayal and language:

> First thing, Orlinda come siding up to Mirandy, asking, "Who gon' be yo' partner?" Mirandy tried not to act excited. "He's real special." Then she added. "I wish you and Ezel luck. Y'all gon' need it." "Me and Ezel? Girl, don't be silly." (unnumbered pages)

Just as important, the culturally conscious authors do not hesitate to present historically accurate portrayals of the horrors of the African American experience in the United States. Although the stories are not designed to frighten children or instill in them a sense of hopelessness, their authors portray aspects of the African American experience rarely seen in children's literature. This is especially true for books in this category that depict slavery or racial discrimination. Arguably, the books represent a "storied tradition of resistance";[23] that is, while accurately portraying historical facts, they do so in ways that highlight African American resistance. For example, in Mildred Taylor's searing novelette set in the South, *The Friendship* (1987a), an elderly African American man, Mr. Tom Bee, goes to the local store to purchase tobacco from a White man, John Wallace, whose life he had saved several years previously. Wallace had promised Mr. Bee that he would never disrespect him in front of Whites. However, in an ugly confrontation in Wallace's store one day, Wallace is urged by some other Whites to put Mr. Bee "in his place," and he shoots Mr. Bee for referring to him as "John." Although wounded, Mr. Bee vows that he will never call Wallace "Mister." The reality and pain of the social dilemmas depicted in this text are rarely approached in children's literature texts generally used in American schools. Thus, in one sense, the culturally conscious books represent the ideal standard for African American children's literature. They provide exceptional aesthetic experiences; they entertain, educate, and inform; and they engender racial pride.

Despite the quality of these works, their full potential has not been met, for a variety of reasons. Since the 1970s the number of books published by African Americans or others about African American experiences has hovered around 200 books per year. Rarely is that number surpassed, and, sadly, many African Americans remain unaware of the existence of these books. Many of these books never reach the hands of African American children. Some have been out of print for significant time periods. Even when the books are available, some teachers are hesitant to use them because they believe that the books depict only bleak ghetto situations, that they might embarrass African American children, or that White children are not interested or may be ill at ease with the books. However, as Harris notes, as recently as 1990 a sixth-grade teacher responded that she was angry that her teacher training failed to expose her to this body of literature; she has since made it available to her students.

What, then, does the future portend for African American children's literature? In some ways, the future looks promising. Several new writers have emerged during the 1980s whose work suggests that African American children's literature will remain a viable, vibrant tradition, albeit one that remains unfairly neglected. From the bedtime story ritual featured in *Tell Me a Story, Mama* (Johnson, 1989), to the day-to-day activities of a middle-class African American family related in *Whose Side Are You On?* (Moore, 1988), and to the frank discussion of the issue of colorism in *The Shimmershine Queens* (Yarbrough, 1989), these books present a range of experiences and intimate portrayals of African Americans. They read as if they were written *for* African American children. Via the language, nicknames, foods, and other aspects and nuances of culture that they present, they implicitly inform their readers that the stories are from the African American community, "the 'hood." There is a naturalness about them—these books do not scream messages or didacticism other than those which inherently stem from the affirmation and celebration of African American culture. To their credit, they also justly criticize negative aspects of African American culture, but not in formulaic fashion.

An argument can be made that the culturally conscious books are essential for African American children specifically and for all children generally. Purves and Beach[24] found that children prefer literary works with subject matter related to their personal experiences, that they engage more with materials related to their personal experiences, and that they seek out works with which they can identify or which contain characters whose experiences reflect their own. Further, recent research in cognition supports the notion that familiarity with and interest in a topic or text facilitates comprehension.[25] Arguably, reading comprehension among African American children would improve if the literacy materials were more meaningful to them.[26]

If African American children do not see reflections of themselves in school texts or do not perceive any affirmation of their cultural heritage in those texts, then it is quite likely that they will not read or value schooling as much. Children need to understand the languages, beliefs, ways of life, and perspectives of others. White children and other children of color need to read African American literature because notions of cultural pluralism are becoming more important as cultural, economic, and geographical barriers are eradicated. The task confronting educators, then, is to provide all children with opportunities to hear, read, write about, and talk about literature, especially literature that affirms who they are.

Notes

1. A. Baker, *Books about Negro Life for Children* (New York: The New York Public Library, 1961); D. Broderick, *Image of the Black in Children's Fiction* (New York: R. R. Bowker, 1973); S. Brown. Negro character as seen by White authors. *Journal of Negro Education,* 2 (1973), 179–203; R. Sims, *Shadow and Substance: Afro-American Experience in Contemporary Children's Fiction.* Urbana, IL: National Council of Teachers of English, 1982.

2. R. Williams, *The Long Revolution* (New York: Oxford University Press, 1961); *Marxism and Literature* (New York: Oxford University Press, 1977).

3. Brown, op. cit.

4. R. Elson, *Guardians of Tradition: American Schoolbooks of the Nineteenth Century* (Lincoln, NE: University of Nebraska Press, 1964).

5. J. Fraser, Black publishing for Black children. *School Library Journal,* 20 (1973), 19–24; D. Muse, Black children's literature: Rebirth of a neglected genre. *Black Scholar,* 7 (1975), 11–15.

6. Fraser, op. cit.; Muse, op. cit.; G. Penn, *The Afro-American Press and its Editors* (Springfield, MA: Wiley, 1891); I would tend to label Dunbar's *Little Brown Baby* the first, though only tentatively. Just as *Iola Leroy,* F. E. W. Harper, *Iola Leroy* (Boston: Beacon Press, 1988; reprint of 1892 edition) previously was believed to be the first published novel by a African American woman until recent research uncovered Harriet Wilson's *Our Nig,* H. E. Wilson, *Our Nig* (New York: Vintage Books, 1983; reprint of 1859 edition), similar shifting circumstances exist with regard to children's literature by and for African Americans.

7. Some researchers [Muse, op. cit.; C. Vaughn-Roberson and B. Hill, *The Brownies' Book and Ebony, Jr.!*: Literature as a mirror of the Black experience. *Journal of Negro Education*, 58 (1989), 494–510] argue that *The Joy*, published by Mrs. Johnson in the 1880s, could be designated the first work created for African American children during this period.

8. J. Anderson, *The Education of Blacks in the South, 1860–1935* (Chapel Hill, NC: University of North Carolina Press, 1988).

9. Brown, op. cit.

10. W. E. B. DuBois (1903), *The Souls of Black Folk* (Greenwich, CT: Fawcett, 1961).

11. W. E. B. DuBois (1940), *Dusk of Dawn* (Millwood, NY: Krause International, 1975).

12. *The Brownies' Book* generally has been designated the first periodical for African American children created by African Americans [R. Kelly, *Children's Periodicals of the United States* (Westport, CT: Greenwood, 1984)] but Fraser (op. cit.) argues that *The Joy* is the first. A comprehensive examination of *The Brownies Book* is found in Harris. [V. Harris, *The Brownies' Book: Challenge to the Selective Tradition in Children's Literature* (Doctoral dissertation, University of Georgia, 1986). (University Microfilms No. AAC-8628882) (1987a).]

13. Harris, op. cit.; and "Jessie Fauset's transference of the new Negro philosophy to children's literature," *Langston Hughes Review*, 6 (1987b), 36–43.

14. Harris, 1987a, op. cit.

15. C. Woodson, *The Mis-Education of the Negro*. Washington, D.C.: The Associated Publishers, 1969).

16. C. Nicholas (ed.), *Arna Bontemps–Langston Hughes letters*. 1925–67 (New York: Dodd, Mead, 1980).

17. S. Alexander, *The Achievement of Arna Bontemps*. Unpublished doctoral dissertation, University of Pittsburgh (1976).

18. Sims, op. cit.

19. N. Huggins (ed.), *Voices from the Harlem Renaissance*. (New York: Oxford University Press, 1976).

20. Hamilton's *M. C. Higgins, the Great* (1974) was the first book written by an African American to win the Newberry Medal. The book also won the National Book Award and the *Boston Globe-Horn Book Magazine Award*, the only children's literature ever to do so.

21. V. Hamilton, The mind of a novel: The heart of a book. *Children's Literature Quarterly*, 8 (1983), 10–13.

22. T. Feelings, Illustration is my form, the Black experience my story and my content. *The Advocate*, 4 (1985), 73–83.

23. The phrase, "storied tradition of resistance," was first coined by Susan Cox and appeared in an unpublished manuscript by Taxel (*Reclaiming the Voice of Resistance: The Fiction of Mildred Taylor*. Unpublished manuscript presented at the annual meeting of the American Educational Research Association, San Francisco, California, 1989).

24. A. Purves and R. Beach, *Literature and the Reader* (Urbana, IL: National Council of Teachers of English, 1972).

25. L. Fielding, P. Wilson and R. Anderson, A new focus on free reading: The role of tradebooks in reading instruction. In T. Raphael, ed., *The Contexts of School-Based Literacy* (New York: Random House, 1984), 149–162.

26. J. Kunjufu, *Developing Positive Self-Images and Discipline in Black Children* (Chicago: African-American Images, 1984); H. Madhubuti. *Black men: Obsolete, Single, Dangerous?* (Chicago: Third World Press, 1989).

Children's Books Cited

Bannerman, H. (1899; 1923). *The Story of Little Black Sambo*. New York: Harper & Row.

Bontemps, A. (1934). *You Can't Pet a Possum*. New York: Morrow.

Bontemps, A. (1941). *Golden Slippers*. New York: Harper & Row.

Bontemps, A. (1954). *The Story of George Washington Carver*. New York: Grosset & Dunlap.

Bontemps, A. (1955, 1986). *Lonesome Boy*. New York: Beacon.

Bontemps, A. (1959). *Frederick Douglass: Slave, Fighter, Freeman*. New York: Knopf.

Bontemps, A. & Hughes, L. (1932). *Popo and Fifina: Children of Haiti*. New York: Macmillan.

Bryant, S. (1907, 1938). *Epaminondas and His Auntie*. Boston: Houghton Mifflin.

Caines, J. (1973). *Abby*. New York: Harper & Row.

Dunbar, P. L. (1895). *Little Brown Baby*. New York: Dodd, Mead.

Finley, M. (1868, 1893). *Elsie Dinsmore*. New York: Dodd, Mead.

Floyd, S. (1905). *Floyd's Flowers*. Atlanta, GA: Hertel & Jenkins.

Golding, W. (1962). *Lord of the Flies*. New York: Putnam.

Graham, L. (1965). *North Town*. New York: Harper Junior.

Hamilton, V. (1974). *M. C. Higgins, The Great*. New York: Macmillan.

Hamilton, V. (1975). *Paul Robeson: The Life and Times of a Free Black Man*. New York: Harper.

Hamilton, V. (1983). *Willie Bea and the Time the Martians Landed*. New York: Greenwillow.

Hawthorne, N. (1983). *The Scarlet Letter*. New York: Penguin.

Haynes, E. (1921). *Unsung Heroes*. New York: DuBois & Dill.

Henderson, J. (1921). *A Child's Story of Dunbar*. New York: DuBois & Dill.

Hunt, B. (1951). *Little Brown Koko*. Chicago: American Colortype.

Jackson, J. (1945). *Call Me Charlie*. New York: Harper Junior.

Johnson, A. (1989). *Tell Me a Story, Mama*. New York: Orchard Books.

Johnson, A. E. (1890). *Clarence and Corrine*. Philadelphia: American Baptist Publications Society.

Lofting, A. (1948). *The Story of Doctor Dolittle*. Philadelphia: J. B. Lippincott.

McCloskey, R. (1941). *Make Way for Ducklings*. New York: Puffin/Penguin.

McKissack, P. *Mirandy and Brother Wind*. New York: Knopf.

Ovington, M. (1913, 1972). *Hazel*. Freeport, NH: Books for Libraries.

Ovington, M. (1931). *Zeke*. New York: Harcourt Brace.

Page, T. (1888; 1932). *Two Little Confederates*. New York: Charles Scribner's Sons.

Paterson, K. (1977). *Bridge to Terebithia*. New York: Crowell Junior Books.

Piper, W. (1954; 1980). *The Little Engine that Could*. New York: Putnam.

Potter, B. (1902, 1989). *The Tale of Peter Rabbit*. London: Fredrick Warne.

Pritchard, M. & Ovington, M. (1920). *The Upward Path*. New York: Harcourt, Brace & Howe.

Steptoe, J. (1987). *Mufaro's Beautiful Daughters*. New York: Lothrop, Lee & Shephard.

Taylor, M. (1976; 1984). *Roll of Thunder, Hear My Cry*. New York: Bantam.

Taylor, M. (1987a). *The Friendship*. New York: Dial Books for Young Readers.

Taylor, M. (1987b). *The Gold Cadillac*. New York: Dial.

Wilder, L. (1953). *Little House on the Prairie*. New York: Harper Junior.

White, E. B. (1952; 1975). *Charlotte's Web*. New York: Harper Junior Books.

Woodson, C. (1928). *African Myths*. Washington, D.C.: The Associated Publishers.

Yarbrough, C. (1989). *The Shimmershine Queens*. New York: G. P. Putnam's Sons.

11

The Passions of Pluralism
Multiculturalism and the Expanding Community
Maxine Greene

There have always been newcomers in this country; there have always been strangers. There have always been young persons in our classrooms we did not, could not see or hear. In recent years, however, invisibility has been refused on many sides. Old silences have been shattered; long-repressed voices are making themselves heard. Yes, we are in search of what John Dewey called "the Great Community"[1]; but, at once, we are challenged as never before to confront plurality and multiplicity. Unable to deny or obscure the facts of pluralism, we are asked to choose ourselves with respect to unimaginable diversities. To speak of passions in such a context is not to refer to the strong feelings aroused by what strikes many as a confusion and a cacophony. Rather, it is to have in mind the central sphere for the operation of the passions: "the realm of face-to-face relationships."[2] It seems clear that the more continuous and authentic personal encounters can be, the less likely it will be for categorizing and distancing to take place. People are less likely to be treated instrumentally, to be made "other" by those around. I want to speak of pluralism and multiculturalism with concrete engagements in mind, actual and imagined: engagements with persons, young persons and older persons, some suffering from exclusion, some from powerlessness, some from poverty, some from ignorance, some from boredom. Also, I want to speak with imagination in mind, and metaphor, and art. Cynthia Ozick writes: "Through metaphor, the past has to capacity to imagine us, and we it. Through metaphorical concentration, doctors can imagine what it is to be their patients. Those who have no pain can imagine those who suffer. Those at the center can imagine what it is to be outside. The strong can imagine the weak. Illuminated lives can imagine the dark. Poets in their twilight can imagine the borders of stellar fire. We strangers can imagine the familiar hearts of strangers."[3]

Passions, then, engagements, and imagining: I want to find a way of speaking of community, an expanding community, taking shape when diverse people, speaking as *who* and not *what* they are, come together in speech and action, as Hannah Arendt puts it, to constitute something in common among themselves. She writes that "plurality is the condition of human action because we are all

185

the same, that is, human, in such a way that nobody is ever the same as anyone else who ever lived, lives, or will live."[4] For her, those present on a common ground have different locations on that ground; and each one "sees or hears from a different position." An object—a classroom, a neighborhood street, a field of flowers—shows itself differently when encountered by a variety of spectators. The reality of that object (or classroom, or neighborhood, or field of flowers) arises out of the sum total of its appearances. Thinking of those spectators as participants in an ongoing dialogue, each one speaking out of a distinct perspective and yet open to those around, I find a kind of paradigm for what I have in mind. I discover another in the work of Henry Louis Gates, Jr., who writes about the fact that "the challenge facing America in the next century will be the shaping, at long last, of a truly common public culture, one responsive to the long-silenced cultures of color." (It is not long, it will be remembered, since the same Professor Gates asked in a *New York Times* article, "Whose canon is it anyway?"). More recently, he has evoked the philosopher Michael Oakeshott and his notion of a conversation with different voices. Education, Gates suggests, might be "an invitation into the art of this conversation in which we learn to recognize the voices, each conditioned by a different perception of the world." Then Gates adds: "Common sense says that you don't bracket out 90% of the world's cultural heritage if you really want to learn about the world."[5]

For many, what is common sense for Gates represents an attack on the coherence of what we think of as our heritage, our canon. The notion of different voices conditioned by different perspectives summons up the specter of relativism; and relativism, according to Clifford Geertz, is the "intellectualist Grande Peur." It makes people uneasy because it appears to subvert authority; it eats away at what is conceived as objectively real. "If thought is so much out in the world as this," Geertz asks, as the uneasy might ask, "what is to guarantee its generality, its objectivity, its efficacy, or its truth?"[6] There is irony in Geertz's voice since he knows and has said that "for our time and forward, the image of a general orientation, perspective, *Weltanschauung,* growing out of humanistic studies (or, for that matter, out of scientific ones) and shaping the direction of the culture is a chimera." He speaks of the "radical variousness of the way we think now" and suggests that the problem of integrating cultural life becomes one of "making it possible for people inhabiting different worlds to have a genuine, and reciprocal, impact upon one another."[7] This is troubling for people seeking assurances, seeking certainties. And yet they, like the rest of us, keep experiencing attacks on what is familiar, what James Clifford calls "the irruption of otherness, the unexpected. . . ."[8] It may well be that our ability to tolerate the unexpected relates to our tolerance for multiculturalism, for the very idea of expansion, and the notion of plurality.

We are well aware, for all that, that Arthur Schlesinger, Jr., among others who (like Schlesinger) must be taken seriously, sees a "disuniting of America"[9] in the making if shared commitments shatter, if we lose touch with the democratic idea. Proponents of what is called "civism"[10] are concerned that pluralism threatens the existence of a democratic *ethos* intended to transcend all differences." The *ethos* encompasses the principles of freedom, equality, and justice, as well as regard for human rights; and there is fear that the new relativism and particularism will subvert the common faith. And there are those like E. D. Hirsch, Jr., who sees the concept of "background knowledge" and the shared content it ensures undermined by "variousness" and the multicultural emphases that distract from the common. What they call "cultural literacy" is undermined as a result; and the national community itself is eroded.[11] At the extreme, of course, are those on the far right who find a conspiracy in challenges to the so-called Eurocentric canon and in what they construct as "Politically Correct," signifying a new orthodoxy built out of oversensitivity to multicultural concerns.[12] As for the religious fundamentalist right, says Robert Hughes (writing in *The New York Review*) one of the motives driving men like Jesse Helms is to establish themselves as defenders of what they define as the "American Way" now (as Hughes puts it) "that their original crusade against the Red Menace has been rendered null and void. . . ."[13] Not only do they argue for their construct against the National Art Endowment's grants to *avant garde* artists; they attack such deviations as multiculturalism. It is important to hold this in mind as we try to work through a conception of pluralism to an affirmation of the struggle to attain the life of "free and enriching communion" John Dewey identified with democracy.

The seer of the life of communion, according to Dewey, was Walt Whitman. Whitman wrote about the many shapes arising in the country in his time, "the shapes of doors giving many exits and entrances" and "shapes of democracy . . . ever projecting other shapes." In "Song of Myself" (in total contradiction to the fundamentalist version of the "American Way") he wrote:

> *Through me many long dumb voices,*
> *Voices of the interminable generations of prisoners and slaves,*
> *Voices of the diseas'd and despairing and of thieves and dwarfs,*
> *Voices of cycles of preparation and accretion,*
> *And of the threads that connect the stars, and of wombs and of*
> *   the father-stuff,*
> *And of the rights of them the others are down upon. . . .*
>
> *Through me forbidden voices. . . .*[14]

He was, from all appearances, the seer of a communion arising out of "many shapes," out of multiplicity. There is no suggestion of a melting pot here; nor is there a dread of plurality.

For some of us, just beginning to feel our own stories are worth telling, the reminders of the "long dumb voices," the talk of "the rights of them the others are down upon" cannot but draw attention to the absences and silences that are as much a part of our history as the articulate voices, the shimmering faces, the images of emergence and success. Bartleby, the clerk who "prefers not to" in Herman Melville's story, may suddenly become exemplary.[15] What of those who said no, who found no place, who made no mark? Do they not say something about a society that closed too many doors, that allowed people to be abandoned like "wreckage in the mid-Atlantic"? What of those like Tod Clifton in Ralph Ellison's *Invisible Man?* A former youth leader in the so-called Brotherhood, he ends up selling Sambo dolls in front of the Public Library. When the police try to dislodge him, he protests; and they kill him. The narrator, watching, wonders: "Why did he choose to plunge into nothingness, into the void of faceless faces, of soundless voices, lying outside history? . . . All things, it is said, are duly recorded—all things of importance, that is. But not quite; for actually it is only the known, the seen, the heard, and only those events that the recorder regards as important are put down. . . . But the cop would be Clifton's historian, his judge, his witness, his executioner, and I was the only brother in the watching crowd."[16] The many who ended up "lying outside history" diminished the community, left an empty space on the common ground, left undefined an aspect of reality.

It is true that we cannot know all the absent ones; but they must be present somehow in their absence. Absence, after all, suggests an emptiness, a void to be filled, a wound to be healed, a flaw to be repaired. I think of E. L. Doctorow painting a landscape of denial at the beginning of *Ragtime,* appealing to both wonder and indignation, demanding a kind of repair. He is writing about New Rochelle in 1906; but he is presenting a past that reaches into the present, into *our* present, whether or not we ride trolleys anymore.

> Teddy Roosevelt was President. The population customarily gathered in great numbers either out of doors for parades, public concerts, fish fries, political picnics, social outings, or indoors in meeting halls, vaudeville theatres, operas, ballrooms. There seemed to be no entertainment that did not involve great swarms of people. Trains and steamers and trolleys moved them from one place to another. That was the style; that was the way people lived. Women were stouter then. They visited the fleet carrying white parasols. Everyone wore white in summer. There was a lot of sexual fainting. There were no Negroes. There were no immigrants.[17]

The story has focally to do with a decent, intelligent black man named Coalhouse Walker, who is cheated, never acknowledged, never understood, scarcely *seen,* and who begins his own fated strategy of vengeance which ends when promises are broken and he is shot down in cold blood. Why is he unseen? Why were there no Negroes, no immigrants? More than likely because of the condition of the minds of those in power, those in charge. Ellison may explain it when he attributes invisibility to "a peculiar disposition of the eyes of those with whom I come in contact. A matter of the construction of their inner eyes, those eyes with which they look through their physical eyes upon reality."[18] But that disposition must itself have been partly due to the play of power in discourse as well as in social arrangements. We may wonder even now what the assimilation or initiation sought by so many educators signified when there were so many blanked out spaces—"no Negroes . . . no immigrants," oftentimes no full-grown women.

Looking back at the gaps in our own lived experiences, we might think of silences like those Tillie Olsen had in mind when she spoke of literary history "dark with silences," of the "unnatural silences" of women who worked too hard or were too embarrassed to express themselves,[19] of others who did not have the words or had not mastered the proper "ways of knowing."[20] We might ponder the plight of young island women, like Jamaica Kincaid's Lucy from Antigua, forced to be "two-faced" in a post-colonial school: "outside, I seemed one way, inside I was another; outside false, inside true."[21] For years we knew no more about people like her (who saw "sorrow and bitterness" in the face of daffodils because of the Wordsworth poem she had been forced to learn) than we did about the Barbadians Paule Marshall has described, people living their fragmented lives in Brooklyn. There was little consciousness of what Gloria Anzaldua calls *Borderlands: La Frontera* on which so many Latinos live,[22] nor of the Cuban immigrants like the musicians in *The Mambo Kings Sing Songs of Love*. Who of us truly wondered about the builders of the railroads, those Maxine Hong Kingston calls "China Men," chopping trees in the Sandalwood and Sierra Nevada Mountains? Who of us could fill the gaps left by such a person as Ah Goong, whose "existence was outlawed by the Chinese Exclusion Acts. . . ."? His family, writes Kingston, "did not understand his accomplishments as an American ancestor, a holding, homing ancestor of this place. He'd gotten the legal or illegal papers burned in the San Francisco earthquake and fire; he appeared in America in time to be a citizen and to father citizens. He had also been seen carrying a child out of the fire, a child of his own in spite of the laws against marrying. He had built a railroad out of sweat, why not have an American child out of longing?"[23] Did we pay heed to a person like Michelle Clift, an Afro-Caribbean woman who felt that speaking in words that were not her own was a form of speechlessness? Or to a child like Pecola Breedlove in Toni Morrison's *The Bluest Eye,* the unloved black child who wanted to look like Shirley Temple so she could be included in the human reality?[24] Or to a Mary Crow Dog, who finds her own way of saying in the autobiography *Lakota Woman?* How many of us have been willing to suffer the experiences most recently rendered in Art Spiegelman's two-volume comic book called *Maus?* He tells about his father, the ill-tempered Vladek, a survivor of Auschwitz, and his resentful sharing of his holocaust memories with his son. Every character in the book is an animal: the Jews, mice; the Germans, cats; the Poles, pigs. It is a reminder, not simply of a particular culture's dissolution ("Anja's parents, the grandparents, her big sister Tosha, little Bibi, and our Richieu. . . . All what is left, it's the photos."[25]). It is a reminder of the need to recognize that everything is possible, something normal people (including school people) either do not know or do not want to know.

To open up our experience (and, yes, our curricula) to existential possibilities of multiple kinds is to extend and deepen what we think of when we speak of a community. If we break through and even disrupt a surface equilibrium and uniformity, this does not mean that particular ethnic or racial traditions ought to replace our own. Toni Morrison writes of pursuing her freedom as a writer in a "genderized, sexualized, wholly racialized world"; but this does not keep her from developing a critical project "unencumbered by dreams of subversion or rallying gestures at fortress walls."[26] In her case, the project involves exploring the ways in which what we think of as our Americanness is in many ways a response to an Africanist presence far too long denied. She is not interested in replacing one domination by another; she is interested in showing us what she sees from her own perspective—and, in showing us, enriching our understanding not only of our own culture, but of ourselves. She speaks of themes familiar to us all: "individualism, masculinity, social engagement versus historical isolation; acute and ambiguous moral problematics; the thematics of innocence coupled with an obsession with figurations of death and hell. . . ." Then she goes on to query what Americans are alienated from, innocent of, different from. "As for absolute power, over whom is this power held, from whom withheld, to whom distributed? Answers to these questions lie in the potent and ego-reinforcing presence of an Africanist population."[27] Even as Americans once defined their moral selves against the wilderness, they began to define their whiteness against what Melville called "the power of blackness"; they understood their achievement of freedom against slavery. Whether we choose to see our history that way or not, she is introducing a vision only she could create, and it offers us alternative vantage points on our world. Indeed, the tension with regard to multiculturalism may be partially due to the suspicion that we have often defined ourselves against some unknown, some darkness, some "otherness" we chose to thrust away, to master, not to understand. In this regard, Morrison says something that seems to me unanswerable: "My project is an effort to avert the critical gaze from the racial object to the racial subject; from the described and imagined to the describers and imaginers; from the serving to the served."

To take this view is not to suggest that curricula should be tailored to the measure of specific cultural groups of young people. Nor is it to suggest, as the Afrocentrists do, that emphasis should be laid on the unique experiences, culture and perspectives of Afro-Americans and their link to African roots. There is no question that what history has overlooked or distorted must be restored—whether it has to do with Afro-Americans, Hispanics, Asians, women, Jews, native Americans, Irish, or Poles; but the exclusions and the deformations have not kept artists like Morrison, Ellison, and James Baldwin from plunging into and learning from western literary works, anymore than it has prevented scholars like Gates and Cornel West and Alain Locke from working for more and richer interchanges between Afro-American and Euro-American cultures. Morrison begins her new book with a verse from Eliot and goes on to pay tribute to Homer, Dostoevsky, Faulkner, James, Flaubert, Melville, and Mary Shelley. It is difficult to forget James Baldwin reading Dostoevsky and haunting the public library, to turn attention from West's critiques of Emerson, to ignore Ellison writing about Melville and Hemingway, even as he drew attention to what he called "the Negro stereotype" that was "really an image of the irrational, unorganized forces in American life."[28] We might think of Maya Angelou as well, of her years of self-imposed silence as a child and the reading she did through those years. We might recall Alice Walker engaging with Muriel Rukeyser and Flannery O'Connor, drawing energy from them, even as she went in search of Zora Neale Hurston and Bessie Smith and Sojourner Truth, and Gwendolyn Brooks. ("I also loved Ovid and Catullus . . . the poems of e. e. cummings and William Carlos Williams."[29]) And we are aware that, as time goes on, more and more Afro-American literature (and women's literature, and Hispanic American literature) are diversifying our experience, changing our ideas of time and life and birth and relationship and memory.

My point has to do with openness and variety as well as with inclusion. It has to do with the avoidance of fixities, of stereotypes, even the stereotypes linked to multiculturalism. To view a person as in some sense "representative" of Asian culture (too frequently grouping together human beings as diverse as Japanese, Koreans, Chinese, Vietnamese) or Hispanic culture or Afro-American culture is to presume an objective reality called "culture," a homogeneous and fixed presence that *can* be adequately represented by existing subjects. (Do Amy Tan's maternal characters embody the same reality as does Maxine Hong Kingston's "woman warrior"? Does Richard Wright's Bigger Thomas stand for the same thing as Miss Celie stands for in Alice Walker's *The Color Purple?*) Do we not *know* the person in the front row of our classroom, or the one sharing the raft, or the one drinking next to us at the bar by her/his cultural or ethnic affiliation.

Cultural background surely plays a part in shaping identity; but it does not determine identity. It may well create differences that must be honored; it may occasion styles and orientations that must be understood; it may give rise to tastes, values, even prejudices that must be taken into account. It is important to know, for example, without embarrassing or exoticizing her, why Jamaica Kincaid's Antiguan Lucy feels so alienated from a Wordsworth poem, and whether or not (and against what norms) it is necessary to argue her out of her distaste for daffodils. It is important to realize why (as in Bharaka Mukherjee's *Jasmine*) Hindus and Sikhs are so at odds with one another, even in this country, and to seek out ways in which (consulting what we believe to be the Western principle of justice) they can be persuaded to set aside hostility. Or perhaps, striving to sympathize with what they feel, we can communicate our own caring for their well-being in such a fashion as to move them provisionally to reconceive. Paulo Freire makes the point that every person ought, on some level, to cherish her/his culture; but he says it should never be absolutized. When it is absolutized, when a person is closed against the new culture surrounding her/him, "you would" (Freire says) "even find it hard to learn new things which, placed alongside your personal history, can be meaningful."[30]

There has, however, to be a feeling of ownership of one's personal history. In this culture, because of its brutal and persistent racism, it has been painfully difficult for Afro-American young people to affirm and be proud of what they

191

choose as personal history. Poverty, hopelessness, the disruption of families and communities, the ubiquity of media images all make it difficult to place new things against a past too often made to appear a past of victimization, shadows, and shame. To make it worse, the mystification that proceeds on all sides gives rise to a meta-narrative of what it means to be respectable and successful in America—a meta-narrative that too often seems to doom minorities to life on the outermost borders, or, as Toni Morrison writes in *The Bluest Eye,* "outdoors" where there is no place to go. ("Outdoors," she writes, "is the end of something, an irrevocable, physical fact, defining and complementing our metaphysical condition. Being a minority in both caste and class, we moved about anyway on the hem of life, struggling to consolidate our weaknesses and hang on, or to creep singly up into the major folds of the garment."[31])

It happens that *The Bluest Eye,* because of its use of the first paragraph of the basal reader *Dick and Jane,* dramatizes (as few works do) the coercive and deforming effect of the culture's official story, the meta-narrative of secure suburban family life. As the novel plays itself out, everything that occurs is the obverse of the basal reader's story with its themes of pretty house, loving family, play, laughter, friendship, cat, and dog. The narrator of the main story, Pecola Breedlove's story, is young Claudia—also black and poor, but with a supporting family, a sister, a mother who loves her even as she complains and scolds. A short preface, ostensibly written after Pecola's baby and her rapist father have died, after the seeds would not flower, after Pecola went mad, ends with Claudia saying: "There is really nothing more to say—except why. But since *why* is difficult to handle, one must take refuge in *how.*"[32] When very young and then a little older, Claudia tells the story; and, in the telling, orders the materials of her own life, her own helplessness, her own longings. She does that in relation to Pecola, whom she could not help, and in relation to the seeds that would not flower and those around her "on the hem of life." She weaves her narrative in such a fashion that she establishes an important connection to the past and (telling about Pecola and her family and her pain) reinterprets her own ethnicity in part through what Michael Fischer calls "the arts of memory." Whatever meaning she can draw from this feeds into an ethic that may be meaningful in the future, an ethic that takes her beyond her own guilt at watching Pecola search the garbage. "I talk about how I did *not* plant the seeds too deeply, how it was the fault of the earth, the land, of our town. I even think now that the land of the entire country was hostile to marigolds that year. . . . Certain seeds it will not nurture, certain fruit it will not bear, and when the land kills of its own volition, we acquiesce and say the the victim had no right to live. We are wrong, of course, but it doesn't matter. It's too late." As Charles Taylor and Alasdair MacIntyre have written, we understand our lives in narrative form, as a quest. Taylor writes: "because we have to determine our place in relation to the good, therefore we cannot be without an orientation to it, and hence must see our life in stories."[33] Clearly, there are different stories connected by the same need to make sense, to make meaning, to find a direction.

To help the Claudias we know, the diverse students we know, articulate their stories is not only to help them pursue the meanings of their lives—to find out *how* things are happening, to keep posing questions about the why. It is to move them to learn the "new things" Freire spoke of, to reach out for the proficiencies and capacities, the craft required to be fully participant in this society, and to do so without losing the consciousness of who they are. That is not all. Stories like the one Claudia tells must break through into what we think of as our tradition or our heritage. They can; they should with what Cornel West has in mind when he speaks about the importance of acknowledging the "distinctive cultural and political practices of oppressed people" without highlighting their marginality in such a way as to further marginalize them. Not only does he call attention to the resistance of Afro-Americans and that of other long-silenced people. He writes of the need to look at Afro-Americans' multiple contributions to the culture over the generations. We might think of the music— Gospel, jazz, ragtime; we might think of the black churches; we might summon up the civil rights movement and the philosophies, the dreams that informed it; we might ponder—looking back, looking around—the images of courage, the images of survival. West goes on to say: "Black cultural practices emerge out of a reality they cannot *not* know—the ragged edges of the real, of necessity; a reality historically constructed by white supremacist practices in North America. . . . These ragged edges—of not being able to eat, not to have shelter, not to have health care—all this is infused into the strategies and styles of black cultural practices."[34] Viewed in connection with the idea of multiculturalism, this does not mean that Afro-American culture in all its variousness can be defined mainly in terms of oppression and discrimination. One of the many reasons for opening spaces in which Afro-Americans can tell their own stories is that they, far more than those from other cultures, can explain the ways in which poverty and exclusion have mediated their own sense of the past. It is true that experiences of pain and abandonment have led to a search for roots and, on occasion, for a revision of recorded history. What is crucial is the provision of opportunities for telling all the diverse stories, for interpreting membership as well as ethnicity, for making inescapable the braids of experience woven into the fabric of America's plurality.

In the presence of an increasingly potent Third World, against the sounds of increasingly eloquent post-colonial (and, now, post-totalitarian) voices, we can no longer pretend that the "ragged edges" are an exception. We can no longer talk in terms of seamless totalities under rubrics like "free world," "free market," "equality," or even "democracy." Like the "wreckage in the mid-Atlantic," like the "faceless faces," like the "unnatural silences," the lacks and deprivations have to be made aspects of our plurality as well as of our cultural identity. Publics, after all, take shape in response to unmet needs and broken promises. Human beings are prone to take action in response to the sense of injustice or to the imagination's capacity to look at things as if they could be otherwise. The democratic community, always a community in the making, depends not so much on what has been achieved and funded in the past. It is kept alive; it is energized and radiated by an awareness of future possibility. To develop a vision of such possibility, a vision of what might and ought to be, is very often to be made aware of present deficiencies and present flaws. The seeds did not flower; Pecola and her baby could not be saved. But more and more persons, paying heed, may move beyond acquiescence. They may say, as Claudia does, "We are wrong, of course . . ." but go on to overcome the "doesn't matter." At that moment, they may reach beyond themselves, choose themselves as who they are and reach out to the common to repair.

Learning to look through multiple perspectives, young people may be helped to build bridges among themselves; attending to a range of human stories, they may be provoked to heal and to transform. Of course, there will be difficulties in affirming plurality and difference and, at once, working to create community. Since the days of de Tocqueville, Americans have wondered how to deal with the conflicts between individualism and the drive to conform. They have wondered how to reconcile the impassioned voices of cultures not yet part of the whole with the requirements of conformity, how not to lose the integrity of those voices in the process, how not to allow the drive to conformity determine what happens at the end. But the community many of us hope for now is not to be identified with conformity. As in Whitman's way of saying, it is a community attentive to difference, open to the idea of plurality. Something life-affirming in diversity must be discovered and rediscovered, as what is held in common becomes always more many-faceted—open and inclusive, drawn to untapped possibility.

No one can predict precisely the common world of possibility, nor can we absolutely justify one kind of community over another. Many of us, however, for all the tensions and disagreements around us, would reaffirm the value of principles like justice and equality and freedom and commitment to human rights; since, without these, we cannot even argue for the decency of welcoming. Only if more and more persons incarnate such principles, we might say, and choose to live by them and engage in dialogue in accord with them, are we likely to bring about a democratic pluralism and not fly apart in violence and disorder. Unable to provide an objective ground for such hopes and claims, all we can do is speak with others as eloquently and passionately as we can about justice and caring and love and trust. Like Richard Rorty and those he calls pragmatists, we can only articulate our desire for as much intersubjective agreement as possible, "the desire to extend the reference of 'us' as far as we can."[35] But, as we do so, we have to remain aware of the distinctive members of the plurality, appearing before one another with their own perspectives on the common, their own stories entering the culture's story, altering it as it moves through time. We want our classrooms to be just and caring, full of various conceptions of the good. We want them to be articulate, with the dialogue involving as many persons as possible, opening to one another, opening to the world. And we want them to be concerned for one another, as we learn to be concerned for them. We want them to achieve friendships among one another, as each one moves to a heightened sense of craft and wide-awakeness, to a renewed consciousness of worth and possibility.

With voices in mind and the need for visibility, I want to end with a call for human solidarity by Muriel Rukeyser, who—like many of us—wanted to "widen the lens and see/ standing over the land myths of identity, new signals, processes." And then:

Carry abroad the urgent need, the scene,
to photograph and to extend the voice,
to speak this meaning.
Voices to speak to us directly. As we move.
As we enrich, growing in larger motion,
this word, this power.[36]

This power, yes, the unexplored power of pluralism, and the wonder of an expanding community.

Notes

1. John Dewey, *The Public and Its Problems* (Athens, OH: The Swallow Press, 1954), 143ff.

2. Roberto Mangabeira Unger, *Passion: An Essay on Personality* (New York: Free Press, 1984), 107.

3. Cynthia Ozick, *Metaphor and Memory* (New York: Alfred A. Knopf, 1989), 283.

4. Hannah Arendt, *The Human Condition* (Chicago: The University of Chicago Press, 1958), 57.

5. Henry Louis Gates, Jr., "Goodbye, Columbus? Notes on the Culture of Criticism," *American Literary History* (Winter 1991): 712.

6. Clifford Geertz, *Local Knowledge* (New York: Basic Books, 1983), 153.

7. Geertz, *Local Knowledge,* 161.

8. James Clifford, *The Predicament of Culture* (Cambridge, MA: Harvard University Press, 1988), 13.

9. Arthur M. Schlesinger, Jr., *The Disuniting of America: Reflections on a Multicultural Society* (New York: W.W. Norton & Co., 1992).

10. Richard Pratte, *The Civic Imperative* (New York: Teachers College Press, 1988), 104–107.

11. E. D. Hirsch, Jr., *Cultural Literacy* (Boston: Houghton Mifflin Company, 1987).

12. Dinesh D'Sousa, *Illiberal Education: The Politics of Race and Sex on Campus* (New York: The Free Press, 1991), 239.

13. Robert Hughes, "Art, Morality & Mapplethorpe," *The New York Review of Books,* 23 April 1992, 21.

14. Walt Whitman, *Leaves of Grass* (New York, Aventine Press, 1931), 53.

15. Herman Melville, "Bartleby," in *Billy Budd, Sailor and Other Stories* (New York: Bantam Books, 1986).

16. Ralph Ellison, *Invisible Man* (New York: Signet Books, 1952), 379.

17. E. L. Doctorow, *Ragtime* (New York: Random House, 1975), 3–4.

18. Ellison, *Invisible Man,* p. 7.

19. Tillie Olsen, *Silences* (New York: Delacorte Press, 1978), 6.

20. Mary F. Belenky, et al., *Women's Ways of Knowing* (New York: Basic Books, 1986).

21. Jamaica Kincaid, *Lucy* (New York: Farrar, Straus, and Giroux, 1990), 18.

22. Gloria Anzaldua, *Borderlands/ La Frontera: The New Mestiza* (San Francisco: Spinsters/ Aunt Lute, 1987).

23. Maxine Hong Kingston, *China Men* (New York: Vintage International Books, 1989), 151.

24. Toni Morrison, *The Bluest Eye* (New York: Pocket Books, 1972).

25. Art Spiegelman, *Maus II* (New York: Pantheon Books, 1991), 115.

26. Toni Morrison, *Playing in the Dark: Whiteness and the Literary Imagination* (Cambridge, MA: Harvard University Press, 1992), 4–5.

27. Morrison, *Playing in the Dark,* p. 45.

28. Ralph Ellison, *Shadow and Act* (New York: Signet Books, 1964), 55.

29. Alice Walker, *In Search of Our Mother's Gardens* (Orlando, FL: Harcourt Brace Jovanovich, 1983), 257.

30. Paulo Freire and Donaldo Macedo, *Literacy: Reading the Word and the World* (South Hadley, MA: Bergin and Garvey, 1987), 126.

31. Morrison, *The Bluest Eye,* p. 18.

32. Morrison, *The Bluest Eye,* p. 9.

33. Charles Taylor, *Sources of the Self* (Cambridge, MA: Harvard University Press, 1989), 51.

34. Cornel West, "Black Culture and Postmodernism," in *Remaking History*, ed. Barbara Kruger and Phil Mariani (Seattle, WA: Bay Press, 1989), 93.

35. Richard Rorty, "Solidarity or Objectivity?" in *Objectivity, Relativism, and Truth* (Cambridge: Cambridge University Press, 1991), 23.

36. Muriel Rukeyser, *The Book of the Dead*. (New York: Covici-Friede, 1938), 71–72.

12

To Fight Swimming with the Current
Teaching Movement History[1]
Ceasar L. McDowell and Patricia Sullivan

hy teach movement history? Over the past year we have put this question to historians, educators and movement veterans as we have developed the ideas in this chapter. Our informal questioning of colleagues suggests movement history is taught to tell the story of how one struggle against oppression—that of African Americans in the United States—was mounted, maintained, resisted, and challenged. This story is told (1) as evidence of how social change occurs, (2) to capture the context in which social change happens, (3) to convey the story of the people who engaged in that struggle, and (4) to provide insight into how the lessons of the past can inform the future. Key among these lessons are the power of collective action, the existence of universal human rights, and the political and social efficacy of every individual. Moreover, Vincent Harding suggest that beyond the general reasons for teaching history mentioned above, there is a particularly compelling reason to tell movement history: to reaffirm the role of the young in shaping the world of today.

> Everywhere we turn the central role of young people is obvious, and we are certainly compelled to ask important questions about why young people in Nashville, Birmingham, Atlanta, and later Prague and Leipzig took such responsibility for the future of their people, their nations. Of course such reflection leads naturally to explorations about young people today, about possibilities for their own development that may take them beyond consumerism, limited horizons, and random rebelliousness to a higher level of responsibility and hope. And we need to be prepared to offer our own personal responses when they raise their calls for living models, humane guides on the path of responsible commitment to the expansion of democracy.[2]

Thus, the teaching of movement history, like the teaching of all history, must not only reflect an understanding of the past; it must also inform the present so that we may enable the young to envision and enact a better future.

Yet, if we examine how movement history is presented, it becomes clear that there is a discrepancy between what we want from movement history and how that history is recorded in American history textbooks. What we find is that movement history is subject to the same critique that Nathan Huggins offered of slave history: frozen in time and space creating the illusion that movement history is "aberrant and marginal to the main story of American History."[3]

This discrepancy between what we want from movement history and how movement history is presented is in part constructed by the desire of many scholars to capture the movement as a clearly definable event or set of events with a beginning, end, and neat chain of cause and effect[4] and, the need within the liberal establishment (who must indeed publish these works and finance these films) to make the story of the movement part of the master narrative of the United States' "great march forward." They have, as Huggins says, "conspired with the Founding Fathers to create a national history, teleologically bound to the Founder's ideals rather than their reality."[5]

Forcibly wedged between 1954 and 1968, movement history has been defined as the history of the civil rights movement, represented by what Adam Fairclough terms the "Montgomery to Memphis time-frame [which] brackets the movement with the leadership of Martin Luther King, Jr., 1955–1968."[6] The history becomes a recounting of national responses to institutional injustices which were surmounted by extraordinary individuals, doing extraordinary things, under extraordinary circumstances. It is little wonder that many young people believe the movement began with Rosa Parks and ended on a hotel balcony in Memphis, and having achieved its primary goal of "voting rights" and the elimination of legalized segregation has little to offer the world of today except for vicarious nostalgic pleasure. In short, our presentation of movement history has robbed it of its most salient purpose: to secure a more promising future.

Clearly, our critique does not apply to every instance in which individuals have captured movement history. However, if the discontinuity between the story movement history has to tell versus the story it is allowed to tell is to be minimized, we will need to reframe the way we define and teach movement history. Part of the reframing will require that we (1) broaden the definition and role of movement history, (2) demarginalize movement history by making it part of American History, and (3) clarify the organizing and mobilizing tradition of the movement.

Redefining Movement History

In the beginning of this chapter we argued that movement history is often defined as the history of the civil rights movement. This limited view of movement history is fed by a belief that in the absence of organized mass demonstration against clear discriminatory practices there is no political movement. But, in fact, movement history has its beginning at that point in time when race was legitimized by whites as a social construct by which Africans and people of African descent could be denied recognition as human beings in the United States of America. Yet, in the midst of the United States' caste system, slaves built and were sustained by their own institution. "The slave," as Huggins says, "created his own means of validation."[7] Accordingly, slaves, in order to create these means of validation, had to engage in what we discuss later as the organizing tradition of the movement.

Locating the beginning of movement history at the first instance of repression is not merely a symbolic redefinition of movement history. Indeed, it is our belief that this redefinition of movement history is the first step in understanding movement history. Embedded in this redefinition are five concepts that stand in direct contrast to the dominant framework by which we understand movement history. First, by locating movement history within the first instance of denial, we suggest that among African-Americans—and supporting whites—there never was a point of wholesale acquiescence and contentment with the conditions of slavery and limited citizenship. Second, the refusal to acquiesce was, in fact, a decision to struggle. Third, the purpose of the struggle was to eradicate the vestiges of legal and economic injustices *and* to build viable and sustainable communities. Fourth, the problems, whether legal or social, could only find their true resolution within the hearts and heads of men and women. Fifth, once located within the hearts of people the problem had no real resolution; communities must always be prepared to engage in resistance and struggle.

If we accept that the movement is ongoing and that the civil rights movement is only part of a long story of movement history, we can then make room for the stories behind the scene that made the well-known events possible. We would begin to deemphasize the work of individuals and focus more on the richness of communities that manage to sustain liberating ideas, values, and commitments in the midst of differential treatment. When we begin to look at movement history this way, we become interested in the influences of individuals—be it Ella Baker, Amzie Moore, Charles Houston, Martin Luther King, Jr., or Malcolm X—because of what it tells us about the collection of people, the community, who informed and supported their efforts and the ideas that united people rather than what it tells us about the greatness of particular individuals. Moreover, in accepting the ongoing nature of movement history we are then forced to demarginalize movement history and recognize it as an integral part of American history and not just post-World War II southern U.S. history.

Revising the Context of Twentieth-Century Movement History

Internal resistance to racial oppression laid the foundation for a continuous movement. As historian Leslie Owens explains:

> . . . for most blacks, resistance to American society's oppressive features has been an almost automatic part of their personality and identity in historical touch with the earliest days of the overseas trade. Whereas Western scholarship has

frequently confused resistance with bloodshed as a fundamental ingredient, Africans have often perceived it as an inner stance coiled to preserve identity. . . . Africans (blacks) have continued to think of themselves as the people of soul and humanity, which is in fact the most forceful resistance they could offer to a hostile environment deceived by its own democratic impulses."[8]

Prior to the Civil War, public resistance was circumscribed by the institution of slavery, and the disfranchisement of free blacks, though it found continuous manifestations in individual acts of resistance, slave rebellions, and political activism among free blacks. Emancipation and the Reconstruction amendments, which secured the guarantees of full citizenship for African Americans, transformed the terrain of struggle. Implementation of the fourteenth and fifteenth amendments was negotiated throughout the Reconstruction period as newly freed black men and women defied southern terror and lawlessness and laid claim to the political rights and responsibilities of citizenship. But the erosion of federal protections and the ascendancy of white supremacy as a national ideology during the late nineteenth century fed the counterrevolution in the South and tested the capacity of black Americans to realize the fruits of freedom. From the late nineteenth century on, boycotts of newly segregated street cars, migration, litigation, accommodation, the founding of the National Association for the Advancement of Colored People in 1909, the Harlem Renaissance, and the mass appeal of Marcus Garvey's United Negro Improvement Association fueled the continuing movement for freedom and human dignity in a society that sanctioned racial oppression and disfranchisement.

The ways in which black people have responded individually and collectively to national developments and initiatives in the post-Reconstruction era suggests a creative and multifaceted struggle in a society which systematically denied Afro-Americans basic citizenship rights and the protection of the law. Commenting on his 1918 editorial "Close Ranks," which called for black Americans to support the war effort, W. E. B. Du Bois explained in 1935: "We were in a raging flood, and our only real choice was to fight swimming with the current or to be drowned in impotent opposition."[9]

During the 1930s, the era of the Great Depression and the New Deal, federal activism in the economic life of the nation once again broadened the public arena for resistance and struggle. Robert Weaver observed that "these experiences, for the first time since Reconstruction, demonstrated the potential and importance of a positive racial program in the federal government."[10] The response of African Americans to the challenges and opportunities inherent in the political tumult of the decade helps to illustrate the dynamic and creative nature of movement history in the twentieth century.

Until World War II, the great majority of black Americans lived in the South (more than 80 percent during the 1930s). They were the poorest of the poor in the poorest region in the nation. Struggle within the community was continuous—to make a living, stay healthy, obtain even the most rudimentary education. How and when should the community divert its efforts toward the pursuit of those basic constitutional guarantees which had been denied them by southern state governments at the turn of the century, with the sanction of the United States Supreme Court? In 1896, Booker T. Washington told his people to "cast down your bucket where you are." Du Bois emerged as Washington's most potent critic early in the century and urged struggle on the legal and political front as well. But three decades later he would ask those national civil rights leaders wed to an exclusive focus on gaining legal equality: "Are we to starve to death until we settle color discrimination, or are we to secure the power to fight before we enter battle?"[11]

The question of when and how to engage the broader battle to secure full constitutional rights and protections has been, to a large extent, the function of national developments providing an opening to extend the struggle into the larger political arena. The depression and the expansion of federal power under the New Deal provided such an opportunity. In the wake of total economic collapse, political action and leadership moved to center stage. Franklin D. Roosevelt invigorated the political process and aroused the interests and hopes of people who had never completely secured representation in the national political arena. The pragmatic, open spirit of the New Deal, along with Roosevelt's frequent endorsement of government as a tool for human betterment, provided a focus for the political currents released by the depression. During the 1930s, a southern movement for racial justice and equality interacted with other democratic movements, initiating a sustained, organized movement to compel federal enforcement of the fourteenth and fifteenth amendments.

In 1933, W. E. B. Du Bois told a group of students at Fisk University, "we are on the threshold of a new era. . . . Unless the American Negro today . . . plans exactly how he is to establish a reasonable life . . . he is doomed to be a suppressed and inferior caste in the United States for incalculable time." There was a widespread sense of anticipation and urgency which Roosevelt and the New Deal engaged and provided a national focus for. The rapid expansion of federal involvement in the life of the citizenry through New Deal programs raised serious questions about what this meant for the nearly 80 percent of the country's black citizens who lived under a racial caste system in the South. Black students, working through the Southern Negro Youth Congress, acted on Du Bois' challenge, and joined in helping to organize their community's response to New Deal initiatives.[12]

During the 1930s, a loosely defined, black-led political movement for full participation in the economic recovery effort developed in Washington and throughout the South, interacting with other movements and organizations with a shared commitment to invigorating and expanding the democratic process, and securing economic justice and security as a national priority. Several scholars have examined various aspects of this process as it related to black Americans. But with the important exception of Ralph Bunche's study, *The Political Status of the Negro in the Age of F.D.R.*, they have focused almost exclusively on political developments in Washington, or in northern urban cities where the black vote was a key component of the New Deal coalition of voters that emerged with the 1936 election. These studies reflect a narrow view of politics and the nature of political change, measured primarily by election returns and competition between the two major political parties. Therefore the South, where the great majority of black people were excluded from traditional forms of political participation, has remained peripheral in much of the scholarship of blacks and the New Deal.

Robert Weaver, in an address before the annual convention of the NAACP in 1937, offers a more effective way for understanding the significance of the New Deal programs in terms of the dynamic, continuous struggle of black people. "More important than the factual representation of New Deal programs is the interpretation and analysis of results . . . and the evolution of techniques for the future. Such techniques are survival factors for minorities. Unless a group like ours is constantly developing, consciously or unconsciously, such techniques it will not only fail to advance, but must rapidly loose ground." "The evolution of techniques for the future" is a concept which comes closest to defining the process that engaged black Americans during the New Deal era.[13]

For an understanding of the movement that developed during the 1930s, the interconnectedness between local movements in the South and national developments needs to be established. Indeed, New Deal activists quickly recognized the importance of supporting and strengthening these connections. During the earliest days of the Roosevelt Administration, black interests were represented on Capitol Hill by the NAACP, the newly formed Joint Committee on Economic Recovery, and increasingly by a handful of black professionals working in New Deal agencies. Headed by John P. Davis and Robert Weaver, the Joint Committee was especially vigilant in monitoring Congressional hearings on New Deal programs, and representing black interests in proceedings for establishing wage and hour codes under the National Industrial Recovery Act (NRA). Davis, a recent graduate of Harvard Law School, and Weaver, a 26-year-old Harvard Ph.D. in Economics, were among a new generation of black political activists, galvanized by the Depression and the New Deal.[14] Through organized pressure, the Joint Committee did succeed in defeating provisions for a racial wage differential, which would have provided federal sanction of southern racial policies. However, white southern subterfuge persisted and implementation of the equal-wage policy accelerated the displacement of black workers in the South. Late in August 1933, 1,200 black Atlantans gathered in a mass meeting to protest the administration of NRA programs which either displaced black workers or persisted in paying them at a lower scale, in violation of federal regulations. The group pledged their support of Roosevelt, but petitioned that the benefits of the New Deal "be accorded to all citizens alike irrespective of race."[15]

The legalization of labor unions, first under the NRA and then by the Wagner Labor Relations Act, forced the issue of racial discrimination in the trade unions and focused attention on the black community's traditional hostility toward the racially exclusive American labor movement. The NAACP, the Joint Committee, and sympathetic members of the Roosevelt administration protested against federal protection for any groups that discriminated. The NAACP lobbied for an amendment to the Wagner Act that would have denied its benefits to any trade union that discriminated on the basis of race. Senator Robert Wagner himself supported the amendment and attempted to accommodate it, but re-treated under intense pressure from the American Federation of Labor (AFL), which sanctioned all-white unions. The passage of the Wagner Act without an antidiscrimination provision bore further evidence of the fact that appeals for equity and justice were easily eclipsed by the claims of better organized, more powerful white interests. However, key black civil rights activists urged black workers to look beyond this temporary defeat and not concede the labor move-ment to the racist AFL. Younger black leaders like Ralph Bunche, Charles Houston, Robert Weaver, John Davis, Abram Harris, and others believed that interracial labor unity was essential if black workers were to make significant economic progress. They led in building toward such a movement by urging black workers to organize and seeking to promote an effective alliance with white unions through education and organization. In 1934, white and black tenant farmers led the way when they organized the biracial Southern Tenants Farmers Union in Arkansas.[16]

It had become increasingly evident that agitation, litigation, and protest, long the primary mode of the national NAACP, was insufficient in meeting the economic plight of black Americans and the challenges and opportunities presented by the New Deal. Access to the process at the national level without the backing of an organized, politically effective constituency placed black people at a great disadvantage, particularly as a counterweight to southern conservatives, the dominant faction within the Democratic Party and one of the strongest forces in Congress. In the spring of 1935, the Joint Committee on National Recovery and the Social Science Division of Howard University sponsored a national conference "devoted to surveying the position of, and of suggesting a way out for, the Negro in the current economic crisis." While a broad range of political ideologies were represented at the meeting, nearly all participants called for a mass-based organization of blacks (either separately or in a class-based alliance with whites) for effective political action and representation.[17]

Such efforts were already underway in the South, having roots in the early years of the depression. Robin Kelley's *Hammer and Hoe: Alabama Commu-nists during the Great Depression* provides the most comprehensive survey of the development of indigenous political movements in a southern state during this period. Kelley chronicles the ways in which Communist Party organizers, having established a regional headquarters in Birmingham, interacted with mostly black working-class people around immediate concerns—unemploy-ment relief, the desperate plight of the rural poor, police brutality—to aid in organizing collective action, and in the development of local leadership. Neighborhood relief committees and the Share Cropper's Union were among the organizations that grew up during the early 1930s. The Scottsboro case enhanced the Party's reputation as a "race" organization among large segments of the black community and demonstrated the Party's effectiveness in focusing national and international attention on racial injustice in the South. The Party also became the lightening rod for antiradical and racist sentiments, targeted by antisedition laws and widespread police repression. From the start, the struggle for economic, racial, and political reform was necessarily accompanied by a continuing effort to maintain and expand civil liberties and constitutional protections.[18]

NAACP Legal Counsel Charles Houston contrasted the effectiveness of Communist Party organizers in the South with the white-collar approach of the NAACP. The NAACP confined "active fighting . . . to a few top leaders." The Communist Party, however "links all of its members into active struggle for the program. Every . . . member . . . feels that he carries the revolution on his shoulders." Through its efforts to organize sharecroppers in Alabama and its activity in the Scottsboro case, Houston observed that the Party had "done a great job of infusing a spirit of courage and action into the Negro masses." He told NAACP Secretary Walter White in 1934 that "the work of the next decade will have to be concentrated in the South." In organizing the protracted legal campaign against unequal education in the South, Houston continually worked to stretch the traditional structure of the NAACP, revive and expand local branches, and make the organization a vehicle for community organizing and political action in the South. For Houston, this was essential to a successful legal campaign. The enforcement of legal victories would depend on an organized and politically active community.[19]

With the active support and encouragement of Charles Houston and Thurgood Marshall, both of whom spent much time visiting communities throughout the South, NAACP membership and branch activity in the region accelerated during the late 1930s. A closer examination of NAACP activity in the South during the 1930s would contribute to a fuller understanding of the origins of sustained, organized movements. In South Carolina, Osceola McKaine, Secretary of the Sumter branch, expanded NAACP membership around the teacher salary equalization campaign. In Birmingham, the Popular Front invigorated the local NAACP branch. NAACP activity in Texas provides an example of how a liberal interpretation of the New Deal's mandate sparked the organization of a statewide network of NAACP branches.

Maceo Smith, head of the Dallas branch of the NAACP, became race relations officer for the Federal Housing Authority in 1938. White housing officials refused to let a black administrator share the FHA office in Fort Worth, so the FHA quartered Smith in a Dallas housing project, assigned him a secretary, and allotted him travel funds to tour projects throughout the state. Interpreting his assignment, he reasoned that racial relations could best be improved by securing equal opportunities for blacks through the work of the NAACP. Smith's superiors in Washington concurred with his assessment. His Dallas office became the nerve center for a statewide NAACP. He maintained a voluminous correspondence with local branch officers, convened frequent exec-utive council meetings at his Dallas office, and helped to mold a working organization of the NAACP's state leaders.[20]

Since the late nineteenth century, legal restrictions, backed up by terror and intimidation, had placed the ballot box beyond nearly all black Southerners. In the South, therefore, the right to vote was essential to securing all other benefits and protections of citizenship. During the 1930s, the effort to participate in the electoral process became primary to the movement, as well as a vehicle for community organizing. Ralph Bunche traveled through the South in the late thirties and reported on mock election campaigns for black mayors in several southern cities, and growing movements among black Southerners to at least attempt to register and vote "despite the hardships frequently imposed by registrars." As early as 1934, blacks in South Carolina and Georgia began to systematically petition State Democratic Committees to break the color bar to primary elections. South Carolina voting rights activist John McCray linked the revival of black political activism in his state directly to Roosevelt and the New Deal. McCray explained that black people, in their desire to endorse the Roosevelt program of jobs and relief, "turned serious thought to voting." They reasoned, he continued, that "just as the government had filled their empty stomachs . . . it might be used to break racial discriminations, remove police brutalities, establish equal opportunity in education, employment, and eliminate jim crowism."[21]

In 1938, President Roosevelt and Southerners in his administration endorsed the political changes that had taken hold in the South and linked them to a national effort to liberalize the Democratic Party. With the emergence of the New Deal coalition of labor, northern black and urban voters in 1936, the Democratic Party became the national majority party, threatening the dominant position of its conservative anti-New Deal southern wing. Roosevelt attempted to hurry Party realignment along in 1938 when he responded directly to southern opponents of the New Deal. Charging that they were wed to a feudal economic system that had long crippled the development of southern resources and people, Roosevelt urged southern voters to turn out three senators and two congressmen. The failure of the "purge" effort underscored the fact that Roosevelt's most loyal constituencies in the South could not vote. The President endorsed plans for a regionwide interracial conference of New Deal supporters and personally urged the organizers to give primary attention to ridding the South of disfran-chisement laws and to expanding political participation. The Southern Confer-ence for Human Welfare (SCHW), founded in Birmingham in 1938, would play an active role in supporting and expanding the "Democratic Front" that had cohered around the New Deal by the late 1930s. During the next decade, movements originating in black communities, among the newly organized industrial unions, and among progressive white Southerners would attempt to build a coalition of voters and organizations that could effectively counter conservative dominance of the Democratic Party in the South, thus making the

Democratic Party an effective vehicle for advancing racial and economic justice. By 1946, an estimated 600,000 black southerners had registered to vote, three times the number that had been registered in 1940.[22]

This brief outline should suggest the ways in which early movement efforts in black communities developed and interacted with other political movements as well as national developments during the 1930s. The Double V for Victory campaign of World War II and the growth of NAACP branches during the war years needs to be understood within this context. Black Americans led in linking wartime rhetoric to movements for freedom and democracy at home. But in doing so, they were building on the democratic political culture that developed during the 1930s, as well as the associations and connections that had grown up during that decade. A fuller exploration of this rich legacy is essential before historians can fully understand the significance of World War II developments in the South, within the Democratic Party, and nationally.

The movement of the 1930s and 1940s succeeded in placing civil rights on the national agenda. During 1948, Harry Truman ordered the desegregation of the armed forces and the Democratic Party adopted a civil rights plank in the national party platform which caused Southern conservatives to bolt the Democratic Party and run their own candidate for president on the States Rights Party ticket. These actions also ensured that Harry Truman would keep the crucial northern black vote in the Democratic Party's column, a key element in the closely contested presidential race that year.

By the late 1940s, the democratic culture of the New Deal era was eclipsed by the Cold War, and this had important consequences for the southern movement. President Truman's halting civil rights initiatives were accompanied by the implementation of a loyalty program which, historian Ellen Schrecker explains, "succeeded in establishing anticommunism as the nation's official political ideology," preparing the way for McCarthyism.[23] Historians and teachers need to examine how domestic Cold War policies effected the democratic, inclusive southern movement that emerged during the New Deal era. What are the connections between civil rights and civil liberties in the struggle for racial justice? In evaluating Truman's civil rights policies, historians must take into account the ways in which anticommunism and the retreat on civil liberties effected movements to expand political participation in the South and reenforced racist and antidemocratic forces in the South. Such an understanding might aid in explaining the dichotomy that existed in 1954, and its consequences. By the time the Brown decision secured legal equity, the democratic activism of the 1940s had been thoroughly eclipsed by a resurgent Southern conservatism; the forces of white supremacy dominated the politics of the region and the national Democratic Party.

Clarifying the Organizing Tradition

Acknowledging the central role of movement history in American history also requires that we expand our understanding of the activity within movement history to include both the mobilizing tradition and the organizing tradition of the movement. The clarification of this distinction is paramount to meeting one of the goals in teaching movement history: to reaffirm the role of the young in shaping the world of today.

When we speak of the mobilizing tradition within the movement, we are addressing those activities that are mounted to bring pressure on existing systems to facilitate change. It is this tradition that is at the heart of the popular portrayal of post-World War II movement history. Accordingly, the civil rights movement—as this era is referred to—is presented as the story of a popular black uprising culminating in mass demonstrations, boycotts, and marches orchestrated by spirited and moving organizers and leaders in response to the common suffering by black Americans. This story then is carried forth by focusing post-World War II movement history on seminal events—Montgomery, the March on Washington, or Selma—and the people and organizations that facilitated these events—Martin Luther King, Jr., James Farmer, Ralph Abernathy, Congress on Racial Equality (CORE), Student Nonviolent Coordinating Committee (SNCC), and Southern Christian Leadership Conference (SCLC).

The focus on the mobilizing activity of post-World War II movement activity is in part a reaction to the advent of television. Television changed the entire political landscape of the United States. Beginning with Edward R. Morrow's broadcast between 1953 and 1954 on the McCarthy hearings to the televised hearings on Clarence Thomas' nomination to the United States Supreme Court, the impact of television on the American consciousness is evident. Perhaps the two most important events in television's influences were the decisions to move from a 15-minute news format to a 30-minute news format in 1963 and to increase network competition through the advent of the rating system.[24] These two events, and the rhetorical liberalism of the 1960s, opened the way for television to depict social conflict even if only as a means of attracting a larger audience.

As television began to bring the American public more and more images of the nation's social conflicts, it inevitably shaped the form in which effective social conflict would be defined. The decision to carry an event on television became more dependent on the dramatic effect of the imagery than the substance of the issues. Moreover, legitimacy would be defined by one's ability to capture the media rather than one's support from or connection to the community. As Kellner notes, "by appearing on television, oppositional movements acquired legitimacy and attracted audiences to their struggles. Such tactics also inspired other oppositional groups to emulate the actions and tactics portrayed" and provided a means for the messages and struggles of the movement to inform the direction of other social groups.[25]

Today, most social movements accept this process of events by acknowledging its debt to the "civil rights movement." In fact, the public perception forged by television that the movement is the story of mobilization for mass demonstration is even articulated as justification for the current efforts of

Operation Rescue. Such an abomination of the movement is in part possible because of the lack of attention to the organizing tradition within the movement, a tradition which is at the heart of the viability and longevity of the movement.

The organizing tradition differs from the mobilizing tradition by one key ingredient: its purpose is to build a political infrastructure within a community that will sustain it over time in its efforts to mount struggles against injustices. In short, the organizing tradition is steeped in the building and sustaining of community and serves as the backbone of the movement. It is what León-Portilla terms the ecosis, "the process of making or building a house" that all cultures under siege must engage in if they are to survive.[26] At the heart of the organizing tradition or ecosis is a recognition of the long haul. This tradition accepts that the process of change while inevitable is in actuality slow, even in the midst of a will to change.[27] What the organizing tradition does is forge the maintenance of community by building a language that makes it possible for communities to continue the struggle amidst great odds and great terror.

This language of transition, as we refer to it, is at the heart of the distinction between the organizing and mobilizing traditions. In each of these traditions there is what is commonly termed a language of critique. It is this form of talk that allows us to understand the injustices that exist in the world. There is also a language of possibility which provides for us the vision of the world for which we strive. Perhaps the most notable example of this is Martin Luther King, Jr.'s "I Have A Dream" speech. But between the critique and the possibility lies change. In the mobilization tradition, the language for this change is the language of action and the language affirmation. It is in the language of action that one hears the call for solutions (legal or political) to pressing problems. The language of affirmation serves to acknowledge the rights of people to make these calls for action. Willie Ricks shouting of "Black Power" is one example of this language of affirmation.

Without disregarding any of these languages, the organizing tradition added and put at center stage another language: the language of transition. The language of transition differs from the others in that it is centered around the process of change. This language recognizes the personal struggle each of us must go through as we hold on to the dream while simultaneously acknowledging the limits of the world we must struggle in. In short, the language of transition is about making real the lived experiences of people who must live with and through changes on a day to day basis. Part of that transitional effort for people is to continue to act in a world which does not support what one believes in.

This language of transition is evident in the organizing tradition through the use of song, celebration, learning, and talk. Through these mediums, communities were able to acknowledge the problems to be dealt with, envision a goal to be achieved, and maintain and build self-respect while living in conditions that were designed to deny self-respect. Perhaps nowhere is this distinction clearer than in the leadership styles of SCLC and SNCC. SCLC was a more centralized organization clearly led by a strong leader: King. SNCC was a loose coordinating committee established to support democratic process and community-based initiatives.[28]

This localization of authority advocated by veterans of the organizing tradition like Charles Houston, Ella Baker, Amzie More, Bob Moses, and Unita Blackwell—who worked throughout the south in various organizations and communities—was based in a belief in the capacity of self-leadership at the local or community level. Accordingly, when one examines the movement effort in Mississippi between 1960 and 1964, one is struck by the centrality of local control in the organization and direction of local action and mobilization. Clearly, this did not mean that in each community or organization everyone was involved in the setting of every agenda or in following through with each action. What the organizing tradition meant was that the process remained open for people to join in and exit from and served to create leadership from within the ranks of the community.

With this focus on the development of local leadership, it is not surprising that the image and the experience of these authentic community efforts, based in the organizing tradition, "provided some of the central visions of the freedom movement and expressed some of its most vibrant hope and direction."[29] In short, the organizing effort had as its goal the building of a foundation on which issues of the day and issues to come could be addressed without diminishing the ability of the community to respond in the future. The legacy of this tradition can be seen today in the Algebra Project and the Mississippi Community Foundation. The Algebra Project is a community-based program developed as a response to the ever-increasing role of mathematical competence as prerequisite for full participation in the economy. Through its curricular process, the Algebra Project seeks to build a network of adults—parents, educators, school administrators, and community leaders—who understand the social and political implications of mathematics education for their children. The aim is to educate the broader minority community to the critical importance of algebra and to organize that community to ensure access to algebra for *all* minority students.

The Mississippi Community Foundation (MCF) is a statewide grass-roots organization established to support the establishment of community development initiatives among African Americans in Mississippi society. Founded in November of 1990, MCF started as a response to efforts by film producers to create a feature-length film on the Mississippi Freedom Movement. Drawing on the organizing tradition that characterized their work in the Movement effort in Mississippi, civil rights workers, freedom fighters, movement families, and community members approached about the film created MCF to ensure that those who made the story of the movement possible would benefit from its telling and retelling and to create a means for movement communities to take ownership of their stories. These stories of peoples lives are their personal capital and MCF provides a way to pool that capital so it has meaning. Each person's story is meaningless outside the story of the community. The pooled capital of people's movement lives also has value. MCF provides a way to use the capital gained from marketing these stories to reinvest in the communities that made the Mississippi movement story possible.

Conclusion

We began this chapter by distinguishing what we believe to be the central reasons for capturing and teaching movement history. Key among these is the legacy of the movement to the hope of future generations. We went on to argue that to secure this legacy, movement history must be redefined and rooted firmly in the context of American history. This redefinition must begin with the recognition that (1) movement history began with the first instance of repression and (2) this resistance manifests itself through both an organizing and mobilizing tradition.

Our adherence to this perspective stems from our recognition that the current approach to teaching movement history as the story of extraordinary individual leadership from 1954 to 1968 robs the African American communities of their pivotal role in the shaping and framing of movement (and American) history, and their potential in shaping the world of today and tomorrow. It is incumbent on historians and educators that they do not continue to contribute to the disenfranchisement of the African American community from its history.

Clearly, this represents a real challenge for the teaching of movement history. As our case study demonstrates, the linkages among issues of race, class, politics, national interest, and ideology are extremely intricate. Yet the intricacy of that particular period is mirrored throughout the movement and American history. Consequently, no matter where you "cast down your bucket" in the study of movement history, the linkages to compelling issues of American history will reveal themselves, if you have framed movement history as we suggest.

Accordingly, no matter where you look in history, you will begin to tap into a process that demonstrates the capacity of ordinary people to mount multiple forms of resistance and construct alternative forms for building a dialectical process that will sustain resistance over time. Such a presentation of history enables students to hold Nathan Huggins' "deforming mirror of truth" to the images of the day that deny them and their communities a sense of political efficacy. Through this reframing of movement history, we can offer the hope that is essential to encourage the young to take hold of their responsibility for the future. For until we can find pride, honor, and hope in the work of the communities of 10, 20, 30, and 70 years ago, we cannot begin to find pride and hope in the communities we live in today. Moreover, unless we as historians and educators have that hope, it is unlikely that we can reframe movement and American history for others. Toward that end, we recommend that you begin your quest for understanding the hope that can be found in movement history by reading Vincent Hardings' *Hope and History*.[30] It is there that you will come to see the centrality of movement history to our understanding of the history of the United States and the possibilities for our future.

Notes

1. This chapter is based on a talk presented at the Annual Conference of the Association for the Study of Afro-American Life and History, Washington, D.C., 31 October–2 November 1991.

2. Vincent Harding, *Hope and History: Why We Must Share the Story of the Movement* (New York: ORBIS, 1990), 8.

3. Nathan I. Huggins, *Black Odyssey: The African American Ordeal in Slavery* (New York: Vintage Books, 1990), xxxiii.

4. Adam Fairclough, "State of the Art: Historians and the Civil Rights Movement," *Journal of American Studies* 24(3) (1990): 398.

5. Huggins, *Black Odyssey,* p. xii.

6. Fairclough, "State of the Art," p. 387.

7. Huggins, *Black Odyssey,* p. xxv.

8. Leslie H. Owens, "The African Garden: Reflections about New World Slavery and Its Lifetime," in *The State of Afro-American History: Past, Present and Future,* ed. Darlene Clark Hine (Baton Rouge, LA: Louisiana State University Press, 1986), 35.

9. W. E. B. Du Bois, "Social Planning for the Negro, Past and Present," *Journal of Negro Education* 16 (1) (1936): 121.

10. Robert Weaver, "The Impact of the New Deal upon Blacks and their Participation in World War II Production," paper delivered before the Association for the Advancement of Science, Washington, D.C., 15 February 1978, p. 13.

11. Du Bois, "Social Planning for the Negro," p. 122.

12. Johnetta Richards, "The Southern Negro Youth Congress," dissertation, University of Cincinnati, 1989.

13. Robert C. Weaver, "The Negro and the Federal Government," speech delivered at the twenty-eighth meeting of the National Association for the Advancement of Colored People, Detroit, MI, 30 June 1937. NAACP Papers (microfilm), reel 9.

Robert Weaver was born in Washington, D.C. in 1907. He was part of a small group of black students at Harvard University in the early 1930s whose personal strivings and social concerns were galvanized by the devastating impact of the depression in the black community. Weaver went on to join the Roosevelt Administration as a Special Advisor on Negro Affairs in November 1933, working with Secretary of Interior Harold Ickes. Weaver developed the first affirmative, no-discrimination policy, which mandated a minimum number of skilled black workers be included in the construction of federally funded public housing projects. Robert Weaver published two major books which document the impact of federal policies, and the persistence and pervasiveness of racial discrimination in employment and housing: *Negro Labour* (1946) and *The Negro Ghetto* (1948). Robert Weaver was a leading figure in the informal "Black Cabinet" within the Roosevelt administration and became the first black person to serve in a Presidential Cabinet when Lyndon

Johnson appointed him Secretary of Housing and Urban Development (HUD). See Robert C. Weaver, "Blending Scholarship with Public Service," *Sage Race Relations Abstract* 16 (Nov. 1991): 4–16.

14. Other members of the group included John P. Davis, Ralph Bunche, and William Hastle. Weaver and Davis organized themselves as the Negro Industrial League (which became the Joint Committee on Economic Recovery) and lobbied the Roosevelt administration and Congress for full inclusion of black workers in the New Deal recovery program.

15. Raymond Walters, *Negros and the Great Depression: The Problem of Economic Recovery* (West Port, CN: Greenwood Publishing Co., 1970), 98, 168.

16. Wolters, "Negros and the Great depression," 183–192.

17. The main papers read at the conference were published in the *Journal of Negro Education* 16 (1) (1936).

18. Robin Kelley, *Hammer and Hoe: Alabama Communists during the Great Depression* (Chapel Hill, NC: University North Carolina Press, 1990); P. Sullivan, interview with Rob Hall, Communist Party district organizer for Alabama, 1934–41, 11 Oct. 1991. For the history of the Scottsboro case, see Dan T. Carter, *Scottsboro: A Tragedy of the American South* (Baton Rouge, LA: Louisiana State University Press, 1969).

19. Extracts from statement by Charles H. Houston in a debate with Bernard Ades before the Liberal Club of Howard University on the Scottsboro case, 28 March 1935, NAACP Papers (microfilm), reel 16; C. H. Houston memo for Mr. White and Mr. Wilkins, 15 July 1935, Box I, G-14, NAACP Papers, Library of Congress. For an account of the life and times of Charles Houston, see Genna Rae McNeil, *Groundwork: Charles Hamilton Houston and the Struggle for Civil Rights* (Philadelphia: University of Pennsylvania Press, 1985).

20. Michael Gillette, "The NAACP in Texas," dissertation, University of Texas, 1984, pp. 14–15.

21. Ralph Bunche, *The Political Status of the Negro in the Age of FDR*, Edited and with introduction by Dewey W. Grantham (Chicago: University of Chicago Press 1973), 72, 87–88; Palmer Webb, "The Negro Vote in the South," *Virginia Spectator* (Nov. 1938), John McCray, "The Changing South: Negro Citizens Seize the Opportunity to Vote," AP News Feature, undated, John McCray Papers, Caroliniana Library, University of South Carolina. Also see Patricia Sullivan, "The New Deal and the Movement's Foundation," in *New Directions in Civil Rights Studies*, eds. Armstead Robinson and Patricia Sullivan (Charlottesville: University Press of Virginia, 1991).

22. Luther P. Jackson, "Race and Suffrage in the South Since the 1940," *New South* (June/July 1948): 4.

23. Ellen Schrecker, *No Ivory Tower: McCarthyism and the Universities* (New York: Oxford University Press, 1986), 4–6.

24. Douglas Kellner, *Television and the Crisis of Democracy* (Boulder, CO: Westview Press, 1990), 46.

25. Kellner, *Television and the Crisis of Democracy*, p. 56.

26. Miguel León-Portilla, *Endangered Cultures* (Dallas, TX: Southern Methodist University Press, 1990).

27. Aldon D. Morris, *The Origins of the Civil Rights Movement: Black Communities Organizing for Change.* (New York: The Free Press, 1984).

28. Morris, *The Origins of the Civil Rights Movement*, p. 120–138.

29. Vincent Harding, "Community as a Liberating Theme in Civil Rights History," in *New Directions in Civil Rights Studies*, eds. A. Robinson and P. Sullivan (Charlottesville: University Press of Virginia, 1991), 18.

30. Harding, *Hope and History*.

Part IV

School Structures that Foster Multicultural Education

Shifting the Power, Shifting the Players

13

One Step Among Many
Affirming Identity in Anti-Racist Schools
Kathy Greeley and Linda Mizell

In their 1989 study of adolescent identity formation, Aries and Moorehead concluded that unlike White teenagers, who tend to be preoccupied with ideological and sexual–interpersonal issues, the single most important factor in shaping Black teens' sense of self is race. Their findings come as no revelation to many educators—Black ones who have accumulated a lifetime of profound personal experience, as well as other astute observers—who also recognize that even before adolescence, the effects of institutional racism begin to eat away at the positive racial identity of black youth and provide a distorted sense of self and of racial superiority to white ones.[1]

Schools play a central role in perpetuating institutional racism and, likewise, can play an equal role in combatting it. Hilliard and Pine offer as a model of anti-racist schools those "characterized by intervention programs to counteract racism, by diverse teaching staffs, by truly multicultural curricula, by appropriate pedagogical practices, by high expectations, and by continuing emphasis on the development of character and self-esteem . . ."[2]

When a school begins to engage in the process of multicultural, anti-racist change, the expectations of all faculty, parents, and children are raised. However, priorities are likely to be different for each of those groups, and even break down along racial lines within the groups. Administrators may be preoccupied, for instance, with the changing demographics of the student body, whereas teachers may think solely in terms of the curriculum, with neither giving a great deal of thought to the overall climate of the school.

But even if the school attempts to address only curriculum, the social fabric of the school is inevitably altered: children of color are given the implicit message, often for the first time, that they have a right to be there and to have their needs met. In an institution where they constitute the racial minority, they—and for that matter, their parents, too—may respond by expressing the need for a racial group identity to confidently interact with the larger group.

The formation of racial affinity groups is fraught with fears and anxieties for all kids. White kids fear the loss of friendships with kids of color and can often articulate that fear. What is more difficult for them to acknowledge and express is their fear of losing the inherent power and privilege that accrue by virtue of race to Whites. How many White children (or adults) are even aware of the fact that unlike their Black or Asian or Latino peers, it is not only possible but probable that they will regularly find themselves in an all-White academic or social grouping without any effort on their part? For children who are unaccustomed to being excluded from anything on the basis of race, an all-Black group can prove threatening.

Conversely, kids of color fear the repercussions of asserting their racial identities and consequently challenging power relationships. Not infrequently, social acceptance by their White peers has been predicated either on their assuming a submissive role in the group, or on providing their White friends access to the seductive aspects of their culture—music, dress, vernacular—while avoiding any allusion to the negative impact of American racism. To even raise such issues is likely to create the perception that they are "preoccupied" with race, or to earn them reputations as troublemakers or divisive elements, from their peers as well as their teachers.

All these responses are understandable given the fact that, in most cases, kids are expected to shift from the prevailing model of multiculturalism which emphasizes either "color-blindness" or a superficial celebration of differences to a model that encourages confrontation of racism and its institutional affect.

Faced with the uncomfortable process of confronting these fears and anxieties, kids (as well as teachers and parents) typically counter with charges of "reverse racism," usually with little or no understanding of what that means. By focusing on the perceived "divisiveness" of racial affinity groups as the primary issue, they tend to diffuse discussion of the issue that prompted the formation of the group in the first place—isolation, exclusion, and lack of affirmation for the kids of color.

A less typical but more productive response is the willingness to risk engaging in the uncertain process of honest confrontation. In such a process, the discussion shifts away from the decision to form racial affinity groups, and instead addresses the larger issue of the social and academic climate for *all* the children in the school. It requires an understanding that final resolution—or even a conflict-free resolution—of any given situation is not always possible or even desirable. Conflict must be seen as part of an ongoing process in which people are likely to offer challenge, to hurt feelings, to make mistakes, but ultimately to learn from them.

Although each institution varies in its particulars, the primary issues and responses will be similar in any setting where kids of color are in a minority. It is important to note, however, that the same underlying attitudes and assumptions are present even—or perhaps *especially*—in an all-White institution. The presence of significant numbers of children of color simply hastens the implementation of some process that brings those issues and assumptions to the surface. That process is evident in the experiences of two progressive elementary schools, one public and one private, both located in Cambridge, Massachusetts.

In each school, the formation of affinity groups for Black kids prompted a series of discussions and actions.

Kathy Greeley is a White teacher who works with her students on a variety of formal and informal extracurricular activities. Her initial role in the creation of a Black Student Union was that of an advocate and supporter, and later as a mediator in the often heated discussion that took place in formal and informal groups.

Linda Mizell helped initiate a group for Black children in her school. She is an African American, and until recently, one of only two adults of color at the school. She describes the process from the perspective of her intimate involvement with the kids' group and the Black parent group, as well as with the larger community in her role as an administrator.

As parents, as educators, as key players in the formation of racial affinity groups and the attendant controversy surrounding their formation, we offer to share those experiences.

*   *   *

As you walk up the front steps of the Graham and Parks Alternative Public School, you are greeted with an intricate mosaic that depicts a multiracial group of children playing together. Phrases from the song, "If I Had A Hammer" punctuate the mural. Go up the steps and you enter the first-floor corridor. There, welcoming visitors into the school, is a larger-than-life size mural that has at its center two Black women. One of them is Saundra Graham, an activist and politician from the neighborhood where the school is located. The other figure is Rosa Parks, the seamstress and civil rights activist who inspired the Montgomery bus boycott in 1956. The artist shows Ms. Parks surrounded by a group of children, Black, White, and Asian. Her hands are reaching out to them. The rest of the mural is a splash of vivid color that depicts scenes from the bus boycott, people marching on Washington, multicolored hands holding up a globe, and a chain being broken by a book. On the left side of the mural are five silhouettes of children in motion. Inside each shadow appears scenes from different cultures: Haitian, Greek, Central American, Irish, and native American.

Graham and Parks is a K–8 alternative public school with a population of 400 students, located in a racially and economically diverse neighborhood in Cambridge, Massachusetts. Classes are multigraded (1st/2nd, 3rd/4th, etc.), and are heterogeneously grouped. Fifty-one percent of the students are of color and 49 percent are White. Approximately one-third of the students in the school are Haitian because the city's primary Haitian bilingual program is housed here. For an urban school, it has a fairly large middle-class population, which is predominantly White.

The school staff is committed to multicultural education. Artwork reflecting a wide variety of cultures is exhibited throughout the building. The library

217

exhibits a broad range of authors and histories. Teachers, most of whom do not use textbooks, are careful to choose a diversity of literature. Students study native American cultures, the civil rights movement, Caribbean culture (particularly Haiti), Africa, and Central America, as well as American history.

Better integration of bilingual and monolingual students has been a goal for several years now. While slow, progress is being made. Morning announcements are made in both English and Haitian Creole. Some monolingual classes are learning conversational Creole. Pairs of classrooms, bilingual and monolingual, are beginning to work together on a variety of curriculum projects.

In spite of the school's commitment to providing a multicultural environment where all children feel welcome and represented, there are still problems. Perhaps given the intersection of racial (and class) tensions with the identity crisis of adolescence, these problems are most intensely manifested in the seventh and eighth grade. Unlike the self-contained classrooms of the lower grades, junior high students are based with a homeroom teacher, but travel to others for some of their subjects. There is an active Student Council, and the peer mediation program has been quite successful. Students feel they have a voice in the school and have been involved in developing school rules and various policies. Various issues are discussed in a biweekly community meeting that involves all seventh- and eighth-grade students and staff. There is very little overt racism. Students know there will be serious consequences for racist or sexist remarks. There are few fights in general, and even fewer are motivated by race. And yet, students comment consistently that teachers are "just not seeing it."

But teachers do see problems. They see the tensions between groups of students, which often break down around racial lines and then are compounded by class differences. Students sit with their friends at lunch and hang out with their buddies at the park during recess. It is the exception rather than the norm for students to cross racial and class lines to form friendships.

The seventh- and eighth-grade teachers have been particularly concerned about academic issues. Students of color seem to lack confidence in their academic ability. Often they are reluctant to express their views in a class discussion. Or they will refuse to read a good essay or poem that they wrote aloud to the class. When asked for his opinion, it is not uncommon for a student to mutter "I don't know" and stare at his desk. Or a student will raise her hand, wave it madly in the air in response to a question and when called on will say "Oh, forget it." And if pushed to answer, a student may offer a wonderful insight to the class discussion and then finish it off with "I know that's wrong."

A couple of years ago, as the seventh- and eighth-grade teacher team evaluated the school year that had just ended, several teachers expressed frustration around these concerns. How could we support these students of color to feel more empowered in school? After discussing a number of ways to positively reinforce students' academic success, the Haitian bilingual teacher proposed, "How about forming a Black Student Union?" It would be a support group for both African American and Haitian children to talk about their experiences growing up Black in America. By providing a forum in which to discuss these issues, the students would feel a greater sense of solidarity and belonging. The rest of the staff was enthusiastic about the idea, and it was decided that it would be introduced to the students in September.

At one of our early community meetings that next September, Josiane (the bilingual teacher) addressed students about the idea of a support group for Black students in the school. As she talked about the differences in experience between White and Black children and the need for Black students to come together to share their stories with each other, the tension in the room grew thick. She had barely finished speaking when the room erupted. Students were all talking at once, arguing with each other, heads were pumping up and down, and hands waved in the air.

"Yeah, we like this idea!"

"You can't do that. It's not fair!"

"It's about time!"

"It's not right to have a separate group like that. That's discrimination!"

"You're only saying that 'cause you're white!"

"That's racist!"

"All our lives you've told us we should get along together. Now you're intentionally driving a wedge between us."

We established some semblance of order and proceeded to have a very heated discussion about the purpose of a Black Student Union, the necessity for such a group, whether or not Whites would be excluded, the ethical issues of exclusion and inclusion, the legal issues of "special interest" groups, the philosophy of the school. A few Black students became vocal defenders of the idea. A number of White students protested vehemently. They felt that all their lives they had been taught the importance of integration. They said they could understand that Black students might experience racism in their lives and be discriminated against, but that school should be one place where those divisions weren't made. The Black students retorted that they didn't see why they should be prevented from getting together just because it made White kids uncomfortable. It didn't mean they hated Whites, they just wanted to be with their own. Some White students countered that that was just reverse discrimination, and anyway, racism wasn't really a problem anymore.

A wide spectrum of views were expressed. Some White students supported the idea. Some Black students seemed indifferent. Some Black students feared the loss of their White friends and felt terribly torn by the discussion. Some White students felt angry that *their* issues and problems were not being addressed. What united all views was pain, pain in struggling to unravel the deep complexities of racism in our society.

The meeting ended unresolved. Some students left the room in tears, others in anger, and others ready to go to lunch and recess. Passionate discussions continued in classrooms, over lunch, and out at the playground. We had one or two more community meetings where students continued to debate the issue, but, over time, most students, Black and White, came to accept the idea. The

BSU began to meet on a biweekly basis during lunch with the support of three Black staff (a kindergarten teacher, the seventh/eighth-grade bilingual teacher, and a classroom aide). About 15–20 students met, some African American, some Haitian, a few Hispanics, and one White. The tension over the group died down considerably, but it did not disappear.

Students active in the BSU decided to produce a play about their history. They worked on it intensively, often on their own time, and that April, they announced that they were ready to perform their original play. The play was about a "nerdy" girl who goes to a school dance. She is so clumsy that no one will dance with her. She persuades two of the "hot" dancers to come over to her house to teach her some steps. When they show up there the next day, they notice that the pictures on her bedroom wall are not of music stars. "Who are they?" they ask. The pictures are of Harriet Tubman, Rosa Parks, and Martin Luther King. As the girl describes the contributions of these people to the struggle for justice and equality, other students act out the stories in front of them. The final scene of the play takes place at the next school dance where the girls talk about the importance of knowing your own history, and the three of them break into fancy dance steps together. The play was so well-received by the junior high students, they urged the Black Student Union to perform it for the whole school.

The following September, a group of students (rather than a staff person) announced at a community meeting that the Black Student Union would begin meeting the next Friday. While there was some discussion and debate reminiscent of the previous year, the response of the majority of the students, Black and White, was quite accepting.

It is unclear whether the existence of this group and the great success of their first dramatic production significantly changed racial dynamics in the school. It clearly has improved relations between many Haitian and African American students, previously a source of great friction. It has also boosted the self-confidence of some of the students. It is difficult to measure these things. However, the staff felt that simply acknowledging the difficult and complex issues of race relations has been an important first step towards creating a more democratic school environment.

* * *

One glance at the exterior walls of Cambridge Friends School lets the visitor know that this is a place which kids call their own. Panel after painted panel boasts abstract designs, scenes from the school's history, and along the rear wall, self-portraits of the lower school children. The front wall, however, the one that surrounds the main entrance to the building, grew out of a popular third- and fourth-grade curriculum unit. Greek gods, goddesses, and heroes, all with fair skin and blue eyes, most with blonde hair, float along a blue-sky background.

A number of people have told me that they found this scene delightful and inviting. Others say that each time they enter the school, the mural strikes them as an overwhelming statement of the school's *whiteness*. An Indian parent confided that she and her husband had first visited the school three years earlier, at the sight of the Greeks, they had looked at each other, gotten back in their car and driven away.

For much of its history, the murals have very nearly reflected the racial makeup of the the student body. Prior to 1988, despite the fact that Black children accounted for more than half the children of color in the school, it was not uncommon to find a lone African American boy and/or girl in each grade. In some classes, there have been no children of color.

As Mary Johnson, Head of School has reflected, our recent anti-racism work, particularly over this past year, helped us to see that although Cambridge Friends School was a fine school, it was not as fine for some students as it was for others.

My son, who until fourth grade was the only African American boy in his grade and one of two in his mixed-grade class, confessed that during those years he had been ashamed of being Black. When I asked why, his answer was simple: "Because I was the only one." His classmates' assumptions about Black people in general and the urban poor in particular made him uncomfortable, and his tenuous acceptance as an exception to the rule did little to ease his discomfort. Nor did he feel good about his efforts to emotionally distance himself from other black people, however negatively they might be defined.

What made the difference that helped him stop being ashamed and start feeling proud again? "Mostly," he said, "having more Black kids around." But there was more too, things he found more difficult to articulate that had to do with being together and talking about feelings and "all the other stuff that's been going on." I finally realized that he was talking about the Black Kids Group.

When Black parents began to meet informally in 1989, nearly every one of them had at least one story to tell of their child being scapegoated, excluded, and marginalized. In some cases, teachers were oblivious to the situation, and in others they seemed incapable of effectively dealing with it. In all cases, parents had been led to believe that the problems were unique to their child, or resulted from such factors as being "the new kid." In fact, the negative experiences of most kids followed a nearly identical pattern: we were able to list 10 common elements, ranging from being the last one picked for a team, to being either physically or verbally assaulted and then being blamed for the incident.

As parents became aware of these patterns, they also became more attuned to the children's perceptions. One devastating discovery was that Black kids thought it was racist to play with other Black kids. They tried hard to never mention race or racism (and were often mortified when their parents did), but there were little indicators that they did indeed notice: "Which Abby?" "The Black Abby."

In the spring of 1990, our many discussions with Black parents contributed to a growing body of evidence that Black children were indeed taking an

221

emotional beating in their classrooms. During a Sunday afternoon Black Families meeting the Black Kids Group met for the first time. Anita Howard, a parent trustee and social psychologist by training, spent half an hour talking with the children about how good it felt to be together. She gave them an illustrated packet of poems by such noted children's writers as Eloise Greenfield and Lucille Clifton that talked about friendships, loneliness, playground politics, and other issues that kids face.

While the children met, the parents discussed their expectations for the new group. Although unanimous in their support for the group, they were adamant that this not be a "let's fix the Black kids" measure, but rather a mechanism for affirming and protecting the kids while the school engaged in the process of fixing itself. Another measure which they wholeheartedly endorsed was the hiring of a Black psychologist to consult with faculty, parents, and the school's resident psychologist.

The impact of the group was immediately obvious. One girl had been described by her parents as "outgoing, confident, a leader." They worried about the gradual change in her over the course of the four years she had been at CFS. In class, she was more often quiet, unsure, reluctant to speak up. As a first grader she had mortified her parents by announcing that "Black people aren't teachers"—a logical assumption, considering the virtual absence of Black teachers in the building.

The day after the kids met, she strode confidently into her language group meeting and announced, "I'm going to read a poem." She read three, to the group's enthusiastic approval; and for the first time, her teacher saw the child that her parents had described.

Following that first meeting, notices were sent to all the Black families who had not attended the Sunday meeting, explaining the purpose and format of the group. The children would meet twice a month for the rest of the term during Open Studio (a 45-minute period which, at least theoretically, was unscheduled time throughout the school). Parents were asked to give written permission for their children to participate in the group, although the final decision still lay with each child. Of the 30 Black children in the school, only 1 was denied parental permission.

Focus groups have been around CFS nearly as long as the school has been in existence. They can be initiated by requests from parents, teachers, or the children themselves. The groups are confidential. In the recent past, there have been groups for children in divorced or separated families, for middle school boys on friendship issues, and for gender groups to discuss sexuality. They convene during the school day under the guidance of a faculty or staff member, often the school psychologist.

This was the same procedure which we followed for the Black Kids Group. The group was led by Anita Howard and by me. As Director of Admissions and Development and as the parent of two lower school children, I had a passing acquaintance with all the children, a personal relationship with most. We also met periodically with Jesse Harmon, the Black psychologist who was hired to consult with parents and faculty.

Most of the children were eager to take part in the group. One first-grade boy whose parents had not been at the meeting and had not yet returned his permission form heard about the meeting and simply showed up, adamant that his father wanted him to be there. Other children, unable to contain their excitement over the group, had barely managed to make it through the first part of the day.

But for some children, leaving their classrooms was difficult. They were afraid that they might be penalized by their teachers and classmates for choosing to come to the group instead of staying behind to finish a project. They worried that their White friends would be angry at them, or would exclude them from work or play groups. And for a few who had found safety in racial anonymity, the risk of this nearly public statement of racial affinity was too risky.

Most of that meeting (the first one held during school hours) was devoted to discussion of why the kids were there, why it was hard for some of them, and each person's right to choose. Several kids chose to return to class, with the group's blessing (albeit after a lively and at times heated debate) and the assurance that they would always be welcomed back into the group.

The group spanned kindergarten through eighth grade, and, not surprisingly, different age groups had different needs: the older children felt an urgency to talk about their issues; the younger children, with shorter attention spans and a less clearly defined sense of race and racism, tended to favor more active expressions. A seventh grader suggested that we separate into two groups. We were surprised by the vehemence with which the children rejected that idea. A first grader spoke very eloquently about the need for unity and affirmation and support of each other. An eighth grader, an extremely popular basketball star, said simply, "We have to stick together."

After that, the challenge to the group facilitators was how to find a balance of activities that worked for all the kids. One day we described the games of our youth to the kids. We talked about the cross-age play, about older siblings and friends taking care of the younger children, and then we taught them to play "Little Sally Walker," a ring game. The kids came up with their own updated, gender-free variation, "Little Homey Walker," and the older kids were just as engaged as the younger ones.

At the end of this enthusiastic and very noisy game, we sat down again and gave them the history of the game. We talked about its roots in slavery, its development as a safe way for enslaved people to publicly show affection to each other, and the ability of the people to triumph in spirit. We told them that each time we play "Little Sally Walker," we're celebrating all those people who came before us. Both sobered and inspired by the story, the children wanted to make the game a part of every meeting thereafter.

The group certainly had its difficulties, scheduling sometimes became a major issue, behavior problems were sometimes magnified in the group, and the kids themselves sometimes struggled with the unsettling nature of some of our discussions. A few children remained on the fringe, checking in periodically, but usually not staying, while a few others were never able to bring themselves even to that point—but for those children as well as the faithful attenders, the mere existence of the group offered affirmation and the opportunity to define a group identity.

At the next Black Families meeting, we offered a progress report and described some of the group's activities, while making it clear that the specifics of the children's discussions were confidential. Most of the parents had heard very little about the meetings from their children and had not pressed for details. All were delighted that their children were participating.

The wholesale disappearance of Black children on every other Tuesday afternoon, their enthusiasm prior to leaving and their usually happy faces upon their return created a stir in some classes. At the end of each meeting, the sixth, seventh, and eighth graders took the youngest children by the hand and escorted them back to their classrooms; that alone was cause enough for envy, especially when one of the eighth graders was Khalil, the basketball star, who was idolized by virtually every child in the school.

The Black Kids Group became an intriguing mystery to many of the White children, a mystery of which they were not and could not be a part. For the Black children, many of whom had been victimized by the subtle and not-so-subtle patterns of exclusion, it was a new and unexpected experience to have access to something wonderful and school-sanctioned which their White peers did not. Their response to this turn of events was gracious; they began to ask if they could bring friends to the meeting.

In response, we planned a special meeting where each of the children in the group would be allowed to invite a friend. In the case where Black children constituted over a third of the class, we decided that they would be allowed to invite two friends; in another where they made up nearly half the class, all of the children would be invited, so that no one would be left behind. A memo was sent to all the teachers advising them of the plan and asking for their feedback.

The morning of the scheduled meeting, we learned that a visiting storyteller would be available. At several teachers' suggestion, the event was moved to the assembly hall and the entire school invited. All of the kindergarten through fourth graders attended. We began by having the members of the group stand, and we acknowledged them as the hosts of the afternoon's joyous, audience-interactive event. Thinking that we had satisfied the need for sharing, we proceeded to plan the group's last meeting.

Mentoring continuity, and affirmation were themes which we had integrated into each of our previous meetings. We thought it appropriate to end the year by celebrating our eight-grade graduates. With money contributed by the Black parents, we bought gift books for each of the eighth graders, whether they had been part of the group or not, and cake and ice cream. We planned a presentation ceremony and a time for sharing feelings.

At the very start of the meeting, however, two or three children expressed their distress over us having "gone back on the promise" that they would have the chance to invite a friend to a meeting. When we reminded them of the big meeting with the storyteller, they said, "That was like an assembly. We still didn't get to invite our friends." When we saw how agitated they were, we realized that we had underestimated the importance of the invitation, and so we agreed that they could go back to class and get a friend.

As it turned out, this had not only been an issue for those three children, but for most of the group. The room nearly emptied, and minutes later, over 60 children were crammed into a small, un-air-conditioned room. The remaining time was taken up with presenting the gifts (all of the eighth graders came, even though they had not known about the gifts or the party in advance) and making sure that all the children got a sliver of cake and a spoonful of ice cream. At the end of the meeting, curious upper schoolers came to investigate. All of the graduates were invited to share the leftover cake.

Since that meeting, the words "ice cream" have come to symbolize the controversy that issued. CFS has a very definite "party protocol," unofficial guidelines about how guest lists are formulated and how invitations are distributed, all designed to minimum exclusion. As long as the Black Kids Group was viewed as a "support" group, it generated very little parental interest or concern about exclusion; by serving ice cream, however, we had crossed the line from "support group" to "party," and a number of White parents, kindergarten parents in particular, felt that the school was sanctioning a form of racial exclusion which had hurt their children. Some parents raised their concerns in thoughtful dialogue. A handful covertly contacted other White parents in the class or demanded answers that violated the confidentiality of the group and would never have been entertained in the context of other focus groups.

In a subsequent racism-awareness workshop for parents, several hours were devoted to a heated discussion of the group's existence. Some parents asked why the community had not been informed of the formation of the group, why it met during school hours and on school premises, and why the school would have a group that by definition excluded most children. In answer, several staff members explained that we had followed standard operating procedure in forming the group: focus groups are never publicly announced, they are always held at the school during school hours, and all of them by definition excluded most children.

The discussion then turned to whether or not it was constructive to have such a group. Although one parent proposed that such racial separation is psychically damaging to Black children, most of the concern centered on the group's impact on White children. "What do you say to the White children who are left behind when all the Black children get up and go?" one parent asked. Another answered, "I don't have to say anything. My daughter knows it's a meeting for Black kids and she knows she's not Black. I asked her about it, and for her, it's as simple as that." A Black parent reframed the debate by quietly declaring that she and other Black parents had collectively decided that the group was something which their children needed, and that she neither sought nor required the permission of the White parents to do it; further, she asserted that the group would continue, opposition or no. Other Black parents in the workshop agreed.

The following day, the faculty held its all-day, year-end meeting with Enid Lee, the same consultant who had led the parent workshop. On a number of points, the faculty discussion was almost identical to the parents'. At the end of the day, Enid pointed out that the better part of two days had been devoted to discussing White fears and concerns about the group, with very little discussion of how the school would affirm and support Black kids. A teacher later said, "I had to face the fact that my inordinate concern over where the group met and how that was communicated was an expression of my unconscious resistance. I'd never been so keenly interested in the logistics of any other group before, but I suppose it was because I was really a little uncomfortable with this one. I didn't like to admit that even to myself."

The most dramatic response came from the seventh and eighth graders. Many of the White students were angry and confused about the group; most of the Black students were disappointed and angered by their friend's reactions. When tensions peaked, an upper school meeting was called, which ended up lasting most of the day. In the meeting, the children expressed their anger, fears, and disappointments. They asked many of the same questions that their parents were asking: why had the group been "kept secret," instead of being announced in an assembly; why did it exclude people, and if it had to happen, why couldn't it happen outside of school instead of taking up "our" time? There was a little bit of shouting and a lot of crying. "I was afraid," said one teacher, "that we would split open at the seams."

The discussion of the Black Kids Group led to the discussion of many other issues—in the world at large and at CFS in particular—and the airing of a number of misconceptions. "I heard that the school is trying to fill all its openings with people of color. I don't think that's right. I think we should hire *good* teachers instead." For the previous three years, the school had had only one teacher of color, and so the hiring committee had worked hard to find others—and had successfully filled two of the three positions with *excellent* teachers of color, the third with an equally good White teacher. "My dad said that the school has this new policy of accepting any students of color that apply. That doesn't seem fair." During the previous year's admissions process, 17 of 23 spaces in the kindergarten had gone to siblings; despite the fact that approximately 75 students of all races had been turned away, including some very strong black applicants, rumors persisted that White kids didn't stand a chance of getting in because all the spaces were going to kids of color, with nary a mention of the sibling policy.

The meeting pointed up the critical need to provide solid information to the students: They themselves asked "Why can't we have workshops like the parents and teachers do?" But the core of the discussion, the major issue for most of the kids, was still the Black Kids Group: "We have problems, too," some of them said, "why can't we have a group? *You can*, we answered. We explained the process for forming focus groups and encouraged them to pursue the idea of a White kids' anti-racism support group. By the time the meeting ended, things were calmer, but it was still difficult to assess the day's impact.

That night, most of the eighth graders showed up at the end-of-the-year All School Picnic. Six of the girls sought me out, their expressions somber and introspective, eager to share their thoughts about the meeting. "The thing I like about this school," one girl said, "is that it keeps on challenging me. Everytime I think I have my mind made up about something, I end up having to rethink it and really question myself and what I believe."

The following week during the graduation ceremony, the eighth grade brought us to tears with the unexpected announcement that their class gift to the school would be a fund to enhance the library's anti-racist collection.

* * *

At Graham and Parks and at CFS, racial affinity groups were formed to address specific needs on the part of Black students. And in both schools, the groups had a positive impact for all the students; even the controversy which they generated resulted in discussion, honest confrontation, and an increased level of understanding among various groups. However, lest the relative success of racial affinity groups in our two schools prompt others to adopt this strategy as a panacea for all of a school's ills, we hasten to point out that these groups were developed within the context of a long-term, schoolwide commitment to multicultural, anti-racist institutional change.

The ultimate measure of success for any school which represents itself as a multicultural, anti-racist institution is how well it prepares all of its students to engage in the school's academic and social life with both confidence and competence. Whether they are highly structured, school-sanctioned gatherings like the ones we've described, or informal groupings initiated by the students (the infamous "Black table" in the cafeteria comes to mind), the emergence of racial affinity groups usually brings a number of issues to the surface—issues that either actively support or impede the school's progress toward its goals. Yet the creation of an affinity group in the absence of any other institutional efforts to address these issues virtually guarantees isolation, exclusion, and divisiveness. The decision to support affinity groups must be only one among many steps which affirm the school's commitment to building a multicultural democracy.

Racism touches a raw nerve for most Americans. Even in the most progressive schools, among people who have put a lifetime of personal and professional energy into struggling against racism, the problems of racism run deep. What steps, then, can be taken to make our schools the embodiment of the truly democratic multicultural society that we envision?

A critical first step toward achieving this goal is to simply acknowledge that no matter how much we have done, a great deal of work still remains. When issues of racism are raised, they are commonly met with considerable resistance, denial, even anger. *Why do you keep harping on this?, We dealt with it last year,* or *Our school is light years better than most!* are common responses. The inability to confront the existence of racism is in itself an indicator that more work is needed. We must be willing to name racism, and we must create an environment in which it is safe for our children to name it, too.

Once we have acknowledged that racism is a problem, there must be a clear, unequivocal commitment to examining in detail both the structures of our schools and the content of our message. Modern-day racism is often difficult to identify because it is so insidiously, so thoroughly, and so subtly integrated into all aspects of our culture. We need to look for patterns. Are students of color spending more time in the office for disciplinary reasons than other students? Are students of color achieving at the same rate as White students? Are more Black and Hispanic students being retained? Are students being tracked into ability groups, with a disproportionate number of children of color in the low groups? Do parents have a voice in the school? Do parents of color exercise that voice? If the statistics reveal a pattern of difference based on race, then we must be prepared to take an unflinching look at why our schools are failing to support these students in achieving success.

Schools need to stop asking what they can do to build the self-esteem of children of color, and instead ask themselves what they are doing that erodes the children's self-esteem. How many good teachers acknowledge that each child has an individual set of social and learning needs, yet when faced with the issue of race, defensively invoke the principle of sameness: "I don't see color—I treat all my kids the same!" As educators, we must get beyond our defensiveness enough to understand that each child brings his or her own issues, be they social, behavorial, or academic, into the school; our concern must be whether the school constructively addresses those issues or exacerbates them.

Schools need to have considerable focus and skill to adequately deal with the complexities of racism. While the cost in time, energy, and sometimes financial resources may seem great, the costs we are incurring by ignoring racism are much, much greater. One simple way to begin is to look at three basic issues: Who is teaching? What are they teaching? How is it being taught?

First, faculties must be diverse. Students need positive role models to relate to. If schools are teaching multiracial groups of children, they should be hiring a multiracial faculty. Even in a racially homogeneous school, children need to see people of color in a variety of roles. A diverse faculty brings a diversity of experiences, attitudes, and practices that strengthen the community as a whole. If it is not possible immediately to diversify the teaching staff, then efforts must be made to bring other members of the community—mentors, human service providers, performing artists, artists-in-residence, guest speakers, or willing parent volunteers—into the school to engage with the children on a regular basis.

Second, we must look closely and critically at the content of the curriculum. Whose pictures are in the textbooks? What information is missing? Whose stories get told? Do we celebrate Chinese New Year, yet fail to mention the

Chinese Exclusion Acts or modern-day racism against Asians? Is Black History taught only in February (if at all), or is history taught as a complex interweaving between many forces and voices in our society? Are the books we read written by a diversity of people from a diversity of perspectives? Do children understand the ways that different groups have been excluded from the mainstream, and yet continue to fight for, and sometimes win, their rights? We are calling for a curriculum of inclusion, where all children can both find their own history and come to understand the uniqueness of other struggles.

Third, and perhaps most important, is the understanding that no curriculum is foolproof, and no curriculum is teacherproof. We must constantly evaluate and reevaluate how our children are being taught. Our unconscious behaviors in the classroom—who we call upon most frequently, how we group students, the subtle ways in which we impart our expectations of students—often break down along racial lines, even among skilled, caring, committed teachers. We must look for these patterns, then develop effective strategies for countering them.

Increasingly, educators are understanding the complexity of learning styles that students bring to the classroom. Schools have traditionally rewarded only those students who can fit into a fairly rigid mold of achievement. When there is only one "right" way to learn, those who have other strengths, skills, and talents are denied access to academic success. Teachers must constantly challenge themselves to find the strengths of each student and to provide a multiplicity of opportunities for each child to succeed. All children can learn. It is up to us to discover the most effective ways to teach them.

Our children live in a world where racism and other forms of discrimination exist. While we may not be able to change the realities of the world that the children bring with them, we can make the place where they spend six or seven hours of each day a community that nurtures, challenges and prepares them to question the order of that world. We can provide a forum, a safe haven for children to share, to struggle, to consider, to debate, to explore their concerns, their hurts, their victories, and to affirm themselves and others. The education we provide must, above all else, empower them—and us—to go back into the world as confident, competent, clear-thinking individuals committed to real democracy.

Notes

1. Elizabeth Aries and Kimberly Moorehead, "The Importance of Ethnicity in the Development of Identity of Black Adolescents," *Psychological Reports* 65 (1989), pp. 83–93.

2. Gerald J. Pine, and Asa G. Hilliard III, "Rx for Racism: Imperatives For America's Schools," *Phi Delta Kappan* (1990), pp. 593–600.

Afrocentric Immersion

Academic and Personal Development of African American Males in Public Schools

Peter Murrell

Introduction

One of our nation's most serious problems concerns educating ever-increasing numbers of underserved urban youth. In particular, it is widely accepted and generally lamented that frighteningly large proportions of African American males are failing in school at every level from kindergarten through twelfth grade. In every large metropolitan school system across the nation, they are disproportionately expelled, suspended, and relegated to programs for learning disabled, emotionally disturbed, and mentally retarded. They have dramatically lower grade point averages and rates of matriculation. Clearly, there is a combination of political, economic, and sociological circumstances that contributes to the demise of educational success among African American males. But the desperateness of the educational problem has focused energy on an educational solution.

The Milwaukee Public Schools (MPS) system is embarking on a controversial experiment in which a middle school and elementary school will offer a comprehensive educational program designed exclusively for African American children and that focuses particularly on promoting the academic achievement and personal growth and development of African American males. It is an idea that has gained support in a number of cities, including Washington, D.C., Baltimore, Detroit, Minneapolis, St. Louis, Miami, New York, and Philadelphia, where there are plans to open similar schools or expand on similar proposals within the year. These schools would be headed by African American principals and, to the degree possible, staffed by Black male faculty; they would operate with an Afrocentric curriculum emphasizing the history, culture, and consciousness of Africans throughout the world.

The idea has its supporters and detractors. Proponents of an immersion school for African American males point to the powerful effect toward building self-esteem, self-confidence, and a love of learning. Criticisms have been leveled on both ideological and pedagogical grounds. For example, the venerable

Kenneth B. Clark, whose research on self-image in black children was instrumental in the *Brown v. Board of Education* ruling, sees not only a danger of setting legal precedent for resegregating public education, but also warns of the potential harm from stigmatizing and separating Black youngsters in special schools. As debate continues, so has the emergence of several programs which already boast success in reversing negative educational trends for Black males.

The concept of educational immersion within the traditions, consciousness, history, and culture of African and African American people is also centrally linked to the national debate about multicultural education. At issue is whether the movement to eliminate Eurocentric hegemony in curriculum will bring on excesses in which African American, and other historically marginalized cultural groups, revise curriculum in ways that too severely discount the traditions of Euro-Western cultures and too liberally assert the primacy and superiority of their own cultures. Ill-informed interpretations of Afrocentricity abound in both popular media and the educational literature, regarding it as little more than an ethnocentric curriculum supported by dubious scholarship and whose primary purpose is to enhance self-esteem and self-respect among black children.

What follows in the remainder of this chapter is an analytic case study of African American Immersion as a holistic educational program designed to address specific needs of African American males in public schools. This discourse has two major aims. The first is to establish human development and growth as the theoretical foundation of Afro-American Immersion schools, where the systematic analysis of the particular cognitive, social, emotional, and moral developmental issues of largely urban, poor African American children constitute the basis for curricular and pedagogical design.

The second aim of this discourse is to examine the way in which an Afrocentric curriculum provides a powerful scaffolding for the renewal of urban schools and for the transformation of traditional programs into significantly more enabling and empowering educational experiences for African American children, particularly young men. Using the Milwaukee Project as an example, I will describe how the Afrocentric focus promotes structural, institutional, and pedagogical change for the renewal quality education.

Before proceeding first to a brief background on the Milwaukee Project, I should alert the reader to what could be seen as a bias against Milwaukee Public Schools. The intent of this analysis is not to indict the public schools by pointing to its failures. However, reference to African American childrens' experience in the public schools cannot be avoided. Because this analysis is predicated on foundational knowledge about human development—what the children need as supports in schools to learn, grow, and develop—my description of this foundation must necessarily include discussion of the particular needs of African American children not being met in the Milwaukee Public Schools and how the Afrocentric curriculum addresses them in a way that traditional approaches cannot.

The Milwaukee Project

The African American Immersion Schools—a middle school and an elementary school—were created by the Milwaukee School Board following the recommendations of a task force. The task force, a body including African American educators, educational scholars, and community activitists, was charged with organizing the evidence revealing the extent to which the public schools were underserving and counterserving African American males in the Milwaukee community. Their final report included a plan for the creation of the immersion schools.

The African-American Immersion Schools are dedicated to a comprehensive program placing on an equal par (1) academic excellence and (2) the promotion of personal growth and development. Toward this end, the programs in both the elementary school and the middle school will draw upon community resources and will structure time and activity so as to create an "expanded school family." Using the expanded school family as a base, the immersion schools will:

1. develop a strong, tangible sense of community among all faculty, staff, parents, and students;

2. develop and support long-term mentoring relationships between community members and students;

3. develop teaching practice which engenders long-term commitments and long-term nuturing/supportive relationships between students and teachers (teachers will retain the same group of students from sixth to eighth grade in the middle school);

4. mold children toward a vision of positive personal, social, and community values and responsible citizenship with an *additional focus on African American males;*

5. draw upon a variety of instructional experiences beyond the school walls, extending into the community.

The African American Immersion Schools are committed to the Afrocentric Idea (cf. Asante[1]). African, pan-African, and African American culture will be the foundation of the schools' multicultural curriculum. The core curriculum, pedagogy, and classroom management approaches will be based on the acknowledged African origins of civilization, the strengths and abilities of children's learning styles, and content areas in mathematics, science, history/social studies, humanities, and physical education.

In this chapter I will argue that the principles the Afrocentric Idea, used as a theoretical framework for teaching, curriculum, and school structuring, is perhaps the best hope of saving the educational futures of young black males served by those schools. I will develop this argument by exploring the following issues in the next two sections:

- What role do/should schools serve in the development of children—academically, intellectually, morally, socially, etc.

- In what ways is this role inadequate for the appropriate and positive development of African American children, particularly black males?

- How do principles of the Afrocentric Idea, when used as a theory of curriculum, pedagogy, and school restructuring, eliminate the intellectual and academic violence done to young black males by inserting an appropriate program of development?

Educational Foundations: Human Development

What Should Schools Do? A Question of Development

About a year ago a young African American woman, a teacher initiate whom I had met at another college in the area, asked me if I would accompany her to a meeting with the principal of her son's school. The woman, requested my presence and counsel because of her anger, outrage, and bewilderment. Her 7-year-old son Jerid was enrolled in the second grade at one of the highly regarded elementary specialty schools. The meeting, requested by the principal, followed on the heels of a bizarre incident in which Jerid had become tangled in window shade cords and had fallen in such a way that he nearly strangulated.

What was troublesome to the mother was her sense that the school people were attempting to absolve themselves of responsibility for Jerid's lack of academic success and were also attempting to use the incident as evidence that he should be removed from the class. In her conversations with the teacher, the mother heard the teacher make a number of statements implying that the incident was due to the absence of "age-appropriate" behaviors. The teacher even insinuated a suicide attempt by asking such questions as "Does Jerid seem depressed?" and "Does he talk about death?" The purpose of the meeting, she feared, was to remove her 7-year-old son from the second-grade class on the basis of psychological instability.

Throughout the semester, the teacher communicated to the mother that Jerid was having problems. The teacher reported that Jerid was uncooperative, would "act out," and would not do assigned work. Moreover, the teacher reported that he sometimes would fly into fits of rage, and that she considered these tantrums so inappropriate that she did not want to risk the effect that it might have on the other children. The mother was puzzled and skeptical about these reports, as she saw nothing in Jerid's behavior at home which indicated moodiness, uncooperativeness, or anything like the emotional displays reported by the teacher.

Increasingly, in these conversations, the teacher began entreating the mother to take Jerid to receive professional help and would include pieces of classroom behavior which seemed to support her suggestion that Jerid was developmentally far behind the other children. The mother told me that the theme of the telephone conversation changed from misbehavior to hints of emotional disturbance and dysfunction a couple of weeks after the incident, and that she was troubled to find that the school psychologist had evaluated Jerid without informing her.

The mother's suspicion that a case was being built against Jerid remaining in class was confirmed by the tone of the meeting. She and I resisted the suggestion, reminding both the principal and the teacher that the issue was still an instructional one, and that the decision would be better informed if I observed Jerid in class. And so it was agreed that I observe Jerid in the classroom.

As I observed Jerid during the class period I did indeed see behaviors not exhibited by other children. Jerid exhibited a high degree of figiting and nervous energy. But I also observed a pattern of interaction between the teacher and Jerid which made his lack of success in the classroom no surprise. I could not escape the conclusion that the root of Jerid's "classroom problems" was that he received far too little attention and instructional contact.

There was something perfunctory in the teacher's interactions with Jerid, as if demonstrating too much warmth would incite him to one of the "outbursts" she claimed he had. In a classroom based on discovery learning, Jerid was assigned to listen to a tape of a story book while he read along silently. At the time he was the only child in the class engaged in a solitary activity. After a few minutes, his attention clearly strayed from the book, so I engaged him in putting together a puzzle map of the United States. When he began working on the puzzle, a couple of other boys came over and cooperated in putting together the map. In those moments of solving the puzzle, Jerid's behavior was briefly transformed from being aimless and withdrawn to purposeful and engaged.

I draw on this narrative because it illustrates a subtle yet critically important factor in the desparate plight of Black boys in public schools. On the surface, the issue may not seem to involve ethnicity, culture, or race. One could speculate on a number of causes for Jerid's lack of educational success, and it is not my intention here to lay blame on the teacher or the school. The point here is that this teacher was not fully equipped to work with an African American boy with the same skill she worked with children who share her cultural frame and class background. This classroom teacher was highly regarded by the school community for her ability to socially draw out children, an ability which was clearly demonstrated in her interactions with other children—but *not with Jerid*. Why wasn't this teacher successful with Jerid? What did she see in him that was "developmentally retarded" that the mother did not see?

The failure of this teacher's knowledge of child development exists in two dimensions. The first concerns the foundations of human development as provided in traditional teacher preparation programs, and the subsequent inappropriateness of a knowledge base predicated on the developmental norms of white, middle-class youngsters when used to assess low-income, urban African American children. The second knowledge failure is an outcome of the first. Lacking the appropriate frameworks for interpreting the developmental patterns of low-income urban black children does not afford teachers trained in traditional teacher preparation programs easy access to relevant understandings about their African American students. Successful teaching in this case would require that teachers accommodate their theoretical knowledge of human development to the lives and cultures of these children.

The irony of Jerid's case is that the basis on which the teacher judged that he should be removed from class were her developmental assessments—her claims that Jerid was *developmentally* behind the other children, and that he lacked the age-appropriate behaviors and developmental readiness for her classroom. I contend that the source of this teacher's inability to reach Jerid was lack of knowledge about the patterns of growth and development of African American children. The basis upon which the teacher judged Jerid to be beyond her classroom help—developmental readiness—is precisely the knowledge domain to which she had the *least access*.

What this teacher lacked was an understanding of the developmental trajectories and learning patterns of African American children. The result was a misreading and misinterpretation of Jerid's abilities and intentions in the classroom, subsequently leading to destructive instructional decisions. For example, for the teacher, Jerid's high activity signaled "developmental immaturity." However, for someone familiar with African American children, the high activity would have been regarded as appropriate. The differences in psychomotor developmental norms between African American and mainstream children may also have signaled advanced development of the African American children.

Marcell Gerber examined the norms of African American infants and found that the average age for mastery of some standard psychomotor tasks vastly preceded those of mainstream youngsters (see Kunjufu[2]). For example, standards such as holding oneself upright appeared at 7 weeks for African American infants, compared to 6 months by the mainstream norms; climbing steps at 11 months compared to the mainstream standard of 15 months; and walking to the Gesell box to look inside at 7 months, compared to the mainstream standard of 15 months. Mainstream teachers who are not aware of the norms of motor development among black children are more likely to judge higher activity in the classroom through their own cultural and experiential lens, resulting in a judgment that a child is "hyperactive."

Because teaching is interactive, the misinterpretation of activity levels may go two ways. In particular, teachers who experience black children as "hyperactive" may, in turn, be regared by the children as boring and lacking verve. In work reported by Harry Morgan comparing samples of African American and middle-class white children in their response to children's television programs, researchers found a differential effect for the programs "Mister Roger's Neighborhood" and "Sesame Street" on the learning performance of each sample. The researchers found that when white children were presented with the slower-paced television program "Mr. Rogers", and then the faster-paced "Sesame Street", the slow-paced program had a more positive effect on their behavior and learning. By contrast, the African American children responded better to "Sesame Street."

The point is that there are unique aspects of development among African American children that differ from the standard norms and expectations drawn from white, middle-class youngsters, and that these aspects need to be understood by teachers. What is just as important are the ways that the experiences and social contexts of poverty, oppression, fear, and violence add to the mix of culturally and ethnically shaped differences in socialization and development. Neither of these two dimensions of foundational knowledge about the development of African American children, the personal and the sociocontextual, are articulated in the practice of the corps of teachers in the Milwaukee community.

Currently, only a small number of teacher education curricula have begun to recognize the importance of specific knowledge about the developmental histories, learning patterns, and specific needs of children of color. Traditionally the approach has been one of remediating "cultural deficits" with little understanding of strengths and culturally defined approaches to thinking and knowing. More critical to the failure of these programs is the lack of understanding of how the culturally linked strengths, ways of knowing, and socialization practices interact with the perspectives held by diverse and poor communities toward authority, poverty, and economic and political oppression.[3]

The models of human development many teachers apply, and to which they were exposed during teacher training, are models based upon the culture and socialization practices of white, middle-class mainstream norms. Not only are these frameworks not inclusive or representative of the experience of an increasingly diverse student population, but foundational knowledge about cognitive, moral, and psychosocial development is not integrated into an understanding of educational issues of children of color. Even now, less than a handful of teacher preparation programs (i.e., Wheelock College, Bank Street, and Pacific Oaks College) specifically work to integrate a foundational understanding of human development into the professional and clinical training of its teachers. Therefore, most teachers when encountering needy African American children, Hispanic children, and other children of color are only equipped to diagnose deficiencies as determined by the developmental benchmarks of white middle-class children.

The primary source of the damage done to the cognitive, social, and emotional development of African American boys in classrooms is an insufficient and incomplete knowledge about the development and socialization of African American children. This proposition seems trivial and obvious until one systematically examines the many ways that schools must support the development of children, and currently undersupport the development of black children.

The following are ways that an insufficient knowledge base about the development and socialization of African American children further exaggerate miscues between teachers and students in the Milwaukee Public Schools[4]:

1. *Attributions of problems to deficits in children, rather than inappropriateness of instruction:* the assumption that the problem is based upon what the child lacks, rather than how the instruction has failed.

2. *Misinterpretation of students intentions, aptitudes, abilities, and motivations:* resulting in otherwise competent teachers selecting inappropriate instructional options.

3. *Classroom management for African American males is based on rules of control:* fueled by the visceral fear and discomfort many teachers have of expressions of "blackness" in African American males, behavior is managed by attempts to suppress those expressions, rather than by demonstrating a model of desired behavior.

4. *Ignorance of, and lack of contact with, community norms of child-rearing practices:* leading to strained, adversarial, and combative relationships with parents.

5. *Invisibility of African American History and culture in the curriculum:* resulting in students feeling that schools are not *about* them, and therefore not *for* them.

Lisa Delpit[5] aptly characterizes the limited parameters of conventional teacher knowledge of mainstream teachers who were themselves socialized within the "culture of power" and within conventional norms of what constitutes good teaching. As she describes her professional awakenings as a culturally responsive teacher with urban black children early in her teaching career,[6] we see that this understanding did not come from books, but rather from her experience as a Black person in this society, from cultural understandings which she shared with her students, from her undying belief that all children can learn, from her willingness to grant legitimacy to the experiences and perspectives of the community, and perhaps most importantly, from her capacity to see the children she taught as extentions of herself. This is a long way for teachers socialized in mainstream communities to come because the transformation requires them to call into question many of their most taken-for-granted and common assumptions about the way things work in the classroom and in the world.

Obviously it is theoretically possible for white teachers socialized within a mainstream cultural frame and conventional teacher preparation programs to work effectively with students whose background is different from theirs. But for the present, few of the conditions necessary for helping them acquire the working knowledge of human development in African American and other ethnic communities exist. Questioning and suspending one's world view and interrogating one's own racism are not actions people do naturally nor engage in spontaneously. Yet, we see that these are necessary steps for the white mainstream teacher in order to even begin a systematic understanding of human development in non-mainstream communities.

Schools and the Development of Children

The importance of schools as socializing institutions has been too easily glossed over in the debates about the African American Immersion Schools. The debate is trivialized by the narrowed focus on self-esteem, and the often stated assumption that the primary benefit of an Afrocentric curriculum to African American children is in bolstering a positive self-concept. Opponents of the concept of an Afrocentric curriculum push this idea further, claiming that the only benefit to black children will be that they will "merely feel better about themselves" and not be able to function within wider society.[7]

The enhancement of self-esteem and self-regard *is* an important element of the Afrocentric curriculum because African American children are exposed to many more positive images of "blackness," learn a world history documenting the extensive contributions of African people to world and "western" civilization, and key upon positive models of African Americans. But to key on self-esteem enhancement as the central thrust of the Afrocentric curriculum is to seriously understate its scope as a holistic program for the cognitive, emotional, spritual, moral, and social development of African American children.

The healthy growth and development of *all* children as they enter school depends in large part upon the continuity of socialization between family life and school life. The quality of children's educational life in school is determined by how well the socialization in school matches, fortifies, and builds on their experiences in the home. Schools play an essential role in the psychosocial development of all children. We know that the processes of psychosocial and moral development are marked by a number of developmental tasks children work through.

Schools also play a central role in the cognitive development of children, as well as the development of thinking abilities they need to reason morally. The classroom, the playground, the groups of children walking to and from school are all situational contexts in which children develop their thinking, their emoting, and their valuing. On a daily basis, children negotiate friendships, use strategies to achieve social or political goals within their peer group, and make decisions about the correctness of conduct.

Much of this interaction takes place in the classroom, organized around teacher's attention and relationships with the teacher. Erickson and Schultz's concept[8] of "classroom underlife" characterizes the dynamic of informal social interaction in the classroom:

> Classroom underlife (its informal social organization) seems to ebb and flow in the recurring periods of darkness and light as the spotlight of teacher attention sweeps around the room. In elementary school the student underlife seems to thrive in the interstices of classroom events (e.g., going to the pencil sharpener, turning in a paper, getting ready to leave the room) . . . . In the high school, underlife is carred out in glances across aisles of desks and to some extent played out in classroom discourse. But the underlife seems also especially vigorous as

it walks out the classroom door and creates interstices in the hallways and on the school's approaches—its sidewalks, lawns, parking lots—and in various sports events sponsored by the school such as football games and the prom.

The point is that the universe of events which shape the intellectual, social, and emotional maturity of our children extends far beyond our design of instruction or curriculum. The Afrocentric Immersion curriculum examines and draws on the multiplicity of contexts of school life, to shape and encourage daily experiences in schools that bring about positive development among African American children. To do this, it is necessary to combine foundational developmental knowledge about black children as discussed above, with an understanding of their experiential lives as they try to situate themselves in "a place called school."

What are the conditions in the children's social environments in schools that support their school success and are they different for African American children from low-income neighborhoods? We know that social efficacy and emotional security are foundations for cognitive growth and learning. Children have few quality learning experiences if they are mistrustful of others, doubt their efficacy in the world, or develop a sense of inferiority. Children in the early school years are developing a sense of *industry* and the developmental task is to develop lasting dispositions about themselves as able "doers."

We know that school environments must support the child's sense of well-being, trust, and self-efficacy. Teachers who have a strong understanding of human development and human learning have a better chance of re-creating these supportive environments in their classrooms. Such teachers also are more likely to avoid making the erroneous, frequently unconscious assumptions about a black child's ability or potential based upon unfamiliar patterns of learning and behavior.

Yet, in cross-cultural interactions, there is much more that needs to be known about the lives, histories, and cultures of children in order to support their development. Given the vast array of situations and interstices in schools that shape the emotional and social development of children, it is important to reexamine the relationship between school structure and the goals of the school in terms of student development. It is also important that the design of an appropriate and effective school environment for the growth and development of children is guided by a framework, mission, or theory.

In the next section of this chapter, Afrocentric pedagogy will be examined as a framework for the educational program in the African American Immersion schools. In the remainder of this section, I will probe futher the conditions under which schools provide an appropriate nurturing environment for the scholastic and personal development of all children, and extend these understandings to a discussion of what gets short-circuited in the educational experiences of African American males. The exposition of the shortcomings in the educational system for African American males will serve as the explanatory framework for how the educational program for the African American Male Immersion schools was constructed to meet unmet needs.

Developmental Pedagogy

Teacher Esteem for Students

Prominent in all discussion about good teaching and the conditions for helping children smoothly adapt to school is the belief that all children can learn. This belief is played out in two sorts of actions leading to quality instruction. One of these is providing a warm, safe, and nuturing emotional environment where children receive expressions of esteem and positive regard from the teacher. Good teachers express caring for the students, advocate for them in relationship negotiation with other children, and generally respond to them as they would their own children.

The other sort of teacher action is the creation of opportunities for children to develop a sense of industry and self-efficacy. Good teachers know how to orchestrate the activities of children so that they experience successes in a variety of tasks. They also know how to recognize special efforts and to encourage special abilities.

The good teaching embodied in these two sorts of teacher actions—creating a safe, warm emotional environment and creating contexts producing a sense of industry, rather than inferiority—depends on the continuity of experience between home and school. Good teachers are trusted and respected by the community. They share with parents and students common cultural assumptions and experiential backgrounds. Unfortunately, the reality in Milwaukee, as in other larger metropolitan school systems, is that the predominantly white middle-class teacher corps cannot create or maintain the same ties with the African American children as they do with mainstream children. They simply have had too little access to the communities, families, and cultures of these children to maintain this continuity of experience as teachers.

Teachers from mainstream backgrounds simply have to overcome too much to be able to express the same degree of esteem, positive regard, and love for African American boys. As indicated above, the primary problem is that lack of requisite knowledge about the growth, development, and socialization of African American males to make appropriate decisions and create sufficiently nurturing learning environments. In addition, to establish the same degree of connectedness, teachers must overcome their:

- visceral *fear* of Black men and boys, a fear fueled by rampant rates of violence, joblessness, and crime among African American males, leading to teacher feelings that "culturally black" behaviors have to be suppressed and eliminated in African American boys before they "turn bad" and become "unteachable";

- lack of connection with, understanding of, and respect for African American family life, leading to teacher feelings that the family life is something African American children need to be rescued from;

- negative perceptions of Black males reflected by images depicted repeatedly in the popular culture, leading to feelings that the disproportionate numbers of suspensions, special education assignments, and academic failures are not the fault of the schools, but due to "bad environments";

- lack of connection with, understanding of, and respect for African American culture, leading to discounting or undervaluing the strengths and abilities African American males bring to school (e.g., oracity and dexterity) to be built on and encouraged;

- attributions of problems to deficits in children, rather than inappropriateness of instruction: the assumption that the problem is based upon what the child lacks, rather than how the instruction has failed;

- lack of requisite knowledge about African American children: resulting in otherwise competent teachers misreading the aptitudes, abilities, and intentions of African American children they work with;

- lack of any clear moral or ethical disposition on racial conflict and oppression, resulting in the absence of a repertoire for helping children reason through and resolve conflicts based on racial antagonism, opting instead to avoid or smooth over problems.

It is impossible to overstate the importance of these barriers white middle-class teachers (and others marginal to African American cultures, lives and experiences) have to overcome to forge the same quality connections with African American boys as they do with other children. Rather than the continuation of socialization and emotional support children need to receive when they enter school, African American boys experience a shocking discontinuity. Rather than experiencing the warm, safe, nurturing environment children need to discover and learn, Black boys experience an emotionally toxic environment where elements of who they are diminished, devalued, and punished. The dramatic statistical evidence is available elsewhere.[9] Here it is more important to more clearly convey the destruction of African American boys in the absence of the critical student–teacher connection necessary for positive primary socialization.

What happens to African American males when teachers and school people fail to establish connectedness to them based upon an understanding of their culture, lives, community, history, and development? This consequence frequently has three elements. The responses educators make to problems of achievement or conduct often (1) are predicated on a misinterpretation of ability, expression, or intention, and (2) followed by an exaggerated or inappropriate course of action based on (3) an insufficient framework for addressing the developmental needs and demands of African American children.

The classroom is the critical scene for appropriate primary socialization. What goes on day-to-day looms as large in the developmental crisis of African American males as disproprotionate special education placements and suspensions. Although the scope of this paper will not permit me to illustrate the experience of African American males in classrooms in any exacting manner, I nonetheless will share the following anectdotes illustrative of apparently benign treatments in the classroom that produce deeply malignant educational consequences for African American males:

While observing a student teacher in an integrated school, highly regarded systemwide for its innovative teaching and educational programs, I noticed that in the class of about 27 fourth graders, there was only one Black male. He was sitting in the back of the room by himself. The magnitude of his exile from the rest of the class was so startling, I had to hide by consternation when I asked the cooperating teacher the reason for his physical separation. She replied that "He's separated from the group to receive special attention." Yet in the 55 minutes I observed the class, he was the *only* child to receive *absolutely no attention*—no interaction whatsoever with teacher or classmates.

While visiting a fifth grade classroom of about 30 pupils with an equal distribution of African American and white students, I noticed that only at one table seating five African American boys was there continuous high-level activity—loudly talking to one another and jumping up from their seats to hit or feign hitting each other. As everyone else was writing quietly at their desks, this behavior clearly stood out, and other children were demonstrably irritated by the distraction. When I asked the teacher why she permitted this she said "Oh, I am teaching them according to their kinetic learning styles." Yet, the lesson was on composing a letter of request.

A colleague of mine told of how she decided to remove her kindergartner from the suburban school to which he was bused. She and her husband were one of many area African American families participating in a busing plan to integrate predominantly white suburban schools. My colleague and her husband were disturbed to discover that none of the white children in the gym class engaged in folk dancing would hold their son's hand, but would instead grasp his sleeves. When the parents confronted the teacher with this information, the teacher said that she had not noticed.

A situation that I have encountered many times, through the narratives of my colleagues, the reports of my teacher initiates, and my own observations in schools is the infamous "misbehavior table" in the school lunch room, where all, or nearly all, of the children placed there are black. When I or my student teachers ask a supervising teacher "Where are the white kids who misbehave?" the assumption is chilling clear: It is mainly the black children who misbehave.

Each of these events illustrates the pattern of an exaggerated, disproportionate, and inappropriate response to the schooling needs of African American boys. Moreover, the fact that these responses did not necessarily result from malintent in no way diminishes the toxic effect on the educational futures of Black boys. When a group of children is identified as being disordered, disadvantaged, and disruptive, almost any policy or intervention can be justified.

Last year, a story that made front-page news in the community was the suspension of a African American boy from kindergarten, allegedly for sexual misconduct with a kindergarten girl. The boy had merely taunted the girl by lifting her dress in the presence of classmates. The incident was coded as 3rd degree sexual assault. The justifiable outcry from the African American community raised the question: What kind of beliefs did the school people harbor about Black boys that would allow them to imagine sexual misconduct from a five year old? The incident dramatically brought to the fore the deep-seated fears white teachers and administrators habored about Black boys. Would they believe that their own five-year-old sons were capable of sexual assault?

The event dramatically illustrates the patterned response to Black males: a misperception of intention or action followed by an exaggerated sanction or intervention that is disproportionate to the problem, followed, in turn, by an inappropriate response to the problem (How does suspension teach a kindergartner appropriate behavior?). To the extent that school personnel cannot view African American children as extentions of themselves, this pattern of interaction with African American children will persist. The statistical evidence supporting this is clear. For example, between 1978 and 1985, 94.4 percent of all students expelled from the Milwaukee Public Schools were African American. The system is third in the nation in its high ratio of the Black-to-White suspension rate.

The point is that even if mainstream teachers were to somehow gain the foundational knowledge of development which is uniquely experienced in the environments of the Black child's early growth and socialization, the nascent fear these teachers have of Black boys precludes application of that knowledge. Without the connections to African American students forged from an authentic understanding of experiences, abilities, and cultural norms, classrooms are not supportive environments but become intellectually, spiritually, and socially destructive environments for African American males. Teachers cannot advocate for them in the same way as their other students because of the tendency to attribute problems as matters of "readiness" or ability, and not to their own teaching. Similarly, without understanding the abilities and strengths African American students bring, teachers are much less likely to create opportunities to extend these abilities and use them as a scaffolding for developing other abilities.

Language Socialization, Culture, and Developing Literacy Skills

Many writers have observed that urban African American youth possess considerable language skill and communicative competence before they enter school (e.g., Gee,[10] Kochman,[11] Labov,[12] Smitherman,[13] Dillard[14]). Although educators have always recognized the importance of school curricula building on the language abilities and strengths of children, accomplishing this for urban African American children has met with little success on a wide scale. In mainstream communities where teachers, parents, and children belong to the same cultural community, teachers are much more successful in building on existing linguistic abilities because the children and the teacher share a common dialect and communicative style. Although it is possible for teachers *who do not already share* the language features of African American children to scaffold their literacy learning in the same way they do with children of similar language background, too few mainstream teachers acquire the requisite cross-cultural pedagogical knowledge and language competence to do so.

In fewer than a handful of schools in Milwaukee has this specific linguistic–cultural knowledge about African Americans been incorporated into pedagogy for African American children. This knowledge is glaringly absent in teacher-preparation programs in the area colleges and universities. There is little recognition of the uniqueness of African American discourse styles or understanding of Black Dialect. In four out of five instances when I have asked teachers to tell me their understanding of Black English, reference is made to its being "slang" or "street talk" despite the fact that linguists have for more than two decades recognized it as a legitimate dialect.

It will be useful at this point to briefly address the question of why the literacy learning opportunities of children from marginalized groups suffer when their teachers come from different language communities and/or cultural communities. The work of Heath,[15] Scribner and Cole,[16] and many other researchers in the field of cultural psychology have provided many meaningful insights into how culture and cognition intertwine in the development of literacy in children. Specifically, from this body of work we have come to better understand of how, for example, the socialization practices of different communities differentially shape the way young learners respond to, and "take meaning" from, written text.

For example, in a well-known study, Heath[17] showed how the contrasting patterns of language socialization in the common practice of reading bedtime stories in mainstream and nonmainstream communities differentially prepares the children for their literacy achievement in school. In a "scaffolding" (cf. Cazden,[18] Tharp and Gallimore[19]) interaction between mother and child reading a bedtime story for example, the mother might ask "What is x?" to which the child vocalizes a response, redirects her attention to the object in the picture, or both. The mother then provides a verbal feedback and a label. In this way, Heath[20] asserts, before the age of 2, the child is being socialized into the most common discourse pattern in school classrooms—the initiation–reply–evaluation (IRE) sequence. The child will be well-prepared cognitively and dispositionally to interact smoothly with teachers when they get to school.

The significance of this study is that in the nonmainstream communities a different pattern of language socialization emerged from the bedtime story literacy event. Heath[21] found that the patterns of literacy learning in the two nonmainstream communities did not have this finely tuned, consistent, repetitive, and continuous pattern of training that was embedded in the literacy events (e.g., the bedtime story) of households in the mainstream community. Heath documented ways in which the differences in school achievement between mainstream and nonmainstream communities was linked to differences in their home experiences with literacy. As mainstream teachers came to understand the specific linguistic patterns and communicative styles of nonmainstream students with the help of Heath, they improved in their ability to connect with the children.

An important insight suggested in, and supported by, this research is that literacy is not one monolithic set of multipurpose skills. Rather, literacy is a set of social practices situated in specific sociocultural contexts.[22] Specific literacies are apparent in the ways people talk, read, write about, and otherwise interact with written discourse. Moreover, the set of literacy skills that Heath[23] observed in the African American community are skills that, if promoted in schools, would benefit *all* children. Heath[24] states:

> The school seemed unable to recognize and take up the potentially positive interactive and adaptive verbal and interpretive habits learned by Black American children (as well as other nonmainstream groups), rural and urban, within their families and on the streets. These uses of language—spoken and written—are wide ranging, and many represent skills that would benefit all youngsters: keen listening and observational skills, quick recognition and nuanced roles, rapid-fire dialogue, hard-driving argumentation, succinct recapitulating of an event, striking metaphors, and comparative analyses based on unexpected analogies.[25]

A number of scholars[26] have examined ways that the language traditions, literacy skills and discourse patterns of African American culture may be drawn upon to support learning in the same way the traditions of Heath's mainstream community supported their learning in mainstream schools. One purpose of the Afrocentric pedagogy in the Milwaukee immersion school is to stimulate inquiry into what literacies derive from the encultured experiences of African American children in the community, and how they might differ from the literacy abilities typically expected of elementary students in Milwaukee's public schools. The question for determining pedagogy is: "How can the discourse practices and the communicative features within the African American community scaffold and promote learning?"

Lee[27] discusses the use of the literacy skills engendered in African American discourse styles to make literary criticism more accessible to African American children. The collective voice and talk of the African American community has been woven into rich literary forms by African American creative writers for many years, and she demonstrates how reading such works provides the pedagogical scaffolding for building skills of literary analysis, particularly for African American youth who already share the literacies invoked in the works of African American writers. She argues that there are routine practices within the cultural life of African American communities on which schools could draw to promote the construction of understanding in literature and the ability to critique literature.

Drawing on this, the elementary African American Immersion School (recently renamed Martin Luther King Elementary School) has begun putting together an extensive collection of literature for children and adults written by African American authors. The reading program has also begun to focus on reading development by integrating aspects of oral competence with written discourse by looking for ways that the figurative and expressive characteristics of African American language enhance children's understanding of the structure of written discourse (cf. Lee[28]).

Discourse practices and the communicative features within the African American community, particularly the powerful oral traditions, can serve an important role in the educative process. In an Afrocentric pedagogy, the literacy abilities engendered by the oral traditions provide a bridge between socially meaningful motifs and their experience in school. In an Afrocentric curriculum the unique and distinct discourse practices of the African American community become the scaffolding to link oral talk with conceptual learning. One example of this in the elementary school is the use of the *narrative*.

Narratives are a universal meaning-making strategy. The way stories are told within a given culture reveals implicit social and linguistic knowledge engendered by that culture. Consider the concept of "signifying" within the African and African American tradition of the communal storyteller. The storyteller, or African griot, is one who is regarded by the community as the possessor of special wisdom and insight and whose role is to provoke introspection and thoughtful reflection through his/her narratives.

Early in the first semester, the implementor of the elementary African American Immersion School assumed the role of the African griot to set the Afrocentric curriculum at the school. In a fifth-grade class studying American history, she used traditional storytelling to examine the arrival of African people to this hemisphere. Dressed in traditional African garb and accompanied by the rhythms of African drums played on a tape player, she tells of the experience of African people brought as slaves to the "new world."

In an assembly of several classes in the gym, an authentic African griot performs his magic. He has gone to great lengths to include the contemporary cultural codes embedded in rap music into his rendition of familiar fables, such as the gingerbread man. The gingerbread man, who gets up and runs away, becomes the little co'nbread man. Little co'nbread man speaks in dialect:

> *Ha, ha, ha! Hee, hee, hee!*
> *Yo may be* bad *but yo can't catch me!*
> *Run! Run! As fast as you can.*
> *But you can't catch me*
> *The little co'nbread man.*

Integrated into his narrative is instruction that promotes moral development, cognitive development, ethical content, and both intercultural and intracultural awareness. For example, at the end of the story where the fox coaxes the cornbread man close enough to grab him, the fox's discourse evokes in the children a sense of social conduct that is anchored in their experience and their language:

> *Boy, what's wrong with you?*
> *Yellin' at me from way ova there!*
> *Din't yo mamma teach you no manners?*
> *You try'na dis (disrespect) me or somethin'?*
> *You come over here and speak to me proper.*
> *If you can't do that, then get out my face!*

Asante[29] notes that the "signifying monkey," which is legendary in the African American "communication memory" is the progenitor of several forms of signifying, to rapping, and to variations of the "dozens" (p. 49). He provides one version of the signifying monkey:

> *Down in the jungle near a dried-up creek*
> *The signifying monkey hadn't slept for a week*
> *Remembering the ass-kicking he got in the past*
> *He had to find somebody to kick the lion's ass.*
> *The monkey said to the lion one bright summer day,*
> *There's a bad motherfucker over the way.*
> *The way he talks about you can't be right.*
> *And when y'all meet there's bound to be a fight.*
> *He talks about your mother in a helluva way.*
> *He call her a no-good bitch and he meant it for a fight.*
>
> *Now if you ask me, I'll say, "man, it ain't right."*
> *Off went the lion in a terrible rage*
> *creating a breeze which shook the trees*
> *and knocked the giraffe to his knees.*
> *He confronted the elephant up under the tree,*
> *and said "motherfucker, it's you or me."*
> *He drove at the elephant and made a pass.*
> *That's when the elephant knocked him flat on his ass.*
> *He kicked and stomped him all in his face*
> *Busted two ribs and pulled his tail out of place.*
> *They cursed and fought damn near all day.*
> *I still dont's see how that lion got away.*

The griot offered the children a similar rendition told in the form of rap (without profanity) and punctuated frequently by a refrain that by the second or third time the children said along with him:

Signifyin' monkey,
Way up in yo' tree,
You always lyin', an' signifyin'
But you better not monkey with me!

The African griot was very careful in setting up his rendition of the signifyin' monkey, told as an African fable explaining why monkeys live in trees. The parallel lesson was about signifying and the role it played in the social relationships among the children. He introduced the term and clarified its meaning in the context of children's common experience. Nearly all the hands shot up when Teju asked "How many of you got into some mess about 'You know what so-and-so said about you cause you said she said . . .' and then you say 'I didn't say nothin' like that' and then it's 'She said you said that I said . . . , but I what I really said . . .' Clearly all the hands went up when he asked "How many of you got into some trouble over something that started by someone sayin' 'yo mama' "?

The repetition of the refrain gave children the opportunity to participate in, and be a part of, the performance. The connection between the speaker and the audience is thus established in the tradition of African storytelling. One could not help but feel the communal power and the sense of unity generated in the room full of kindergartners, first, second, and third graders, vocalizing the "signifyin' monkey" refrain in one collective voice.

The griot used the fable as an anchor to key strategies for cognitive and social self-monitoring. The social development was set up with the question: "Now what are you going to do if someone comes up in your face with that stuff?" Children learn as a cognitive (metacognitive) strategy to think about the signifyin' monkey, and to hum the melody of the refrain as a meta-cognitive reminder not to "get into it" with another trouble-making child. Children learned to invoke in memory the story and the melody of the refrain as a strategy for dealing with conflict situations that test their ability to maintain self-control.

Perhaps the most important implicit lesson is that children learn how to conduct themselves with signifying peers without regarding the *discourse form itself* as negative. Where mainstream teachers may have simply said "This is what signifying leads to so don't do that," this mode provides a code of conduct which does not disconfirm signifyin' as a cultural marker. Smitherman[30] identifies the formal properties of signifying as follows

> . . . indirection, circumlocution; metaphorical-imagistic (but images rooted in the everyday, real world); ironic; rhythmic fluency and sound; teachy but not preachy; directed at a person or persons usually present in the situational context (siggers [signifiers] do not talk behind yo back); punning, play on words, introduction of the semantically or logically unexpected. (p. 121)

The value toward signifyin' is not presented as a negative, and so avoids disaffirming it as an aspect of African American culture. The axiology expressed in the fable is that some people will do it, and maybe everyone does it at some time or another, but there is virtue in not letting yourself be controlled by "siggers," placing the responsibility for appropriate action with the individual.

Teachers Who Help Students with Self-Definition and Search for Identity

We know that children fashion a vision of themselves based on the responses and expectations directed toward them in the process of growing up. Children tend to be the kind of people they think parents, teachers, and other socially significant people expect them to be. One of the most important developmental tasks our students encounter as they move through adolescence toward adulthood is forming a sense of self—an identity. The process is marked by the experimentation with different, sometimes conflicting, roles. Numerous identities can be drawn from the surrounding culture. The young people who successfully cope with these conflicting identities during adolescence emerge with a new sense of self that is both stable and acceptable to them. On the other hand, those who are not successful in resolving this identity crisis become confused and frustrated, suffering identity confusion.

But what happens to children who are presented roles with contradictory perspectives and meanings? The available evidence suggests that identity formation is indeed more difficult for children of color to the extent that: (1) they come from a different cultural frame than that engendered by their schools and (2) they cannot select a role without it creating contradictory aspects across culture. For example, we all remember the scene in the film "Stand and Deliver" where Angel arranged with Jaime Escalante to have several math textbooks so that his peers would not assume he was cooperating with "the man" and reject him for being studious. Angel's choosing to be a "good student" carried the price of rejection by his peers.

Angel Guzman, of course, was able to resolve this relatively minor role conflict (gang member versus good student) by disguising that fact that he studied. But this sort of culturally linked role conflict frequently is a profoundly more disturbing element in the schooling experience of African Americans in predominantly white, middle-class settings, described by Fordham and Ogbu[31] as the "burden of acting white":

> Specifically, blacks and other minorities (e.g., American Indians) believe that in order for a minority person to succeed in school academically, he or she must learn to think and act white. Furthermore, in order to think and act white enough to be rewarded by whites or white institutions like the schools, a minority person must give up his or her minority-group attitudes, ways of thinking, and behaving, and, of course, must give up or lose his or her own minority identity. That is, striving for success is a subtractive process: the individual black student following school standard practices that lead to academic success is perceived as adopting

a white cultural frame of reference . . . as "acting white" with the inevitable outcome of losing his or her black identity, abandoning black people and black causes, and joining the enemy, namely, white people. (pp. 25–26)

The purpose here is not to evaluate this conception of identity conflict. The psychological consequences of conflicts posed by contradictions of group membership and personal identity is the subject of some important work which examines not only the cultural markers of urban Black males (e.g., the "cool pose"[32]), but also the revisioning of past research on African American identity toward a more powerful discourse for examining the full range of experience of African Americans (e.g., Cross[33]). The point here is that, because of contradictions set up by contrasts in the expectations of home and school cultures, the resolution of role conflicts is considerably more difficult and complicated for children of color.

The construction of one's identity is more problematic for children of color since, unlike mainstream white youngsters, racial identity is not a choice selected from among competing roles. Moreover, one's membership in a racial group also necessarily involves choosing from among competing perspectives and ideologies as well. Therefore, the conflicts experienced by African American children are *ideological* as well as *developmental* as they try to balance the sometimes conflicting needs to define themselves within their cultural frame versus "fitting in" or doing well at school.

Central to fashioning an identity is the selection of a societal role that validates the young person's vision of herself in the world and relates to how she defines herself. The identity conflict described by Du Bois almost a century ago— the conflict posed by achieving in the "White man's world" while remaining "culturally Black" is, in one sense, a contradiction never resolved. It is the persistence of what Du Bois[34] calls dual consciousness: the special sort of identity confusion African American adolescents face when they are forced to choose from among roles that sometimes counterpose their "blackness" with symbols they want to adopt. The importance of role models, reaffirmed time and again in the educational research literature, is critical for children of color. They need to see adults of color *modeling successful resolutions* of the inherent contradictions of living in an unjust, oppressive, and racist society.

As George McKenna points out in an example about teaching contemporary history, there is a profound difference in the rhetorical force between saying "Blacks had to ride in the back of the bus" and being able to say "*We* had to ride in the back of the bus." Children still need access to the cultural roots through an Afrocentric world view. More importantly, African American children need guidance through the rough terrain of dual socialization that all nonmainstream children must face. Few mainstream teachers are prepared to understand, much less guide children through, this rough developmental terrain.

The duality of socialization actually creates a three-way quandry (cf. Boykin and Toms[35]) as African American children in public schools must respond to, and struggle with, three socialization agendas: (1) to the mainstream culture extant in public schools; (2) to the cultural motifs of blackness; and (3) to a dynamic of resistance (to oppression and cultural hegemony) versus participation (in the culture of power) experienced as an intensified sort of identity confusion (Murrell[36]).

It is this latter aspect of socialization that is critically important in the development of African Americans in both schooling and life experiences. Unlike most mainstream youngsters, for African American children (as well as children of other marginalized ethnic groups), socialization is not merely toward contemporary mainstream culture. These youngsters are also biculturally socialized to the extent their families attempt to prepare them to assume roles in the "culture of power," but this biculturality may be fraught with conflict as youth struggle with some of the inherent contradictions that assuming these roles pose with respect to their culture of origin. Praeger[37] captures the problematic in these words:

> [I]t is not the mere fact that Blacks hold a dual identity in this country which has constrained achievement; to one degree or another, every ethnic group and racial group has faced a similar challenge. The Black experience in America is distinguished by the fact that the qualities attributed to Blackness are in opposition to the qualities rewarded in society. The specific features of Blackness as cultural imagery are, almost by definition, those qualities which dominant society has attempted to deny in itself, and it is the difference between Blackness and whiteness that defines, in many respects, American cultural self-understanding. For Blacks, then, the efforts to reconcile into one personality images that are diametrically opposed poses an extraordinarily difficult challenge. (p. 111)

Fordham,[38] in conversations with academically talented African American high school students, has identified tendencies of these youngsters to deny and diminish both black cultural motifs and academic behaviors too closely associated with "acting white." Clearly, neither form of denial and suppression of self is healthy. But what chance does a teacher from a mainstream perspective have of helping children recognize the "warring ideals" within themselves, much less how to deal with the conflict? What in traditional curriculae will help children work this through?

Despite the multicultural competence of their teachers, African American children still need guidance to interpret experiences rooted in cultural hegemony. I remember a Black boy in a classroom I was observing get up and walk to the pencil sharpener. He was made to go back and walk across the room again the "correct way" by his teacher. How does a seven-year-old child come to understand that the verve and rhythm in his walk, an expression of joy, are somehow "wrong"? How does he interpret the denial of this expression as "correct"? This event, I am sure, was regarded by the teacher (and perhaps the reader) as one of many occasions where one helps the children and as not particularly significant. But it was clear that the event *was* significant to the young man, whose facial expression continued to show resentment some minutes after he sat back down. What is his defense against cultural hegemony?

How does he learn not to care whether someone does not approve of his expression of self?

African Americans (and members of other geopolitical groups) who develop positive identities also manage to externalize the conflicts inherent in their experiences as a person of color in a racist, sexist, and unjust society. They are able to stand apart from it and recognize that it really exists in the structural inequities of society. Moreover, they develop a strong perspective with which to interpret social reality and act morally in the world. Du Bois[39] referred to this perspective as a second sight through which to view "one's self through the eyes of others." (p. 45). Asante[40] refers to the development of this perspective as moving from the *rhetoric against oppression* to the *discourse of resistance to oppression*. Gay[41] characterizes positive identity formation of African Americans this way:

> We know when we are in the presence of individuals who have clarified their Blackness and integrated it into their being, not so much by any specific, isolated behaviors as by the sense of security, self-direction, confidence, assurance, and comfort with their ethnic selves they radiate. They neither apologize for nor proselytize about their Blackness. They simply fuse it with all other dimensions of their being. They are, in the words of perceptual and humanistic psychologists, self-actualized—ethnically actualized. (p. 64)

The important questions here concern how we move young Black scholars beyond identity confusion when they are in White schooling environments. What are the developmental markers signifying resilient maturity? What takes place developmentally that allows minority students to move beyond simply balancing conflicting expectations of their culture-of-origin with the school culture? What role models must teachers be able to provide African American boys? What complicates the issue still further is the extreme difficulty of preparing mainstream teachers to help African American children develop self-identity. Even if we do prepare that rare individual teacher who acquires an understanding of the interplay between pattern and individual expression, there is still the issue of how they position themselves politically and rhetorically with respect to the community they serve.

Recall Asante's distinction between the "rhetoric of *protest* to oppression" versus the "rhetoric of *resistance* to oppression." Despite their skills as culturally responsive teachers, if they are not African American, they can only assume the former rhetorical stance, but not the latter. To many readers this may seem a trivial point, but it is difficult to overestimate its importance when it comes to guiding young African American men to an integrated identity in the face of the contradicting roles he must assume to be successful in school (cf. Fordham and Ogbu[42]).

The problem of rhetorical stance and the political stance of the mainstream teacher of African American students emerges in any number of important ways. For example, I recall an occasion when one of my student teachers was going to teach a unit on the structure of poetry by using rap music. Rather than having her students introduce the rap discourse to be examined, she handed out copies of a rap song about school that she had prepared for discussion, and proceeded to encourage the same sort of analysis the English class typically does when analyzing a poem from their texts.

The resentment and anger this generated in the predominantly African American classroom was palpable. She usually did not have to coax responses, as the class was very participatory. This day nobody volunteered, nobody responded to her attempts to elict discussion. When called on, several students would ignore the question asked, but would begin signifying to the inappropriateness of the lesson with questions of their own such as: "Miz B., where'd you get this from?" and "Say, Miz B., when did you start listening to rap music?" and "Why don't we analyze something that *you* listen to?" The teacher did not pick up on the indirection, apparently intepreting and responding to the signifying questions as though they were genuine expressions of curiousity.

What is required in situations like these is not only an understanding of the complex mixture of language, culture, and thought, but also a sense of how one situates oneself within a cultural scene where the politics of power are shaped by racial membership. My student teacher created a breech with her students on two bases: a problematic rhetorical stance as well as a problematic political stance. By introducing rap discourse as an object of study in her English classroom, this student teacher had tacitly claimed authority over a language form in which she, in fact, had *no* expertise. Rap is, after all, a language form based in *performance*. It is not a form available to her as means of expression or communication, and therefore, as the basis of teaching. It is a platform from which she cannot speak.

The second basis of the breech concerns what "teaching about rap" represented in terms of cultural politics. My student teacher was not aware that she had communicated disrespect and the specter of putting her students "under the microscope" by making their music and forms of expression the subject of formal study. The students easily and correctly surmised that because she was white and from a priviledged background, she had no occasion to listen to rap music other than to create a lesson. She had invoked the sense of violation among the students by "taking over" a cultural form and discourse style that, for many, is a part of personal identity—one of the few ways they had of maintaining an "identity of resistance" toward school to the extent it represented oppression of Black people. So here was their language being co-opted by the school and transformed into a potential instrument of continued oppression.

Where did this student teacher go wrong? By all accounts she is to be commended for attempting to incorporate aspects of her students lives and culture in her teaching. Yet she was not successful in that lesson because she did not anticipate reactions that come out of the rhetoric of resistance to oppression. Could we have prepared this teacher to anticipate this conflict? Probably not. Could we provide her with the skills to ascertain where she had gone wrong and how to repair her relationships? Definitely so. But the ability to become politically aware and sensitive to the cultural politics of one's classroom is extremely difficult by itself. Add to this the difficulty of deciding what one *ought* to do ethically to serve the best interests of one's students, given that one's political and cultural interests may not coincide with theirs.

The bottom line is that the importance of role models for African American boys, as well as all children of color, cuts much deeper than providing someone "to be like." Children of color need to see models of people who have successfully resolved conflicts and contradictions en route to forming an integrated identity. Mainstream teachers simply do not experience "the burden of acting white" and therefore cannot model a person who has dealt with that problem of self-definition.

Summary

Let me summarize the case for Afrocentric immersion by the arguments made thus far. The purpose of the African American Immersion Schools is to create a school program that identifies and builds on the experiences and culture of African American students. The central theme is *human development*, preparing African American students intellectually, socially, and morally to further their education or immediately become constructive forces in the community. The concept leads us to place the total development of the African American child at the center of curriculum and instruction. Afrocentricity is the foundation of the curriculum and pedagogy for the African American Immersion Schools in Milwaukee.

I began this essay framing the educational problem: African American children, and males in particular, are seriously and dramatically underserved by public schools. I argued that the goal of improving schooling experiences for African American children, as well as other marginalized ethnic-minority groups, cannot be separated from the larger questions surrounding the purposes of education. Moreover, given the extensive social and economic factors placing African American males particularly "at risk," I argued that schools must support and promote the personal development and well-being of children *in addition to* academic achievement—a goal explicitly adopted by the African American Immersion Schools.

Second, I argued that the goal of creating more culturally responsive, developmentally appropriate, and experientially relevant school experience for African American children is not being met by conventional approaches to education. More importantly, I showed why public schooling, as it presently is constituted, is *congenitally incapable* of providing developmentally appropriate and culturally responsive education for children of color. The basis from which I argued this point concerned the importance of primary socialization—how both school and home educate and enculturate the young to become participants in the social world.

For all children, success in school depends in large measure on continuity of primary socialization—the complex and often overlooked process of communication whereby a young person (learner) acquires from an experienced, more knowledgeable significant other (parent, teacher, caretaker) ways in which to think about, talk about, and *participate in* the social world (Bowers and Flinders,[43] p. 10). The development of children cognitively, socially, and emotionally requires that their experiences with school extend and build on the foundations of learning in the child's home and community. For African American children, there is a *discontinuity* between the primary socialization of the home and community on one hand, and how it is experienced in school on the other hand.

I argued that the cultural–experiential discontinuity experienced by African American children cannot be successfully remedied by public schools as they are presently constituted because, by and large, mainstream teachers are not prepared to connect with and teach African American children in the same way as they can children like their own. The reasons I identified—the visceral fear of African American males based in part on distorted images, racism, ignorance of the lives, history, culture, and language of African American people—make it impossible to form the same warm, supportive, scaffolding relationships that are essential for primary socialization to continue in school. In addition, I noted several ways that sparse grounding in African American culture and language undercuts opportunities for linguistic–cognitive scaffolding. Finally, I noted the problematic of "rhetorical stance" for teachers who must assist African American students in identity integration given the conflicts and contradictions posed for them by political, social, and economic realities.

Conclusion

I began this discourse with two aims in mind. One was to firmly establish a thorough-going understanding of human development as the foundation for revisioning educational programs for so-called "at risk" youngsters in urban public schools. Toward that end, I used the African American Immersion Schools in Milwaukee as a case analysis to illustrate the need for this foundational professional knowledge and the relationship between the dearth of critical developmental understanding about Black children and their lack of academic success. The other aim was to articulate the vision of Afrocentric immersion as an educational program, again drawing upon the in-progress work of the Milwaukee Project. This discourse was framed by an illustration of how Afrocentricity as a theory of curriculum and pedagogy addresses educational needs of the African American community.

With this established, I want to restate the case for Afrocentric immersion more emphatically and forcefully. In looking after the development of children, we need to be as attendant to the critical–intellectual stresses in their environments as we are to the physical stresses. With the same vigor as we ensure that our children are not cold and hungry, we must look after the devastating effects that America's cultural hegemony and ideologies of oppression can have on their cognitive and moral development.

To enable and empower African American boys, a central focus of their educational experience must be a critical discourse of what it means to be Black in America. Situating this critical discourse in the extensive history of African people is essential, not as a palliative to flagging self-images, but as an essential component of careful critical analysis.

The dynamic of society's complicity in the perpetuation of racism, racial self-hatred, and cultural hegemony must be made explicit and examined critically in the curriculum. Unless schools engender resilient development of our young Black men in the face of culturally hegemonic and racist images of Blacks in the popular culture, public schools will continue to be toxic environments for African American boys. Moreover, this toxicity poisons everyone sooner or later, as lost souls in the schools become predators on the streets.

African American children must be socialized in the context of the positive values and traditions of African culture and the Black community. Let us be realistic about the possibilities of traditional educational models providing the continuation and enrichment of socialization experience. To squarely face realities of black children in urban settings, schools must be places that engender and extend the strongest positive elements of the adult Black community. The Afrocentric Immersion Schools program is designed to do just that.

Notes

1. M. K. Asante, *The Afrocentric Idea* (Philadelphia: Temple University Press, 1987).

2. Jawanza Kunjufu, *Developing Positive Self-Images and Discipline in Black Children.* (Chicago: African American Images, 1984). ISBN O-913543-01-2; *A Talk with Jawanza* (Chicago: African American Images, 1989). ISBN O-913543-14-4

3. J. King and G. Ladson-Billings, "The Teacher Education Challenge in Elite University Settings: Developing Critical Perspectives for Teaching in a Democratic and Multicultural Society," *The European Journal of Intercultural Education* (to appear); P. C. Murrell, "Cultural Politics in Teacher Education: What's Missing in the Preparation of African-American Teachers?" *Readings on Equal Education* 11(6) (1991): 205–225.

4. L. D. Delpit, address at the Association of American Colleges of Teacher Education, Atlanta, GA. Fall 1991.

5. L. D. Delpit, "The Silenced Dialog: Power and Pedagogy in Educating Other People's Children." *Harvard Educational Review* 58(3) (1988): 280–298.

6. L.D. Delpit, "Skills and Other Dilemmas of a Progressive Black Educator." *Harvard Educational Review* 56(40) (1986): 389–395.

7. D. Ravitch, "Multiculturalism: E Pluribus Plures," *American Scholar* (Summer 1990).

8. F. Erickson and J. Schultz, "Students' Experience of the Curriculum," in *Handbook of Research on Curriculum*, ed. P.W. Jackson (New York: Macmillan, 1991).

9. African American Male Task Force, Milwaukee Public Schools Internal Document, "Educating African American Males: A Dream Deferred," May 1990.

10. J. Gee, "The Narrativization of Experience in the Oral Style," *Journal of Education* 171(1) (1989): 75–96.

11. T. Kochman, *Black and White Styles in Conflict* (Chicago: University of Chicago Press, 1981).

12. W. Labov, *Language in the Inner City* (Philadelphia: University of Pennsylvania Press, 1972).

13. G. Smitherman, *Talkin' and Testifying': The Language of Black America* (Boston, MA: Houghton Mifflin, 1977).

14. J. L. Dillard, *Black English: Its History and Usage in the United States* (New York: Random House Press, 1972).

15. S. B. Heath, "What No Bedtime Story Means: Narrative Skills at Home and School," *Language and Society* 11 (1982): 49–76; "Oral and Literate Traditions among Black Americans Living in Poverty," *American Psychologist* 44(2) (1989): 367–373.

16. S. Scribner and M. Cole, *The Psychology of Literacy* (Cambridge, MA: Harvard University Press, 1981).

17. S. B. Heath, *Ways with Words: Language Life and Work in Communities and Classrooms* (Cambridge: Cambridge University Press, 1983).

18. C. Cazden, *Classroom Discourse* (Portsmouth, NH: Heinemann, 1988).

19. R. G. Tharp and R. Gallimore, *Rousing Minds to Life: Teaching Learning, and Schooling in Social Context* (Cambridge: Cambridge University Press, 1988).

20. Heath, op. cit. (Ref. 17).

21. Heath, op. cit. (Ref. 14).

22. Scribner and Cole, op. cit. (Ref. 16).

23. Heath, op. cit. (Ref. 15).

24. Heath, op. cit. (Ref. 15).

25. C. D. Lee, "Big Picture Talkers/Words Walking Without Masters: The Instructional Implications of Ethnic Voices for an Expanded Literacy," *Journal of Negro Education* No. 3 (1991): 291–304.

26. H. L. Gates III, *The Signifying Monkey: A theory of Afro-American Literary Criticism* (New York: Oxford University Press, 1988); Lee, op. cit. (Ref. 25).

27. Lee, op. cit. (Ref. 25).

28. Lee, op. cit. (Ref. 25).

29. Asante, op. cit. (Ref. 1).

30. Smitherman, op. cit. (Ref. 13).

31. S. Fordham and J. Ogbu, "Black Students' School Success: Coping with the Burden of 'Acting White,' " *The Urban Review* 18(3) (1986): 1–31.

32. R. Majors and J. M. Billson, *Cool Pose: The Dilemmas of Black Manhood in America* (New York: Lexington Books, 1992).

33. W. E. Cross, Jr., *Shades of Black: Diversity in African American Identity* (Philadelphia: Temple University Press, 1991).

34. W. E. B. Du Bois, *The Souls of Black Folk* (New York: New American Library, 1969).

35. A. W. Boykins and F. D. Toms, "Black Child Socialization," in *Black Children: Social, Educational, and Parental Environments*, eds. H. P. McAdoo & J. L. McAdoo, (Beverly Hills, CA, Sage Publications, 1985), 33–51.

258

36. P. C. Murrell, "Coping in the Culture of Power: Resilience As a Factor in Black Students' Academic Success," paper presented at the annual meeting of the American Educational Research Association, San Francisco, CA, April 1991.

37. J. Prager, "American Racial Ideology As Collective Representation," *Ethnic and Racial Studies* 5 (1982): 99–119.

38. S. Fordham "Racelessness As a Factor in Black Students' Success: Pragmatic Strategy or Pyrrhic Victor," *Harvard Educational Review* 58(1) (1988): 29–84.

39. Du Bois, op. cit. (Ref. 34).

40. Asante, op. cit. (Ref. 1).

41. G. Gay, "Ethnic Identity Development and Black Expressiveness," in *Expressively Black: The Cultural Basis of Ethnic Identity*, eds. G. Gay and W. L. Baber (New York: Prager, 1987), 35–74.

42. Fordham and Ogbu, op. cit. (Ref. 31).

43. C. A. Bowers and D. J. Flinders, *Responsive Teaching: An Ecological Approach to Classroom Patterns of Language, Culture, and Thought* (New York: Teachers College Press, 1990).

15

"I Am Still Thirsty"*

A Theorization on the Authority and Cultural Location of Afrocentrism

Imani Perry

Afrocentrism. From the national headlines generated by Father George Stallings draping of African *kente* cloth at the front of a Catholic church renamed the "Imani Temple" and calling for an Afrocentric black Catholic community, to articles in a *Boston Globe Magazine* issue on multiculturalism referring to the Afrocentric movement in terms suggesting a racist thought-police,[1] Afrocentrism has entered the American national consciousness dramatically. It has been adopted by African Americans across class, geographic, and gender lines. It has been met by nonblacks with a variety of responses, including imitation, adaptation, and negation.

Two Perspectives on Afrocentrism

As with any cultural movement, finding a concrete definition is an arduous task. One begins with locating its roots. Molefi Kete Asante of Temple University presides as the progenitor with his texts *Afrocentricity* and *The Afrocentric Idea,*[2] in which he presents a philosophy of existence for Africans in the Diaspora based upon what he terms the African Cultural System. Since he is, at the very least, the creator of the term "Afrocentricity," any definition of it must somehow be born of his work. However, Afrocentricity has been consciously adopted as a popular black urban movement, and there are critical points of divergence between Asante's delineations and those that popular culture has set. (Henceforth, popular culture will refer specifically to popular black urban culture.) This chapter will consider several of these points of divergence, examining the degree to which the perceived viability of Afrocentricity is dependent on Asante's construction and critically inquiring whether his theory is historically optimal or even feasible.

Asante's work will be compared with rap music, the medium most appropriate

*This quote is from the song "Tennessee" by Arrested Development.

261

for making significant comparisons with Asante's text *Afrocentricity*. Rap serves as *the* revolutionary literature of young urban black America. This writer can state as a member of that generation that this is where we see "our" voice most present in all of society. Additionally, rap artists can very well be deemed the closest phenomena to freelance intellectualism in the current society, because rap exists overwhelmingly as "uncut and uncensored" (rapper KRS-1 interview for Yo! MTV Raps).[3] It is as literary as it is oral and musical, with complex linguistic constructions and subtly distinguishable poetic patterns and rhythms of speech. The rap referred to in this chapter is not the mainstreamed "pop" rap (i.e., Hammer and Vanilla Ice), but rather the creative cutting edge of the art form that frequently deals specifically with Afrocentricity. To quote Q-Tip, noted rapper and member of A Tribe Called Quest in a rap entitled "Check The Rhime"—"What you say Hammer, proper? Rap is not pop if you call it that then stop."[4] In Hazel Carby's 1991 lecture on Afrocentricity to a "Problems in Cultural Criticism" class at Yale University, she spoke of the "street" manifestation having a great deal to do with dress style, with physical accoutrements. Videos of randomly sampled cable television rap shows will be cited here as part of an analysis of the visual presentation of Afrocentricity.

Convergent Perspectives

It is important to look to Asante to see if the nature of this contemporary art fits into his definition of Afrocentricity significantly enough for comparisons to be made. He describes the spiritual and meditative element of Afrocentricity, Nija, as having a series of components which are (1) Libation to Ancestors, (2) Poetry and Music, Creativity and Expression, (3) Nommo: Generative Word Power, (4) Affirmation, (5) Teaching from Nija, and (6) Libation to Posterity.[5] These components are essentially met in the presentation and culture of rap music, despite a context which is not explicitly ceremonial. "Poetry and Music, Creativity and Expression," are obviously present, yet several of the other elements of Nija are as well. Repeatedly, rappers pay homage to political and spiritual leaders of the past, with visual images and references to figures such as Malcolm X, Marcus Garvey, and Black Panther Party members—a "libation" of sorts to ancestors.

"Generative Word Power" and "Affirmation" are fundamental to rap. Braggadocio and self-empowering descriptions are present in almost every rap one encounters. Take a line from Special Ed's "I Got It Made": "Think just blink and I've made a million rhymes just imagine if you blink a million times, damn I'd be paid—I Got It Made";[6] his words enable him to be paid (to make lots of money and be greatly respected), as well as granting himself the capacity to create an astounding number of poetic constructions (in this context, rhymes refer to entire verses of a rap), both affirming himself and emphasizing the power his words contain.

Asante speaks of the language of Ebonics, black American dialect, as the principal language of the Afrocentric individual.[7] No other intellectual vehicle uses Ebonics to the degree rap music does. In fact, with its widespread appeal to African American youth, rap has critically changed Ebonics by guiding the development of new terms and sentence constructions. "MC," a term now almost generic in its frequency of usage by rap artists, previously referred to the master of ceremonies in some celebratory event of mainstream culture. It now refers to the master of ceremonies in every rap musical event.

Afrocentricity, as postulated by both Asante and the popular culture that rap represents, consciously affirms the African cultural roots of Africans throughout the Diaspora. Critical to both perspectives on Afrocentricity is the reclaiming and embracing of what Asante terms the African Cultural System: "I speak of it [Afrocentricity] as a transforming agent in which all things that were old become new and a transformation of attitudes, beliefs, values and behavior results."[8] Similarly, the rapper Afrika of the Jungle Brothers in a song entitled "Learn Your History" from the *Forces of Nature* album says

Look back into your past sister, look back into your past brother,
My forefather was a king, he wore fat gold chains and fat ruby rings
nobody believed this to be true, maybe it's because my eyes ain't blue,
You ain't gonna find it in you history books,
come here young blood and take a look and dig down inside this hardcover,
don't you know that you was barred brother,
All you read is slavery, never 'bout the Black man's bravery,
You look at the pictures and all they show is, African people with bones in they
  noses.
That's not true, that's a lie, You didn't get that from our lemon pie.[9]

Divergent Perspectives

These lines give an image of the old, the forefather, and it becomes new with the call to dig down and renew a study and recognition of the past.

However, the revolution of the old to the location of the new takes different scopes in the two conceptualizations of Afrocentricity presented. Asante's philosophy demands an African cultural purity. He says that the Judeo-Christian religions are not constructed for Africans, and thus cannot be adopted by an Afrocentric person. He asserts that Afrocentric people should have African names, and that the problems we encounter result from our failure to vigilantly follow the guidelines set by our African heritage.[10] Beyond positing this African purity, Asante negates the possibility of a creolized African culture. ". . . Experiences are rooted in our ancestral home and defined by social and legal sanctions of four hundred years in America."[11] As an argument supporting African naming, he says, "My case is that Whites have never had to react to us as a people with a history apart from slave history. . . . All African people participate in the African Cultural System although it is modified according to specific histories and nations."[12] In various constructions such as these, Asante trivializes the African American experience as not uniquely cultural, and as one that is fundamentally defined by slavery alone. This is problematic, because it immediately excludes the 100-plus years of history since emancipation, and disallows any legitimate history or culture to oppressed people; this has been a central point of contention that black intellectuals have had for years with the dominant society.

Contrary to Asante's assertions, Afrocentricity in popular culture is at its core a creolized African movement. The cultural transformations that Africans have undergone in the United States and the Caribbean are manifested as part of reclaiming our African heritage. Clothing and hairstyles as well as elements of Judeo-Christian religious symbolism are conspicuous evidence. Cable television rappers who are generally defined as Afrocentric have Afrocentric physical manifestations. Dreadlocks, a hairstyle derived from Rastafarians, a religious and cultural group of Jamaica, shortened, thinned, and styled in ways particular to African Americans, are a signature style of Afrocentrism. Women and men wear braids derived from traditional African braiding styles and modern West African (particularly Senegalese) innovations, as well as the larger plaits and twists first seen in the Americas. The traditional African crowning of the head with some type of wrap or headwear is a near-universal cultural retention of African Americans; in every video screened for this chapter at least one of the performers wore some type of hat or scarf. The list of significant rap artists in whose videos these styles are present is lengthy: A Tribe Called Quest, Public Enemy, Brand Nubian, PM Dawn, etc. Additionally, all these artists wear "European" dress with African-inspired accessories and draping. Beaded necklaces or leather medallions with the outline of Africa, often in red, yellow, black, and green at some time or another adorn the necks of all these rappers. (The colors are meant to signify aspects of the African world. The red is for the blood that has been shed in oppression. The yellow represents the sun that shines upon Africa; also, as the color of gold, it represents the riches that were robbed of Africa. The black signifies the people, and the green the rich land of Africa.) But these Afrocentrists are African *Americans,* and there is no necessity for them to physically adorn themselves solely in African-inspired attire at all times: more jeans and jerseys are seen than dashikis or tailored *kente*-cloth pants and shirts.

In the video of "Can't Truss It" by Public Enemy (a rap group highly publicized as nationalistic and as having politically extreme views), the notion of reclaiming an African American heritage is central.[13] Parallels between slave and current African American experiences are drawn; both periods are shown as times of resistance. One of the rappers, Flavor Flav, is portrayed on the slave block taking the money he is purchased with, and is also portrayed as a butler putting poison into his master's coffee. The enslaved persons are not depicted as cultureless, rather they are shown dancing, and the woman central to the video wears a modern braided hairstyle. A particularly poignant scene depicts why we are at the most basic level not only African. The woman is raped by her master and gives birth to a child that appears white yet is not acknowledged as the master's child. The impact of miscegenation has been so great that there are countless African Americans that are considered black who do not appear as Africans. Asante attributes racism in this country to a matter of color, but it is evident that Black America has not been defined by anyone on the basis of color, but rather as a question of African ancestry and membership in a particular cultural group. Here again, Asante is willing to negate culture when defining African Americans, whereas he continually seeks to define all Africans by a single culture.

Afrocentricity and Religion

> Adoption of Islam is as contradictory to the Diasporan Afrocentricity as Christianity has been. Christianity has been dealt with admirably by other writers, notably Karenga; but Islam within the African American community has yet to come under Afrocentric scrutiny. Understand that this oversight is due more to a sympathetic audience than it is to the perfection of Islam for African-Americans. While the Nation of Islam under the leadership of Elijah Muhammad was a transitional nationalist movement, the present emphasis of Islam in America is more cultural and religious.[14]

This statement of Asante's is shocking: he has eliminated as viable Afrocentric belief systems the two religious institutions most central to Africans the world over. If Afrocentrism disallows the belief systems commonly held (at the very least by African Americans) from whence does one derive spirituality and the will to struggle? Asante provides no other substantial school of religious thought, and even if he were to provide one, the question arises, Is not the African mind defined by what Africans think rather than by a *perception* of what we once thought? Every major political movement of African Americans from slave revolts on have been guided by religious leaders who follow one of these two faiths.

Asante finds these religions problematic because, he says, all religions come from nationalism and neither of these nationalisms is our own. This seems a sophisticated explanation of a simplistic construction, namely, that those are the white man's and the Arab man's religions. He designates subscribing to Islam as submitting to a strange god because Arabic is the language of Islam, not a "black" language, and prayer is directed to Mecca, in an Arab country. This neglects to consider that even after the Black Muslim movement became more religious as opposed to nationalist, it was attractive to many as a result of Malcolm X's experience of Mecca as the first primarily spiritual rather than racial interaction he had had, one that awarded him faith in the brotherhood of humanity. Asante neglects as well that many Africans who came to this country enslaved and were followers of Islam. Additionally, the intense spirituality of African Americans, who often go into states of religious ecstasy in Protestant churches, is enough to contest Asante's simplistic racializing of these religions.

Rapper PM Dawn's video to the song "Set Adrift on Memory Bliss" has Roman crosses constantly decorating the screen amidst dreadlocked, braided, and beaded individuals wearing clothing in environs suggestive of an island location. This song is on an album entitled *Of the Heart, Of the Soul and Of the Cross: The Utopian Experience*.[15] The title is suggestive of the power of a trinity, and subscribes significantly to Christian symbolism. Even in a song that has no explicit religious symbolism, "Check the Rhime" by A Tribe Called Quest, the line occurs, ". . . So play the resurrector and give the dead some life, okay if knowledge is the key then just show me the lock . . ."[16] True, there have been visual and linguistic barriers in Judeo-Christian religions that have historically excluded Africans due to racism or systems of oppression. But rap artists have done interesting things in response to these racist formulations. Inherent in reclaiming African history and cultural heritage has been the reclaiming of religious history, a movement forefathered by rapper KRS-1:

Genesis Chapter 11 verse 10 explains the genealogy of Shem, Shem was a Black Man in Africa,
if you repeat this back they can't laugh at ya'
Genesis 14 verse 13 Abraham steps on the scene being a descendant of Shem which is a fact,
means Abraham too was Black
Abraham born in the city of a Black man named Nimwar descended from Ham,
Ham had four sons, one was named Canaan
here let me do some explaining, Abraham was the father of Isaac, Isaac was the father of
Jacob, Jacob had 12 sons, for real, and these are the children of Israel.[17]

In addition to claiming historic Christianity, there is a widespread trend among Afrocentric rappers to become members of various branches of Islam. Lyrics by Poor Righteous Teachers and Brand Nubian refer frequently to praising Allah and guiding life by the principles set by Islam.[18]

Part and parcel of embracing existence in the Americas is the other point of divergence from Asante-defined Afrocentricity: the nature and development of philosophy in the individual. In *Afrocentricity* Asante states

> [W]e must appreciate the fact that the acquisition of consciousness is part peda-
> gogical and part phenomenological. We learn from our teachers who have studied
> our history and given attention to our traditions and revolutionary possibilities;
> as we learn from the lowest stages of conflict with a racist opposition whenever
> we assert ourselves. Our consciousness grows at each stage until we are finally
> clear in our afrocentricity.[19]

It is here that the two conceptualizations diverge. Pedagogy is essential to rap's Afrocentrism; the KRS-1 video corresponding to a song entitled "You

Must Learn" places the rapper at the front of a schoolroom, teaching until the administrators throw him out and remove the map of Africa.[20] The song goes on to stress the active process of reading and learning about the elements of one's history and culture masked by the Eurocentrism of American education and intellectual thought. This tone of teaching and learning is repeated throughout rap; in fact, rappers could be called the critical pedagogues of Afrocentricity. In a guest host appearance on the program "Rap City" on the Black Entertainment Television network, Wise Intellect, a rapper in the group called Poor Righteous Teachers, Afrocentric Muslims who frequently use a West Indian Patois in their raps, stated the following (paraphrased: "We're here at the University of Maryland where all these people are supposed to be learning, but they aren't really learning their history. So all you people in school don't forget what you need to learn about yourself too."[21] (Wise Intellect's fellow rapper in Poor Righteous Teachers is called Culture of Freedom.) The pedagogy is one in which the teacher, the rapper, is engaged with the student, the listener, in exploring the lesson and achieving some greater knowledge. The notion of rap as didactic is universal to all segments of the art form, as evidenced in the categorizing of rappers and rap movements as "Old School" or "New School," connoting schools of thought particular to time periods. One identified with the "Old School," with a history in the art form, a forefather, is given a significant degree of respect.

It is the process itself of actively learning and reading that is considered Afrocentric, in addition to the stylistic expression, rather than Asante's notion that that process merely leads one to an ideal of Afrocentric existence. In the popular concept it is the *process* of learning and self-expression *itself* that brings one liberation, because the element of oppression being confronted is the suppression of a learning of history and expression of culture. What is liberatory is performing those actions, not some ideology, that those actions might lead to. The notion that one can create a philosophy of Afrocentrism built around a central statement of values is arguable. If the robbery of history and absence of cultural exploration has occurred to the tragic degree that Afrocentric thinkers including Asante have overwhelmingly stated it has, how can an African American dictate the philosophy of what has been lost before it has been found by the people? How does one know that the philosophy would necessarily function in opposition to the way we currently guide our lives? It is impossible to know, and that is why a more viable model would appear to be one in which Afrocentrism is a cultural movement that grants a power of knowledge and affirmation that is liberatory in its acquisition as much as in its possession. Historically, the acquiring of knowledge and literacy have been central to how African Americans liberate themselves, dating back to slavery when literacy was denied to the majority of African Americans, often at the penalty of death, and more recently to such a leader as Malcolm X, who only through his experience of study was able to transcend his existence as a thief without active intellectual thought.

Criticisms of Afrocentrism

Among the criticisms of Afrocentrism most frequently presented by white and black, left- and right-wing authors, are the following: It negates the experience of Africans in America; it is parallel to Eurocentrism in that it seeks cultural purity and superiority; and it is fundamentally sexist. These criticisms are valid with regard to Asante's theories, but questionable in the context of popular culture.

The issue of sexism is complex. Asante makes such insignificant references to women that they are virtually negligible. The majority of rappers are male; however, some semblance of parity between men and women is evident in the videos depicting Afrocentrism. In Chubb Rock's "Just the Two Of Us"[22] women move back and forth from African to American clothing; in "Bonita Applebum" by A Tribe Called Quest[23] images of men and women are paired or flashed separately, but are equally engaging and Afrocentric. Poor Righteous Teachers' newest release, "Shakiyla,"[24] is dedicated to the black woman because "she has been neglected . . . the mother of civilization and queen of the universe."[25] The portion of a release compiled by several independent rappers, entitled "H.E.A.L., Human Education Against Lies," speaking to issues of education, is done by a woman, MC Lyte.[26] She speaks about African-focused education not having any place in young people's formal education as it was beginning to have in the seventies. One of the most famous women rappers, Queen Latifah, has worn pieces of African clothing to emphasize her claim of a queenly status; in her "Ladies First" video[27] she flashes images of African American female leaders such as Frances Ellen Watkins Harper and Ida B. Wells as a claim to her heritage. Latifah's fellow woman rapper, Monie Love, in her song "Ladies First," says in part

Praise me not for being simply what I am, born in L.O.N.D.O.N. and down
    American,
you dig exactly where I'm coming from, you want righteous rhyming I'm a' give you
    some,
to enable you to see the meaning which is displayed . . . pay me every bit of your
    attention like
mother like daughter I would also like to mention
I wish for you to bring me to the, bring me to the, rhythm
which is now systematically given
desperately stressing I'm the daughter of a sister who's a mother of another plus
    one more
On tour, have a job to do we're doing it,
Respect due to the mother who's the root of it
and next up is me the M.O.N.I.E. L.O.V.E. and I'm first cause I'm a L.A.D.I.E.[28]

Rappers frequently explore African, African American, and Caribbean histories and cultures, emphasizing the range of the Diaspora that Asante intends to address. So there is nothing ahistorical about claiming an *entire* history (for

Asante, 400 years of existence, struggle, and development is a significant elimination). This claim in popular culture does not negate traditional formal education, even though it *is* largely Eurocentric, because the emphasis on staying in school is enormous. Leaders of The New School, who are highly critical of the educational system in songs such as "Teacher's, Don't Teach Us Nonsense,"[29] frame their entire album as a day in school, and thus posit formal education as the norm even as they criticize it. Rather than dismiss formal education, popular Afrocentrism requires one to supplement it significantly with texts that assist in creating a framework for world identity. From Du Bois to rapper Dougie Fresh, it has been said (in different ways), "A person without history is like a tree without roots."

Who Shall Be the Authority?

The final question becomes, To whom do we award the authority to define the terms of Afrocentricity and consequently our response to it? To a professor at Temple University who writes in traditional scholarly language while saying that Africans must search for cultural purity even to the point of giving up the languages of Europeans? Or to those who "speak the language" and are culturally and socially located within the majority of African Americans, and who recognize the creolized nature of African America? It is obvious to this writer that it is the latter group that we should look to, and that scholarly work must be done, inquiring into Afrocentricity as it is popularly manifested, in order for a generally accessible, historical documentation to be made of this significant movement.

Notes*

1. Multiculturalism article, *Boston Globe Magazine,* Oct. 13, 1991. The New World, A Special Issue on Multiculturalism, 13–16.

2. Molefi K. Asante, *Afrocentricity: The Theory of Social Change,* (Africa World, 1980) and *Afrocentric Idea,* (Temple University Press, 1988).

3. Interview with KRS-1 on "Yo M.T.V. Raps."

4. Lecture by Professor Hazel Carby in "Problems in Cultural Criticism Course" Fall, 1991, Yale University.

*These notes do not conform to the *Chicago Manual of Style*. The videos referenced were selected through sampling rap videos being shown on television, particularly two shows, Yo MTV Raps and RAp City. References to interviews with rap artists are not dated. It was impossible to determine while watching these interviews if they were reruns.

5. Asante, *Afrocentricity*.

6. "I Got it Made" by Special Ed.

7. Asante, *Afrocentricity*.

8. Ibid, p. 2.

9. "Learn Your History", *Forces of Nature*, by Afrika of the Jungle Brothers.

10. Ibid, p. 26.

11. Ibid, p. 27.

12. Ibid, p. 2.

13. "Can't Truss It" by Public Enemy.

14. Asante, *Afrocentricity*, p. 10.

15. "Of the Heart, of the Soul, and of the Cross: The Utopian Experience," by PM Dawn

16. "Check the Rhime" by A Tribe Called Quest.

17. "We Must Learn", by KRS-1.

18. See *Rock Dis Funky Joint,* by Poor Righteous Teachers and *One For All,* by Brand Nubian.

19. *Afrocentricity,* by Molefi Asanta, p. 25.

20. "We Must Learn," by KRS-1.

21. Quote by Wise Intellect, a member of the group, Poor Righteous Teachers," in an interview on Rap City.

22. "Just the Two of Us" by Chubb Rock.

23. "Bonita Applebum" by A Tribe Called Quest.

24. "Shakiyla" by Poor Righteous Teachers.

25. Interview with Wise Intellect on "Yo MTV Raps."

26. "Human Education Against Lies" by MC Lyte.

27. "Ladies First" by Queen Latifah.

28. "Ladies First" by Queen Latifah.

29. "Teachers Just Don't Teach" by Leaders of the New School.

16

"Choice" for the Chosen
The False Promise of Market-Driven Education
Robert Lowe

For nearly 150 years, public education has been deeply embedded in the civil landscape of the United States. Though long enshrined as a fundamental public good, public schools have been called on to serve contradictory aims: to engender critical citizenship and demand blind patriotism, to further group identity and promote assimilation, to stimulate economic mobility and reproduce the class order, to enlarge equality of opportunity and maintain preserves of privilege.

These tensions have led to contentious politics and periods of intense criticism of public education. But there remained an underlying recognition that public schools were essential to a democratic society. That recognition stood unassailed—until recently. Building on a decade of national power that has radically redefined the nature of public responsibility, conservatives under the aegis of "choice," have proposed the substitution of markets for public schools. Further, they have made their arguments plausible to diverse constituencies. Despite the grave inadequacies of public education today, however, throwing schools open to the marketplace will promote neither excellence nor equality for all. Rather, it will enhance the freedom of the privileged to pursue their advancement unfettered by obligation to community.

Current efforts to promote an educational marketplace through choice trace directly to the work of conservative economist Milton Friedman. Writing in the mid-1950s, Friedman proposed that every family be given a voucher of equal worth for each child attending school. Under this plan, families could choose any school that met rudimentary government oversight (which Friedman likened to the sanitary inspection of a restaurant). Parents could add their own resources to the value of a voucher, and, presumably, schools could set their own tuition level and admission requirements.[1]

At the time, Friedman's proposal failed to attract widespread support. While some people excoriated public schools during the 1950s for curricular laxity that allegedly gave Russians the jump in the space race, optimism prevailed that curriculum innovation and more attention to advance placement classes would remedy the problem. Further, for the first decade after the 1954 *Brown v. Board of Education* decision, optimism remained high that public schools could create equality of educational opportunity. In fact, it was school desegregation that most underscored the conservative nature of Friedman's stance.

The first choice program provided white students in Virginia public funds to attend private academies to avoid attending public schools with Blacks.[2] Friedman addressed this matter in his proposal. Although he expressed his personal desire for integration, he believed that state-imposed desegregation violated parents' freedom to choose. Thus Friedman asserted the primacy of freedom over equality and finessed the lack of freedom the less-than-equal possessed.

During much of the 1960s, confidence prevailed that public education could promote both excellence and equality. But by the 1980s such confidence had seriously deteriorated in a political climate that identified the state as the perpetrator rather than the ameliorator of social and economic ills.[3] A wave of national reports contributed to this climate by maintaining that the United States was losing its competitive edge because schools were inadequately developing students' skills.[4] At the same time, sustained inequities in educational outcomes between white students and students of color seriously undermined faith in the public schools' capacity to provide equal educational opportunity. In such an environment, a new private school choice program that emphasizes opportunities for low-income students of color was linked with a new, more public relations oriented defense of the educational marketplace. This new approach met considerable success in creating the illusion that choice would serve all.

The link was forged publicly in June, 1990 when Wisconsin State Representative Annette "Polly" Williams, the African American sponsor of the highly publicized Milwaukee Parent Choice Program, traveled to Washington, D.C. as a featured participant in the unveiling of *Politics, Markets, and America's Schools* by John Chubb and Terry Moe.[5] Rarely do scholarly works become media events, but this event signified the launching of a vigorous campaign to promote educational choice. It also implied the existence of far broader support for opening schools to the marketplace than the historically conservative constituency for choice would suggest. Although it would be a mistake to conclude that support for "choice" represents a consensus among diverse political forces, it rapidly is becoming the major policy issue affecting schools in the United States today.

At the cutting edge of this issue are the choice program in Milwaukee and Chubb and Moe's *Politics, Markets, and America's Schools*. The former, a modest program that provides public funds for private education, appears to demonstrate in practice that choice expands equality of opportunity. The latter attempts to theoretically justify the abandonment of all public education on the grounds that choice will produce educational excellence.

Taken together, the program and the book suggest that choice will provide both equity and excellence. Yet nothing could be farther from the truth. While the Milwaukee program—a kind of affirmative action effort—may indeed provide greater opportunity for some of its participants, Chubb and Moe's brief for providing all individuals with vouchers to attend private schools fails to sustain its thesis and has dire implications for equality of educational opportunity.

The Milwaukee Parent Choice Program has received attention far out of proportion to its immediate impact. In a district that enrolls nearly 100,000 students, the program was originally intended to provide 1,000 low-income students with approximately $2,500 each so that they might attend a nonsectarian private school. Only 558 students applied for the 1990–91 school year, and merely 341 ultimately enrolled in the seven schools that agreed to participate.

Despite the program's small scale, nationally prominent conservatives vocally endorsed it. Even before the school term began, it won praise from the Bush administration, the *Wall Street Journal,* Wisconsin's Republican Governor Tommy Thompson, and the head of the powerful Bradley Foundation. And despite the questionable success of the program thus far, many advocates persist in seeing it as a first step in restoring the nation's educational health. They believe this only can be accomplished by breaking up the public school monopoly.

The program also has spawned vocal opposition. Some antagonists, like Wisconsin Superintendent of Public Instruction Herbert Grover, view Polly Williams as the unwitting accomplice of right wing business interests bent on destroying a public good.[6] Others oppose the program because they fear that it presages an end to a variety of perceived goods, including desegregation, teachers' unions, a common curriculum, and provisions for children with special needs.

Thus, both proponents and opponents rightly see the Williams initiative as an entering wedge in a national battle over the future shape of education in the United States. It is important, however, to see the Milwaukee Choice Program on its own terms. That many conservatives support the plan does not make Polly Williams their agent. Rather, she has responded to the sustained failure of the Milwaukee Public Schools to provide an acceptable education to low-income children of color. During 1989–90, for instance, Hispanics maintained an average GPA of 1.47 and African Americans averaged 1.31. In three high schools, between 36 percent and 40 percent of blacks were suspended. The previous year, the annual dropout rate was 17.8 percent for African Americans and 17.4 percent for Hispanics.[7]

In the face of miserable average grades and appalling suspension and dropout rates, Williams has enabled a small number of students to seek an education elsewhere—partly in community-based schools that have long served African Americans and Hispanics. Under the circumstances, it makes little sense to berate the program for violating the ideal of the common school or the goal of an integrated society. Such unrealized visions are inadequate justifications for denying a few children a potential opportunity to pursue an education of value. As advocates of choice are quick to point out, the Milwaukee program gives some options to low-income families that the well-to-do have long exercised, and virtually no one challenges the right of the privileged to either move to their schools of choice in the suburbs or to attend private schools.

Yet the program does raise questions. While the $2,446 each student could bring as tuition to a private school did expand choice during the program's first year, this relatively small voucher meant that parents could not choose, if they desired, elite, overwhelmingly white prep schools. Second, those who applied for the program were probably among the most aggressive about pursuing quality education for their children and, consequently, among the most enfranchised.[8] Third, more than 200 students were turned away due to space limitations, leaving fewer than 400 who enrolled. Admission was to be based on a lottery system, but without the Department of Public Instruction monitoring the process, it might have been difficult for participating schools to resist taking the strongest applicants. Even if the program were an outstanding success, it would not constitute a brief for substituting the marketplace for public schools.

The continuing praise of the Bush administration notwithstanding, there were troubling signs during the program's first year. Most important, the Juanita Virgil Academy, the one school essentially created in response to the voucher-bearing clientele, suffered inadequate books and supplies from the outset and soon closed, disrupting the lives of the 63 "choice" students who had enrolled. In addition, some 15 students were dismissed for disciplinary reasons or learning problems, so that only 259 completed the first semester in schools of choice.[9] Finally, nearly 100 nongraduating members of that group elected not to participate in the program during its second year.[10] Problems within the Milwaukee Choice Program, as the following analysis of Chubb and Moe's book will indicate, multiply when choice expands to include everyone.

In *Politics, Markets, and America's Schools,* Chubb and Moe offer an elaborated version of Milton Friedman's argument. Like Friedman, they say little about equality of educational opportunity *per se,* but hold that education will improve for all through opening it to the competition of the marketplace. They go so far as to maintain that public schools generally are incapable of providing effective education because the way they are governed limits their capacity to remedy shortcomings.

Chubb and Moe point out numerous problems that afflict public education today. They observe that principals cannot hire or fire teachers. They note that teachers run a gauntlet of irrelevant certification requirements, possess limited autonomy in the classroom, and are denied colleagues who share a common purpose. And they recognize that parents have little influence over the schools their children must attend. The authors identify such unsatisfactory conditions as key contributors to what they perceive as the degenerate character of education in the United States.

They further contend that many of the educational reforms mandated in the 1980s—such as longer school terms, more homework, and increased academic requirements for high school graduation—were guaranteed to fail because they were imposed bureaucratically. In fact, they see bureaucracy as the central impediment to effective schools. They believe it strangles the capacity of principals and teachers to fashion schools after their own vision and renders them unresponsive to the interests of parents. The solution to poor education, according to Chubb and Moe, is not the futile effort to impose quality through increased bureaucratic controls but to eliminate such controls.

Chubb and Moe hold that public schools are necessarily bureaucratic since, in democratically controlled organizations, bureaucracy is the means through which competing political interests institutionalize their influence. They argue that private schools, in contrast, tend to be autonomous because accountability does not spring from bureaucratic regulation, but from the market mechanism. If a private school fails to do an effective job, according to their reasoning, clients will leave it for another. Chubb and Moe consequently look to the marketplace to create excellence in education.

To summarize their argument, Chubb and Moe assert that public schools provide inadequate instruction because they lack the autonomy necessary to create effective education; they lack autonomy because they are bureaucratic; and they are bureaucratic because politics shapes them. Thus, they claim the way to create effective schools is to substitute the market for politics. The clarity of their argument and the simplicity of their solution, apparently buttressed by the analysis of massive databases, may seem persuasive. But problems with their formulations abound.

First, Chubb and Moe assume that *A Nation at Risk,* along with less influential reports of the 1980s, provides such telling evidence of educational malfeasance that drastic measures are justified.[11] Serious questions might be raised about the test results marshalled to document this state of affairs. It is questionable whether standardized test scores can accurately gauge the nation's educational health, a point Chubb and Moe themselves make in another context.

Even assuming such scores have value, the strategy of *A Nation at Risk* to document both declining scores within the United States and unfavorable comparisons of scores with other countries hardly withstands close scrutiny. Its authors fail to note that their data suggest only a modest decline in scores since the 1960s. They do not acknowledge the upward trajectory of scores on several tests in the 1970s and 1980s, and they also ignore tests that showed no decline.[12] Furthermore, the report inappropriately contrasts the achievement of twelfth graders in the United States with those of other countries since the groups are not comparable. Most students in the United States reach the twelfth grade and a high percentage progresses beyond. In many other countries, only an elite group completes high school. Thus, international comparisons beneath the collegiate level have limited utility.[13]

Lack of evidence indicating "a rising tide of mediocrity," to use the unfortunate phrasing of *A Nation at Risk,* in no way suggests that children of color are receiving an adequate education. But it undercuts the justification of a market-based educational system for all based on the assumption that nothing could be lost by dismantling public schools. More important, Chubb and Moe fail to prove that private schools do a better job than public ones. Scholars have raised a number of questions about the data Chubb and Moe relied on, including whether a brief multiple choice test adequately documented student performance and whether the private school sample overrepresented elite preparatory schools.[14] Although many Black and Latino families have avoided the degradations of miserable public schools by enrolling their children in Catholic institutions, the mere fact of private status obviously does not confer excellence on schools. Thus it is hardly surprising that recent data on achievement in Milwaukee's Catholic schools point out a vast chasm in student achievement between those serving high income and low income neighborhoods, and they suggest racial differences in performance that closely parallel those of the Milwaukee Public Schools.[15]

Even setting aside problems with their data, Chubb and Moe's claims far outstrip their findings. Despite their argument that the autonomy they associate with private schools profoundly affects student performance, in their model autonomy accounts for a tiny percentage of variance in achievement. Thus as scholars Gene Glass and DeWayne Matthews note, "A school that moves from the 5th percentile to the 95th percentile on autonomous organization would be expected . . . to climb a month or so in grade equivalent units on a standardized achievement test."[16] Furthermore, Chubb and Moe cannot even truly determine whether greater autonomy creates better students or whether better students permit more autonomous schools.[17] In addition, they cannot demonstrate that higher achievement in private schools stems from the way they are organized or from the select group of students who attend them.[18] Finally, they fail to confront the hypothesis that the real issue is not autonomy but wider reliance on an academic curriculum in private schools—something that can be replicated in public institutions.[19]

Chubb and Moe also overstate the advantages of private schools in supporting teacher professionalism. Principals tend to have greater power in private schools, but it scarcely follows that teachers are more able to act as professionals. Unprotected by unions, the jobs of private school teachers are precarious. This vulnerability can exert greater constraints on teachers' autonomy than the bureaucratic regulations common to public schools. In addition, there is nothing professional about most private school teachers' salaries. Compensation typically too meager to support a family has meant that private school positions have been most acceptable to the independently wealthy, to members of religious orders, and to families with more than one wage earner.[20]

Overblown bureaucracies, of course, do limit institutional change and absorb huge financial resources for little direct educational service. Chubb and Moe correctly argue that many private schools are relatively free of bureaucracy, yet Catholic schools, which enroll a high percentage of nonpublic students in the United States, are certainly bureaucratic institutions. More broadly, the organization of the private sector as a whole fails to confirm Chubb and Moe's notion that bureaucracy characterizes public rather than private institutions. Intricately bureaucratized corporations produce a high percentage of the nation's wealth. Business influence, in fact, had much to do with the development of bureaucratic, centralized systems of public education.[21] Recent developments, however, hold out the possibility that public schools, like innovative corporations, can balance bureaucracy with autonomy.[22] Chubb and Moe offer scant attention to reform efforts in many communities that have moved toward various forms of school-based management.[23]

Furthermore, Chubb and Moe exaggerate when they suggest that public schools are rendered incoherent by the variety of political influences that shape them. Their pluralistic notion of educational politics fails to recognize that through most of the twentieth century, schools were elite-dominated. Bureaucratic structures in part were designed by elites at the turn of the century to remove schools from popular political control.[24] Yet altered power relations can inspire bureaucratic measures that protect the rights of minorities and the poor. Thus, recent bureaucratic regulations, engendered by the civil rights movement of the 1960s, are the real objects of conservative complaint. These have promoted desegregation, bilingual education, and education of the handicapped, institutionalizing a modicum of equity in public schools as a response to the demands of those traditionally denied power. That such regulations cannot adequately secure equality of educational opportunity does not mean that the market can do any better.

Chubb and Moe assume that the market will create quality education for everyone through the mechanism of choice. Yet choice certainly has not accomplished this in the private sector of the economy. If the affluent can choose health spas in the Caribbean and gracious homes, the poor must choose inadequate health care and dilapidated housing. To the extent that those with limited resources have won forms of protection, it has not been guaranteed by the play of the market, but from governmental regulation. The conservative agenda of deregulation over the past decade has eroded those protections and greatly increased the disparity between the wealthy and the poor in the United States. A market system of education is merely an extension of deregulation and promises to compound social inequities.

In the market system promoted by Friedman, Chubb and Moe, and conservative political and corporate leaders, public taxation would guarantee relatively modest vouchers worth the same amount for every student in each state. Families, acting as consumers, would then choose the schools their children would attend. But unlike the Milwaukee Program where a lottery determines admission, schools may choose as well. Chubb and Moe are adamant about this:

> Schools must be able to define their own missions and build their own programs in their own ways, and they cannot do this if their student population is thrust on them by outsiders. They must be free to admit as many or as few students as they want, based on whatever criteria they think relevant—intelligence, interest, motivation, behavior, special needs—and they must be free to exercise their own, informal judgement about individual applicants.[25]

It is in their interest to choose those students who are already high achievers, and it is in their interest—especially for smaller schools—to accept those whose families can supplement the amount of the voucher they are given. Friedman's version of the plan would allow individual families the right to add their own cash to a voucher. Chubb and Moe would allow local districts to augment the value of vouchers through increased local taxation. In either case, the wealthy would have greater choice than the poor.

Advocates of an educational marketplace, then, have won a significant ideological victory by successfully labeling their program "choice" rather than the more neutral sounding "voucher." While no one in their right mind would deny families educational options, "choice" obscures the reality that those who come from economically empowered families are those most likely to be chosen by good schools. As in the marketplace writ large, what one can purchase depends on how much currency is brought to the transaction.

Choice also obscures how the already advantaged would financially benefit at the expense of the less fortunate. A reduced tax rate would provide the well-to-do with a voucher for part of their tuition for private schools. This contrasts favorably with the current situation which requires them to pay higher taxes for public schools in addition to relying solely on their own resources if they choose private institutions. Such a tax advantage, obvious in the Friedman plan, would obtain in the Chubb and Moe variant as well since wealthy districts' decisions to raise taxes above the lower limit would be offset by the abolition of federal and state-level taxation that redistributes resources to poor districts. For the poor, in contrast, the baseline vouchers would be difficult to add on to, creating a situation reminiscent of Southern jim crow education where vast differences existed between per pupil expenditures for black and white schools.

Under Jim Crow, it was common for African Americans to supplement meager public funding by constructing schoolhouses with their own donated labor and paying teachers out of their inadequate incomes.[26] But Blacks could not rectify these inequities despite extraordinary sacrifices. As the scholar W.E.B. Du Bois maintained, if some of these starved schools managed to achieve excellence through unusual efforts, greater funding would have made such excellence far more widespread.[27]

A voucher system of education can provide support for long-established community-based education programs that have effectively served children of color on shoestring budgets. But as the failure of the Juanita Virgil Academy suggests, the notion that choice would create a nation of small, effective schools is a construction as mythical as the notion that the market can maintain a nation of shopkeepers. A high level of capitalization and economies of scale would be necessary to construct buildings, to conduct advertising campaigns, to maintain staffing with an unpredictable number of students, and to make do with the unsupplemented vouchers those without wealth would bring. A likely result would be educational versions of fast-food conglomerates, with scripted teacher behaviors similar to the standardized patter of McDonald's order clerks. Like nineteenth-century charity schools, such schools would compose the bottom tier of an educational hierarchy based on privilege.

Aside from the inequities associated with a market-based approach to schooling, such a strategy raises fundamental issues of educational purpose. Should taxpayers contribute to financing schools that have no public accountability, no matter how objectionable many might find their goals? Should the public subsidize elite prep schools, schools run for profit, schools with racist ideologies, and schools run by corporations to train future workers? Should families be regarded as entrepreneurial units charged with maximizing their children's educational opportunities? This market ethos ignores any sense of responsibility for other children's education, any obligation for community control of education, any commitment to schools as sites of democratic discourse, any need for the new common curriculum some educators are forging out of the cultural works and political struggles of the diverse peoples who have shaped the United States.

It is no small irony that so many conservatives have accused the multiculturalist movement of balkanization when their own policies have profoundly exacerbated the real differences that exist between groups in the United States. Certainly Republicans are not solely responsible for a long history of governmental policies that have developed suburban preserves for middle-class whites at the expense of urban economies inhabited by the poor and people of color.[28] Yet since the early 1980s regressive tax reform, diminished social services, and a benign attitude toward the flight of manufacturing jobs beyond U.S. borders have significantly increased the disparity between the wealthy and the poor. Already by 1983, according to historian Robert Weisbrot, "the cumulative impact of Reagan's policies involved a $25 billion transfer in disposable income from the less well-off to the richest fifth of Americans, and a rise in the number of poor people from 29.3 million in 1980 to 35.3 million."[29]

There are now signs that the strategy of suburbanization is yielding to urban gentrification as professional jobs in the service sector replace blue collar positions. Historian Kenneth Jackson has indicated that rising fuel, land, and housing costs, along with changes in family organization, make suburban living less desirable.[30] In addition, privatization is a major incentive for the affluent to resettle in cities where inadequate revenues are starving public services. Increasingly in cities, where deindustrialization and reduced federal aid have devastated public spaces, urban professionals are paying only for those services that benefit themselves. These enclaves of privilege support private country clubs, private security guards, private road repair services, and private schools.[31]

Adding to such services, choice is a way of subsidizing urban professionals' taste for private education in environments where even the best public schools do not always accommodate them. Although virtually every city has magnet schools which disproportionately concentrate school districts' resources on college preparatory programs for middle-class children, they typically practice at least a rudimentary form of equity that requires some degree of racial balance, and they cannot guarantee admission to all white middle-class applicants. As choice invites suburbanites back to the city to enjoy their private pursuits at the expense of reinvigorated public services, they will displace and further marginalize the poor.

In the conservative imagination, the divestment of state redistributive functions does not terminate responsibility for the less fortunate. Rather, such responsibility becomes voluntary, an act of private choice. Much, in fact, is made of the public spiritedness of the affluent who voluntarily participate in contributing to the common good. Enormous publicity, for instance, has attended the offer of New York businessman Eugene Lange and several others to guarantee college scholarships to low-income school children, as well as to provide various supportive academic and counseling services to see them through high school. Oddly, we hear little about the federally funded TRIO programs that realized such practices worked decades ago. They have a long record of demonstrated success limited only by funding that is inadequate to reach more than a small percentage of the eligible population.[32] Massive federal support of such initiatives, in fact, is paramount because Lange and a few other philanthropists devoted to equity are exceptions. As policy analyst Robert Reich has pointed out, the wealthy contribute a lower percentage of their incomes to charitable purposes than the poor, and what they do give is disproportionately dispensed on elite cultural activities and institutions that serve them. Further, Reich notes that the much ballyhooed support of corporations for public schools is less than what they receive in the tax breaks they have successfully won.[33] Choice in giving, like choice in selecting private schools, provides a poor case that private spending will support public goods.

None of this is to say that public schools are beyond reproach. If they adequately served children of color, interest in "choice" would be limited and efforts to secure multicultural education unnecessary. Typically, students in public schools have suffered curricula that are ethnocentric and unquestioningly nationalistic. They also have experienced a wide variation in academic quality based on their race and class. Author Jonathon Kozol, for instance, poignantly describes such grave inequities between public schools, underscoring the obvious unfairness of favoring the already advantaged with disproportionate resources.[34] Thus, it might make sense to restrict choice programs to the underserved.[35]

This clearly is not what the Bush administration had in mind, however, since it steadfastly opposed affirmative action. Leading Republicans and conservative groups like the Landmark Legal Center for Civil Rights, which defended the Milwaukee Choice Program in the courts while it opposed the 1990 Civil Rights Act, merely view the Milwaukee program as an opening gambit in an effort to institute vouchers for everyone.[36] This agenda is explicit in the activity of the Excellence Through Choice in Education League of California. Its agenda to place on the ballot a state-wide measure mandating vouchers for all was at first tactically articulated as a measure to serve low-income families only.[37]

If public education has inadequately fulfilled its responsibilities to educate all, market-driven educational enterprise cannot fulfill them. At best, the popularity of choice among those with the least privilege should send a powerful message to public school educators that the common school for many remains a myth. It highlights the need to support a multicultural agenda that widens public discourse on equity issues and transforms public education in ways that enable people of color to exercise co-ownership of society. Yet the very idea of schools that educate people in common—drawing on the richness of diversity—is antithetical to the intent of the conservative leaders and foundations advocating choice.

Early in the twentieth century, corporate elites claimed to take the schools out of politics by creating expert-run centralized and bureaucratic public schools. Their demand for efficiency and impartial expertise masked a politically motivated effort to replace working-class influence over education with their own influence. Today, Chubb and Moe articulate the position of corporate elites who rail against the bureaucratic schools their predecessors were so influential in creating, once more claiming they want to take schools out of politics. Yet their desire to open them to the marketplace is also an inherently political strategy. It will enable the more affluent to free themselves from the yoke of all the legislative and legal safeguards people have won through the freedom struggles of the 1960s. It, furthermore, will free the rich from all public educational responsibility, striking a major blow against the current multiculturalist effort that seeks a radical expansion of democracy and a reinvigorated vision of community. The implementation of "choice" would be a victory for narrow class interest over community, accelerating the drastic maldistribution of opportunity that exists today.

Notes

1. Milton Friedman, "The Role of Government in Education," in Robert A. Solow *Economics and the Public Interest* (New Brunswick, NJ: Rutgers University Press, 1955).

2. The most notorious instance of this occurred in Prince Edward County, where public schools were closed for five years. Blacks too were offered vouchers, but committed to desegregation, they refused and many children received no formal education during that period. See J. Harvie Wilkinson III, *From Brown to Bakke: The Supreme Court and School Integration, 1954–1978* (New York: Oxford University Press, 1979), 98–100.

3. See Charles Murray, *Losing Ground: American Social Policy, 1950–1980* (New York: Basic Books, 1984); Diane Ravitch, *The Troubled Crusade: American Education, 1945–1980* (New York: Basic Books, 1983).

4. National Commission on Excellence in Education, *A Nation at Risk: The Imperative for Educational Reform* (Washington, D.C.: Government Printing Office, 1983).

5. John E. Chubb and Terry M. Moe, *Politics, Markets, and America's Schools* (Washington, D.C.: The Brookings Institution, 1990).

6. See, for instance, *The Milwaukee Journal*, 23 July 1990.

7. *Milwaukee Sentinel*, 20 October 1990, p. 7; 22 October 1990, p. 8.

8. There is evidence, in fact, that choice parents were more educated and had been more actively involved in the Milwaukee Public Schools than both other low-income parents and parents in general. See John F. Witte, "First Year Report: Milwaukee Parent Choice Program," University Wisconsin-Madison, November 1991, pp. 5, 7.

9. *New York Times,* 12 June 1991, p. B9.

10. *Wisconsin DPI Bulletin* 2 (August 16, 1991): 3. The most dramatic drop in returning students took place at the Harambee Community School where only 19 returned of the 79 nongraduating participants. See *Milwaukee Journal,* 3 October 1991, p. A21.

11. National Commission on Excellence in Education, *A Nation at Risk.*

12. See Lawrence C. Stedman and Carl F. Kaestle, "The Test Score Decline Is Over: Now What?" *Phi Delta Kappan* (November 1985): 204–210; Lawrence C. Stedman and Marshall S. Smith, "Weak Arguments Poor Data, Simplistic Recommendations," in *The Great School Debate* eds. Beatrice and Ronald Gross (New York: Touchstone, 1985), 83–105.

13. Stedman and Smith, *The Great School Debate,* p. 90.

14. See, for example, Peter H. Rossi and James D. Wright, "Best Schools—Better Discipline or Better Students? A Review of High School Achievement," *American Journal of Education* 91 (November 1982): 82; comments on John Witte's unpublished paper presented at 1990 meeting of American Political Science Association, *Education Week,* 14 November 1990, p. 20.

15. *Milwaukee Journal,* 1 August 1991, pp. 1, 8.

16. Gene V. Glass and DeWayne A. Matthews, "Are Data Enough?" *Educational Researcher* 20 (April 1991): 26.

17. Glass and Matthews, "Are Data Enough?" p. 25.

18. On this issue, see Richard Murname, "Evidence, Analysis, and Unanswered Questions," *Harvard Educational Review* 51 (November 1981): 485–487.

19. *Education Week,* 14 November 1990, p. 20; also see Douglas Willms, "Do Private Schools Produce Higher Levels of Academic Achievement," in *Public Dollars for Private Schools: The Case of Tuition Tax Credits,* eds. Thomas James and Henry M. Levin (Philadelphia: Temple University Press, 1983), 230–231.

20. See Peter W. Cookson, Jr. and Caroline Hodges Persell, *Preparing for Power: America's Elite Boarding Schools* (New York: Basic Books, 1985), 84–93. Also, for high turnover of teachers and administrators in Milwaukee choice schools, see Witte, "First Year Report: Milwaukee Choice Program," pp. 12–13.

21. David Tyack, *The One Best System: A History of American Urban Education* (Cambridge, MA: Harvard University Press, 1974), part IV.

22. Thomas J. Peters and Robert H. Waterman, Jr., *In Search of Excellence: Lessons from America's Best Run Corporations* (New York: Harper and Row), 318.

23. Richard Elmore and Associates, *Restructuring Schools: The Next Generation of Educational Reform* (San Francisco: Jossey-Bass, 1990).

24. Tyack, *The One Best System,* pp. 132–133.

25. Chubb and Moe, *Politics, Markets, and America's Schools,* pp. 221–222.

26. James Anderson, *The Education of Blacks in the South, 1861 to 1935* (Chapel Hill, NC: University of North Carolina Press, 1988).

27. W.E.B. Du Bois, "Pechstein and Pechsniff," *The Crisis* 36 (September 1929): 314.

28. Policies have included federal highway subsidies, segregationist FHA loans, zoning ordinances, and legal standing for restrictive covenants. See Kenneth T. Jackson, *Crabgrass Frontier: The Suburbanization of the United States* (New York: Oxford University Press, 1985), 293. Ira Katznelson and Margaret Weir, *Schooling for All: Class, Race, and the Decline of the Democratic Ideal* (Berkeley: University of California Press, 1985), 217.

29. Robert Weisbrot, *Freedom Bound: A History of America's Civil Rights Movement* (New York: Plume, 1991), 302.

30. Jackson, *Crabgrass Frontier*, pp. 297–303.

31. See, for instance, Robert B. Reich, "Secession of the Successful," *New York Times Magazine,* 20 January 1991, p. 42.

32. See *Chronicle of Higher Education,* 3 July 1991, p. A17.

33. Reich, "Secession of the Successful," pp. 43–44.

34. Jonathan Kozol, *Savage Inequalities: Children in America's Schools* (New York: Crown Publishers, 1991).

35. For advocacy of choice programs with redistributive goals, see John E. Coons and Stephen D. Sugarman, *Education by Choice: The Case for Family Control* (Berkeley: University of California Press, 1978), 31; Henry M. Levin, "Educational Choice and the Pains of Democracy," in *Public Dollars for Private Schools,* pp. 36–37.

36. The Landmark Legal Center is funded in part by the Bradley Foundation, *Milwaukee Journal,* 23 July 1990, pp. 1, 4; for its opposition to the 1990 Civil Rights Act, see *New York Times,* 21 October 1990, p. 15.

37. *Education Week,* 18 September 1991, p. 1.

17

The Politics of Teaching Literate Discourse

Lisa D. Delpit

I have encountered a certain sense of powerlessness and paralysis among many sensitive and well-meaning literacy educators who appear to be caught in the throes of a dilemma. Although their job is to teach literate discourse styles to all of their students, they question whether that is a task they can actually accomplish for poor students and students of color. Furthermore, they question whether they are acting as agents of oppression by insisting that students who are not already a part of the "mainstream" learn that discourse. Does it not smack of racism or classism to demand that these students put aside the language of their homes and communities and adopt a discourse that is not only alien, but that has often been instrumental in furthering their oppression? I hope here to speak to and help dispel that sense of paralysis and powerlessness and suggest a path of commitment and action that not only frees teachers to teach what they know, but to do so in a way that can transform and subsequently liberate their students.

Discourse, Literacy, and Gee

The chapter got its start as I pondered the dilemmas expressed by educators. It continued to evolve when a colleague sent a set of papers to me for comment. The papers, authored by literacy specialist James Paul Gee ("Literacy, Discourse, and Linguistics: Introduction" and "What Is Literacy?"), are the lead articles of a special issue of the *Journal of Education*[1] devoted solely to Gee's work. The papers brought to mind many of the perspectives of the educators I describe. My colleague, an academic with an interest in literacy issues in communities of color, was disturbed by much of what she read in the articles and wanted a second opinion.

As I first read the far-reaching, politically sensitive articles, I found that I agreed with much that Gee wrote, as I have with much of his previous work. He argues that literacy is much more than reading and writing, but rather, that it is part of a larger political entity. This larger entity he calls a Discourse, construed as something of an "identity kit," that is, ways of "saying–writing–doing–being–valuing–believing," examples of which might be the Discourse of lawyers, the Discourse of academics, or the Discourse of men. He adds that one never learns simply to read or write, but to read and write within some larger Discourse, and therefore within some larger set of values and beliefs.

Gee maintains that there are primary Discourses, those learned in the home, and secondary Discourses, which are attached to institutions or groups one might later encounter. He also argues that all Discourses are not equal in status, that some are socially dominant—carry with them social power and access to economic success—and some nondominant. The status of individuals born into a particular Discourse tends to be maintained because primary Discourses are related to secondary Discourses of similar status in our society (for example, the middle-class home Discourse to school Discourse, or the working class African American home Discourse to the black church Discourse). Thus, the status of the institution to which one's Discourse is connected can define the status of the individual in a stratified society. Status is also maintained because dominant groups in a society apply frequent "tests" of fluency in the dominant Discourses, often focused on its most superficial aspects—grammar, style, mechanics—so as to exclude from full participation those who are not born to positions of power.

These arguments resonate in many ways with what I also believe to be true. However, as I reread and pondered the articles, I began to get a sense of my colleague's discomfort. I also began to understand how that discomfort related to some concerns I have about the perspectives of educators who sincerely hope to help educate poor children and children of color to become successful and literate, but who find themselves paralyzed by their own conception of the task.

There are two aspects of Gee's arguments which I find problematic. First is Gee's notion that people who have not been born into dominant Discourses will find it exceedingly difficult, if not impossible, to acquire such a Discourse. He argues strongly that Discourses cannot be "overtly" taught, particularly in a classroom, but can only be acquired by enculturation in the home or by "apprenticeship" into social practices. Those who wish to gain access to the goods and status connected to a dominant Discourse must have access to the social practices related to that Discourse. That is, to learn the "rules" required for admission into a particular dominant Discourse, individuals must already have access to the social institutions connected to that Discourse—if you're not already in, don't expect to get in.

This argument is one of the issues that concerned my colleague. As she put it, Gee's argument suggests a dangerous kind of determinism as flagrant as that espoused by the geneticists: Instead of being locked into "your place" by your genes, you are now locked hopelessly into a lower-class status by your Discourse. Clearly, such a stance can leave a teacher feeling powerless to effect change, and a student feeling hopeless that change can occur.

The second aspect of Gee's work that I find troubling suggests that an individual who is born into one Discourse with one set of values may experience major conflicts when attempting to acquire another Discourse with another set of values. Gee defines this as especially pertinent to "women and minorities," who, when they seek to acquire status Discourses, may be faced with adopting values which deny their primary identities. When teachers believe that this acceptance of self-deprecatory values is *inevitable* in order for people of color to acquire status Discourses, then their sense of justice and fair play might hinder their teaching these Discourses.

If teachers were to adopt both of these premises suggested by Gee's work, not only would they view the acquisition of a new Discourse in a classroom impossible to achieve, but they might also view the goal of acquiring such a Discourse questionable at best. The sensitive teacher might well conclude that even to try to teach a dominant Discourse to students who are members of a nondominant oppressed group would be to oppress them further. And it is this potential conclusion which concerns me. While I do agree that Discourses may embody conflicting values, I also believe there are many individuals, who have faced and overcome the problems that such a conflict might cause. I hope to provide another perspective on both of these premises.

Overcoming Obstacles to Acquisition

One remedy to the paralysis suffered by many teachers is to bring to the fore stories of the real people whose histories directly challenge unproductive beliefs. Mike Rose[2] has done a poignantly convincing job detailing the role of committed teachers in his own journey toward accessing literate Discourse, and his own role as a teacher of disenfranchised veterans who desperately needed the kind of explicit and focused instruction Rose was able to provide in order to "make it" in an alien academic setting. But there are many stories not yet documented which exemplify similar journeys, supported by similar teaching.

A friend and colleague who teaches in a college of education at a major mid-Western university told me of one of her graduate students whom we'll call Marge. Marge received a special fellowship funded by a private foundation designed to increase the numbers of faculty holding doctorates at black colleges. She applied to the doctoral program at my friend's university and traveled to the institution to take a few classes while awaiting the decision. Apparently, the admissions committee did not quite know what to do with her, for here was someone who was already on campus with a fellowship, but who, based on GRE scores and writing samples, they determined was not capable of doing doctoral level work. Finally, the committee agreed to admit Marge into the master's program, even though she already held a master's degree. Marge accepted the offer. My friend—we'll call her Susan—got to know Marge when the department head asked her to "work with" the new student who was considered "at risk" of not successfully completing the degree.

Susan began a program to help Marge learn how to cope with the academic setting. Susan recognized early on that Marge was very talented, but that she did not understand how to maneuver her way through academic writing, reading, and talking. In their first encounters, Susan and Marge discussed the comments instructors had written on Marge's papers, and how the next paper might incorporate the professor's concerns. The next summer Susan had Marge write weekly synopses of articles related to educational issues. When they met, Marge talked through her ideas while Susan took notes. Together they translated the ideas into the "discourse of teacher education." Marge then rewrote the papers referring to their conversations and Susan's extensive written comments.

Susan continued to work with Marge, both in and out of the classroom, during the following year. By the end of that year, Marge's instructors began telling Susan that Marge was a real star, that she had written the best papers in their classes. When faculty got funding for various projects, she became one of the most sought after research assistants in the college. And when she applied for entry into the doctoral program the next fall, even though her GRE scores were still low, she was accepted with no hesitation. Her work now includes research and writing that challenge predominant attitudes about the potential of poor children to achieve.

The stories of two successful African American men also challenge the belief that literate Discourses cannot be acquired in classroom settings, and highlight the significance of teachers in transforming students' futures. Clarence Cunningham, now a Vice Chancellor at the largest historically black institution in the United States, grew up in a painfully poor community in rural Illinois. He attended an all-African-American elementary school in the 1930s in a community where the parents of most of the children never even considered attending high school. There is a school picture of a ragtag group of about 35 children hanging in his den. As he shows me that picture, he talks about the one boy who grew up to be a principal in Philadelphia, one who is now a vice president of a major computer company, one who was recently elected Attorney General of Chicago, another who is a vice president of Harris Bank in Chicago, another who was the first black pilot hired by a major airline. He points to a little girl who is now an administrator, another who is a union leader. Almost all of the children in the photo eventually left their home community, and almost all achieved impressive goals in life.

Another colleague and friend, Bill Trent, who is a professor and researcher at a major research university, has told me of growing up in inner-city Richmond, Virginia, "the capitol of the Confederacy" in the 1940s and 1950s (personal communication, April, 1991). His father, a cook, earned an eighth-grade education by going to night school. His mother, a domestic, had a third-grade education. Neither he nor his classmates had aspirations beyond their immediate environment. Yet, many of these students completed college, and almost all were successful, many notable. There are teachers, ministers, an electronics wizard, state officials, career Army officers, tennis ace, Arthur Ashe, and the brothers Max and Randall Robinson, the national newscaster and the director of Trans-Africa, respectively.

How do these men explain the transformations that occurred in them and their classmates' lives? Both attribute their ability to transcend the circumstances into which they were born directly to their teachers. First, their teachers successfully taught what Gee calls the "superficial features" of middle-class Discourse—grammar, style, mechanics—features that Gee claims are particularly resistant to classroom instruction. And the students successfully learned them.

These teachers also successfully taught the more subtle aspects of dominant Discourse. According to both Trent and Cunningham, their teachers insisted that students be able to speak and write eloquently, maintain neatness, think carefully, exude character, and conduct themselves with decorum. They even found ways to mediate class differences by attending themselves to the hygiene of students who needed such attention—washing faces, cutting fingernails, and handing out deodorant.

Perhaps more significant than what they taught is what they believed. As Trent says, "They held visions of us that we could not imagine for ourselves. And they held those visions even when they themselves were denied entry into the larger white world. They were determined that, despite all odds, we would achieve." In an era of overt racism when much was denied African Americans, the message drilled into students was "The one thing people can't take away from you is what's between your ears." The teachers of both men insisted that they must achieve because "You must do twice as well as white people to be considered half as good."

As Cunningham says, "Those teachers pushed us, they wouldn't let us fail. They'd say, 'The world is tough out there, and you have to be tougher' " (personal communication, April, 1991). Trent recalls that growing up in the "inner-city," he had no conception of life beyond high school, but his high school teachers helped him to envision one. While he happily maintained a C average, putting all of his energy into playing football, he experienced a turning point one day when his coach called him inside in the middle of practice. There, while he was still suited up for football, all of his teachers gathered to explain to him that if he thought he could continue making C's and stay on the team he had another thought coming. They were there to tell him that if he did not get his act together and make the grades they knew he was capable of, then his football career would be over.

Like similar teachers chronicled elsewhere (for example, Ladson-Billings,[3] and Walker[4]), these teachers put in overtime to ensure that the students were able to live up to their expectations. They set high standards and then carefully and explicitly instructed students in how to meet them. "You can and will do well," they insisted, as they taught at break times, after school, and on weekends to ensure that their students met their expectations. All of these teachers were able to teach in classrooms the rules for dominant Discourses, allowing students to succeed in mainstream America who were not only born outside of the realms of power and status, but who had no access to status institutions. These teachers were not themselves a part of the power elite, not members of dominant Discourses. Yet they were able to provide the keys for their students' entry into the larger world, never knowing if the doors would ever swing open to allow them in.

The renowned African American sociologist E. Franklin Frazier also successfully acquired a Discourse into which he was not born. Born in poverty to unschooled parents, Frazier learned to want to learn from his teachers and from his self-taught father. He learned his lessons so well that his achievements provided what must be the ultimate proof of the ability to acquire a secondary dominant Discourse, no matter what one's beginnings. After Frazier completed his master's degree at Clark University, he went on to challenge many aspects of the white-dominated oppressive system of segregation. Ironically, at the time Frazier graduated from Clark, he received a reference from its president, G. Stanley Hall, who gave Frazier what he must have thought was the highest praise possible in a predominantly white university in 1920. "Mr. Frazier . . . seems to me to be quite gentlemanly and *mentally white*" (emphasis added, quoted in Platt,[5] p. 15). What better evidence of Frazier's having successfully acquired the dominant Discourse of academe?

These stories are of commitment and transformation. They show how people, given the proper support, can "make it" in culturally alien environments. They make clear that standardized test scores have little to say about one's actual ability. And they demonstrate that supporting students' transformation demands an extraordinary amount of time and commitment, but that teachers *can* make a difference if they are willing to make that commitment.

Despite the difficulty entailed in the process, almost any African American or other disenfranchised individual who has become "successful" has done so by acquiring a Discourse other than the one into which he or she was born. And almost all can attribute that acquisition to what happened as a result of the work of one or more committed teachers.

Acquisition and Transformation

But the issue is not only whether students can learn a dominant secondary Discourse in the classroom. Perhaps the more significant issue is, should they attempt to do so? Gee contends that for those who have been barred from the mainstream, "acquisition of many mainstream Discourses . . . involves active complicity with the values that conflict with one's home and community-based Discourses." There can be no doubt that in many classrooms students of color do reject literacy, for they feel that literate Discourses reject them. Keith Gilyard, in his jolting autobiographical study of language competence,[6] graphically details his attempt to achieve in schools that denied the very existence of his community reality:

> I was torn between institutions, between value systems. At times the tug of school was greater, therefore the 90.2 average. On other occasions the streets were a more powerful lure, thus the heroin and the 40 in English and a brief

visit to the Adolescent Remand Shelter. [I] . . . saw no middle ground or more accurately, no total ground on which anomalies like me could gather. I tried to be a hip schoolboy, but it was impossible to achieve that persona. In the group I most loved, to be fully hip meant to repudiate a school system in which African-American consciousness was undervalued or ignored; in which, in spite of the many nightmares around us, I was urged to keep my mind on the Dream, to play the fortunate token, to keep my head straight down and "make it." And I pumped more and more dope into my arms. It was a nearly fatal response, but an almost inevitable one." (p. 160)

Herb Kohl,[7] writes powerfully about individuals, young and old, who choose to "not-learn" what is expected of them rather than to learn that which denies them their sense of who they are:

Not-learning tends to take place when someone has to deal with unavoidable challenges to her or his personal and family loyalties, integrity, and identity. In such situations there are forced choices and no apparent middle ground. To agree to learn from a stranger who does not respect your integrity causes a major loss of self. The only alternative is to not-learn and reject the stranger's world. (pp. 15–16)

I have met many radical or progressive teachers of literacy who attempt to resolve the problem of students who choose to "not learn" by essentially deciding to "not teach." They appear to believe that to remain true to their ideology, their role must be to empower and politicize their most disenfranchised students by refusing to teach what Gee calls the superficial features (grammar, form, style, and so forth) of dominant Discourses.[8] Believing themselves to be contributing to their students' liberation by deemphasizing dominant Discourses, they instead seek to develop literacy *solely* within the language and style of the students' home Discourse.

Feminist writer, bell hooks, writes of one of the consequences of this teaching methodology.[9] During much of her post-secondary school career she was the only black student in her writing courses. Whenever she would write a poem in black Southern dialect, the teachers and fellow students would praise her for using her "true authentic voice" and encourage her to write more in this voice (p. 11). Hooks writes of her frustration with these teachers who, like the teachers I describe, did not recognize the need for African American students to have access to many voices and who maintained their stance even when adult students or the parents of younger students demanded that they do otherwise.

I am reminded of one educator of adult African American veterans who insisted that her students needed to develop their "own voices" by developing "fluency" in their home language. Her students vociferously objected, demanding that they be taught grammar, punctuation, and "standard English." The teacher insisted that such a mode of study was "oppressive." The students continued venting their objections in loud and certain tones. When asked why she thought her students had not developed "voice" when they were using their voices to loudly express their displeasure, she responded that it was "because of who they are," that is, apparently because they were working class, black, and disagreed with her. Another educator of adults told me that she based her teaching on liberating principles. She voiced her anger with her mostly poor, working-class students because they rejected her pedagogy and "refused to be liberated." There are many such stories to recount (see, also, Yorio[10]).

There are several reasons why students- and parents-of-color take a position that differs from the well-intentioned position of the teachers I have described. First, they know that members of society need access to dominant Discourses to (legally) have access to economic power. Second, they know that such Discourses can be and have been acquired in classrooms because they know individuals who have done so. And third, and most significant to the point I wish to make now, they know that individuals have the ability to transform dominant Discourses for liberatory purposes—to engage in what Henry Louis Gates calls, "changing the joke and slipping the yoke" (quoted in Martin[11] p. 204), that is, using European philosophical and critical standards to challenge the tenets of European belief systems.

bell hooks[12] speaks of her black women teachers in the segregated South as being the model from which she acquired both access to dominant Discourses and a sense of the validity of the primary Discourse of working-class African American people. From their instruction, she learned that black poets were capable of speaking in many voices, that the Dunbar who wrote in dialect was as valid as the Dunbar who wrote sonnets. She also learned from these women that she was capable of not only participating in the mainstream, but redirecting its currents: "Their work was truly education for critical consciousness. . . . They were the teachers who conceptualized oppositional world views, who taught us young black women to exult and glory in the power and beauty of our intellect. They offered to us a legacy of liberatory pedagogy that demanded active resistance and rebellion against sexism and racism" (p. 50).

Carter G. Woodson called for similar pedagogy almost seventy years ago. He extolled teachers in his 1933 *Mis-Education of the Negro* to teach African-American students not only the language and canon of the European "mainstream," but to teach as well the life, history, language, philosophy, and literature of their own people. Only this kind of education, he argued, would prepare an educated class which would serve the needs of the African-American community.

Acquiring the ability to function in a dominant Discourse need not mean that one must reject one's home identity and values, for Discourses are not static, but are shaped—however reluctantly—by those who participate within them and by the form of their participation. Many who have played significant roles in fighting for the liberation of people of color have done so through the language of dominant Discourses, from Frederick Douglass to Ida B. Wells, to Mary McCloud Bethune, to Martin Luther King, to Malcolm X. As did bell hooks' teachers, today's teachers can help economically disenfranchised students and students-of-color both to master the dominant Discourses and to transform them. How is the teacher to accomplish this? I suggest several possibilities.

What Can Teachers Do?

First, teachers must acknowledge and validate students' home language without using it to limit students' potential. Students' home Discourses are vital to their perception of self and sense of community connectedness. One Native American college student I know says he cannot write in standard English when he writes about his village "because that's about me!" Then he must use his own "village English" or his voice rings hollow even to himself. June Jordan[13] has written a powerful essay about teaching a course in black English and the class's decision to write a letter of protest in that language when the brother of one of the students was killed by police. The point must not be to eliminate students' home languages, but rather to add other voices and Discourses to their repertoires. As bell hooks[14] and Henry Gates[15] have poignantly reminded us, racism and oppression must be fought on as many fronts and in as many voices as we can muster.

Second, teachers must recognize the conflict Gee details between students' home Discourses and the Discourse of school. They must understand that students who appear to be unable to learn are in many instances choosing to "not learn" as Kohl puts it, choosing to maintain their sense of identity in the face of what they perceive as a painful choice between allegiance to "them" or "us." The teacher, however, can reduce this sense of choice by transforming the new Discourse so that it contains within it a place for the students' selves. To do so, they must saturate the dominant Discourse with new meanings, must wrest from it a place for the glorification of their students and their forbears.

An interesting historical example is documented by James Anderson.[16] Anderson writes of Richard Wright, an African American educator in the post-Reconstruction era, who found a way through the study of the "classical" curriculum to claim a place of intellectual respect for himself and his people. When examined by the U.S. Senate Committee on Education and Labor, one senator questioned Wright about the comparative inferiority and superiority of the races. Wright replied:

> It is generally admitted that religion has been a great means of human development and progress, and I think that about all the great religions which have blest this world have come from the colored races—all. . . . I believe, too, that our methods of alphabetic writing all came from the colored race, and I think the majority of the sciences in their origin have come from the colored races. . . . Now I take the testimony of those people who know, and who, I feel are capable of instructing me on this point, and I find them saying that the Egyptians were actually wooly-haired negroes. In Humboldt's Cosmos (Vol. 2, p. 531) you will find that testimony, and Humboldt, I presume, is pretty good authority. The

same thing is stated in Herodotus, and in a number of other authors with whom you gentlemen are doubtless familiar. Now if that is true, the idea that the negro race is inherently inferior, seems to me to be at least a little limping." (p. 30)

Noted educator Jaime Escalante prepared poor Latino students to pass the tests for advanced calculus when everyone else thought they would do well to master fractions. To do so, he also transformed a new Discourse by placing his students and their ancestors firmly within its boundaries. In a line from the movie chronicling his success, *"Stand and Deliver,"* he entreated his students, "You *have* to learn math. The Mayans discovered zero. Math is in your blood!"

And this is also what those who create what has been called "Afrocentric" curricula do. They too seek to illuminate for students (and their teachers) a world in which people with brown and black skin have achieved greatness and have developed a large part of what is considered the great classical tradition. They also seek to teach students about those who have taken the language born in Europe and transformed it into an emancipatory tool for those facing oppression in the "new world." In the mouths and pens of Bill Trent, Clarence Cunningham, bell hooks, Henry Louis Gates, Paul Lawrence Dunbar, and countless others, the "language of the master" has been used for liberatory ends. Students can learn of that rich legacy, and they can also learn that they are its inheritors and rightful heirs.

A final role that teachers can take is to acknowledge the unfair "Discourse-stacking" in which our society engages. They can discuss openly the injustices of allowing certain people to succeed, based not upon merit, but upon which family they were born into, upon which Discourse they had access to as children. The students, of course, already know this, but the open acknowledgment of it in the very institution which facilitates the sorting process is liberating in itself. In short, teachers must allow discussions of oppression to become a part of language and literature instruction. Only after acknowledging the inequity of the system, can the teacher's stance then be "Let me show you how to cheat!" And of course, to cheat is to learn the Discourse which would otherwise be used to exclude them from participating in and transforming the mainstream. This is what many black teachers of the segregated South intended when they, like the teachers of Bill Trent and Clarence Cunningham, told their students that they *had* to "do better than those white kids." We can again let our students know that they can resist a system that seeks to limit them to the bottom rung of the social and economic ladder.

Gee may not agree with my analysis of his work, for, in truth, his writings are so multifaceted as not to be easily reduced to simplistic positions. But that is not the issue. The point is that some aspects of his work can be disturbing for the African American reader, and reinforcing for those who choose— wrongly, but for "right" reasons—not to educate black and poor children.

Individuals *can* learn the "superficial features" of dominant Discourses, as well as their more subtle aspects. Such acquisition can provide a way both to turn the sorting system on its head and to make available one more voice for resisting and reshaping an oppressive system. This is the alternative perspective I want to give to teachers of poor children and children of color, and this is the perspective I hope will end the paralysis and set teachers free to teach, and thereby to liberate. When teachers are committed to teaching all students, and when they understand that through their teaching change *can* occur, then the chance for transformation is great.

Notes

1. James P. Gee, *Journal of Education: Literacy, Discourse and Linguistics, Essays by James Paul Gee*, Vol. 171, No. 1, 1989.

2. Mike Rose. *Lives on the Boundary* (New York: The Free Press, 1989).

3. Gloria Ladson-Billings and Annette Henry. "Blurring the Borders: Voices of African Liberatory Pedagogy in the United States and Canada," *Journal of Education*, Vol. 172, No. 2, pp. 72–88, 1990.

4. Emilie V. Siddle Walker, "Caswell County Training School, 1933–1969: Relationships Between Community and School," *Harvard Educational Review*, in press.

5. Anthony M. Platt, *E. Franklin Frazier Reconsidered* (New Brunswick, NJ: Rutgers University Press, 1991).

6. Keith Gilyard, *Voices of the Self* (Detroit: Wayne State University Press, 1991).

7. Herb Kohl, *I Won't Learn From You! The Role of Assent in Education* (Minneapolis, MN: Milkweed Editions, 1991).

8. Gee's position here is somewhat different. He argues that grammar and form should be taught in classrooms, but that students will never acquire them with sufficient fluency as to gain entry into dominant Discourses. Rather, he states, such teaching is important because it allows students to gain "meta-knowledge" of how language works, which in turn, "leads to the ability to manipulate, to analyze, to resist while advancing" (p. 13).

9. bell hooks. *Talking Back* (Boston, MA: South End Press, 1989).

10. Carols Yorio, "The Other Side of the Looking Glass," *Journal of Basic Writing*, Vol. 8, No. 1, 1989.

11. Reginald Martin, "Black Writer as Black Critic: Recent Afro-American Writing," *College English*, Vol. 52, No. 2, Feb. 1990.

12. hooks, op. cit.

13. June Jordan, "Nobody Mean More to Me Than You and the Future Life of Willie Jordan," *Harvard Educational Review*, Vol. 58, No. 3, 1988.

14. hooks, op. cit.

15. Henry L. Gates, *Race, Writing and Difference* (Chicago: University of Chicago, Press, 1986).

16. James D. Anderson, *The Education of Blacks in the South, 1860–1935* (Chapel Hill, NC: University of North Carolina Press, 1988).

About the Authors

Chapter 1

Theresa Perry is Associate Professor of Education and Undergraduate Dean at Wheelock College, Boston, Massachusetts. She previously taught in the philosophy and theology department at Xavier University in New Orleans, Louisiana, and in the African American studies department at Northeastern University in Boston, Massachusetts. She is currently completing a book on the development of a theoretical perspective on African American school achievement.

James W. Fraser is Professor of Education and History and Director of the Center for Innovation in Urban Education at Northeastern University, Boston, MA. He has previously taught at Public School 76 (Manhattan), Wellesley College, Boston University, the University of Massachusetts at Boston and Lesley College. He has written extensively in the fields of history of education and public policy issues in education, and he has been active in desegregation efforts with the Boston Public Schools for the past twenty years.

Chapter 2

Linda Mizell is the Director of Admissions and Development at Cambridge Friends School, and author of *Think About Racism* (Walker, 1992), a text book for young readers. She consults to schools in the Boston area, and has organized and facilitated conferences, workshops and presentation for parents and educators. She has two sons, Bakari and Lateef. In her spare time, she fantasizes about becoming rich and famous by writing critically acclaimed, best-selling historical novels.

Susan Benett has taught middle school and high school English for the past five years, most recently at Cambridge Friends School, Cambridge, MA. She has an M.F.A. from the University of Iowa's Writer's Workshop.

Berit "Bisse" Bowman teaches first and second graders at the Cambridge Friends School in Cambridge, MA, where she frequently supervises graduate students in education. She has assisted schools around the country in developing and assessing curriculum, and is particularly interested in the history and culture of American Indians. Each summer she and her husband Byron head off to the woods with groups of children to teach low impact camping and outdoor education. Bisse is a long-time member of Stampandet, a Scandinavian vocal band.

Laraine Morin teaches fifth and sixth grades at the Cambridge Friends School in Cambridge, MA., and is a lecturer in the Department of Education at Regis College, Weston, MA. She has taught middle school students in multiethnic, multilingual Catholic schools in the Archdiocese of Boston. She is a workshop presenter in teaching/learning styles and multicultural education at all levels, and is active in a number of Boston-area organizations which attempt to make resources available to wide range of educators.

Chapter 3

Judith J. Richards is a teacher at the Saundra Graham and Rosa Parks School in Cambridge, MA. She is also an adjunct faculty member at Wheelock College, where she teaches courses in mathematics education and multi-cultural learning and teaching. Her research interests and prior publications have been in the areas of classroom discourse of mathematics and science and on alternative assessment.

Chapter 4

Sandra Dickerson is a high school English teacher at the Cambridge Rindge and Latin School and an adjunct faculty member at Wheelock College, Boston, MA. She is a poet and a prize-winning writer. She has consulted nationally on multicultural education. She recently received her doctorate from Boston University. Her dissertation is entitled: "Is Sapphire Still Alive: The Image of Black Women in Television Situation Comedies." Her educational philosophy is "All children can learn, and all children have gifts/talents."

Chapter 5

bell hooks is one of the leading feminist and cultural critics. She is the author of several books including *Yearning: Race, Gender and Cultural Politics* and *Breaking Bread: Insurgent Black Intelligent Life*. She is a Professor of English and Women's Studies at Oberlin College.

Chapter 6

Nitza M. Hidalgo is an Assistant Professor of Education at Wheelock College, Boston, MA. She teaches in the areas of multicultural education and on urban school reform. Current research involves an ethnographic investigation of Puerto Rican families' influence on their children's school achievement. She was the past Chairperson of the *Harvard Educational Review,* and the co-editor of "Facing Racism in Education."

Chapter 7

Sau-ling Cynthia Wong is Associate Professor in the Asian American Studies Program, Department of Ethic Studies, University of California at Berkeley. She has published on both Asian American literature and Asian American language education issues. She co-edited *Language Diversity: Problem or Resource?* (1988), and her *From Necessity to Extravagance: Contexts and Intertexts in Asian American Literature* is forthcoming in 1993 from Princeton University Press.

Chapter 8

Edna Acosta-Belén is a Professor of Latin American and Caribbean Studies, and Women's Studies at the University at Albany, SUNY. She has published the volumes *The Puerto Rican Women: Perspectives on Culture, History, and Society; The Hispanic Experience in the United States* (with B. Sjostrom), *Researching Women in Latin America and the Caribbean* (with C. Bose), *Integrating Latin and Caribbean Women into the Curriculum and Research* (with C. Bose), and *In the Shadow of the Giant: Colonialism, Migration, and Puerto Rican Culture* (forthcoming). Dr. Acosta-Belén received her Ph.D. from Columbia University and has been a postdoctoral fellow at Princeton and Yale Universities.

Chapter 9

Susan Asai is a Professor of Music at Northeastern University in Boston and a performer of the Japanese koto (13-stringed zither). She has both a bachelor's and master's degree in music education and a doctorate in ethnomusicology. Susan's area of expertise is Asian music and the development of popular music styles in this part of the world. Her range of knowledge and her primary interests are reflected in the courses she teaches which include "Music of East Asia," "Music in Latin America and the Caribbean," "Music as a Means of Social Expression," and "Introduction to World Music." She has written articles about the folk performing arts in Japan, the Asian American connection jazz, and Japanese American taiko drumming. Susan has strong links to the Asian artist community in Boston and serves on the boards of both the Asian American Artist Association and the Refugee Arts Group, Country Roads, Inc.

Chapter 10

Violet J. Harris is Associate Professor of Education, University of Illinois, Champaign. Prior recipient of a Spencer Fellowship, she has lectured extensively on the African-American oppositional multicultural children's literature for several publishing houses.

Chapter 11

Maxine Greene is Professor of Philosophy and Education (emer.) and William F. Russell Professor in the Foundations of Education at Teachers College, Columbia University. She has lectured and taught widely in critical philosophy, educational theory, literature, aesthetic education, and curriculum. For the last several years, she has been drawing from these fields in various papers and articles on multiculturalism. A past-president of AERA and other professional organizations, she holds a number of honorary degrees and continues to publish in the full range of educational journals. Her books include *Teacher as Stranger, Landscapes of Learning, Public School and the Private Vision,* and most recently *The Dialectic of Freedom.*

Chapter 12

Ceasar L. McDowell teaches in the Department of Human Development and Psychology, Harvard Graduate School of Education. He is co-editor of *Facing Racism in Education* (Harvard Educational Review Press) and 1992 recipient of the national Kellogg Fellowship award.

Patricia Sullivan teaches history at the University of Virginia, and serves as Assistant Director of the Center for the Study of Civil rights. She is co-editor of New Directions in Civil Rights Studies (University Press of Virginia, 1991) and author of *To Preserve Liberty and Promote Justice: The New Deal, The Sought, and the Politics of Civil Rights* (forthcoming).

Chapter 13

Linda Mizell (see Chapter 2)

Kathy Greeley is a 7th and 8th grade teacher of language arts and social studies at the Saundra Graham and Rosa Parks School in Cambridge, MA, and has worked there since 1985. She previously taught at the Robert White School, a special needs high school in Boston. She has been active in a variety of anti-racist organizations and is currently working with the Education Task Force of the Cambridge Rainbow around issues of excellence, equity, and access in the Cambridge Public Schools.

Chapter 14

Peter Murrell is Assistant Professor in the School of Education and Department of Psychology at Alverno College in Milwaukee, WI. He has previously taught psychology at the secondary (Milwaukee Public Schools) and postsecondary (Milwaukee Area Technical College) levels, and taught educational psychology at graduate and undergraduate level at the University of Wisconsin-Milwaukee and Marquette University. He has written about the preparation of urban teachers and is active on state and local task forces on student assessment. He is currently investigating the analytic/interactional competences and strategic thinking that underlie pedagogical excellence of effective teachers of African American students.

Chapter 15

Imani Perry is a Junior at Yale University in New Haven, CT, where she is a double major in Literature and American Studies. She is author of "A Black Student Reflects in the Difference Between Public and Private Education," Harvard Education Review, Journal 58, no. 3, p. 332–336, August, 1988. She is Editor in Chief (1992–1993) for the "Observer", a Yale student publication, and a member of Alaafia, a dance collective.

Chapter 16

Robert Lowe teaches at National-Louis University. With David Tyack and Elisabeth Hansot he is co-author of *Public Schools in Hard Times* (Harvard University Press, 1984). He currently is completing a book on the search for racial justice in the post-*Brown* era.

Chapter 17

Lisa D. Delpit is Senior Research Associate, Institute for Urban Research, Morgan State University in Baltimore, MD. The focus of her work is teaching and learning in multicultural contexts. She has lived and worked in Papua, New Guinea, rural Alaska, and various urban sites in the United States.

Index